UNITED STATES

Since 1865

UNITED STATES
Since 1865

NINETEENTH EDITION

John A. Krout and Arnold S. Rice

BARNES & NOBLE BOOKS
A DIVISION OF HARPER & ROW, PUBLISHERS
New York, Cambridge, Philadelphia,
San Francisco, London, Mexico City,
São Paulo, Sydney

LIBRARY OF CONGRESS CATALOG CARD NUMBER: 76–18396

INTERNATIONAL STANDARD BOOK NUMBER: 0–06–460168–4

90   20 19 18 17 16 15 14 13

ABOUT THE AUTHORS

John A. Krout received his A.B. degree from the University of Michigan and his A.M. and Ph.D. degrees from Columbia University. From 1922 until his retirement in 1962 he served at Columbia University successively as instructor in, to professor of, history, Dean of Graduate Faculties, and Vice-President. He is a trustee of the Museum of the City of New York and of the New York State Historical Association, and belongs to numerous other historical groups—among these the American Historical Association and the Society of American Historians. He was a member by presidential appointment of the Civil War Centennial Commission. His published works include *The Origins of Prohibition*, *Annals of American Sport*, *American History for Colleges* (with D. S. Muzzey), *Approaches to American Social History* (W. E. Lingelbach, editor), *The Completion of Independence* (with D. R. Fox), *Great Issues in American History*, and *United States to 1877* (a companion Outline).

Arnold S. Rice holds a B.A. degree from the State University of New York at Albany, an M.A. from Columbia University, and a Ph.D. from Indiana University. He is Professor of History and the Chairperson of the Department of History at Kean College of New Jersey. During the 1964–1965 academic year he was a Fulbright Exchange Professor in the Netherlands. He belongs to the American Historical Association and to the Organization of American Historians. In addition to having made many contributions to a variety of journals and reference works, he is the author of three books, *The Ku Klux Klan in American Politics*, *Herbert Hoover*, and *Newark, 1666–1970*.

PREFACE

In preparing this edition of *United States Since 1865* we have tried to give appropriate emphasis to the events of the past fifteen years. Although we have sought to avoid the temptation to exaggerate the significance of contemporary trends, at the same time we have accorded thorough recognition to the political, economic, and social changes taking place in the 1970s, some of which may well serve as guides to the future of the nation. Thus two new last chapters treat comprehensively the Vietnam War and its aftermath, the policy of détente with the Communist nations, the struggle by blacks and other minority groups for equality, the women's liberation movement, the exploration of space, the Watergate scandal, the resignation of Richard M. Nixon, the succession of Gerald R. Ford, and the election of Jimmy Carter.

Since chronology is the framework of history, a chronological arrangement determines the pattern of this book. In addition, a topical sequence for all important subjects can easily be traced through use of the index.

The bibliography lists general works with which every attentive observer of American history should become acquainted; it also provides special studies for each chapter.

We hope that students will find that *United States Since 1865* will not only serve as an ample digest of material for courses in American history but also provide a historical framework for courses in American government and in American literature.

JOHN A. KROUT
ARNOLD S. RICE

TABLE OF CONTENTS

1. THE RECONSTRUCTION PERIOD   1
   The Prostrate South, 1. Framing a Reconstruction Policy, 2. Radical Republicans versus the President, 3. The South in Transition, 7. The Legacy of Reconstruction, 10.

2. FROM GRANT TO CLEVELAND: DOMESTIC AFFAIRS   13
   Grant and Scandals, 13. Republican Dominance and Intraparty Strife, 17. The Return of the Democrats to Power, 23. A Republican Revival, 26. A Democratic Reappearance, 29.

3. SETTLEMENT OF THE WEST   32
   The Indians, 32. The Mining Frontier, 34. The Cattle Country, 36. The Farmers' Frontier, 37.

4. THE RISE OF BIG BUSINESS   40
   The Shape of Industry, 40. Devices of Industry, 44. The Regulation of Industry, 46. The Railroad Systems, 47. Abuses of the Railroads, 51. Control of the Railroads, 53.

5. THE STATUS OF INDUSTRIAL WORKERS   56
   Aims and Tactics of Management and Labor, 56. Some Influential Labor Unions, 57. Management Labor Conflict, 60.

6. THE REVOLT OF THE WEST   64
    The Farmers' Grievances, 64. The Agrarian Reaction, 65.

7. THE UNITED STATES AS A WORLD POWER   74
    Political Diplomacy in Action, 74. Relations with
    Great Britain, 76. Relations with Latin America,
    78. The Lure of the Pacific, 79. War with Spain, 83.
    A Colonial Empire, 88.

8. THE ERA OF THEODORE ROOSEVELT   94
    The Progressive Movement, 94. The Square Deal,
    98. Taft and Reform, 103. An Agressive Foreign
    Policy, 107.

9. WILSONIAN LIBERALISM   113
    The New Freedom, 113. The New Diplomacy, 119.

10. WORLD WAR I   123
    A Neutral in Difficulty, 123. United States Entry
    into War, 127. "Over There," 128. The Home
    Front, 130. The Lost Peace, 132.

11. THE 1920s: PEACETIME PURSUITS   138
    Return to "Normalcy," 138. Domestic Issues, 144.
    Foreign Affairs, 154.

12. THE NEW DEAL   159
    The Great Depression, 159. The First New Deal,
    162. The Second New Deal, 169. Evaluation of the
    New Deal, 177. Toward Solidarity with Latin
    America, 178.

13. WORLD WAR II   181
    The Approach of War, 181. United States Entry
    into War, 189. "G.I.'s," 189. The Home Front,
    190. The War in Europe, 193. The War in the Pa-
    cific, 197. The Defeated Nations, 201. The United
    Nations, 203.

14. THE QUEST FOR STABILITY AT HOME AND PEACE
    ABROAD   207
        Truman and the Domestic Scene, 207. Eisenhower
        and Moderate Republicanism, 215. The Cold War,
        222.

15. THE NEW FRONTIER AND THE GREAT SOCIETY   232
        Kennedy and the New Frontier, 233. Johnson and
        the Great Society, 239. Continuance of the Cold
        War, 248.

16. THE NIXON AND FORD ADMINSTRATIONS—
    AND PRESIDENT CARTER   253
        Nixon and the Domestic Scene, 253. Ford and a
        Post-Watergate Nation, 264. Foreign Affairs, 269.
        Carter and a New Direction, 273.

PRESIDENTS AND SECRETARIES OF STATE   278

SUGGESTED BOOKS FOR FURTHER READING   280

INDEX   292

MAPS

Emancipation and Restoration of Southern States	6
Political Organization of the West and Land Grants to Railroads	49
The Election of 1896	72
The United States as a Colonial Power, 1900	90
Mexico and the Caribbean	121
Tennessee Valley Authority, 1959	168
Europe and North Africa, 1942	195
Pacific Fronts in World War II	199
The United States	266–267

Chapter 1

THE RECONSTRUCTION PERIOD

The Civil War worked a revolution in the life of the American people in many respects more profound than did the War for Independence. During the Reconstruction period, which lasted from the surrender of the Confederate forces in 1865 to the removal of the last Union occupation troops in 1877, the South was the scene of bitter strife regarding its status in the federal government and the plans for its rebuilding. From the Reconstruction period emerged new patterns of government, economy, and society that transformed the southern states.

As for the readmission of the former Confederate states to the Union, the approaches of Presidents Abraham Lincoln and Andrew Johnson on the one hand and of the Congress on the other were so opposed that a rift between the executive and the legislative branches of the government occurred that was unprecedented in the nation's history.

THE PROSTRATE SOUTH

War always disfigures. And a civil war often scars the face of society so greatly that it is hardly recognizable. This was true of the South during the Reconstruction period. Confederate soldiers, returning home after the surrender of General Robert E. Lee, found destruction, poverty, and hopelessness all about them.

Economic Chaos. From Virginia to Texas, farmhouses, barns, and mills had been burned; bridges and railroad tracks had been destroyed; towns had been looted and their inhabitants driven out. Plantation owners had lost their slaves, and they did not have the means to borrow the capital for agricultural equipment to replace slave labor. Business was at a standstill, save for speculative enterprises which preyed on people left destitute by war.

1

Social Confusion. The war destroyed the whole structure of southern society. In many sections aristocratic planters, shorn of wealth and power, yielded reluctantly to the growing influence of bankers, merchants, and small farmers. The changing status of blacks, as they made the transition from slaves to wage earners, created serious social tensions between them and whites.

Political Uncertainty. The collapse of the Confederacy stopped all political processes in the South. State and local governments had to be organized; the new state governments had to establish normal relations within the Union. In the nation's capital and throughout the North political leaders differed sharply over what should be done and how it should be done. There were bitter quarrels among the leaders of the dominant Republican party concerning the proper basis for political reconstruction.

FRAMING A RECONSTRUCTION POLICY

The views among the political leaders who tried to formulate a program for the former Confederate states were so mixed that the American people were badly confused.

The "Conquered Provinces" Theory. Some members of Congress argued that secession was an illegal act and that southerners must pay a heavy penalty for having committed it. By having engaged in this crime, the southern states had placed themselves outside the protection of the Constitution. They must now be treated as "conquered provinces," which Congress had the constitutional power to govern.

Lincoln's 10 Percent Plan. President Abraham Lincoln brushed aside the conquered provinces theory, although he knew it had support from such influential Republican leaders as Representative Thaddeus Stevens of Pennsylvania and Senator Benjamin F. Wade of Ohio. Lincoln believed that the right to secede did not exist; therefore, despite attempts to sever relations by force of arms, the southern states had never left the Union but were merely "out of their proper practical relation" with it. (In 1869 this position was upheld by the Supreme Court in its *Texas* v. *White* decision that the Union was constitutionally indestructible.) Convinced that he should aid the southern people to resume quickly their former status in the Union, Lincoln in December, 1863, presented a plan for Reconstruction that, first, pardoned all southerners (except high Confederate officials and those who had left United States government or military service to aid the Confederacy) who would swear allegiance to the United States and accept "all acts of Congress passed during the existing rebellion with reference to slaves"; second, it authorized the establishment of a new government for any state if one-tenth of its qualified voters of 1860 would take the required loyalty oath.

The Wade-Davis Bill. Lincoln's moderate plan ran into strong opposition among the congressional leaders of his own party who feared that the President would "let the South off too easily" and that former Confederate officials would return immediately to political power in their states. In July, 1864, Congress passed the stringent Wade-Davis Bill. Named after its sponsors, Senator Wade and Representative Henry W. Davis of Maryland, it provided that a majority of white male citizens had to take a loyalty oath before a civil government could be organized in a seceded state, and it excluded from the electorate of such states former Confederate officeholders and military personnel who had "voluntarily borne arms against the United States." Lincoln pocket-vetoed[1] the bill. Thereupon, Wade and Davis issued a manifesto accusing him of "dictatorial usurpation."

The Johnson Plan. The assassination of President Lincoln on April 14, 1865, was a particular blow to those who favored a policy of moderation. His unfinished work fell into the hands of Vice-President Andrew Johnson, a pro-Union Democrat from Tennessee who in the 1864 election had been placed with Lincoln on the ticket of the Republican party (temporarily calling itself the Union party) to emphasize unity and attract wide support. The new President attempted to carry forward his predecessor's plan with minor changes, but the tactless Johnson had little skill in handling strong-willed members of Congress. He granted amnesty to all former Confederates (except certain high leaders and large property-holders) who were willing to take an oath to uphold the Constitution. By successive proclamations he set up provisional (adapted to current conditions and of a temporary nature) governments in a number of states that had composed the Confederacy. He authorized the loyal white citizens to draft and ratify new state constitutions and to elect state legislatures, which were to (1) repeal ordinances of secession; (2) repudiate the Confederate state debts; (3) ratify the Thirteenth Amendment to the Constitution, prohibiting slavery. (This amendment was passed by Congress in February, 1865, and ratified the following December.)

RADICAL REPUBLICANS VERSUS THE PRESIDENT

Opponents of the Johnson plan in the Republican party came to be called Radicals. The Congress that convened in December, 1865, soon came under the domination of this group, which was led by Senator Charles Sumner of Massachusetts and Representative Thaddeus Stevens. The motives of the Radical Republicans in opposing the President's policy were a curious blend of high moral purpose and partisan self-interest, in which the

---

[1] A pocket veto is the retention of a bill unsigned under such conditions that it does not become law.

following were important factors: (1) personal animosity toward Johnson on the part of senators and representatives who believed him unworthy of the presidency; (2) fear of executive encroachment on the authority of Congress; (3) the desire to safeguard the interests of freedmen (blacks freed from slavery as a result of the Civil War); (4) resentment over the speedy return of former Confederates to political power in the South; (5) the determination of the Republican politicians to establish their own party in the South; (6) the hope of northern business enterprise that the removal of southern influence from Congress would result in a program of government aid to industry.

The Black Codes. Beginning in November, 1865, and during 1866 southern legislatures that had been elected under Johnson's lenient Reconstruction plan passed laws called "Black Codes" that regulated the status of the freedmen. Although these laws conferred some rights of citizenship upon the newly freed slaves, they helped to ensure white supremacy by narrowly restricting the political, economic, and social activities of blacks. The Black Codes varied in severity from state to state. Blacks were, for example, denied the right to hold public office, to serve on juries, to bear arms, or to engage in any occupation other than farming without obtaining a license. The immediate effect in the North of the Black Codes was increased support for the Radical Republican position.

The Joint Committee on Reconstruction. In December, 1865, Congress refused to seat the senators and representatives who had been elected by the provisional state governments set up under the Johnson plan. (According to the Constitution, each house of Congress is empowered to judge the election and qualifications of its own members.) Instead, the Republicans in Congress, led by Representative Stevens, immediately created the Joint Committee on Reconstruction, with a total of fifteen senators and representatives, which examined the whole question of political Reconstruction and made new proposals for congressional action.

The Freedmen's Bureau. In March, 1865, Congress created the Bureau of Refugees, Freedmen, and Abandoned Lands (popularly called the Freedmen's Bureau) to provide the newly emancipated blacks with the basic necessities of life and to protect their civil rights, as well as to care for the abandoned lands of the South. In February, 1866, the legislators passed a bill extending the life of the bureau indefinitely. Johnson vetoed this bill on the grounds that states affected by it had not been represented in Congress when it was passed and that its provision for the military trial of civilians violated the Constitution. However, a later bill, enlarging the powers of the Freedmen's Bureau, was passed over Johnson's veto in July, 1866.

The Civil Rights Act. In April, 1866, Congress passed over the President's veto the Civil Rights Act, conferring citizenship upon blacks and assuring them equal treatment with whites before the law. Johnson had maintained that the measure invaded states' rights and would revive the spirit of rebellion.

The Fourteenth Amendment. As the quarrel with Johnson grew more violent, the Radical Republican faction insisted upon the political punishment of former Confederates. The basis of their attack took the form first of a proposal to amend the Constitution. The Joint Committee on Reconstruction proposed the Fourteenth Amendment to the Constitution, which Congress passed in June, 1866, and promptly referred to the states for ratification. By its provisions (1) citizenship was conferred upon every person born or naturalized in the United States and state laws that abridged the privileges of any citizen or deprived any person of "life, liberty, or property without due process of law" were prohibited; (2) a state that deprived any of its male inhabitants of the ballot (the concern was for blacks) was to suffer a reduction of representation in Congress proportionate to the number denied the right to vote (this provision could have been carried out only with enforcement legislation, which Congress never enacted); (3) former Confederates were barred from holding federal and state offices if they had filled similar posts before the Civil War (this disability could be removed by a two-thirds vote of each house of Congress); (4) the Confederate debt was repudiated and the United States debt affirmed. Tennessee quickly ratified the Fourteenth Amendment and was readmitted to the Union. All the other states of the Confederacy rejected the amendment upon the advice of Johnson, who considered it unconstitutional. Even so, by July, 1868, the Fourteenth Amendment had been ratified by the required number of states and was incorporated into the Constitution.

The 1866 Congressional Elections. The President and the Radical Republicans fought for political supremacy in the congressional elections of 1866. The supporters of the administration denounced the Fourteenth Amendment and urged a policy of conciliation toward the defeated South. But in many congressional districts the voters found that their only choice on the ballot was between a Radical Republican and a Democrat who had opposed Lincoln's wartime policies. The result was scarcely in doubt, and the Radicals scored an overwhelming victory.

The Reconstruction Acts. Some months after the congressional elections, in March, 1867, Congress passed, over the President's veto, the Reconstruction Act, dividing the ten states still unreconstructed into five military districts with a major general in command of each. For these states to be restored to the Union, the following procedures were required: (1) constitutional conventions, elected by blacks and loyal whites, were to frame constitutions guaranteeing male suffrage, including blacks; (2) these constitutions were to be approved by Congress; (3) qualified voters were to elect state legislatures pledged to ratify the Fourteenth Amendment; (4)

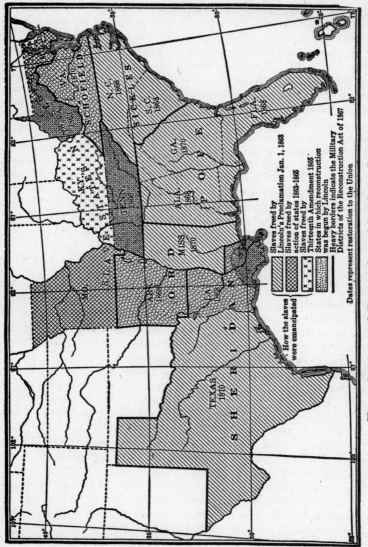

Emancipation and Restoration of Southern States

with the ratification of the Fourteenth Amendment the state could apply for representation in Congress. Later that year and in the following year Congress passed three supplementary Reconstruction Acts that outlined administrative and legal procedures.

The Congressional Challenge. The leaders of the Radical faction in Congress were hindered by their inability to control the presidential office. Realizing that Johnson was personally unpopular, they determined to humiliate him and thus remove any constitutional check on their policies.

IMPEACHMENT OF JOHNSON. In the Tenure of Office Act, passed in March, 1867, over Johnson's veto, Congress forbade the President to remove federal officeholders, including members of his own cabinet, without the consent of the Senate. When Secretary of War Edwin M. Stanton, who was in sympathy with the Radicals, refused to carry out a presidential order, Johnson dismissed him without the Senate's consent. The House of Representatives promptly impeached the President for "high crimes and misdemeanors," which consisted of eleven charges, including the violation of the Tenure of Office Act.

JOHNSON'S TRIAL. At the trial, which took place during March–May, 1868, with Chief Justice Salmon P. Chase presiding, Johnson was ably defended by his lawyers, who argued that the Tenure of Office Act was unconstitutional. In the final vote of the Senate, sitting as the jury, the Radicals failed by one vote (35 to 19) to secure the two-thirds majority required by the Constitution for conviction. Seven moderate Republicans voted with the Democrats to acquit the only president ever impeached by the House of Representatives.[2] Johnson's victory helped preserve the authority and independence of the presidential office. (In 1887 Congress repealed the Tenure of Office Act, and in 1926 the Supreme Court in its *Myers* v. *United States* decision upheld the president's right to remove officials appointed by the president.)

THE SOUTH IN TRANSITION

The policy of miltary reconstruction, which was pushed vigorously by the Radicals, hastened changes in the economic and social life of the South and took political power from the upper classes that had been dominant before the Civil War.

The Changing Political Scene. After the registration of voters, under the Reconstruction Acts of 1867, there were approximately 700,000 blacks

[2]In 1974 the House Judiciary Committee passed three articles of impeachment against President Richard M. Nixon, who resigned from office before the full House of Representatives was to take up the matter.

on the lists and about 625,000 whites. In some districts the black vote was marshaled and controlled by ambitious but unprincipled whites.

"CARPETBAG" GOVERNMENTS. Blacks sat in most of the conventions that drafted the new state constitutions, making up about one-third of the total membership. In the state legislatures there were many inexperienced, yet on the whole able and honest, representatives, both white and black. Making up the group of white legislators were the "carpetbaggers" and "scalawags." The former were northerners who had gone South after the Civil War. Since a number of them carried cheap traveling bags made of carpeting material, they were scornfully called "carpetbaggers." The motives of the carpetbaggers were mixed. Many wanted to help blacks adjust to freedom; others anticipated power and fortune through business and political enterprises. Those southern whites who cooperated with the carpetbaggers and the freedmen to aid the Radical program were dubbed "scalawags" (a slang term for "rascal"). As with the carpetbaggers, their motives were mixed. Many were eager to help both blacks and lower-class whites achieve security in a rebuilt South, while others were interested in political preferment and lucrative contracts during a period of deep confusion. Twenty-two blacks from eight states were elected to Congress; two of them—Hiram R. Revels and Blanche K. Bruce, both from Mississippi— served in the Senate. Some legislatures elected in the southern states in 1868–1869 indulged in extravagance and fraud that left an aftermath of public debts and burdensome taxes. But as supporters of Radical reconstruction pointed out, the carpetbag governments were no more corrupt than a number of northern municipal administrations, some northern state legislatures, and the executive branch of the federal government under President Ulysses S. Grant.

REFORMERS. There were in the southern states a number of white and black leaders who were determined to make life better for the average citizen of the region. All of the state constitutional conventions drafted liberal documents that guaranteed civil liberties and universal male suffrage. In almost every state an attempt was made to base representation in the legislature on electoral districts substantially equal in population. Several legislatures enacted laws providing for an enlarged system of courts. Although fraud tainted some of the appropriation bills passed by the Reconstruction legislators, many other expenditures were for worthy purposes. Greater state support for hospitals and asylums was authorized. Notable were the efforts to build more schools and to provide better educational opportunities for both whites and blacks.

The Fifteenth Amendment. Virginia, Georgia, Mississippi, and Texas were not able to satisfy Congress on rejoining the Union until 1870, when they were readmitted on condition that their legislatures ratify the Fifteenth Amendment, passed by Congress in February, 1869, forbidding any state to deny suffrage on the grounds of "race, color, or previous condition of servitude." Approval of the amendment by the required number of states had been obtained by March, 1870, and it thus became part of the Constitution.

Restoration of "White Supremacy." By 1868 most southern states had ratified the Fourteenth Amendment and had thus been permitted to rejoin the Union. Southern whites soon turned to nonpolitical methods in their efforts to undo the results of Radical Reconstruction.

Secret societies, such as the Ku Klux Klan, the Knights of the White Camelia, and the Boys of '76, were used by southern whites as the instruments of a policy of ugly terrorism designed to frighten blacks and compel them to renounce their new political power and economic and social gains. The Klan became the most notorious of these organizations. Taking refuge under white hoods and robes, its members, on gruesome "night-riding" missions, wielded with abandon on blacks and even their white supporters, too, whips, branding irons, ropes, torches, guns, and knives.

Southern whites who disliked the violent tactics of the Klan and other secret societies turned to more subtle forms of coercion. Blacks were denied employment and were kept from the polls not by force but by psychological intimidation.

The "Force Acts." Southern resistance led to three laws, called the "Force Acts," for the enforcement of the congressional program. The Enforcement Act of May, 1870, imposed heavy penalties for violations of the Fourteenth and Fifteenth amendments. The Enforcement Act of February, 1871, placed congressional elections under the control of federal authorities. The Enforcement Act (also called the Ku Klux Klan Act) of April, 1871, gave the President military powers to suppress violence in the southern states. In 1871 President Grant used these powers to subdue the Klan in South Carolina.

The Return of the Conservatives. Despite the Fourteenth and Fifteenth Amendments to the Constitution and the Enforcement Acts, the Radical Republicans lost ground in the South after 1870.

THE GENERAL AMNESTY ACT. A combination of Democrats and moderate Republicans, who disliked the severity of military Reconstruction, in 1872 pushed through Congress the General Amnesty Act, which restored political privileges to thousands of former Confederates and hastened the collapse of the governments based on black votes. By 1876 only South Carolina, Florida, and Louisiana were still in the hands of the Radical Republicans.

WITHDRAWAL OF FEDERAL TROOPS. As a result of a compromise between certain elements in the Republican party and some leaders of the southern Democrats arising out of the disputed presidential election of 1876, President Rutherford B. Hayes withdrew the federal troops from the

South in 1877; the state governments still in Republican hands quickly fell to the southern Democrats.

SUPREME COURT DECISIONS. In 1873 the Supreme Court, deciding cases that arose from a disputed grant of a state legislature to a slaughterhouse company, restricted the application of the Fourteenth Amendment. It held that the amendment was not intended to protect civil rights in general but only United States citizenship rights. In 1875 Congress passed a Civil Rights Act that prohibited racial discrimination in public places, such as restaurants, hotels, and theaters. The measure was never enforced, and in 1883 the Supreme Court declared it unconstitutional on the ground that the Fourteenth Amendment prohibited acts of discrimination by the states but did not prohibit acts of discrimination by private persons.

THE LEGACY OF RECONSTRUCTION

It is hard to balance the good and the evil features in the congressional program of Reconstruction. It is even difficult to determine whether the policies of the federal government during the Reconstruction era were responsible for all of the political, economic, and social developments of the post–Civil War years in the former states of the Confederacy. Less vigorous northern control might have resulted in similar political, economic, and social changes.

Political Readjustments. The most obvious political consequence of congressional policies in the South was the adherence of the great majority of southern whites to the Democratic party.

THE SOLID SOUTH. In the immediate postwar years most southern whites came to believe that the Republican party as a whole was the party of blacks and corrupt whites, despising the South. As a result, many areas in the former slave states knew only the one-party system. Whoever captured a Democratic nomination on the state or local level was virtually certain of winning the ensuing election. From 1876 to 1920 the Republican party never carried any of the former Confederate states in a presidential election.

THE "BOURBONS." Within the one-party system the leaders of the Democrats came to be known as "Bourbons" (from the name of a European royal family, whose descendants were known for clinging obstinately to ideas adapted to a past order). This extremely conservative faction consisted of some of the former planter class and many southern whites who had made money during the Reconstruction period.

DISFRANCHISEMENT OF BLACKS. By ways that avoided violence, the Democratic leaders steadily reduced the number of blacks who could meet the qualifications for the suffrage. Several devices were used: (1) the literacy test, so constructed that most blacks could not pass; (2) the poll tax (a tax levied on adults, the payment of which was required for voting); (3) property requirements; (4) the "grandfather clause" of newly revised state constitutions, granting the suffrage only to those whose fathers or grandfathers had voted before 1867. (The last device, of course, barred blacks but made it possible for uneducated whites to vote.)

Economic Rehabilitation. The political confusion of the postwar decade retarded all the southern states in their efforts to promote the economic well-being of their citizens.

DISRUPTION OF THE PLANTATION SYSTEM. The revolutionary changes brought about by the war compelled southern landholders to reduce the size of their plantations. Having insufficient money to hire laborers, some landowners sold off large portions of their acreage, but the majority preferred to try a plan of cultivation with tenants, white or black, who themselves did not possess enough money to pay a cash rental. In this system of tenant farming known as sharecropping, the tenant, called a sharecropper, agreed to give the landowner as rent a portion (usually half) of the crop he raised by his labor.

RISE OF THE MERCHANT. If the landowner did not supply the tools, seed, and draft animals that the sharecropper needed, the latter frequently was forced to pledge another share of his crop to the local merchant in order to secure credit for his working requirements. This was called the crop-lien system. Many small farmers who owned their land were forced to engage in the crop-lien system, often pledging their entire crop to the merchant in return for supplies. This proved to be an expensive system of credit. The small farmers were compelled to confine their production to crops having a widespread and constant demand, such as cotton or tobacco. And they became in a sense economically enslaved to the merchant-creditors.

INDUSTRIAL DEVELOPMENT. As the South of the great plantations disappeared, a new industrial order arose. The exploitation of coal, iron, phosphates, and lumber slowly gathered momentum. The less prosperous people in the rural districts drifted into towns to work in factories located where cheap water power was available. The increase in railroad mileage began to keep pace with the output of coal and iron and with the multiplication of cotton mills.

Social Tensions. It is not easy to measure the effect of the Reconstruction years in the process of social readjustment throughout the South.

STATUS OF BLACKS. In many communities the bitterness engendered by imposed government and military occupation under the Radical Republicans brought conflicts between the native whites and the newly liberated blacks that curbed the blacks' development. The breakup of the large plantations into smaller farms often meant the loss of work for blacks. Those who drifted into mill towns or got employment in mines and factories found that their labor was exploited almost as vigorously as it had been during the years of slavery.

CLEAVAGES AMONG NATIVE WHITES. The independent small farmers, heavily in debt, and the sharecroppers grew ever more hostile toward the Bourbon representatives of the former planter aristocracy and the new merchant-creditor group.

"The New South." In 1886 Henry Grady, editor of the *Atlanta Constitution*, used a phrase, "The New South," that gained wide acceptance, to denote developments, primarily economic, in the region after the Reconstruction period. Grady asserted that the South, instead of bemoaning the past, looked to the future with hope and confidence. But the phrase told only part of the story at the close of the nineteenth century. Although southerners made successful efforts to balance agriculture with new industries, much needed to be accomplished.

There was a vigorous leadership trying to remake the South economically, but many critical problems remained: (1) the southern economy had not escaped from control by northern financiers; (2) southern political leaders remained far more interested in sectional than in national problems; (3) many farmers, both white and black, still lived in poverty; (4) mindful of heavy personal losses during the Civil War and the Reconstruction period, most southern voters refused to accept tax programs that would have provided funds for the social services needed to rebuild from war's destruction.

Chapter 2

FROM GRANT TO CLEVELAND: DOMESTIC AFFAIRS

In the last third of the nineteenth century each administration—whether Democratic or Republican—was marred by factional quarrels or lack of constructive leadership, or both. From the beginning of Ulysses S. Grant's first term of office in 1869 to the end of the second Grover Cleveland term in 1897 the professional politicians were slow to face the new issues that arose out of economic changes. They appeared to be more interested in winning elections and dispensing patronage. Since the most important national problems—the regulation of industry, the control of the railroads, the settlement of management-labor disputes, the support of beneficial tariff schedules, the maintenance of a satisfactory currency system—were apt to cut across party lines and impair party discipline, the political leaders either avoided them or dealt with them in evasive generalizations. Demand for reform met with response slowly and over strong opposition from the politicians.

GRANT AND SCANDALS

The period of Grant's presidency was marked by scandals. Corruption, which many believed resulted from the effects of the Civil War, pervaded the times. No event serves as a nation's watershed more than does a war. The Reconstruction period witnessed the rise of big business. And the unprecedented growth of industrial enterprise with the attendant seeking of more and more profits meant, among other things, the discarding by many of an old-fashioned absolute moral code in favor of a freer or "looser" personal one. Corruption existed not only on the federal level of government but also on the state and local levels. Exposed to the American people were the corrupt activities of some members of the southern carpetbag state

13

governments and of the New York City ring of politicians headed by "Boss" William M. Tweed. Although Grant was personally honest, his reputation as Chief Executive suffered from his failure to attempt the reestablishment of a moral tone to government.

Election of 1868. During the campaign the Radicals within the Republican party emerged not only as the champions of a vigorous Reconstruction policy but also as the defenders of northern manufacturing, banking, and railroad interests against the agricultural interests of the West and South.

DEMOCRATS. The delegates to the Democratic national convention adopted a platform that denounced as unconstitutional the congressional program of Reconstruction and pledged support to the "Ohio Idea," an inflationary proposal originating in the Midwest that government bonds, whenever possible, be paid not in gold but in greenbacks (the popular name for the paper money issued during the Civil War). But Democratic support of this midwestern-oriented financial policy was weakened by the nomination for president of Governor Horatio Seymour of New York, who repudiated the greenback plank of the party platform. Chosen to run for vice-president was Francis P. Blair, Jr., of Missouri, a former representative who had contributed greatly to keeping his border slave state loyal to the Union.

REPUBLICANS. The delegates to the Republican national convention adopted a platform that endorsed congressional Reconstruction and demanded payment in gold of the public debt. The Radicals, having made certain that General Ulysses S. Grant was one of their number, succeeded in moving the party to nominate him for president and Speaker of the House Schuyler Colfax for vice-president.

THE CAMPAIGN. Republicans reiterated throughout the campaign that their party had saved the Union. The image of Governor Seymour paled alongside that of General Grant, the symbol of strength and success during the Civil War.

GRANT'S VICTORY. In the electoral college Grant defeated Seymour by 214 to 80 votes. The votes of 650,000 newly enfranchised blacks in the southern states under the military power of the federal government helped to give the Republican candidate his 310,000 popular-vote majority.

The Grant Administration. Grant's naiveté and lack of political experience proved severe handicaps to him and the nation.

THE PRESIDENT. Grant was inclined to regard the presidential office as a gift bestowed upon him by the American people in gratitude for his military service to the nation. Neither by temperament nor by training was he qualified to set a high standard of political ethics.

THE CABINET. Grant's cabinet initially included three men of outstanding ability: Secretary of State Hamilton Fish, Secretary of the Interior Jacob D.

Cox, and Attorney General Ebenezer R. Hoar. However, Cox and Hoar soon retired in disgust, and the President came under the influence of such shrewd politicians as Senator Roscoe Conkling of New York and Representative Benjamin F. Butler of Massachusetts. Civil service positions were filled with Grant's relatives and friends and with minor party workers and their protégés.

Political Corruption. Businessmen sought and received favors from government officials for a price; politicians shamelessly used public office as a source of private profit.

"BLACK FRIDAY." Grant's admiration for and association with men of wealth involved him unwittingly in the attempt by financiers James Fisk and Jay Gould in 1869 to get command of a large part of the nation's gold supply in order to dictate their own price for the precious commodity. While spreading the rumor that Grant was against the government's selling its own gold, Fisk and Gould bought much of the gold privately held, thus shooting up the price of the dwindling supply on the market. Many businesses that needed gold in their transactions were being ruined. On September 24, 1869 ("Black Friday"), when the price of gold was at its highest, the Grant administration took belated action. Secretary of the Treasury George S. Boutwell sold $4 million in government gold, and the price plummeted, bringing ruin to a number of speculators.

THE CRÉDIT MOBILIER. In 1872 rumors were partially verified of graft and political corruption in connection with the Crédit Mobilier, a construction company which in the 1860s had built the Union Pacific Railroad. The principal stockholders of the Union Pacific had been the founders of the Crédit Mobilier, in which capacity they took exorbitant profits for building the line. A congressional investigation in 1873 produced evidence that Democratic Representative Oakes Ames of Massachusetts, in order to influence legislation benefiting railroad interests, had placed shares of Crédit Mobilier stock among congressional leaders, including Vice-President Colfax, who at the time had been serving as Speaker of the House of Representatives.

THE TWEED RING. Symptomatic of business and political corruption were the frauds, totaling perhaps as much as $100 million, committed against the residents of New York City by a group of politicians headed by "Boss" William M. Tweed, the leader of Tammany Hall (the Democratic political machine in Manhattan). The persistent investigative work sponsored by the *New York Times* and the striking cartoons of Thomas Nast in *Harper's Weekly* finally helped to bring about the destruction of the Tweed Ring in 1871.

Election of 1872. Some members of the Republican party, calling themselves Liberal Republicans, were critical of the policies and tactics of the Grant administration and strove to prevent the President's reelection.

LIBERAL REPUBLICANS. The center of the anti-Grant movement in the Republican party was in Missouri, where such Liberal Republican leaders as Senator Carl Schurz and Governor B. Gratz Brown favored a more conciliatory attitude toward former Confederate supporters in the state and resented the dominance of the Radical Republicans in national affairs. These Republicans were especially critical of Grant's policy toward the South. The Liberal Republican national convention included champions of a variety of political reforms. Besides the opponents of Radical Reconstruction policies, there were civil service reformers and advocates of lower tariff rates as well as crusaders against the corruption of the Grant administration. The delegates passed over such reformers as diplomat Charles Francis Adams of Massachusetts and Senator Lyman Trumbull of Illinois to select *New York Tribune* editor Horace Greeley as their standard-bearer. Governor Brown of Missouri was named for second place on the ticket.

DEMOCRATS. The delegates to the Democratic national convention followed the Liberal Republicans in nominating Greeley for president and Governor Brown for vice-president. Although the brilliant but eccentric Greeley had been a vitriolic critic of the Democrats, they accepted him as their candidate because a fusion with the Liberal Republicans seemed the only chance to prevent Grant from succeeding himself.

REPUBLICANS. The Republican national convention nominated Grant for president and Senator Henry Wilson of Massachusetts for vice-president.

THE CAMPAIGN. Rather than forcefully coming to grips on the basic issues of the day, virtually all party speakers—although not the two presidential candidates—rapidly descended to mudslinging. Greeley was castigated for, among other things, an attitude toward the South so "soft" that it bordered on treason. Grant was denounced as an obtuse drunken tyrant.

GRANT'S LANDSLIDE VICTORY. Grant carried all but three border states (Missouri, Kentucky, and Maryland) and three southern states (Georgia, Tennessee, and Texas). Major factors in Grant's overwhelming victory were Greeley's personal unpopularity and the control of the South by the Republican party. The Liberal Republican movement, however, was not without results. It threw a sufficient scare into the administration to cause the President to advocate civil service reform, downward revision of the tariff, and modification of the recent policy toward the South.

Continuance of Political Corruption. Despite the promises he made during his bid for reelection, Grant was either unwilling or unable to put the political house in order, and his second term was marked by a series of government scandals.

THE "SALARY GRAB." The nation was incensed in 1873 by congressional action voting salary raises to members of all three branches of the federal government, including a 50 percent increase for senators and representatives to be retroactive for the preceding two years. Public protest made

Congress repeal its own "back-pay steal" the following year, although the increases voted for the President and Supreme Court justices, for constitutional reasons, were not rescinded.

THE SANBORN CONTRACTS. In May, 1874, a committee of the House of Representatives reported that Secretary of the Treasury William A. Richardson had permitted a friend, John D. Sanborn, to retain exorbitant commissions for collecting unpaid internal revenue taxes for the Department of the Treasury. Richardson promptly resigned in order to escape a vote of censure by the House of Representatives.

THE WHISKEY RING. By ingenious probing, Benjamin H. Bristow, who had succeeded Richardson as secretary of the treasury, revealed the existence of a conspiracy of revenue officials and distillers, and including Grant's private secretary, to defraud the government of internal revenue taxes on whiskey.

THE BELKNAP SCANDAL. In March, 1876, Secretary of War William W. Belknap abruptly resigned in order to escape impeachment for having accepted bribes to grant post-traderships in the Indian Territory.

REPUBLICAN DOMINANCE AND INTRAPARTY STRIFE

Factional rivalries within the dominant Republican party seemed more important to many professional politicians of the party than did the many and serious national issues that needed attention during the period from 1876 to 1884.

Election of 1876. The voting returns in 1876 produced the most disputed election in the nation's history.

DEMOCRATS. The Democratic national convention chose as its standard-bearer Governor Samuel J. Tilden of New York, who had won national fame for his successful prosecution of the Tweed Ring in New York City. Governor Thomas A. Hendricks of Indiana was named for second place on the ticket.

REPUBLICANS. The Republican party, avoiding several prominent leaders who had been too closely linked to the Grant administration, selected as its nominee the honest and conscientious governor of Ohio, Rutherford B. Hayes. Chosen to be his running mate was Representative William A. Wheeler of New York.

THE CAMPAIGN. Both candidates were straightforward representatives of American business interests. During the campaign Tilden focused on the corruption of the Grant administration, while Hayes asserted that the Republican party had saved the nation during the Civil War and the Reconstruction period.

COMPROMISE OF 1877. Tilden won 4,300,000 popular votes to Hayes's 4,036,000. Tilden carried states with a total of 184 votes in the electoral college, one short of the necessary majority. Hayes received 165 votes. In dispute were twenty electoral votes, which both candidates claimed. In Oregon the Democratic governor declared one of the Republicans named to the electoral college technically ineligible to cast his ballot. In South Carolina, Florida, and Louisiana there were charges of fraud involving nineteen electoral votes. (Those southern states were just passing from the control of carpetbaggers, scalawags, and freedmen into the control of the Bourbons.)

To avert any possibility of serious disturbances, Congress created the Electoral Commission of fifteen persons to pass judgment on the disputed votes. Five members of the Senate (three Republicans and two Democrats), five members of the House of Representatives (three Democrats and two Republicans), and five justices of the Supreme Court (three Republicans and two Democrats) were named to the commission. (It had been expected that Justice David Davis, an independent, would be selected by his colleagues on the Supreme Court as the fifteenth member of the commission, but having just been chosen to the Senate from Illinois, he was ineligible.) The decision was eight to seven—along straight party lines—on every disputed point in favor of the Republican Hayes. The nation acquiesced in the decision after southern Democratic leaders had received informal assurances from Republican politicians that federal troops would be withdrawn from the South.

The Hayes Administration. Hayes's term of office was far from tranquil. Relations with the Democrats in Congress were difficult; the Republican party was troubled by factionalism; and constant demands were made by its reform wing that the Republican party be scourged of unscrupulous individuals.

THE PRESIDENT. Although Hayes was no crusading reformer, he worked hard to give the nation honest and efficient leadership. In economic matters he represented the views of business America.

THE CABINET. The members of Hayes's official family were unusually able. Reformers were particularly pleased by the selection of noted lawyer and former attorney general William M. Evarts of New York as secretary of state, Senator John Sherman of Ohio as secretary of the treasury, and former senator Carl Schurz of Missouri as secretary of the interior. The President's appointment of David Key, a Democratic senator from Tennessee, as postmaster general demonstrated his conciliatory attitude toward the South.

Stalwarts and Half-Breeds. Within the Republican ranks there were bitter quarrels between the Stalwarts and the Half-Breeds. The former were staunch supporters of the recent Grant regime and looked to Senator Roscoe Conkling of New York for leadership. The latter (so called because of their "half-breed" Republicanism) were of a more liberal bent, favoring Hayes's southern policy and civil service reform, and they rallied around the authority of Senator James G. Blaine of Maine. Important members of the Stalwart faction were Representative Benjamin F. Butler of Massachusetts, former senator Zachariah Chandler of Michigan, and Senator John A. Logan of Illinois. Prominent Half-Breeds were Representative James A. Garfield of Ohio and Representative George F. Hoar of Massachusetts. This intraparty rivalry gave the reform element within Republicanism an occasional chance to determine party action. Factional strife, however, had more to do with power than with policy.

An Opposition Congress. The President's relations with Congress were far from happy, for the Democrats controlled the House of Representatives during his entire term and the Senate for the latter two years. In the lower house the Democratic majority set up a committee that investigated the disputed election of 1876 in order to embarrass Hayes. The President in return vetoed congressional appropriation bills when the Democrats, attempting to repeal the Enforcement Acts compelling the observance of the Reconstruction program, attached what he considered to be one or another objectionable rider.[1] This partisan quarreling prevented the passage of a sound program of legislation.

Election of 1880. Hayes's refusal to seek reelection seemed to remove the chief obstacle in the way of the Stalwarts, who were making a vigorous attempt to control the Republican organization and force former President Grant on the party and the nation for another term.

DEMOCRATS. The Democratic national convention nominated for president a distinguished Civil War general, Winfield S. Hancock of Pennsylvania. Chosen as Hancock's running mate was former representative William H. English of Indiana.

REPUBLICANS. In the Republican national convention a deadlock developed between the Stalwart supporters of Grant and the Half-Breed supporters of Blaine. On the thirty-sixth ballot Grant's opponents concentrated their strength and led a stampede of delegates to a compromise candidate, Representative James A. Garfield of Ohio. Since Garfield was a member of the Half-Breed faction of the party, the anti-Grant delegates attempted to pacify the Stalwarts by nominating for vice-president one of Senator Conkling's most trusted lieutenants, Chester A. Arthur of New York, who two years earlier had been removed from a New York Custom House post in a reform maneuver by Hayes.

THE CAMPAIGN. Early in the campaign Republicans were alarmed be-

---

[1] A clause appended to a bill to secure a goal entirely distinct from that of the bill itself.

cause the animosities of their convention were not easily forgotten. But Grant and Conkling finally agreed to speak for Garfield and thus present a united front against the Democrats. At a time when the voters could have profited from some guidance in deciding important economic and social issues, they received little help from the two presidential candidates. In ability and achievement there was little difference between Garfield and Hancock, and both men were essentially conservative in their views on national questions. Partisan strife and personal rivalries still held the center of the political stage.

GARFIELD'S NARROW VICTORY. Garfield was elected with 9,000 more popular votes than Hancock received. However, in the electoral college Garfield achieved a more substantial success; he received 369 votes to Hancock's 155.

The Short-Lived Garfield Administration. Garfield was unable to prove himself as president; he was assassinated a few months after assuming the office.

THE INFLUENCE OF BLAINE. As soon as Garfield had been elected, he indicated that Senator Blaine, whom he appointed secretary of state, would exercise a commanding influence in the new administration. The result was an unseemly quarrel between Senator Conkling and the President. When Garfield used the control of political appointments in New York in such a way as to build a Garfield-Blaine machine, Conkling defied the administration. The controversy became ever more acute.

ASSASSINATION. On July 2, 1881, Garfield was shot in the Washington, D.C., railroad station by a crazedly disappointed office seeker, Charles T. Guiteau, who was heard to shout: "I am a Stalwart and Arthur is President now." The President died two months later.

The Arthur Administration. The death of Garfield elevated to the presidency Vice-President Chester A. Arthur. As president, Arthur quickly surprised those who believed that as a machine-oriented politician he would not be equal to the tasks of the office.

THE PRESIDENT. Arthur refused to use the presidency to reward his former political cronies, and he expended much energy in attempting to end the factional strife within the Republican party.

THE CABINET. Gradually the new President changed the membership of his cabinet so that the influence of Blaine and his intimates declined. Senator Frederick T. Frelinghuysen of New Jersey replaced Blaine as secretary of state and jurist Charles J. Folger of New York became secretary of the treasury. Robert T. Lincoln, son of President Lincoln, was retained as secretary of war.

"Pork-Barrel" Appropriations. As the government's income from various taxes piled up a surplus, members of Congress yielded to the temptation to support one another's proposed legislation for expensive

public works in their districts. During the 1870s there was a more than doubling of "pork-barrel"[2] appropriations. Arthur forthrightly criticized what he considered to be wasteful expenditures of government funds even when it was argued that the money was available. When an appropriations bill authorizing the use of $18 million for river and harbor improvements of doubtful need was sent to him to sign, he vetoed it. Although his veto was overridden, he won the esteem of a large part of the nation for his sober action.

Reform of the Civil Service. The assassination of President Garfield, which seemed a consequence of factional quarrels over political appointments, shocked the nation into a realization of the evils of the spoils system.[3]

PLANNING THE MERIT SYSTEM. After the Civil War the merit system of appointing and promoting civil service employees slowly made headway. In 1865 Republican Representative Thomas A. Jenckes of Rhode Island, who had conducted a systematic study of the British civil service, introduced a bill in Congress to set up competitive examinations for specific federal government offices. In 1871 President Grant appointed a commission that experimented, unsuccessfully, with examinations for some positions. President Hayes cast his lot with the enemies of the spoils system. He issued an executive order forbidding the extraction of political contributions from federal officeholders; he gave Secretary of the Interior Carl Schurz a free hand to try the merit system in his department; he renamed Thomas L. James, a champion of civil service reform, to the postmastership of New York City; he removed two of Conkling's leading supporters from New York Custom House posts for violating a regulation against political campaigning by government employees. The National Civil Service Reform League, founded in 1881 by George William Curtis, the editor of *Harper's Weekly*, served to unite the efforts of those in favor of the merit system.

THE PENDLETON ACT. Indignation became widespread as revelations of political corruption marked the trial of President Garfield's assassin. In his first message to Congress President Arthur indicated his willingness to cooperate with the legislative branch in stopping the practice of granting civil service positions as rewards to supporters of the party that won an election. The result was the Pendleton Act. Named after its sponsor, Democratic Senator George H. Pendleton of Ohio, the measure was passed in January, 1883, by a Republican-controlled Congress that was motivated, in part, by the hope that the measure would safeguard Republican office-

[2]Expenditures for projects, such as building roads and bridges, deepening rivers and harbors, and establishing military installations, which are allocated more for local political patronage than for needed improvements.

[3]The practice of regarding public offices and their financial rewards as plunder to be distributed to members of the victorious party in an election.

holders in the event of Democratic successes in the 1884 congressional elections.

The Pendleton Act provided for the appointment by the President of a bipartisan commission of three to draft and administer competitive examinations that would determine on a merit basis the fitness of applicants for office. The act also prohibited the collection of funds from federal officeholders for party campaign purposes. A list of federal positions (approximately 10 percent) obtainable through the merit system was established, and the President was authorized to expand the number as he saw fit. By substituting merit for political influence in federal appointments, the Pendleton Act established the basis for the present-day federal civil service system.

Tariff Legislation. A tariff is a system, or schedule, of taxes, or duties, placed by the federal government on imported goods. In the post-Civil War period the Republican party, when in control of Congress, redeemed its campaign pledges by passing legislation increasing tariff rates.

TRADITIONAL PARTY POSITIONS. The tariff has played a significant role in American politics. The Republican party has traditionally advocated a protective tariff, one that protects domestic manufacturers from foreign competition by imposing high rates on foreign goods so as to discourage their importation. The Democratic party has traditionally supported a revenue tariff, one that provides income for the federal government and therefore has low rates so as not to discourage imports. But Republicans have endorsed the tariff not only for protective purposes but also as a favored means of raising revenue for the government. And some Democrats have even subscribed to free trade, the international exchange of goods unimpeded by any restrictions.

"TINKERING WITH THE SCHEDULES." Protection, initially justified as a help for "infant" industries that were being developed in the face of established foreign competition and subsequently justified as compensation to industry for increased internal revenue taxes, was generally accepted as an important factor in the growth of American industry. Such modification of rates as occurred in 1870, 1872, and 1875 was designed to respond to the protests of the nonindustrial West and South without abandoning the protective principle.

THE TARIFF OF 1883. During the presidential campaign of 1880 there was much discussion about taking the tariff out of politics and revising schedules to meet the needs of domestic manufacturers on a scientific basis. Two years later a congressionally-sponsored fact-finding tariff commission, after conducting a thorough investigation, surprised the nation by recommending a substantial reduction of duties. Congress, however, ignored the advice of the experts and in 1883 passed an act that was a caricature of genuine reform. The reductions in rates averaged scarcely 2 percent.

Exclusion of the Chinese. Immigration from China increased rapidly after 1850. Chinese laborers were welcomed on the West Coast so long as they were needed for such work as the construction of the Central Pacific Railroad. The Burlingame Treaty of 1868 between the United States and China granted Chinese subjects the right of unlimited immigration to the United States. In the 1870s, as it became apparent that, especially in California, the Chinese were competing with native Americans for jobs, a movement developed in that state for a revision of the policy of unrestricted immigration. The Chinese, it was maintained, were socially unassimilable, and their low economic life-style endangered the American standard of living. In 1879 Congress passed a bill restricting Chinese immigration, but President Hayes vetoed it. He then sent a commission to China to secure modification of the Burlingame Treaty. As a result of the negotiations, in 1880 the immigration of Chinese laborers was regulated but not prohibited. In 1882 President Arthur signed the Chinese Exclusion Act, which suspended immigration from China for ten years. The exclusion principle was renewed periodically thereafter, until 1965, when the entire body of American immigration regulations was overhauled.

THE RETURN OF THE DEMOCRATS TO POWER

The balloting in the election of 1884 brought a political upheaval that enabled the Democrats to secure the presidential office for the first time in twenty-eight years.

Election of 1884. Ever since the scandals of the Grant administration the Republicans had been on the defensive. They could win the election only if they held the independent voters who since the Civil War had tended to support their ticket. But in 1884 the Republicans suffered defeat, and contributing to it were defections from their own ranks.

DEMOCRATS. The Democratic national convention chose as its presidential nominee Governor Grover Cleveland of New York, who was widely known as a competent and courageous administrator. For vice-president the delegates named Thomas A. Hendricks, Tilden's running mate in the disputed election of 1876.

REPUBLICANS. The Republican national convention refused to give the nomination to the incumbent Arthur, although he desired it and, it was widely held, deserved it on the basis of his creditable accomplishments as president. Instead, the delegates, disregarding the small but vigorous reform element, yielded to the magnetism of Blaine and on the fourth ballot selected him in a frenzy of rejoicing. Senator John A. Logan of the former Stalwart faction was chosen for second place on the ticket.

THE CAMPAIGN. Many reformers within the Republican ranks announced that they would bolt their party if the Democrats chose a nominee whom they could support. Cleveland was such a candidate. The regular Republicans sneeringly nicknamed the bolters "mugwumps" (from the Indian for "great chief").

CLEVELAND'S NARROW VICTORY. The election was close, with Cleveland receiving only 60,000 more popular votes than did Blaine. In addition to the active support of Cleveland by the mugwumps, reasons for the Democratic victory included (1) the unenthusiastic campaigning for Blaine on the part of former Stalwarts; (2) the belief that Blaine had used his political position to further his own financial interests (in 1876 the "Mulligan Letters" had pointed to his acceptance of money for securing a land grant for an Arkansas railroad); (3) the resentment of Catholic voters, particularly in the pivotal state of New York, over the Reverend Samuel D. Burchard's campaign remark that the Democrats were the party of "rum, Romanism, and rebellion."

The Cleveland Administration.
Although Cleveland soon made it known that he regarded public office as a public trust, he had difficulty in persuading others that his administration would conduct itself accordingly.

THE PRESIDENT. Cleveland was generally considered the ablest Chief Executive since Abraham Lincoln. He was honest, efficient, imbued with common sense, and above all not subject to control by others. Cleveland was stronger than his party, for he embodied the hopes of most political reformers, regardless of party affiliation.

THE CABINET. In choosing his official family, Cleveland sought men of ability, even if they lacked experience in government office. Outstanding appointees were former senator Thomas F. Bayard of Delaware as secretary of state, New York City financier William C. Whitney as secretary of the navy, and Senator L. Q. C. Lamar of Mississippi as secretary of the interior.

Cleveland's Independent Actions.
As a person of great integrity, Cleveland was frequently embarrassed by partisan pressure in dealing with legislative matters and patronage (the control of political appointments). Many of his recommendations to Congress, such as those to revise the tariff rates and to conserve the diminishing acreage of public lands, were either ignored by the legislators or blocked by the Republican leaders.

EXTENDING THE CIVIL SERVICE LIST. With the Democratic leaders enjoying their first national victory in twenty-eight years and insisting that 100,000 federal jobs be given to faithful party workers, Cleveland reluctantly permitted the removal of some Republican officeholders for this purpose. He showed his interest in reform, however, by adding almost 12,000 positions to the list of offices obtainable on a merit basis.

REPEAL OF THE TENURE OF OFFICE ACT. When Cleveland dismissed a federal district attorney in Alabama, the Senate, invoking the Tenure of Office Act passed during the Andrew Johnson administration, demanded that

Cleveland submit the papers relating to the removal. This Cleveland refused to do, insisting that the removal of federal officers was an executive prerogative. Thereupon the Senate censured the President. But in 1887 Congress repealed the Tenure of Office Act. By his action Cleveland had helped to strengthen the independence of the presidency.

THE PENSION CONTROVERSY. The mounting surplus in the Treasury Department prompted Congress to be generous in granting pensions to Union veterans of the Civil War. The modest appropriations for pensions to disabled veterans increased greatly with the passage in 1879 of the Arrears of Pension Act, which granted back payments for service-connected disabilities. Soon pension agents were touring the nation persuading veterans to file claims. By 1885 the pension roll contained close to 350,000 names. Claimants whose cases were not approved by the Bureau of Pensions turned to Congress, where willing legislators sponsored private pension bills, many of which were frauds. Cleveland attempted to investigate each of those bills, and his research led him to veto more than 200, although he approved more private pension bills than had any of his predecessors. Congress abandoned the test of service-connected disability in the Dependent Pension Bill (1887), which provided that any veteran who had served for three months and was incapable of earning a livelihood could receive a pension. But Cleveland vetoed the bill on the grounds that it would tend to "pauperize" the former servicemen and that it was too soon after the war for so comprehensive a pension policy.

Government Reorganization and Reform. The Cleveland administration saw the need to improve the workings of government. Measures were enacted in a spirit of nonpartisanship unusual for the period.

THE PRESIDENTIAL SUCCESSION ACT. In November, 1885, the death of Thomas Hendricks, the fifth vice-president to die in office, prompted the legislators to take action. In 1886 Congress passed the Presidential Succession Act, providing that in case of the removal, death, resignation, or inability to serve of both the president and the vice-president, the members of the cabinet, in order of the creation of their offices, should succeed to the duties of the presidency.

THE ELECTORAL COUNT ACT. Intended to prevent a disputed presidential election (such as that of 1876), the Electoral Count Act, passed by Congress in 1887, authorized each state to decide contests over the appointment of its electors and the reporting of its electoral returns. If opposing sets of returns were submitted, the Senate and House of Representatives, voting separately, were empowered to decide which result to approve; if the two houses of Congress disagreed, the returns certified by the state's governor were to be accepted.

DEPARTMENT OF AGRICULTURE. In 1889 Congress enlarged the Department of Agriculture and made its head a member of the cabinet. The new department was established to gather and distribute information on farming matters and to administer laws dealing with all aspects of agriculture.

The Tariff in Fiscal Policy. The Cleveland administration regarded the tariff as one facet of the government's overall fiscal policy, which had resulted in the accumulation of a surplus of funds through an extensive program of taxation.

SURPLUS OF FUNDS. During the 1880s the excess of federal government income over expenditures averaged $100 million annually. The surplus was embarrassing because it indicated to the taxpayers that they were bearing an unnecessary burden; it reduced the amount of currency in circulation and thus available for normal business needs; and it encouraged Congress to make pork-barrel appropriations.

CLEVELAND'S TARIFF MESSAGE. President Cleveland was opposed to using the surplus funds for large-scale government expenditures; he believed that reduction in internal revenue taxation would lower the surplus sufficiently. In his view, the tariff remained as the obstacle in the way of tax reform. In his third State of the Union Message to Congress, in December, 1887, the President not only denounced the existing tariff duties as a "vicious, inequitable, and illogical source of unnecessary taxation" but also maintained that the protective principle was responsible for the growth of large business combinations that eventually increased prices by stifling competition. The only solution, he emphasized, was the downward revision of tariff rates. Presidential pressure persuaded the Democratic-controlled House of Representatives to pass in 1888 the Mills Bill, providing for a drastic reduction of tariff rates, but the Republican-controlled Senate soon replied with the Aldrich Bill, containing the elements of high protection. There was a stalemate.

A REPUBLICAN REVIVAL

In the election of 1888 both major parties tried to make enough concessions to the discontented farmers and laborers to keep their ranks solid against a protest vote. The Republicans were more successful than the Democrats in convincing the nation that their party was the protector equally of all three elements of economic society—businessmen, factory workers, and farmers.

Election of 1888. The issue in the campaign had been largely set by Cleveland's demand in his message to Congress the preceding year for a general lowering of tariff rates.

DEMOCRATS. The Democratic national convention renominated Cleveland by acclamation. For vice-president the delegates named former senator Allen G. Thurman of Ohio.

REPUBLICANS. After Blaine declined to become a candidate, the Republican national convention selected as its nominee Benjamin Harrison of Indiana, a corporation lawyer and grandson of President William Henry Harrison. Levi P. Morton of New York, a banker who had served as minister to France, was chosen for second place on the ticket.

THE CAMPAIGN. To a remarkable degree the tariff issue overshadowed all others. Party lines held relatively firm, with the Democrats proposing a lowering of tariff duties and the Republicans advocating the maintenance of high protective rates. The Democrats were placed on the defensive by the aggressive and well-financed Republican drive. Cleveland was accused, without justification, of subscribing to a policy of removing all restrictions on trade, including tariffs, and thus benefiting British manufacturers at the expense of American manufacturers. The Republicans also made a strong appeal to Union veterans, whom Cleveland had antagonized by his views on pensions and by his order for the return to the southern states of Confederate battle flags captured in the Civil War. Neither Cleveland nor Harrison addressed himself to the needs of laborers and farmers.

HARRISON'S VICTORY. Although Cleveland received a plurality of more than 100,000 popular votes, he lost such pivotal states as New York, Pennsylvania, and Ohio, with their large number of electoral votes. In these states the Republicans had effectively mobilized the strength of businessmen behind their ticket. Harrison achieved victory with 233 votes in the electoral college to Cleveland's 168.

The Harrison Administration. The executive branch under Harrison reflected the views and had the enthusiastic support of the business interests of the nation.

THE PRESIDENT. Harrison was dignified in demeanor and conservative in opinion; he was an able lawyer but an inept politician.

THE CABINET. Rather than relying upon the advice of his cabinet members, most of whom were fairly competent, the new President depended heavily on the counsel of three prominent Republicans (one of whom did serve in the cabinet): James G. Blaine, once again secretary of state; Thomas B. Reed of Maine, Speaker of the House of Representatives; and William McKinley of Ohio, chairman of the House Committee on Ways and Means. [4]

High Protection. The deadlock on the tariff between the Democratic-controlled House of Representatives and the Republican-controlled Senate that had developed during the last year of the Cleveland administration was broken during the Harrison administration.

THE MCKINLEY TARIFF. The tariff matter was settled after the Republi-

---

[4]The committee concerned with methods and resources for raising the necessary revenue for the expenses of the nation.

cans gained control of the House of Representatives and retained their majority in the Senate in the 1888 election. The result was the McKinley Tariff of 1890, named after William McKinley, who guided the legislation through the House of Representatives. On the theory that prosperity flowed directly from protection, McKinley and his colleagues raised the level of duties to a new peak, attaining an average rate of approximately 50 percent. Rates in the woolen goods, cotton goods, and steel products schedules were increased, while the protective principle was extended to some farm products, including wheat, potatoes, butter, and eggs. To soothe consumers, raw (unprocessed) sugar was put on the free list (the American Sugar Refining Company was a beneficiary of this move), and as a unique concession to the domestic producers of raw sugar, they were granted a bounty of two cents a pound on their product. This strategy reduced revenues and thus decreased the federal surplus. The act also included innovative reciprocity provisions. The President was empowered to impose duties on commodities on the free list, such as sugar, molasses, coffee, tea, and hides, if the nations exporting these items discriminated against the products of the United States.

OPPOSITION TO PROTECTION. As soon as the McKinley Bill was signed into law (October, 1890), prices of protected commodities were raised by producers in anticipation of the effect of the protective schedules. The Democrats used an "increase in the cost of living" argument as an effective weapon against the Republicans in the congressional elections of 1890. The Democratic landslide was partly a result of the voters' repudiation of the Republicans because of the apparent effects of the protective tariff.

Extending the Civil Service List. Harrison's support of the merit system was at first nominal. Mass replacements of Post Office Department workers brought protests even from some Republican leaders. In late 1892 the President, by then defeated for reelection, added a few positions to the merit system.

The Reed Rules. By parliamentary tactics permissible under the rules of the House of Representatives the Democratic minority attempted to obstruct the President's recommendations for legislation. Speaker Reed changed the rules to speed up legislative processes, an action considered arbitrary by the Democrats. After a sharp controversy between the two parties in the lower house, the new rules that Reed had unilaterally imposed were adopted as standard procedure. They provided that the Speaker should entertain no dilatory motions and that physical attendance should be sufficient basis for determination of a quorum. (Under the old rules, when the Democrats had wanted to delay action on a matter, they had refused to answer roll call although physically present, thus preventing a quorum.) The new rules increased the efficiency of conducting the business of the House of Representatives, but in so doing they greatly enlarged the power of the Speaker. As the initiator and vigorous wielder of the new rules, Reed soon gained the title of "Czar."

The "Billion Dollar Congress." Despite Harrison's plea that the "problem" of a surplus of federal funds be solved by reducing taxes, the Republican-controlled Congress actually dissipated the surplus through increased expenditures. During 1889–1891, Congress appropriated a total of $1 billion, the largest sum yet spent by a peacetime session. Among the appropriations were those for the return to the northern states of the direct tax collected during the Civil War; an extensive program of river and harbor improvements; the building of additional steel ships as part of a naval modernization program begun during the Arthur administration; and implementation of the Dependent Pension Act (1890), which was similar to the bill vetoed by Cleveland three years earlier. The Fifty-first Congress thus became known as the "Billion Dollar Congress."

A DEMOCRATIC REAPPEARANCE

The vote in the election of 1892 directed that Grover Cleveland reassume the presidency. During his second term the hostility of the agrarian West and South toward the industrial East grew more intense as a result of a severe economic depression and the policies of the government in financial matters.

Election of 1892. The dramatic feature of the election was the emergence of the Populists as a strong minor party of protest. Nevertheless, the overwhelming number of voters remained loyal to the major parties.

DEMOCRATS. Having Cleveland's permission to promote his candidacy, a group of eastern bankers and businessmen marshaled state delegations pledged to the former President. In an unusual manifestation of party unity, he received on the first ballot the two-thirds vote required by the convention rules for nomination. The midwestern segment of the party was given consideration in the naming of former representative Adlai E. Stevenson of Illinois for vice-president.

REPUBLICANS. Blaine, whose record as secretary of state had commanded general admiration, permitted his name to be presented for the presidential nomination. But Harrison, although unpopular among the Republican party workers, who considered him too reserved and unsympathetic, controlled enough delegate votes to win the nomination on the first ballot. Chosen as his running mate was Whitelaw Reid, editor of the *New York Tribune*.

POPULISTS. Composed of western and southern farmers and eastern laborers, the new third party nominated agrarian-oriented politician James B. Weaver of Iowa for president and agrarian reformer James G. Field of Virginia for vice-president. The Populist platform advocated a variety of reforms to help the farmers and laborers.

THE CAMPAIGN. Although the two major parties differed on the tariff issue, with the Democrats advocating a general lowering of rates and the Republicans supporting the continuance of highly protective duties, there was slight difference in their platforms or in the candidates' statements on any other matter. However, the Republicans were considerably weakened by a number of factors: (1) the hostility of reformers to Harrison's neglect of the merit system; (2) widespead resentment over higher prices following the McKinley Tariff of 1890; (3) anger in the South about the Republican attempt to force federal control of elections on the southern states (a federal election bill had passed the House of Representatives but had not come to a vote in the Senate); (4) disgust with the Republican-controlled Congress for using up the federal surplus at a time when it was feared that an economic depression was beginning.

CLEVELAND'S VICTORY. In popular votes, Cleveland received 5,556,000 and Harrison 5,176,000. The Democrats won a complete victory, capturing the presidency and control of both the Senate and House of Representatives for the first time in thirty-six years. The Populists received 1,041,000 popular votes, thus making their party a force to be reckoned with.

The Second Cleveland Administration. When Cleveland took the oath of office for the second time he became the first and so far has been the only Chief Executive to serve two nonconsecutive terms.

THE PRESIDENT. After leaving the White House four years earlier, he had engaged quite successfully in the practice of law. He returned to office a much more conservative man.

THE CABINET. The membership of Cleveland's official family was strikingly conservative. Walter Q. Gresham of Indiana, a Republican leader who had criticized some of his party's positions, was secretary of state; John G. Carlisle of Kentucky, who had served with distinction in both houses of Congress, was secretary of the treasury; Richard Olney of Massachusetts, a highly successful corporation lawyer, was attorney general.

The Panic of 1893. Cleveland had scarcely been inaugurated, in March, 1893, before the nation found itself in the grip of a panic comparable to that of 1873, the beginning of a severe depression that lasted four years. Certain factors had foreshadowed economic trouble: (1) the enormous increase in government expenditures, while income remained stationary, until the federal surplus was changed to a deficit; (2) the hoarding of gold as investors in Europe, already experiencing a depression, began to sell their American stocks and bonds in order to secure the precious metal; (3) the acute uneasiness of the business community when in April, 1893, the gold reserve in the Treasury Department fell for the first time below the $100 million mark.

BUSINESS FAILURES. The panic was precipitated in May, 1893, by the failure of the National Cordage Company, a rope manufacturing concern.

Within six months thousands of business firms became insolvent, hundreds of banks closed, and scores of railroads went into bankruptcy. By the spring of 1894 close to 20 percent of the work force was unemployed.

"COXEY'S ARMY." Bands of jobless men, organized as "armies," roamed the countryside. Some sought relief measures from state and local governments. "Coxey's Army," led by "General" Jacob S. Coxey, an Ohio businessman, marched on Washington, D.C., in April, 1894, presenting to Congress a petition for inflation of the currency and a federal program of public works. But after Coxey and two aides were arrested for walking on the Capitol lawn, their "army" quickly disbanded.

The Wilson-Gorman Tariff. Early in 1894 the House of Representatives passed the Wilson Bill, which provided for the inclusion of raw materials such as coal, iron ore, lumber, wool, and unprocessed sugar on the free list; the reduction of the rates on such finished products as iron and steel wares, cotton and woolen goods, silk and linen articles; the repeal of the bounty granted under the McKinley Tariff to the domestic producers of unprocessed sugar; and the imposition of a tax of 2 percent on incomes of $4,000 and over, in order to make up the loss of revenue from the reduced duties. The Senate added to the Wilson Bill 634 amendments, removing some raw materials from the free list and raising the protective rates to an average of approximately 40 percent. The resulting Wilson-Gorman Bill bore a marked resemblance to the McKinley Tariff. After acrimonious debate the House accepted the amendments. Although Cleveland did not veto the bill, he refused to sign it, allowing it to become law in 1894 without his signature. In 1895 the Supreme Court in *Pollock* v. *Farmers' Loan and Trust Co.* declared the income-tax provision of the Wilson-Gorman Tariff unconstitutional on the ground that it was a direct tax and therefore subject to the requirement in the Constitution that such a tax must be apportioned among the states according to population.

Chapter 3

SETTLEMENT OF THE WEST

While the South was being humbled during the Civil War and the Reconstruction years, foundations of a new economic order were established in the West. Several factors contributed to the settlement of the West. Among them were the courage and perseverance of the pioneers; the skill of business interests possessed of abundant capital and an adequate labor supply; and a government policy of support and encouragement. The domain of prairie, plateau, mountain, and desert beyond the Mississippi River possessed remarkable resources. Before they could be utilized, however, the West had to be made safe and accessible for settlement. The building of transcontinental railroads made it possible to transport people and goods to and from the region. In topography and climate the West offered a wide range of opportunities for mining, ranching, and large-scale farming. There were three waves of migration: first came the miners; then the cattlemen; and lastly the farmers.

THE INDIANS

The arrival of white people in the West quickly changed Indian life. War, the introduction of diseases such as measles and tuberculosis, extensive killing of the bison, being forced onto reservations—all these created near-unendurable hardships for the Indians of the western plains.

Overcoming the Indians. Complete utilization of the vast natural resources of the western regions was impossible so long as the nomadic Indian tribes, which relied for subsistence on the bison (commonly called buffalo) herds of the Great Plains, retained their hunting grounds. These Plains Indians, probably numbering more than 225,000 at the end of the Civil War, were skilled fighters and often resisted the encroachments of the white settlers.

FRONTIER HOSTILITIES. While some tribes, such as the Crow and northern Arapaho, were generally friendly to the whites, the more militant southern Arapaho, Cheyenne, Comanche, and Kiowa were determined to halt the advance of settlers into the Great Plains and the intermountain areas farther west. During the decade after the Civil War, hundreds of skirmishes took place between United States military forces and the Indian tribes. At times as many as 30,000 troops were in the field to protect emigrants moving along the Missouri River and westward.

COLLAPSE OF THE SIOUX. The Sioux nation in the northern Great Plains constituted one of the most difficult problems for the army commanders; it was large, powerful, and ably led. Skirmish after skirmish occurred. In 1876 General George A. Custer and all under his immediate command were killed in battle by the Sioux at the Little Bighorn River in Montana. However, the Sioux's courageous campaign against United States troops was slowly contained, and by 1880 the northern frontier was relatively quiet. But the price had been high in lives and in money, shocking the government into a reconsideration of its Indian policy.

EXTERMINATING THE BUFFALO. The Plains Indians depended upon the flesh of buffalo for food, upon their hides for clothing, and upon many other parts for additional articles of daily use. An important factor in the decline of militant resistance on the part of the Indians was the slaughter by professional hunters and by sportsmen of the buffalo herds. Buffalo robes were in great demand during the quarter-century after the Civil War. Scout and showman William F. ("Buffalo Bill") Cody claimed that he had shot 4,280 in the northern herds within less than two years. By 1885 only a few straggling herds remained of the more than 15 million animals that had roamed the plains twenty years earlier. Although the species survived under government protection, the main economic support of the nomadic Indians was gone.

Formulating a National Policy for the Indians. A more enlightened policy of dealing with the Indian tribes slowly took shape. But it was framed only after the record had been filled with needless wars and massacres, fraudulent seizures of Indian lands, and speculations of dishonest traders. For many years the Department of War, which advocated "extermination," worked at cross-purposes with the Bureau of Indian Affairs within the Department of the Interior, which at times supplied the Indians with hunting guns, usable of course in combat.

THE RESERVATION SYSTEM. As actual warfare between United States troops and Indian warriors diminished, the government forced tribes onto reservations where they were almost completely dependent on the taxpayers' bounty, never adequate for their needs. The aim of the reservation policy was to assimilate the Indians into an agricultural economy. By 1885 there were 171 reservations in more than a score of states and territories.

But the administration of the reservation system was notoriously corrupt. Government agents made fortunes by supplying Indians under their jurisdiction with shoddy goods, selling them prohibited liquor, and cheating them out of their rightful lands through fraudulent real-estate deals. Meantime, traders, miners, cattlemen, and railroad builders prodded the government into unwarranted encroachments on Indian reservations.

THE REFORM MOVEMENT. Humanitarians, stirred in part by Helen Hunt Jackson's *A Century of Dishonor* (1881), a report on the degradation of reservation Indians, tried to modify or supplant the system. Among the reformers there was a sharp division between those who wanted to preserve old tribal customs and others who desired to hasten the assimilation of the Indians.

THE DAWES ACT. Initially, government action was confined to a program of increased appropriations for schools to train young Indians in arts and crafts, farming, and animal husbandry. Congress partially accepted the idea that Indians should be more adequately prepared for a place in American society when it passed the Dawes Act in 1887. This measure modified the reservation system by granting 160 acres of land and United States citizenship to the heads of Indian families who would agree to abandon their tribal allegiance. The right of disposal of the land was withheld for twenty-five years. The motive behind this legislation was twofold: first, the desire to encourage Indians to become assimilated into the nation and, second, the willingness of the federal government to satisfy the land hunger of white settlers. Land on the Indian reservations not needed for allotment to former members of the tribe was opened to settlement.

THE BURKE ACT. Cattlemen and farmers, seeking new homesteads in the trans-Mississippi West, profited more from the Dawes Act than did the Indians. After some thirty years even the reformers admitted that title to private property and the rights of citizenship had not improved the status of many Indians. The Burke Act, designed to correct the defects of the Dawes Act, was passed in 1906. It provided new incentives for those making the transition from tribal membership to individual citizenship. Citizenship was generally not granted to Indians receiving land allotments until they had completed the twenty-five-year probationary period specified in the Dawes Act, but those who proved competent in managing the land could become citizens in a shorter time. (In 1924 legislation was passed conferring citizenship on all Indians.)

THE MINING FRONTIER

One of the magnets pulling settlers westward through the Indian barriers and drawing squatters[1] into the regions where nomadic tribes had long

[1]Those who occupy land without possessing a legal title.

roamed was the discovery by venturesome prospectors of the rich mineral deposits beyond the Mississippi River.

The "Boom." During the third quarter of the nineteenth century the mineral resources of the West were rapidly discovered and almost as rapidly exploited.

"STRIKES." A discovery of a rich mineral deposit was called a "strike." Gold was found not far from present-day Sacramento, California, in 1848, leading to the "rush" there the following year by prospectors not only from all over the United States but also from overseas. More deposits of gold were revealed in 1858 in the Pikes Peak district of what is now Colorado. The Comstock Lode[2] discovered in 1859 on the site of present-day Virginia City, Nevada, produced large amounts of both gold and silver. In 1874 gold was discovered in the Black Hills section of what is now South Dakota. Copper was found in 1881 near present-day Butte, Montana. A number of abundantly rich silver deposits were unearthed during the 1880s in the Coeur d'Alene Mountains district of what is now Idaho.

MINING CAMPS. In their writings, Bret Harte and Mark Twain, among others, captured the mood and manner of the settlers who threw up the hastily built wooden towns that provided shelter and recreation for enthusiastic seekers of wealth. There saloons, dance halls, hotels, and gambling houses were apt to be established earlier than schools or churches. Indeed, some of the "boom towns" had enjoyed a brief prosperity and been largely abandoned before law and order could be established.

After the "Boom." Despite the usual pattern of discovery and boom (in many a case it was discovery and "bust"), mining soon became the chief industry of the mountainous regions of the West. Upon it rested the economic structure of many communities.

GETTING OUT THE WEALTH. Some mining booms, such as the one at Pikes Peak, ended quickly. The resources of gold, silver, lead, copper, and other minerals were abundant in the West, but it required more than enthusiasm and the techniques of placer mining,[3] such as panning at a stream, to get out the ore. In Montana and Idaho, as in Colorado and Nevada, the greatest wealth came after placer mining had been replaced by more elaborate processes, requiring heavy machinery and considerable outlay of money. As a result, profits went more often to absentee capitalists than to resident prospectors.

THE IMPACT OF THE MINING FRONTIER. Before the pioneer days had ended, the mining frontier produced enduring influences by (1) stimulating settlements that brought new states into the Union (Nevada in 1864, Colorado in 1876, Montana in 1889, Idaho and Wyoming in 1890); (2) providing gold and silver in such quantities that the volume of currency kept pace for

---

[2]A lode is an ore deposit that fills a fissure in rock.
[3]Extracting mineral particles from surface deposits.

a time with the increasing needs of business enterprise; (3) offering new opportunities for the investment of capital in speculative, but often highly profitable, mining ventures; (4) emphasizing the need for the reorganization of the structure of American business so that larger amounts of capital could be used under the corporate form of investment; (5) giving many settlers in new communities a chance to work out procedures of self-government necessary to combat violence and social anarchy; (6) leading to an increased demand for better transportation, which was met by stage coaches, pony expresses, and finally railroads.

THE CATTLE COUNTRY

The westward thrust of rail facilities brought boom times to the Great Plains once the threat of Indian attack was removed. Cattlemen discovered that the treeless grasslands were ideal for grazing livestock and rapidly exploited their lush growth. After the Civil War, cattle were driven from Texas in ever larger herds to rail centers in Wyoming, Kansas, and Missouri for shipment to the East.

The Life of the Cowboy. The difficult and lonely work of the cowboy (also known variously as a cowhand, cowpoke, or cowpuncher) has become one of the most colorful facets of American folklore. "Living in the saddle" and wearing his utilitarian garb consisting of such items as Levi's, a broad-brimmed sombrero, neckerchief, and high-heeled boots, the cowboy was equipped with a revolver and a length of rope to catch cattle. His main job was to protect the cattle as they grazed on the range and as they were driven to market. Although the cowboy had many duties to perform on the ranch and on the roundup,[4] perhaps the most strenuous work of all was on the "long drive"—moving hundreds of cattle hundreds of miles from the range to the "cow towns."

Trails and "Cow Towns." The cattlemen of Texas soon discovered the advantages of fattening their stock, called Texas longhorns, on the free, open range of the plains, which were still part of the public domain. There were four main trails to the cow town rail centers northward: (1) the Goodnight-Loving Trail (named after Charles Goodnight and Oliver Loving, the two cattlemen who laid it out) ending at Cheyenne, Wyoming; (2) the Western Trail ending at Dodge City, Kansas; (3) the Chisholm Trail (named after Jesse Chisholm, a trader who had previously established the route for trading purposes) ending at Ellsworth, Abilene, or Wichita, all in

[4]Gathering cattle together on the range by riding around them and driving them in. This was done when calves needed branding or older animals were to be selected for shipment to market.

Kansas; (4) the Sedalia Trail ending at Sedalia or Kansas City, both in Missouri.

Peak and Decline of the Cattle Business. The period from 1875 to 1885 was the heyday of the long drive, cowboys, the open range, and the cattle barons. During this time almost 300,000 cattle annually were fattened on the free pasturage and shipped to eastern stockyards. At the peak, profits rose to as high as 40 percent.

Good times, however, did not survive the following factors: (1) the advance of the farmers' frontier, which meant fencing of the grazing lands; (2) legislation of some states providing for the close inspection of the Texas longhorns or prohibiting driving the animals across their boundaries; (3) competition from the livestock raisers on the farms of the Midwest; (4) the ability of the cattle buyers in the cow towns to determine prices and the railroad owners to set freight rates; (5) overexpansion of the cattle industry on a speculative basis. With the disappearance of the open range, western cattle raising lost its most picturesque feature.

THE FARMERS' FRONTIER

The farmers, rather than the miners or the cattlemen, gradually became the dominant force in the "taming of the wild West." Government benefits, new inventions, and rail facilities opened the West to an agricultural population.

Land Policies. In the disposal of its public lands the United States had always been generous, and that generosity reached its zenith during the period following the Civil War.

THE HOMESTEAD ACT. This act, passed in 1862, provided that any head of a family who was a citizen, or declared his intention of becoming a citizen, could acquire 160 acres of surveyed land by paying a small registration fee and residing on the land for five years. So rapid was the response to this invitation that by 1880 almost 20 million acres had been entered by those who claimed to be homesteaders. Despite a number of fraudulent entries, most of this land was soon under cultivation by bona fide settlers.

ADDITIONAL LEGISLATION. The Homestead Act was chiefly beneficial in bringing farmers into the forested and humid areas of the national domain. Its emphasis on the small-acreage farm proved a handicap to those who desired to cultivate the treeless and semiarid region of the Great Plains. Congress yielded to pressure from the exploiters of the trans-Mississippi West and passed the Timber Culture Act in 1873 and the Desert Land Act in 1877 to encourage the staking out of larger holdings by prospective homesteaders. The Timber Culture Act provided additional land allotments to persons who used a portion of their original allotments for tree-planting.

The Desert Land Act authorized as additional land allotments semiarid land to be sold at $1.25 an acre to persons who agreed to irrigate it. However, neither act contributed greatly to the westward advance of the farmers' frontier.

OTHER OPPORTUNITIES TO SECURE LAND. Many settlers could not qualify under the Homestead Act or found the land allotment by such legislation insufficient for large-scale agriculture on the Great Plains. But they had other opportunities to secure land. The state governments, which under the Morrill Act (1862) had received generous allotments of land for the endowment of agricultural and mechanical colleges, sold their acres on satisfactory terms, and the transcontinental railroads that had received grants of land offered much of theirs at reasonable rates. All too often, however, prospective settlers seeking to buy land were victimized by speculative interests.

New Methods and Tools. To move homesteaders into the vast areas of the Great Plains required more than the assistance of the federal government through legislation. The open ranges of the cattle country had to be enclosed, and neither deep furrows nor high hedges proved satisfactory substitutes for wooden fences, the timber for which the region lacked. Cheap barbed wire, patented in 1874, finally provided the necessary fencing. At the same time, plows and mowers suitable to the plains appeared on the market. But agriculture was not practicable in the semiarid sections until the twentieth century, when sophisticated irrigation techniques came into use.

Cattlemen versus Farmers. The ranchers viewed the farmers, whom they called "nesters," as their natural enemies. The fences, so necessary for an agricultural economy, broke up the open ranges of the West, and the farmers' search for water took from the grazing cattle easy access to customary water holes. The rivalry in some districts turned into open warfare in the 1880s. But the nesters had found their decisive weapon in the barbed wire that could be used to set off their homesteads from the open range.

Agrarian Immigrants. The bulk of the settlers in the "prairie states" of the Mississippi Valley and in the Great Plains came from the older states. They were attracted to the West by cheap land, improved rail transportation, and the opportunity to harvest the large crops that agricultural machinery made possible. Thousands of additional settlers were foreign immigrants, principally Germans and Scandinavians, who swelled the population of Wisconsin, Minnesota, Iowa, Nebraska, Kansas, North Dakota, and South Dakota.

Closing of the Frontier. The farmers, who had followed the miners and cattlemen, formed the last group to settle the West. Between 1870 and 1880 an area equal to that of Great Britain was brought under cultivation, and the agrarian frontier was pushed close to the limits of arable land. In

1890, although much western land still remained to be settled, the Bureau of the Census announced the end of a frontier line. (By definition a frontier region was a large inhabitable area having fewer than two people per square mile.) The frontier was held by some historians, notably Frederick Jackson Turner, to be the greatest force in the shaping of American democracy. The existence of free, open territory with abundant natural resources was perhaps most important in forming American tendencies to individualism, inventiveness, and expansionism. However, Turner's idea that the frontier served as a "safety valve" during periods of economic distress in the cities of the East was disputed by his critics: they argued that the frontier was of limited value to most urban laborers, who lacked the means to move to the West. After 1890 the West became a place for consolidation and conservation. Expansion was then sought overseas.

Chapter 4

THE RISE OF BIG BUSINESS

In the quarter-century after 1865, the nation witnessed the rise of big business. The tremendous expansion of business enterprise was significantly accelerated by the influence of the dominant economic theory of the period, which favored the free play of individual initiative. However, the monopolistic practices of the large industrial firms and the abuses of the railroads—both of which powers the states were constitutionally prohibited from controlling because of their interstate nature—eventually forced the federal government to take action in the public interest.

THE SHAPE OF INDUSTRY

Industrial enterprise is a pursuit that has for its end the producing and supplying of commodities. It is a form of business activity that is distinguished by being on so large a scale that major problems of capital and labor are often involved. Following the Civil War the development of American industry was so extensive that the entire population was affected by it.

Manufacturing. A handful of significant characteristics marked manufacturing in the post–Civil War years. Readily observable was the evolution of the small shop into the large factory.

A NATIONAL MARKET. The opening of the West brought the entire territory of the United States into a domestic market. The development of a far-flung transportation system put all parts of the market within reach of the manufacturing centers of the East. The enactment by Congress of tariff barriers protected many goods from foreign competition.

ABUNDANT RESOURCES. The discovery and utilization of the nation's natural resources also aided the growth of manufacturing. The mining frontier contributed gold, silver, and copper. Large deposits of iron ore

40

were found in Pennsylvania and in the Great Lakes region, where the Mesabi range of Minnesota was especially accessible. Oil was discovered in Pennsylvania and in the Southwest. The great northwestern forests were added to the source of lumber. Coal, which became of vital importance to power producers, could be mined in a number of regions, especially in the central Appalachian Mountains.

AN ADEQUATE LABOR SUPPLY. Following the Civil War the supply of labor was augmented by veterans seeking jobs and by persons, including many women and children (whose employment was not at the time restricted), attracted from farms to the new manufacturing centers. The largest source of factory labor, however, came from millions of immigrants—mostly from eastern and southern Europe—who arrived in the United States during the last quarter of the nineteenth century. Political unrest and religious persecution abroad, inducements offered by American manufacturing firms, and generally nonrestrictive immigration policies were factors that caused foreigners to flock to the United States. Lacking skills or bargaining power, most of those immigrants had to work long hours for low wages.

TRANSPORTATION. Advances in transportation in the latter part of the nineteenth century were crucial to manufacturing. The railroads carried raw materials to the manufacturing centers and carried finished goods to the domestic markets and to ports for shipment overseas. And such refinements as the air brake, various signal devices, and the refrigerator car increased the value of railroads to manufacturing.

TECHNICAL IMPROVEMENTS AND INVENTIONS. The records of the Patent Office tell an impressive story of how old businesses were revolutionized and new ones created by the invention and improvement of machinery and processes. The process for making steel by blowing air through cast iron in its molten state was discovered in the 1850s by the Englishman Henry Bessemer and the American William Kelly. Thomas A. Edison and his laboratory associates were responsible for such significant inventions as the dynamo, the incandescent lamp, and the alkaline storage battery. Charles Goodyear's process for the vulcanization of rubber to make it stronger and resistant to heat and cold and Eli Whitney's system of interchangeable parts (although both inventors had accomplished their work earlier) came into widespread use after the Civil War. All these devices enabled manufacturers to produce goods more cheaply and in ever-increasing quantities.

Of clear importance to manufacturing were developments in communication. The amount of telegraph wire in use throughout the nation tripled within six years after the close of the Civil War. As the telegraph helped unite the remote sections of the nation, the trans-Atlantic cable, successfully laid in 1866 by Cyrus W. Field, brought other countries of the world into closer business contacts with the United States. Within a few years after its invention in 1876, Alexander Graham Bell's telephone, in addition to becoming a familiar convenience in thousands of American homes, revolutionized business routines throughout the nation.

CORPORATE ORGANIZATION. The form of business organization changed rapidly after 1850. The individual proprietorship and the partnership gave way to the corporation chartered under state law. During the 1850s and 1860s the obvious advantages of the corporate form—relative permanence of the organization, limited liability of the stockholders, and opportunity for the promoters to acquire large amounts of capital—induced the manufacturers to seek corporate charters for their enterprises. Upon these foundations were later erected the elaborate structures designed to insure monopolistic control by particular business firms.

TERRITORIAL EXTENSION. Although the northeastern states, which had been the first to feel the impulse of industrialization, still retained their primacy in the production of commodities, manufacturing rapidly expanded into other sections of the nation. For example, the beginning of population shifts in the 1870s made Chicago the center of the meat-packing domain, carried flour-milling from northern New York to Minneapolis, and brought part of Pennsylvania's great iron and steel mills into Ohio and Illinois. In the 1880s manufacturing also began to occupy an important place in the economic life of the South, where the textile, tobacco, and lumber industries benefited from the cheap labor and accessibility to raw materials.

The Growth of Cities. A significant characteristic of industrial expansion was the growth of cities, with an accompanying influence on national thought and action.

"NEW IMMIGRANTS." The urban population grew rapidly as opportunities in the United States drew millions of immigrants from Europe. Beginning in the 1880s the "new immigrants," coming from eastern and southern Europe, predominated. (Most previous immigrants had come from northern and western Europe.) Many, notably Jews, fleeing from political and religious persecution in the Old World, filled the factories and shops of the United States. The immigrants built bridges, laid railroad tracks, strung telegraph and telephone wires, and dug mines. They also gave to the older American culture an awareness of Europe's treasures in art, literature, and music.

THE URBAN MIDDLE CLASS. Some of the foreign-born joined the native-born to swell the ranks of the middle class, composed principally of business and professional people, bureaucrats, and some skilled craftsmen. A segment of this class acquired wealth through ingenious manipulation of investments in factories, banks, railroads, and mines. Their business methods were generally admired and widely imitated by those who had not attained great financial success. Their power was recognized in all parts of the nation, even if their standards of social conduct and canons of cultural taste left much to be desired. The term "The Gilded Age" (the title of Mark Twain and Charles Dudley Warner's novel, published in 1873, on the obsession with wealth and power) was used to describe the ostentatious, vulgar, and frequently corrupt way of life that characterized the surface aspects of the postwar period.

MUNICIPAL PROBLEMS. While most business leaders were involved in adding to their fortunes, acquiring townhouses and country estates, and winning social recognition and prestige, a small group of other Americans in a variety of professions grappled with the difficult problems presented by the disorderly growth of the cities. They strove mightily, if not always effectively, to provide satisfactory housing, transportation, fire protection, and police service. A few individuals persisted in attacking the poverty, disease, alcoholism, and crime that thrived in the congested byways of the cities. Among the reformers in a variety of fields were Henry George in politics; Joseph Pulitzer in journalism; Clara Barton in public nursing; Susan B. Anthony in the temperance crusade; Frederick Law Olmsted in public architecture; and William Graham Sumner in sociology.

THE URBAN INFLUENCE. If much of the city's population was drawn from the rural districts, conversely the farms and villages fell more and more under the influence of urban manners and standards. Despite the antagonism toward cities often manifested by rural people, they succumbed gradually to urban standardization in habits of thought as well as to uniform factory-made goods.

The Business Cycle. In every part of the world where the process of industrialization was relatively rapid, speculative enterprises intensified the fluctuations in the business cycle—a recurring succession of prosperity, crisis, liquidation, depression, and recovery. Thus prosperous years were swallowed up in crisis, quickly followed by depression. The United States had experienced depression periods in 1819, 1837, and 1857, but the collapse that followed the post–Civil War flourishing years was more severe than usual, for it was on a wider front and in a more highly industrial economy.

THE PANIC OF 1873. The collapse of business prosperity in the United States was but a phase of the world depression resulting mainly from the following conditions: (1) a series of international conflicts, culminating in the Franco-Prussian War of 1870–1871; (2) the too-rapid expansion of railroads in central and eastern Europe; (3) the inflation of national currencies, which adversely affected international exchange. In the United States the panic terminated a period of increasing production of farm commodities, raw materials, and manufactured goods; excessive construction of railroads and public works; and inflated currency and rising prices which had persuaded investors to put their savings into speculative enterprises. Precipitating the panic in September, 1873, was the sudden insolvency of the Philadelphia banking and brokerage firm controlled by Jay Cooke, who had gained fame and huge profits by helping the Union government sell its bonds during the Civil War. Cooke and his associates had formed a syndicate to finance the Northern Pacific Railroad. Their operations brought more capital into railroad building than the receipts from passenger and freight traffic warranted. The attempts of creditors to collect on their loans threw some 5,000 firms into bankruptcy within a year of the Jay Cooke failure. In September, 1873, the New York Stock Exchange was forced to close for ten days. Prices plummeted. In the following year 3 million men were thrown into the ranks of the unemployed. Farmers were forced to sell their grain and livestock below the cost of production.

PROPOSALS FOR INFLATION. Price levels remained low for several years after the crisis. As a result, numerous proposals were offered to secure an inflation of the currency in order to raise prices artificially and thus stimulate trade. Many wanted the government to issue paper money backed not by a set amount of precious metal such as gold or silver but by "the faith and resources of the nation." Others demanded that the total amount of coins in circulation be increased by laws that would compel the government to mint coins of silver (then being mined in large quantities) as freely as it minted gold coins. Both groups maintained that prosperity could be induced by cheapening the value of the dollar through greatly increasing the amount of paper money in circulation, and thus lifting the value of the businessmen's commodities, the farmers' crops, and the workers' labor. Farm groups, as well as labor organizations, gave strong support to inflation as the solution to the business cycle.

THE DEVICES OF INDUSTRY

It was generally believed that freedom of competition in industry would compel efficient methods on the part of the producer and insure fair prices for the consumer. But as industrial competition became more intense, businessmen, fearing its effect on profits, sought to limit it by combinations and concentrated control in ever-larger corporations.

Laissez Faire. This was the motto of eighteenth-century French economists who protested excessive government regulation of industry. The phrase means "to let [people] do [as they choose]." The doctrine of laissez faire emphasized that government, although responsible for the maintenance of peace and the protection of property rights, must not interfere with private enterprise either to hinder by regulation or to help by subsidy. In other words, government should pursue a "hands-off" policy. In the United States laissez faire as an economic theory was popularly summarized: "The government of business is no part of the business of government."

As a matter of fact, the American government pursued a hands-off policy that soon turned into a "hands-outstretched" one. During the quarter-century following the Civil War, politicians—whether Democratic or Republican—seldom opposed the generosity of the government in its support of businessmen. This help took various forms: (1) government grants of land and loans to the railroad builders; (2) high tariff rates maintained to protect American industrialists against foreign competition; (3) banking and financial policies that benefited investors at the expense of other elements in the nation. Thus individual initiative often realized its objectives only with government support.

Many Americans during the late nineteenth century seemed to believe that individual businessmen, by being permitted to pursue their own self-interest without external restrictions, were responsible for the great industrial progress of the nation. They were inclined to admire the more prominent leaders of business—John D. Rockefeller and Stephen V. Harkness in oil, Andrew Carnegie and Elbert H. Gary in steel, Cornelius Vanderbilt and James J. Hill in railroads, and John P. Morgan and Jay Cooke in banking—and to excuse the sharp practices in which such men often engaged.

The Trend toward Monopoly. Various devices were used by the large corporations as they strove to secure dominant positions in their particular fields of production. Businessmen argued that unrestrained competition had become so intense that they had been compelled to correct the "evils of competition" by mergers and consolidations.

THE POOL. Early used by the railroads, the pool took the form of an agreement by which several supposedly competing companies established prices, regulated output, and divided markets among themselves. Since such agreements were not recognized by law, they could be easily broken and thus proved unsatisfactory to firms that tried them.

THE TRUST. This form of combination was first tested when John D. Rockefeller, the founder of the Standard Oil Company, organized the Standard Oil Trust in 1879. Rockefeller's ingenious attorneys worked out a plan whereby a group of corporations that engaged in the refining and transportation of petroleum entrusted their stocks to a small board of trustees, which was authorized to control the new combination. The original stockholders of the various corporations received in return for their stock "trust certificates" on which they were entitled to dividends from the earnings of the trust. As revised in 1882 the Standard Oil Trust included seventy-seven companies, whose total stock was held in trust by a board of nine persons. These companies represented 90 percent of the oil refineries and pipelines of the nation. The oil trust device was followed in modified form by business groups that organized the steel trust, the sugar trust, the beef trust, and a score of others.

THE HOLDING COMPANY. When some of the states prosecuted the trustees on the ground that they were restraining trade, leaders of industry began to abandon the trust device and experiment with the holding company. This was a corporation that neither manufactured a product nor engaged in a service but controlled one or more subsidiary companies that did produce goods or perform services by holding a sufficient share of stock in the latter companies. The holding company became important in the 1890s, after such states as New Jersey, Delaware, and West Virginia modified their corporation laws to permit the chartering of this kind of combination.

THE REGULATION OF INDUSTRY

An increasing number of voters during the 1880s and 1890s came to doubt the prevailing theory that government should abstain from meddling in business affairs. They vigorously questioned the assumption that the individual left to his own discretion would always adopt plans and procedures in the public interest. They insisted that there was a public interest that had to be protected against the private interest. Many Americans were suspicious of all big corporations. They idealized earlier generations when production was on a small scale and most business firms were individual proprietorships or partnerships. To them big corporations meant trusts and trusts meant the threat of monopolistic control.

Criticism of Laissez Faire. Although Americans generally appreciated the cheaper prices made possible by large-scale production, they feared that most business managers were more interested in monopolistic control of prices than in quality production under conditions of maximum efficiency.

MOLDERS OF PUBLIC OPINION. During the 1880s and 1890s the popular magazines and sensational newspapers reported on the unfair practices of monopolistic corporations. Among the leading proponents of government regulation of industry, usually for the purpose of maintaining freedom of competition, were a number of economists and journalists, such as Henry George, Edward Bellamy, and Henry D. Lloyd.

SMALL PRODUCERS. Farmers complained that the power of the large corporations to determine prices resulted in high transportation rates for the produce they shipped and excessive charges for the manufactured goods they purchased. Small businessmen accused their more powerful competitors of using unfair methods, based on monopoly, to force them out of business.

CONSUMERS. Impressed by the congressional investigations into the monopolistic methods of the great railroad systems, many consumers demanded equally searching examinations of the way in which large corporations used their control of the market to charge exorbitant prices. They called upon the government to restore that freedom of trade which would permit the law of supply and demand to operate.

Antitrust Legislation. Since corporations received their charters from states, the early response to demands for action by small producers and consumers came from the state legislatures. Later the federal government took steps.

STATE ACTION. The states did little more than apply the rules of common law forbidding agreements, written or unwritten, in restraint of trade. By 1890 fifteen states had passed laws defining in somewhat specific terms various practices of corporations that would be punished as actions in restraint of trade. However, those laws were of little effect, since corporations chartered in states that had no restrictive legislation could trade across state lines. Also, since the plea of former senator Roscoe Conkling before the Supreme Court in *San Mateo County* v. *The Southern Pacific Railroad* (1882), the federal courts had tended to interpret the Fourteenth Amendment so as to protect corporations against any state legislation that might deprive them of "life, liberty, or property without due process of law." (Corporations were considered "persons" under the law.)

THE SHERMAN ANTITRUST ACT. So powerful was the popular sentiment against the trusts that in 1889 Republican President Benjamin Harrison recommended action by Congress, and in 1890 the legislature followed his suggestion by passing the Sherman Antitrust Act. Named after its sponsor, Republican Senator John Sherman of Ohio, the act, using a principle of the English common law, declared illegal "every contract, combination in the form of trust or otherwise, or conspiracy, in restraint of trade or commerce among the several states, or with foreign nations." It authorized prosecutions by federal district attorneys and suits for damages by any individual or firm injured by a company in violation of the act's provisions. During the first decade of the act's existence, the federal government was not aggressive in seeking criminal indictments. This inactivity can be blamed neither on the conspicuously loose phrasing of the statute nor on the attitude of the judiciary. Although the Supreme Court held in *United States* v. *E. C. Knight Company* in 1895 that the control by the sugar trust of 95 percent of the refining of sugar was not an illegal restraint of interstate trade, in subsequent decisions handed down by the Supreme Court the majority opinion prepared the way for successful prosecution. But the Harrison, Cleveland, and McKinley administrations did not want to undertake a vigorous campaign against the trusts.

THE RAILROAD SYSTEMS

Of paramount importance in the process of industrialization were the railroads, which united all sections of the nation, bringing raw materials and foodstuffs to the industrial centers and carrying finished products to the domestic markets and to ports of shipment for foreign trade. Eastern manufacturing firms, western mining companies, and the growing communities on the Pacific coast enthusiastically sponsored plans to bind together distant parts of the nation with miles of steel rails.

Railroads East of the Mississippi. In the eastern states, railroad construction, which had proceeded rapidly in the 1850s, was checked by the Civil War, but even before the cessation of hostilities building was resumed.

NEW LINES AND INVENTIONS. Between 1865 and the financial panic of 1873, more than 30,000 miles of track were laid; by 1880, despite the depression years, mileage in operation had reached 93,000. During the same period the railroad companies began to substitute steel for iron, to adopt a standard gauge for their tracks, to improve their engines, to introduce the air brake perfected by George Westinghouse in 1868, and to use Pullman cars, invented by George Pullman (his sleeping car was introduced in 1859, his dining car in 1868, and his parlor car in 1875).

DOMINANT LINES. During the 1860s and 1870s the trend toward consolidation of the shorter rail lines established many of the nation's great rail systems: (1) the New York Central, organized by Cornelius Vanderbilt, which ran from New York City to Chicago; (2) the Erie, which expanded its service across New York State, until its director, Daniel Drew, together with financiers Jay Gould and James Fisk, engaged in stock manipulations that threw the line into bankruptcy; (3) the Pennsylvania, which reached Cleveland, Chicago, and St. Louis; (4) the New York, New Haven, and Hartford, which came to dominate New England; (5) the Baltimore and Ohio, which pushed steadily beyond the Ohio River to Chicago; (6) the Illinois Central, managed by Edward H. Harriman, which traversed the Mississippi Valley from Chicago to New Orleans; (7) the Atlantic Coast Line, formed out of more than 100 small independent roads.

The Transcontinental Union Pacific and Central Pacific. Even before the Civil War, eastern businessmen had campaigned for a transcontinental railroad. In Congress there was opposition from the southern legislators who feared that such a railroad, which most people assumed would be constructed over a northern route, would not benefit the South.

GOVERNMENT AID. In 1862, while the southern states were unrepresented because of the Civil War, Congress granted a charter to the Union Pacific Company to construct a railroad from the western border of Nebraska to the eastern border of California. The promoters of the company were to receive a right of way (the land occupied by the railroad for its tracks), free use of timber and minerals on public land, and a grant of ten square-mile sections of public land for every mile of track they laid. (Two years later the land grant was doubled.) In addition, Congress agreed to

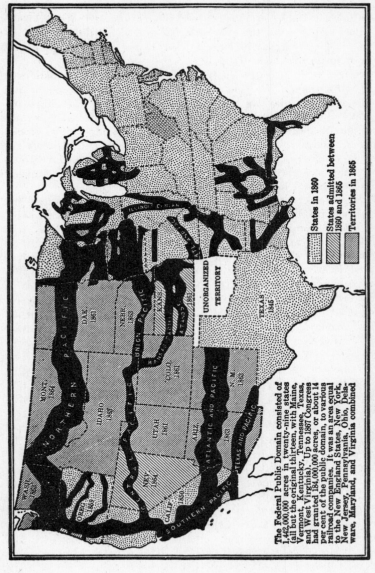

The Federal Public Domain consisted of 1,442,000,000 acres in twenty-nine states (all but the original thirteen, with Maine, Vermont, Kentucky, Tennessee, Texas, and West Virginia). Up to 1867 Congress had granted 184,000,000 acres, or about 14 per cent of the public domain, to various railroad companies. It was an area equal to the New England States, New York, New Jersey, Pennsylvania, Ohio, Delaware, Maryland, and Virginia combined

Political Organization of the West and Land Grants to Railroads lend the company $16,000 for every mile built across the plains, $32,000 for every mile across the plateau region, and $48,000 for every mile across the mountains. At the same time similar terms were accorded the Central Pacific, a California corporation formed to build a line from within that state eastward to meet the Union Pacific.

CONSTRUCTION METHODS. In 1867 the building of the transcontinental line began in earnest. The construction gangs (including thousands of Irish immigrants who worked for the Union Pacific and thousands of Chinese immigrants who worked for the Central Pacific) labored feverishly to overcome the difficulties inherent in spanning a region of desert wastes, wooded plateaus, and precipitous mountains. The promoters, whose ingenuity was tested in meeting engineering problems, were richly rewarded for their efforts. The Union Pacific and the Central Pacific met near Ogden, Utah, in May, 1869, and the first transcontinental railroad was completed.

Other Western Railroads. By 1890 twelve important rail systems had pushed into the region between the Mississippi River and the Pacific coast. They were organized by a few shrewd and powerful entrepreneurs, who frequently used unscrupulous methods to secure domination.

Five of the new railroads in the West, in addition to the Union Pacific–Central Pacific combination, were transcontinental lines: (1) the Great Northern under James J. Hill; (2) the Northern Pacific, organized by Jay Cooke and then taken over by Henry Villard; (3) the Southern Pacific, organized by the controllers of the Central Pacific, Collis P. Huntington and Leland Stanford, and then taken over by Jay Gould; (4) the Atchison, Topeka, and Santa Fe under Cyrus K. Holliday; (5) the Chicago, Milwaukee, St. Paul, and Pacific under Alexander Mitchell.

PATTERNS OF FINANCING. The financial arrangements that made possible the building of the Union Pacific set the pattern for those of the many other early western railroads. Capital for construction came from the sale by the railroads of much of the land granted them by the federal and state governments, loans from federal and state governments, loans from county and municipal governments eager for rail facilities, and private investments by Americans and Europeans.

GOVERNMENT STIMULUS. Land grants from the federal and state governments greatly supplemented the aggregate of their loans to the western railroads. More than 130 million acres owned by the federal government and approximately 55 million acres owned by the various state governments were granted to railroad corporations. For every three dollars invested by private individuals, government authorities advanced two dollars in the form of loans for the building of the western lines. Later, government on the various levels decided to refrain from exacting repayment of the balance (in many cases a considerable amount) of the loans.

Effects of the Transcontinental Rail System. The completion of the transcontinental railroads had important and varied effects on many aspects of American society.

INFLUENCE ON MANUFACTURING AND TRADE. The transcontinental lines slowly created a national market within which farm commodities, raw materials, and manufactured goods could be freely exchanged. Frontier farms and western mining communities could supply urban centers of the East. Manufacturers were encouraged by the expanding market and easy access to raw materials to seek higher profits in mass production at lower cost per unit. Foreign trade also expanded rapidly. Within three years after the completion of the Union Pacific, exports to and imports from China and Japan had risen more than 100 percent.

INFLUENCE ON POPULATION. The high cost of construction caused many transcontinental-railroad promoters to dispose of great portions of their land grants as rapidly as possible. Aggressively making known the availability of dwellings, at reasonable prices and along newly built rail lines, they sold off to enterprising cattle ranchers, sheepherders, and farmers land that the federal and state governments had given them, thus stimulating migration into the trans-Mississippi West. Through advertising and by sending agents abroad, railroad companies actively sought immigrants as railroad construction workers and as land purchasers. Large groups of Europeans and Asians were thereby brought to the American West.

INFLUENCE ON POLITICS. As many Americans moved farther westward, new territories were organized to become states. In the federal government the influence of the new states was felt especially in the Senate (where each state, regardless of population, has two votes). A political revolt of the West against eastern business interests soon developed, climaxing in the 1890s.

ABUSES OF THE RAILROADS

Those responsible for the management of the great rail systems were charged with committing a number of abuses in their promotion, construction, and operation of the lines.

Speculative and Political Abuses. The accusations against many railroad owners and managers cited speculative trickery and political pressure, the latter frequently of an exceedingly immoral kind.

SPECULATIVE PROMOTION. Even the imaginative skill of a railroad operator such as James J. Hill of the Great Northern, or the efficiency of one such as Edward H. Harriman of the Illinois Central, could not obscure the fact that too many American railroads were constructed by speculators who knew little about the needs of the nation and paid scant attention to the requirements of the law. They were guilty of (1) promoting lines in regions where absence of competition enabled them to charge exorbitant rates;

(2) selling large quantities of securities (stocks and bonds) of unsuccessful roads to the residents of the localities that the roads pretended to serve; (3) imposing excessive expenses on railroads undertaking new projects by paying huge profits to themselves as directors of the construction companies that were commissioned to lay the tracks.

POLITICAL CORRUPTION. There was a growing concern during the 1870s and 1880s over the interference with the course of state legislation by powerful railroad lobbyists.[1] Pressure was exerted in various ways to secure legislation favorable to the railroads or to block legislation restrictive of them. By resorting to extensive distribution of free passes among officeholders, generous contributions to party campaign funds, and outright bribery of legislators, the railroads gained "protection" but also incurred ill will.

Financial Abuses. The practices of some owners and managers embraced a wide range of financial dishonesty.

FRAUDULENT SALE OF SECURITIES. European investors were successfully approached to put their money into American lines that had sold more stock than the law permitted. In a few instances powerful directors sold bonds and pocketed the proceeds, thus increasing the corporation's liabilities without adding to its assets.

MARKET MANIPULATION. Daniel Drew, Jay Gould, and James Fisk, who controlled the Erie, were typical of those owners who used valuable railroad properties as devices for building up private fortunes through the unscrupulous manipulation of securities on the stock exchange. They knew little, and cared less, about managing a transportation system.

"STOCK-WATERING." Investors complained that there were railroad directors who engaged in the practice of overcapitalization, or "stock-watering" (the phrase originally referred to feeding salt to livestock to make them thirsty, and then having them fill themselves with water before being weighed for market). By selling more stock than was represented by the actual physical value of the railroad, those directors had given investors stock containing "water"; that is, the par (nominal) value of each share of stock was higher than what it should have been to indicate the true assets of the line.

Unfair Rate-Making. In the view of the shippers the greatest sins of the common carriers (public transportation systems) were their rate-making policies.

POOLING AGREEMENTS. In order to prevent cutthroat competition, such as rate wars, many of the roads entered into pooling agreements, which provided either for a division of territory among the members of the pool or for

---

[1]Persons who solicit members of a legislative body in the lobby or elsewhere in an effort to influence them to pursue a certain course of action.

a proportionate division of the profits at the end of the business year. Thus genuine competition among the roads was eliminated and rates remained as high as the traffic would bear.

DISCRIMINATION BETWEEN PLACES. The "long haul–short haul evil" grew out of a tendency of the roads to favor shippers who operated from important terminal points (stations central to considerable areas), where there was competition among lines. As a result, the shipper using two terminal points paid low rates, while the shipper using way stations (intermediate stations between principal stations), where there was no competition between carriers, paid a proportionately higher rate for the same service. For example, the same shipment could be sent from New York City to Chicago at a lower rate than was charged for the shorter distance between Rochester, New York, and Toledo, Ohio.

REBATES. The small shipper bitterly complained that his larger competitor was the recipient of favors from the railroads in the form of secret rebates (parts of payments returned after open fee transactions), which brought freight costs far below the rates advertised by the roads in their published schedules. The carriers maintained that as a result of the growth of big business, this practice was forced upon them by the powerful industrial entrepreneurs in their war on the independent producers.

CONTROL OF THE RAILROADS

Despite the obvious benefits resulting from the rapid extension of railroad lines into all parts of the nation, protests against the methods of the owners of the transportation systems continually increased, resulting eventually in a variety of regulatory measures.

State Regulations. Mounting protests finally brought attempts by several state legislatures to control the practices of the common carriers.

RAILROAD COMMISSIONS. In 1869 Massachusetts created the first commission with supervisory powers. Its record of correcting abuses through investigation and conference caused other eastern states, notably New York and New Hampshire, to set up similar bodies to hear complaints and report discriminatory practices.

FIXING MAXIMUM RATES. Primarily because of the lobbying of an association of farmers called the Patrons of Husbandry, or, popularly, the Grange, western states passed laws fixing maximum rates for the transportation of passengers and freight. Illinois set up a commission that was given power to prepare rate schedules; Wisconsin, Minnesota, and Iowa established carrying charges by direct legislative action; several other states adopted constitutional amendments empowering the legislature to deal with railroad abuses, including excessively high rates.

Judicial Review of State Legislation. The railroads appealed to the courts to protect them against state regulations, but the trend of early decisions was against the carriers. During the 1870s, in the so-called Granger cases, the Supreme Court held that when property became "clothed with a public interest" its owner must "submit to be controlled by the public for the common good."

MUNN V. ILLINOIS. In 1877 the Supreme Court decided that an Illinois law fixing the maximum rates for the storage of grain in elevators did not deprive the warehouse owners of property rights without due process of law.

PEIK V. CHICAGO AND NORTHWESTERN RAILROAD. In 1877 the Supreme Court, distinguishing between intrastate (within the boundaries of a state) commerce and interstate (between two or among many states) commerce, maintained the right of Wisconsin to regulate railroad rates within the state even though such regulation might incidentally affect persons outside the state. A majority of the justices believed that the states should be permitted to handle their railroad problems without judicial interference "until such time as Congress should legislate on this matter."

THE WABASH RATE CASE. The principles established in the Granger cases were apparently reversed by the Supreme Court in 1886 when it handed down the decision in *Wabash, St. Louis, and Pacific Railway Company* v. *Illinois*, known as the "Wabash Rate Case." A statute of Illinois which attempted to prevent rate discrimination by railroads that passed through its territory was held unconstitutional on the ground that the power over interstate commerce was exclusive to Congress. The effect of the decision was to limit each state's jurisdiction to intrastate commerce and to render ineffective most of the rate-making legislation of the previous fifteen years.

Congressional Action. For a number of years before the Wabash Rate Case decision crippled the power of the states over interstate commerce, Congress had been considering proposals for federal control of the railroads. Every presidential campaign after 1868 was marked by the demand of the minor parties that Congress regulate railroad rates. The Labor Reform party in 1872, the Prohibition party in 1876, the Greenback party in 1880, and the Greenback-Labor party in 1884 cited the outstanding railroad abuses and called upon the federal government to take action. Within the two major parties there was considerable sentiment favoring congressional legislation. The Windom Report to the Senate in 1874, the McCrary Bill passed by the House of Representatives in 1874 but defeated in the Senate, and the Reagen Bill which was passed by the House of Representatives in 1878 but which the Senate refused to consider, all kept the issue alive.

THE CULLOM COMMITTEE INVESTIGATION. In 1885 the Senate appointed a special committee of five, headed by Republican Senator Shelby M. Cullom of Illinois, to investigate the subject of federal control of interstate commerce. The committee, after protracted hearings in every section of the nation, filed a 2,000-page report which concluded that "upon no public question is public opinion so nearly unanimous as upon the proposition that Congress should undertake in some way the regulation of interstate commerce."

THE INTERSTATE COMMERCE ACT. The congressional debates over the Cullom Report resulted in the Interstate Commerce Act—the first attempt of the federal government to control private business enterprise in the public interest. The act, passed by Congress in 1887, forbade the railroads (1) to form pooling agreements; (2) to charge more for a short haul than for a long haul under the same conditions of traffic; (3) to grant secret rebates. It also required them to post their rates and to give a ten-day public notice of any rate change. A bipartisan commission of five, called the Interstate Commerce Commission, was created to supervise the accounting systems, rate schedules, and business methods of the roads; to hear complaints from shippers; and to assist the attorney general in prosecuting offenses against the law. However, under the act even an able and conscientious commission found its efforts ineffective for several reasons: (1) its inability to compel witnesses to testify; (2) the numerous appeals to the courts from commission rulings; (3) the success of the attorneys representing the railroads in winning appeals from the commission's orders; (4) the Supreme Court's tendency to interpret the Interstate Commerce Act in such a way as to restrict the commission's control over the long haul–short haul system and secret rebates. For years the nation waited for Congress to remedy the situation by further regulatory legislation, but that did not come until the first decade of the twentieth century.

Chapter 5

THE STATUS OF INDUSTRIAL WORKERS

By the 1870s the American workingman had learned that so far as he was concerned, the most important effect of industrialization was the transformation of the skilled craftsman into a factory worker. The consequences of this change for the worker included the loss of the bargaining power that his skills and tools had given him; the impersonality of employer-employee relations in the new corporations; and increased competition for jobs resulting from the entry into the labor force of former slaves, women, and immigrants. For unskilled laborers weekly wages of ten dollars or less and a workday of ten hours or more were common. In addition, working conditions in factories were unhealthy and often dangerous.

AIMS AND TACTICS OF MANAGEMENT AND LABOR

In their interest in prosperity for the nation, management and labor have shared a common desire. But they have had historically—and, to be sure, naturally—divergent sets of aims and tactics to get their own cuts of the economic "pie." And this condition has made for an adversary relationship.

Management. The operators of business firms have always sought to achieve the greatest profits possible by increasing production through the most efficient use of materials and labor.

Most employers of the late nineteenth century distrusted labor's attempts to organize and took active measures to hinder them. Among their tactics were (1) the "yellow-dog" contract (a worker's agreement not to join a union during the period of his employment); (2) the blacklist (a list circulated among employers of workers reputed to hold opinions or engage in actions contrary to the employers' interests); (3) the injunction (an order issued by a court whereby one is required to do or refrain from doing a specified act) to restrain unions from actions harmful to employers; (4) the open shop (an establishment in which employment is not determined by union membership or nonmembership); (5) company police and company spies; (6) use of strikebreakers (called "scabs" by workers) to fill the jobs of strikers.

Labor. American workers strove to adjust themselves to the new industrial order of the latter part of the nineteenth century and to organize effectively to improve their status.

During the half-century following the Civil War the labor movement had three principal aims: higher wages, shorter hours (the common demand was for an eight-hour workday), and safe and sanitary working conditions. But the labor movement was concerned with more than these goals. Among its secondary aims were (1) establishment of federal and various state bureaus of labor; (2) abolition of child labor; (3) abolition of contract labor (laborers imported by an employer from a foreign nation); (4) recognition of the principle of collective bargaining (negotiation for the settlement of terms of the collective agreement between an employer or group of employers on one side and a union or number of unions on the other); (5) institution of compulsory arbitration of management-labor disputes; (6) laws providing for workmen's compensation (insurance for pay that a worker may recover from an employer in case of an accident arising out of performing his duties).

Among the tactics of organized labor were (1) the strike; (2) picketing; (3) the boycott (engaging in a concerted refusal to have anything to do with the products or services of an employer—and attempting to convince consumers to do the same—in order to force acceptance of certain conditions desired by a union); (4) the closed shop (an establishment in which the employer by agreement hires and retains in employment only union members in good standing).

Because their task was a more difficult one, the leaders of labor were often less successful than the leaders of industry in mobilizing their forces. In their attempts to weld the workers of the nation into a united and class-conscious group, the labor leaders had to cope with (1) the entrance of blacks, both skilled and unskilled, into the ranks of paid labor; (2) the presence of many poorly paid women in certain crafts; (3) the increase in numbers of foreign-born workers, divided by language, religion, and national tradition; (4) the activities of radicals holding to abstract theories for the reorganization of the social order without sufficient regard for practical difficulties.

SOME INFLUENTIAL LABOR UNIONS

As industrialists formed ever-larger business units, the factory workers tried to create organizations large and strong enough to bargain on equal terms with employers. Eventually their small local craft unions (also called horizontal unions), the membership in which was limited to workmen following the same craft, gave way to large national industrial unions (also called vertical unions), which admitted to membership workmen in an entire industry irrespective of their occupation or craft.

The National Labor Union. The earliest instance of bringing various craft unions into a single national organization was the establishment in 1866 of the National Labor Union, mainly through the efforts of William H. Sylvis, head of the iron molders' union. But since many of Sylvis's associates were allied with skilled craftsmen, they often failed to win the confidence of the factory workers.

OBJECTIVES. In its program the National Labor Union demanded the elimination of monopoly in industry, the establishment of a federal department of labor, the abolition of contract labor, the arbitration of labor conflicts, and the enactment of laws providing for the eight-hour workday in factories.

GROWTH AND DECLINE. The leaders of the union turned to politics to further their organization's objectives, entering the political field as sponsors of the National Labor Reform party. However, in the presidential election of 1872 the party made a notably poor showing, contributing significantly to the rapid dissolution of the National Labor Union.

The Knights of Labor. For more than a decade after the collapse of the National Labor Union, the forces of labor were represented mainly by the Noble Order of the Knights of Labor, founded in 1869 under the leadership of Uriah S. Stephens, a tailor who had helped organize the garment cutters of Philadelphia.

OBJECTIVES AND METHODS. The Knights of Labor stressed (1) industrial unionism; (2) the inclusion of all workers—skilled and unskilled, regardless of the craft or industry—in a single great organization; (3) the formation of local assemblies of workers on the basis of their residence rather than their occupational affiliation; (4) highly centralized control of the local assemblies by the national body. In furthering industrial solidarity, members pledged themselves "to secure for the workers the full enjoyment of the wealth they create, and sufficient leisure in which to develop their intellectual, moral, and social faculties."

Their programs included such specific objectives as (1) the eight-hour workday; (2) equal pay for equal work for men and women; (3) the abolition of labor of children under fourteen; (4) the prohibition of contract foreign labor; (5) the arbitration of labor disputes; (6) the establishment of bureaus of labor statistics on both the federal and state levels; (7) safety and sanitary codes for industry; (8) laws compelling employers to pay laborers on a weekly basis; (9) the creation of cooperatives;[1] (10) the imposition of an

---

[1]Associations for buying or selling goods to the better advantage of its members by eliminating the middlemen's profits.

income tax; (11) government ownership of railroad and telegraph lines.

Although the Knights of Labor held as one of their main tenets that disputes should be arbitrated, they relied increasingly upon strikes and boycotts to win victories. In the political arena the organization fought aggressively for its program, but not until its influence began to wane did it view favorably the idea of a labor party.

GROWTH AND DECLINE. The Knights of Labor expanded rapidly under the leadership of Terence V. Powderly, a former machinist, reaching their greatest strength in 1886 when 5,892 local chapters reported over 700,000 members. However, a series of unsuccessful strikes in 1886 marked the beginning of the union's decline. Its complete collapse was hastened by (1) the growing public belief that many members favored the use of violence in industrial disputes; (2) the hostility of skilled workers toward an organization that minimized the interests of the craft union; (3) the failure of most of the producers' cooperatives in which the Knights of Labor had invested funds; (4) the confusion of aims among the leaders, the majority of whom were largely concerned with the direct goals of higher wages, shorter hours, and good conditions of employment, while others focused on idealistic social reform measures; (5) the revolt by many of the local assemblies against centralized control by the national body; (6) the organization's ineffective handling of the large numbers of unskilled workers, many of whom were transient.

The American Federation of Labor. The increasing dissatisfaction of skilled craftsmen with the objectives and methods of the Knights of Labor resulted in the formation in 1881 of the Federation of Organized Trades and Labor Unions of America and Canada, reorganized in 1886 as the American Federation of Labor (AFL).

OBJECTIVES AND METHODS. Samuel Gompers and Adolph Strasser, who together had revived the Cigarmakers' Union, were influential in organizing the American Federation of Labor and formulating its philosophy. The AFL was a league of separate and quite autonomous craft unions, each of which retained strong local powers, with the authority of the central body strictly limited. The specific objectives of the AFL were quite similar to those of the Knights of Labor, and for a time the two organizations cooperated. Gradually, however, the AFL concentrated its efforts upon a campaign for the "bread and butter" issues—higher wages, shorter hours, and safer and more sanitary conditions of employment within the various crafts. The organization also vigorously advocated the restriction of immigrants, who competed with native Americans for jobs.

The weapons of the AFL came to be the strike, the boycott, and collective bargaining. Refusing to sponsor an American labor party or to ally with any one political party, it used its political power to secure immediate objectives rather than to champion a comprehensive program of the reorganization of society.

GROWTH AND ACHIEVEMENT. Elected first president of the AFL, Gompers held that position except for one term until his death almost forty years later. Despite the pressure of a small Socialist minority among its members, the AFL remained conservative, defending the capitalist system while criticizing its imperfections. Membership increased from 190,000 in 1890 to 550,000 in 1900 to more than 2 million in 1915. However, since the vast majority of the nation's industrial workers did not belong to the AFL, its victories had little direct effect on American labor in general. AFL achievements included (1) the development within the national organization of strong craft unions with effective programs, aided by large funds, for sickness and unemployment benefits; (2) the establishment of the eight-hour workday in several trades; (3) the recognition by an increasing number of employers of labor's right to bargain collectively; (4) the slow but steady growth of labor's influence with the federal and state legislatures.

The Industrial Workers of the World. In 1905 leaders of the radical wing of unionism together with militant Socialists founded the Industrial Workers of the World (IWW) to oppose conservative policies in the labor movement. William D. ("Big Bill") Haywood, who had been an officer in the Western Federation of Miners, was its most prominent head.

OBJECTIVES AND METHODS. The IWW sought to bring all the workers of the nation into a single industrial union. It strove to overthrow the capitalist system and establish in its place a socialist one. Spurning the middle-class reformers and moderate Socialists alike, the IWW championed direct action—the mass strike and sabotage.

GROWTH AND DECLINE. The IWW appealed chiefly to migratory laborers in the lumber camps, mines, and the harvest fields of the Far West. Various states proceeded against the organization because of its radical views and actions, and in 1918 the federal government sentenced to prison its most influential leaders for opposition to American entry into World War I. By the mid-1920s the membership, which at its height numbered 60,000, had disintegrated.

MANAGEMENT-LABOR CONFLICT

In the unequal struggle between the employers, powerful and always well organized, and the unions, weak and often without experienced leaders, workers resorted to strikes, picketing, and boycotts as their only effective weapons.

Confrontation. From 1880 to 1900 there were close to 25,000 strikes involving more than 6 million workers. Almost half ended in failure while another 15 percent ended in compromise.

RAILROAD STRIKES. Symptomatic of the extensive management-labor unrest in the 1870s were the railroad strikes of 1877, which started when employees of the Baltimore and Ohio Railroad struck because of a reduction in wages. Soon most of the roads east of the Mississippi, and eventually some western lines, were involved. Rioting, resulting in bloodshed and destruction of railroad property, was more than the local authorities could handle, and state militia companies were called into action. Finally President Hayes sent federal troops to restore order and to protect non-striking workers who crossed the picket lines.

THE HAYMARKET INCIDENT. Despite the failure of the railroad strikes, industrial warfare grew more intense. On May 4, 1886, a mass meeting organized by anarchists was held in Chicago's Haymarket Square to protest tactics of the police against strikers at the local McCormick Harvester Company plant. When the police tried to disperse the crowd, someone threw a bomb at them. Seven policemen were killed and a number were injured. Both sides then opened fire, resulting in the deaths of two civilians and injuries to both policemen and civilians. Although the person who hurled the bomb was never identified, eight anarchists were convicted of inciting a crowd to riot and four were hanged. The Haymarket Square incident injured the labor movement throughout the nation, for public opinion, unwarrantedly, accused the Knights of Labor of affiliating with anarchists, condoning violence, and being responsible for the so-called Haymarket Riot.

THE HOMESTEAD STRIKE. The wave of antilabor hysteria that followed the Haymarket affair had scarcely subsided when violence flared in June, 1892, at the Homestead, Pennsylvania, plant of the Carnegie Steel Company, where members of the Amalgamated Association of Iron, Steel, and Tin Workers, a relatively strong and conservative union, struck to protest a reduction in wages. In an attempt to destroy the union, the company employed some 300 Pinkerton detectives to protect strikebreakers. (In the late nineteenth century the Pinkerton National Detective Agency was actively engaged in supplying armed men to employers in management-labor disputes.) In desperation the strikers fired on and killed several Pinkerton detectives. After the state militia had restored order, the strike was called off and the Amalgamated Association of Iron, Steel, and Tin Workers, its spirit and funds exhausted after a five-month walkout, collapsed.

THE PULLMAN STRIKE. In the depression year of 1893 the Pullman Palace Car Company, near Chicago, sought to prevent the loss of dividends to its stockholders by reducing the wages of its employees and dismissing many workers. As a result, in June, 1894, the employees struck. The members of the American Railway Union tried to help the strikers by refusing, at first in the Chicago area, to handle any trains carrying Pullman cars. As the boycott spread over the Middle and Far West, the Railroad Managers' Association fought back vigorously. The attorneys for the Railroad Managers' Association secured a federal court injunction, under the Sherman Antitrust Act, to prevent the strikers from interfering with the carrying of the United States mail and with interstate commerce "as a conspiracy in restraint of trade." When the strikers ignored the court order, the government made two moves: first, President Grover Cleveland sent federal troops into the Chicago area, ostensibly to assure delivery of the United States mail but actually to maintain order, a presidential action which Governor John P. Altgeld of Illinois protested as unnecessary; second, Attorney General Richard Olney instructed government attorneys to press charges against officers of the American Railway Union on the ground that they were in contempt of court. Eugene V. Debs, president of the union, was sentenced to a six months' prison term for refusing to obey the injunction. The strike disintegrated. (While in prison Debs spent much time reading about socialist theory; he emerged an ardent opponent of capitalism and some years later became the head of the Socialist Party of America.)

Debs sought a writ of *habeas corpus*[2] in the Supreme Court, which in 1895 the justices denied, basing their decision not on the Sherman Antitrust Act but on the ground that the jurisdiction of the federal government over interstate commerce and the carrying of the mail authorized use of the injunction to prevent obstruction of those activities. This marked the first effective use of the injunction against a union.

Effects of Confrontation. More significant than the failure of any one set of actions by workers was the evidence that public opinion was opposed to the tactics of unions involving strikes, picket lines, and boycotts. Organized wage earners were fully aware of the fact that the force of government on both the federal and state levels usually entered management-labor disputes in support of the employers.

PUBLIC OPINION TOWARD LABOR. Most Americans were unhesitatingly responsive to the individual laborer's grievances concerning long hours, low wages, and unsafe and unsanitary working conditions, but they were suspicious of unions conducting a strong offensive against the employing class as a whole. Many people believed, in accordance with the basic tenets of laissez faire, that collective bargaining could not determine wages, which were set by economic competition. Holding an individualistic view of society, many were slow to admit that labor could win shorter hours, higher wages, and satisfactory working conditions without defying the operation of "natural" economic laws, or that it could organize without resorting to vio-

[2]An inquiry into the lawfulness of the restraint of a person who is imprisoned.

lence. Not until the 1920s did the labor movement enjoy a favorable climate of public opinion.

JUDICIAL RESTRICTIONS ON LABOR. If labor leaders had long found it hard to defend a union's right to bargain collectively, their task became much more difficult after the passage of the Sherman Antitrust Act (1890). The law, designed to prevent corporations from engaging in monopolistic practices, was eventually turned against unions as "combinations in restraint of trade." The federal courts repeatedly held that the Sherman Antitrust Act was applicable to unions, and attorneys for employers used the act to secure injunctions against strikes and boycotts.

LABOR LEGISLATION. Despite the obstacles encountered by the labor movement, some of its objectives were enacted into law. The eight-hour workday was instituted in 1868 for federal employees engaged in public works projects and established in 1892 for all federal employees. The immigration of Chinese laborers, who had been competing for jobs with native-born workers in the Far West, was suspended in 1882. The Erdman Act, passed by Congress in 1898, provided for the mediation of disputes involving railroads engaged in interstate commerce and their employees, and it prohibited the use of the yellow-dog contract by interstate railroads. (Ten years later the Supreme Court declared the latter provision unconstitutional on the ground that it violated the freedom of contract and property rights of the railroads.) Although the Supreme Court generally maintained that state laws regulating employment were unconstitutional, it upheld certain of those laws as valid exercises of the states' police power. Thus in 1898 the Court sustained in *Holden* v. *Hardy* a Utah law establishing maximum working hours for miners and in 1908 in *Muller* v. *Oregon* an Oregon law setting maximum working hours for women. In 1907 Congress passed the Hours of Service Act, limiting, in the interest of public safety, the number of consecutive hours that railroad employees could work.

Chapter 6

THE REVOLT OF THE WEST

Growing dissatisfaction with the failure of both major parties to come to grips with the serious economic issues affecting their welfare caused the farmers to engage in a political revolt in the 1890s. The political power of the business interests was seriously threatened during that decade as the farmers of the West and South, joined by many wage earners of the East, launched proposals for radical reform measures against the bulwark of big business. Although the conservative forces won the important election of 1896, the demands of the farmers and laborers had to be reckoned with thereafter, and many were eventually adopted by both the Democratic and Republican parties.

THE FARMERS' GRIEVANCES

Fundamental to the discontent of the farmers was their belief that they were not receiving a share of the national income commensurate with their contributions to American life.

Farm Environment. During the last third of the nineteenth century most farmers in the United States lived either along the frontier of settlement or in comparative isolation on small farmsteads in more populous areas. From planting time to harvest the average farmer was a hard worker in the fields, and his leisure was usually as monotonous as his toil. Though independent, he was too often isolated and thus denied advantages and conveniences that his fellow Americans in towns and cities took for granted.

The farmer had always been the recipient of nature's bounty and the victim of its uncertainties. In a particular way this was the fate of the western farmer in the post–Civil War period. Many ambitious tillers of the soil had pushed into areas where the average annual rainfall was insufficient for farming without irrigation. In the early 1880s rainfall on the western plains was abnormally heavy, but from the mid-1880s to the mid-1890s an extended drought ruined thousands who had gambled that the rains would continue.

Economic Conditions. During the last third of the nineteenth century the farmer complained bitterly of the low prices for his products and of the high prices of the manufactured goods, including agricultural equipment, that he had to buy.

FINANCIAL COSTS. Constantly in need of loans between harvests, with their accompanying profits, in order to buy new or repair old farm machinery and tools, fertilizer, and other supplies, the farmer grew more and more indignant that he had to pay high interest rates for the bank loans that he was compelled to seek. Because of a higher rate of taxation on landed property (which was always visible to the tax assessor) than on personal property, the farmer's taxes were higher in proportion to his ability to pay than were the taxes of the financier and the factory worker. The farmer was charged excessive railroad freight rates compared with those required of industrial shippers. He also objected to economic discrimination created by tariffs; he bought protected products and sold unprotected ones.

INCREASED PRODUCTION. The growing number of new farms, cultivated more efficiently with better machines, such as the gang plow, disk harrow, thresher, and grain binder, made for a tremendously increased production. This large supply was responsible for the declining prices of the farmer's crops because of the operation of the supply-and-demand principle in an unprotected market. Furthermore, there was increasing competition from Canadian, Russian, and Argentine wheat growers.

FARM OWNERSHIP. As a result of the farmer's unfavorable economic situation during the last third of the nineteenth century, mortgage foreclosures increased greatly. The number of persons working farms as tenants rather than owners also increased as farms became larger, more specialized, and more dependent on ready cash. Prevalent in the South was sharecropping, in which the landlord furnished tenants with land, equipment, and shelter for much of the proceeds from the crops, and the crop-lien system, in which the farmer pledged a portion or all of his crop to a merchant for supplies.

THE AGRARIAN REACTION

The declining prices of agricultural products in the post–Civil War period brought into sharp focus the protest of the farmers. They insisted that new machines, more acres, and larger markets were not enabling the farm population to keep its proportionate share of the national income. To help themselves they began to join a number of organizations and to support different movements.

The Grange. Popularly known as the Grange (the name given to the local chapter), the Patrons of Husbandry was a ritualistic society formed in 1867 through the efforts of Oliver H. Kelley, a Post Office Department clerk, to promote rural social activity as an antidote to the loneliness and monotony of farm life. It was not long before the Grangers began engaging in a program that had economic and political objectives as well as social aims. Within a few years the Grange had approximately 700,000 members, most of whom were from the midwestern grain-growing states.

THE COOPERATIVE MOVEMENT. The Grangers organized cooperatives to reduce the cost of the commodities that they purchased and to increase the price of the crops that they produced. In the 1870s the Grangers were operating plow and harvester factories, elevators for the storage of grain, meat-packing plants, loan companies, and retail stores. However, most of those cooperatives were wrecked by inexperienced and inefficient management, internal dissension, and the aggressive hostility of private competitors.

POLITICAL ACTION. By supporting sympathetic candidates, most of whom were affiliated with minor party movements, the Grangers fought for influence in many state legislatures—and won a number of notable triumphs. Illinois passed a law fixing the maximum rates of railroads and the maximum charges of grain storage companies; Wisconsin and Iowa, whose legislatures were under tight Granger control, enacted laws regulating railroad freight rates; Minnesota established a commission to supervise all public utilities, including railroads. The political power of the Grangers in some of the prairie states enabled them to send to Congress senators and representatives who acted as their spokesmen. In the 1870s, in the Granger cases, the Supreme Court upheld a state's right to establish maximum fees to be charged by railroads and public utilities, but in the 1880s the Court reversed itself regarding the competence of a state to regulate railroad traffic. By that time, however, the farmers had turned to organizations and movements other than the Grange.

The Greenback Movement. Historically farmers are debtors. During the quite extended periods between harvests, when profits are realized, they find themselves borrowing money to repair old machinery and buy new machinery, to make mortgage payments, and to pay for a host of articles that a family needs.

To halt the trend of decreasing prices for agricultural products, the farmers advocated inflation. The debtor class generally—and the farmers particularly—supported strongly the Greenback movement, which would have the government issue paper money to bring about inflation of the currency, a cheapening of the value of money. This would not only increase prices but also ease the payment of debt. (If wheat sold at $1 a bushel, a farmer would need to sell 1,000 bushels to settle a $1,000 loan—disregarding, of course, the interest. If, however, wheat sold at an inflated $2 a bushel, a farmer would need to sell only 500 bushels to repay a $1,000 loan.) Although the farmer would have to pay more for manufactured products, he would still be at an advantage because, while he received higher prices for his crops, his debts would remain the same. Attaining inflation by increasing the amount of currency in circulation could be done in two ways: by issuing more paper money without the backing of gold or silver or by issuing silver coins.

REDEMPTION OF GREENBACKS. During the Civil War the federal government issued approximately $430 million in paper money to help pay for its military operations. These paper notes were called "greenbacks," from the color of the ink used to print them. The greenbacks were not supported by gold or silver as security but were buttressed solely by the confidence of the people in the government.

After the Civil War the creditor class generally, and eastern business interests particularly, demanded a government policy of "sound money," by which they meant removing from circulation most of the paper money and making that which remained redeemable in gold. On the other hand, the western farmers became ever more active in a movement for cheaper money.

Disregarding the sharp protests from the agricultural West, in January, 1875, Congress passed the Resumption Act, providing that of the total amount of greenbacks, $300 million worth should remain in circulation and that after January 1, 1879, they should be redeemable at face value in gold. A reserve of $100 million in gold was set up by the government for this purpose. By bringing greenbacks up to the value of gold-backed money, the Resumption Act produced deflation and a consequent lowering of prices. But in 1878 the lobbyists of the inflationist-minded farmers succeeded in having Congress modify the measure by halting the redemption of greenbacks into gold when the amount of paper money in circulation was $346,681,016—an amount that was allowed to remain in the currency.

THE GREENBACK PARTY. The extreme inflationists answered the federal deflationary policy by organizing the National Greenback party in 1875. The following year the Greenbackers nominated Peter Cooper, a New York City iron manufacturer and philanthropist who believed in an inflationary policy, for president. In 1878 the Greenback party merged with the National Labor Reform party and the new Greenback-Labor party received approximately 1,000,000 votes in the congressional elections and sent fourteen representatives to the lower house. In 1880, 1884, and 1888 the Greenback-Labor party offered presidential candidates to the American people, but its standard-bearers made poor showings and the strength of the third party quickly declined.

The Silver Movement. The advocates of cheap money eventually came to the conclusion that the free and unlimited coinage of silver would provide a more satisfactory currency than would a further issuance of greenbacks.

The Democratic and Republican parties were both divided over the silver issue, with westerners apt to be more sympathetic than easterners toward inflationary proposals. Regardless of party affiliation, the debt-ridden farmers argued for cheapening the value of the dollar by having the government mint silver coins as freely as it minted gold ones.

THE "CRIME OF '73." In 1873 Congress passed the Coinage Act, ending the minting of silver dollars. This demonetization (abandoning the use of a metal as money) abolished bimetallism (the use of two metals, ordinarily silver and gold, for coinage) and placed the nation on the gold standard, having gold as its currency's only base. Some years later the silver advocates blamed declining prices on the scarcity of "hard" (metallic) money and traced this lack to the Coinage Act, calling it the "Crime of '73."

THE BLAND-ALLISON ACT. Silverites called for the government to resume promptly the coinage of silver. Farmers of the West and South and western silver-mine owners allied themselves in lobbying for congressional action. The farmers' case was well known to the nation. The tillers of the soil now had effective allies. Silver-mine owners and those interested in the development of the regions where silver was produced loudly demanded that "something be done for silver." They pointed out that the price of commercial silver had been sharply declining, since the working of new deposits in Nevada and Colorado made larger quantities available on the market and exports of the metal had fallen off because of its decreased use in European and Latin American coinage systems.

A combination of western Republican and southern Democratic voters carried through Congress the Bland-Allison Bill, authorizing the Treasury Department to purchase between $2 million and $4 million worth of silver bullion[1] each month at the prevailing market price and to coin it into silver dollars. President Hayes vetoed the bill on the ground that it allowed dollars of cheaper value to be used in the payment of preexisting debts, but the measure was passed over his veto in 1878. The Bland-Allison Act, however, did not provide the inflation hoped for by the farmers. A succession of conservative "sound money" secretaries of the treasury, using the discretionary power granted them under the terms of the act, authorized monthly purchases of silver bullion only at the $2 million minimum amount.

THE SHERMAN SILVER PURCHASE ACT. Farmers and western silver-mine owners continued to press for a large increase of silver coinage. In 1890 Congress acquiesced with the Sherman Silver Purchase Act, authorizing

[1] Metal in the mass as opposed to being in a coined state.

the Treasury Department to purchase 4.5 million ounces of silver bullion each month at the prevailing market price, paying for it in newly issued Treasury paper notes called silver certificates, which would be redeemable at face value in either gold or silver.

REPEAL OF THE SHERMAN SILVER PURCHASE ACT. Vast numbers of silver certificates were redeemed in gold, draining the gold reserve, which by June, 1893, had fallen below the generally accepted "safe" mark of $100 million. In August President Cleveland, a longtime foe of inflationary policies, informed a special session of Congress that the beginning financial panic was directly traceable to the fear that the nation was going to substitute silver for gold as its monetary base. Cleveland called for the prompt repeal of the Sherman Silver Purchase Act. With the aid of the eastern Republicans in Congress the President won, but he incurred the bitter animosity of the western and southern wings of his own Democratic party.

Populists. The political climax of agrarian discontent of the 1870s and 1880s was the organizing of the Populist party, which enrolled Grangers, Greenbackers, and Laborites, plus many who had been active in the inflationist ranks of the two major parties.

FORMING THE PARTY. During the 1880s there was a phenomenal growth in the western and southern states of numerous agrarian organizations under various titles. These groups were soon consolidated into two powerful associations—the Northwestern Alliance and the Southern Alliance. Such colorful leaders emerged as Jerry ("Sockless Jerry") Simpson and Mary Ellen Lease, both of Kansas, James B. Weaver of Iowa, Ignatius Donnelly of Minnesota, Benjamin R. ("Pitchfork Ben") Tillman of South Carolina, and Thomas E. Watson of Georgia. These organizations and leaders finally united to form a political party to compete with the two major parties. In February, 1892, at St. Louis, Missouri, delegates formally organized the People's Party of the U.S.A., known as the Populist party, which held its first national nominating convention the following July at Omaha, Nebraska, to choose presidential and vice-presidential candidates.

THE PLATFORM. The new third party, amidst a wild ovation, adopted a platform expressing the grievances of decades. The planks dealing with economic reform called for (1) free and unlimited coinage of silver and gold at the ratio of sixteen to one (in minting coins the government had considered sixteen ounces of silver to be equal in value to one ounce of gold); (2) increase of the currency in circulation (then approximately twenty dollars per person) to fifty dollars per person; (3) enactment of an income tax that was graduated (increasing in rate with increase in earnings); (4) reduction of various kinds of federal and state taxes; (5) government ownership and operation of railroads, and telegraph and telephone lines; (6) appropriation by the government of all land held by corporations in excess of their actual needs; (7) prohibition of alien ownership of land; (8) establishment by the government of a postal savings system; (9) use of government funds to facilitate marketing of farm products and to extend short-term rural loans. As an invitation to the industrial wage earners of the East other planks favored (1) restriction of "undesirable" immigration (to lessen competition for jobs); (2) establishment of the eight-hour workday for government employees; (3) abolition of the Pinkerton detective system. The planks that were politically based advocated (1) a single term for the president and vice-president; (2) direct election of United States senators (then appointed by state legislatures); (3) use of the secret ballot; (4) adoption by the states of the initiative (see p. 96) and the referendum (see p. 96).

THE FIRST CAMPAIGN. The Populists presented their first ticket to the nation in the election of 1892, nominating former Greenback representative James B. Weaver of Iowa for president and agrarian reformer James G. Field of Virginia for vice-president. Weaver's popular vote was 1,041,000. He received the entire electoral vote of Kansas, Colorado, Idaho, and Nevada, and one vote each from North Dakota and Oregon, making a total of twenty-two. In accordance with third-party strategy, in the Midwest the Populists allied with the Democrats against the dominant Republicans, while in the South they cooperated with the Republicans in an effort to defeat the dominant Democrats.

Election of 1896.

The battle for the presidency in 1896 was the most momentous since the election in 1860, on the eve of the Civil War. The farmers of the West and South and the laborers of the East made a strong bid for power against the business interests.

DEMOCRATS. Bitterness and confusion were rife at the Democratic national convention. The delegates from the West and South, particularly those from rural areas, were in open revolt against the Cleveland administration, then drawing to a close. From the outset the convention was dominated by the supporters of silver coinage. In the Nebraska delegation was a young former representative who had become well known as a gifted crusader for inflation—William Jennings Bryan. At one point in the proceedings Bryan made an impassioned plea for silver coinage, the last words of which achieved fame: "You shall not press down upon the brow of labor this crown of thorns, you shall not crucify mankind upon a cross of gold." So deeply stirred were the delegates that on the fifth ballot Bryan was nominated for president. As a conciliatory gesture to the East, Arthur Sewall, a Maine banker, was nominated for vice-president. The platform repudiated the Cleveland administration. Adopted after spirited debate, it demanded the free and unlimited coinage of silver and gold at the present legal ratio of sixteen to one. The other planks included (1) a demand that tariff schedules be imposed solely to provide federal revenue; (2) criticism of the Supreme Court for declaring unconstitutional the income tax provision of the 1894 Wilson-Gorman Tariff;(3) denunciation of the government's use of the injunction in management-labor disputes; (4) a demand for the enlargement of the powers of the Interstate Commerce Commission in dealing with the railroads.

REPUBLICANS. The most influential leader at the Republican national convention was Mark Hanna, a Cleveland businessman with large coal and iron interests, whose career in Ohio politics had demonstrated his conviction that there should be an intimate affiliation between the business community and the Republican party. He was determined that the presidential nominee should be his close friend William McKinley, who after having been a seven-term representative from Ohio had served as governor of that state. So effectively had Hanna lined up the Republican delegates that the convention required only one ballot to nominate McKinley for president. Named for second place on the ticket was Garret A. Hobart of New Jersey, a businessman, lawyer, and state legislative leader. Hanna was determined that the platform should pledge the maintenance of the gold standard. He adroitly handled a threatened revolt of the western advocates of unlimited coinage of silver. In the end a plank supporting gold was adopted and only thirty-four delegates, led by Senator Henry M. Teller of Colorado, bolted the convention. In addition, the platform contained planks favoring a protective tariff, generous pensions for veterans of the Civil War who had fought for the Union, enlargement of the navy, and federal arbitration of management-labor disputes involving interstate commerce.

POPULISTS. The adoption of the Democratic party platform was an open invitation to the Populists, who held their national convention two weeks after Bryan was nominated, to join the Democratic ranks. Such a fusion was opposed by some of the most devoted Populist leaders, but the general membership, eager for victory, nominated the Democratic Bryan for president and former Populist representative Thomas E. Watson of Georgia for vice-president. In twenty-six of the forty-five states the Populist and Democratic tickets were combined.

THE CAMPAIGN. The Republican campaign, astutely controlled by Mark Hanna, appealed to the propertied classes and emphasized the "dangerous radicalism" of the Democrats. McKinley, gracious and dignified, received delegations of voters at his home in Canton, Ohio. In contrast to the Republican candidate's "front-porch" campaign, Bryan traveled approximately 15,000 miles, making more than 600 speeches in twenty-nine states, exhorting masses of debt-ridden farmers, poorly paid industrial workers, and small shopkeepers.

MCKINLEY'S VICTORY. McKinley won 7,111,000 popular votes to Bryan's 6,509,000 (227,000 of which were Populist). In the electoral college, McKinley captured 271 votes to Bryan's 176; he took every state east of the Mississippi River and north of the Ohio River, as well as West Virginia, Kentucky, Minnesota, Iowa, North Dakota, Oregon, and California. Most

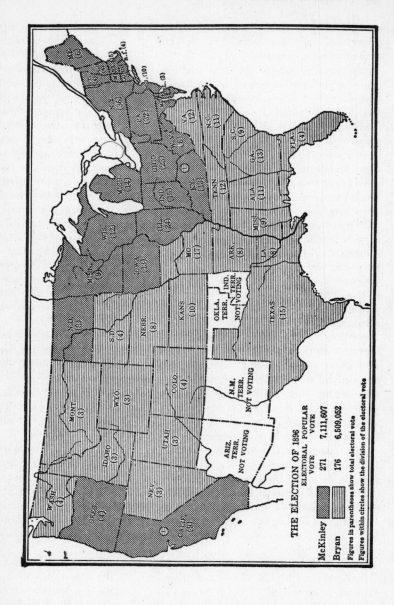

THE ELECTION OF 1896

ELECTORAL   POPULAR
VOTE   VOTE

McKinley   271   7,111,607
Bryan   176   6,509,052

Figures in parentheses show total electoral vote

Figures within circles show the division of the electoral vote

of the West and South went to Bryan. It was believed by many contemporary political analysts that the fact that the season was an especially good one for farmers caused Bryan to lose many votes. All told, the decisive Republican victory meant the defeat of the farmers and laborers in their greatest struggle against the industrialists, the continuing dominance of business interests in government affairs, and the triumph of conservative financiers of the East in the realm of monetary policy. The agrarian crusade had been transformed for a time into a battle over the currency. Although the farmers and laborers were defeated in their fight with the businessmen, within fifteen years their demands would be sponsored by both the Democratic and Republican parties.

The McKinley Administration. The manufacturing and trading interests of the nation looked to the executive branch of the government, with McKinley at its head, for assistance and encouragement. They were clearly not disappointed with the support they received.

THE PRESIDENT. William McKinley was unfailingly dedicated to his church, his invalid wife, and his party. As Chief Executive he made good use of his long-standing habit of compromise and conciliation to achieve his political objectives.

THE CABINET. The McKinley cabinet was, not surprisingly, a model of conservatism. The elderly, and increasingly forgetful, Republican Senator John Sherman of Ohio became secretary of state. (Mark Hanna was appointed to Sherman's vacated Senate seat.) Heading the Department of the Treasury was Chicago banker Lyman J. Gage, a staunch defender of the gold standard. McKinley later made changes in his cabinet, appointing the widely experienced diplomat John Hay as secretary of state and the highly successful New York City corporation lawyer Elihu Root as secretary of war.

Chapter 7

THE UNITED STATES AS A WORLD POWER

For some time after the Civil War the United States attempted to pursue its past intention—professed, at least—of isolationism. But Americans gradually turned their attention from internal events to active participation in international affairs and overseas expansion. By the beginning of the twentieth century this course had given rise to political conflicts at home between those who favored and those who opposed it; to tensions with rival powers, culminating in the Spanish-American War of 1898; and to a basic constitutional issue as to how newly acquired territories should be governed. The United States had finally emerged as an empire-rich world power.

POLITICAL DIPLOMACY IN ACTION

During the three decades following the Civil War the United States had no purposeful foreign policy. Relations with other nations were either determined by events in domestic politics or accidental.

Isolation—Reality or Myth? Although isolation was only a state of mind in the United States from 1865 to 1898, to the inhabitants of the nation it was nothing less than stark reality. Americans were aware of the importance of foreign markets for the products of their factories and farms, but they were little concerned with the stakes of international diplomacy.

THE POLITICIAN AS SECRETARY OF STATE. Remoteness from the main currents of world affairs was evidenced in the activities of the secretaries of state who served between 1865 and 1898. With the possible exceptions of William H. Seward in the Johnson administration and Hamilton Fish in the Grant administration, they were all politicians much more concerned with events at home than with developments abroad. Unimaginative they may have been, and perhaps aggressive in some controversies, but they practiced a diplomacy that was straightforward and peaceful in its objectives.

THE FOREIGN SERVICE. American ambassadors and ministers[1] were too often chosen because they enjoyed enough wealth to entertain foreign dignitaries lavishly or had rendered conspicuous service to the party in power. Occasionally they were men of ability. So inconsequential were the stakes of diplomacy, however, that few of them had a chance to distinguish themselves. The changing administrations in Washington were more concerned with the work of consular officials charged with the care of the commercial interests of American citizens.

Traditional Policies in Foreign Relations. From the pre–Civil War period two traditional policies persisted in American foreign relations—the adherence to the principles of the Monroe Doctrine and the expansion of American commercial interests in the Pacific.

ENFORCING THE MONROE DOCTRINE IN MEXICO. The statement of foreign policy issued by President James Monroe in 1823 and since known as the Monroe Doctrine declared in essence that the Western Hemisphere was no longer open to colonization by European nations; that the United States would not interfere in purely European affairs; and that European nations were not to interfere in the affairs of existing Western Hemisphere republics. During 1863–1864 Emperor Napoleon III of France, in flagrant violation of the Monroe Doctrine, invaded and conquered the republic of Mexico and placed Archduke Maximilian of Austria upon an unstable throne. Secretary of State Seward protested, but in vain since the United States was then involved in the Civil War and could not enforce the Monroe Doctrine. With the conclusion of hostilities the American government ordered troops to take up positions along the Mexican border. War seemed imminent. But Seward was able to achieve a diplomatic victory when Napoleon III's troubles in Europe caused him to withdraw his military forces from Mexico in 1867. Without French support Maximilian lost the throne and was executed by his former subjects. Thus the attempt of a European power to intervene in the affairs of an independent Western Hemisphere republic was thwarted.

DEFINING A POLICY FOR THE PACIFIC. Secretary Seward stated clearly the traditional basis of his nation's commercial interests in the Pacific. In 1867, finding Russia eager to divest itself of its outpost on the North American continent, he persuaded Congress to purchase Alaska for $7.2 million. This base with rich natural resources would, Seward hoped, start the United States on an expansionist policy. In 1867 he also arranged for the United States to occupy formally the Midway Islands, and at the same time he urged eventual acquisition of the Hawaiian Islands.

---

[1]Diplomatic representatives ranking below ambassadors and usually accredited to nations of lesser importance.

RELATIONS WITH GREAT BRITAIN

The attitude of Great Britain toward the United States government during the Civil War left a legacy of bitterness. Relations between the two nations were far from friendly during the last third of the nineteenth century. American ill will toward Great Britain in this period can be attributed to several factors: (1) the belief, growing out of the Revolutionary War and the War of 1812 and perpetuated by many American historians and publicists, that Great Britain was the traditional enemy of the United States; (2) the fact that the governing classes in Great Britain had apparently desired the permanent dissolution of the United States to result from the Civil War; (3) the view of many politicians that the best way to cultivate the Irish-American vote was to "twist the British lion's tail"; (4) resentment of the patronizing attitude of many British commentators on things American.

The *Alabama* Claims and the Treaty of Washington. Great Britain's failure during the Civil War to strictly enforce its neutrality laws made possible the construction in British shipyards of vessels that were to fly the Confederate flag. The claims pressed by the United States against Great Britain for damages inflicted upon northern shipping by these cruisers, the most famous of which was the *Alabama*, came to be known as the *Alabama* claims. Secretary Seward was ignored by the British government when he called for a diplomatic settlement. Great Britain, however, changed its attitude when it watched the United States deal effectively with the Fenian Brotherhood, a secret organization of Irish-Americans intent upon achieving the independence of Ireland. In 1865 the Fenians were using the United States as a base for sporadic raids into Canada. The Department of State was so vigilant in suppressing these violations of Canada's frontiers that British leaders finally responded by settling all outstanding differences between Great Britain and the United States.

Negotiations extended over several years. In 1869 Reverdy Johnson, the American ambassador to Great Britain, and Lord George Clarendon, the British foreign secretary, reached an agreement, known as the Johnson-Clarendon Convention, providing for the settlement of demands outstanding on both sides since 1853. The Senate refused to ratify the agreement, but Secretary of State Hamilton Fish reopened negotiations successfully. The Treaty of Washington, ratified by the Senate in 1871, authorized: (1) the submission of the *Alabama* claims to an international tribunal; (2) the making of a new arrangement for the rights of American fishermen operating off the shores of Canada; (3) the settlement by arbitration of the disputed water boundary between British Columbia and Washington state.

Meeting at Geneva, Switzerland, in 1872 the tribunal that had been created under the terms of the Treaty of Washington to adjudicate the *Alabama* dispute refused to accept United States claims for indirect damages by the British-built Confederate vessels but awarded $15.5 million for direct damages, which Great Britain promptly paid.

The Newfoundland Fisheries Dispute. For decades fishermen from Maine and Massachusetts operated off the shores of Newfoundland (a Canadian province), basing the right to fish on a treaty between the United States and Great Britain dating from the early nineteenth century. Resenting the American fishermen, the Newfoundland legislature passed irksome restrictions upon their activities. Quarrels over fishing rights were halted by the Treaty of Washington, but in 1885 when the fisheries clauses of the treaty were terminated, Canada began seizing American fishing vessels in Canadian waters. In response, an angry Congress authorized President Cleveland to close American ports to Canadian ships and goods. The State Department finally worked out an informal agreement with the British government that remained in effect until 1912.

The Bering Sea Controversy. During Cleveland's first term the United States, in an attempt to protect the herds of seals in the Bering Sea, west of Alaska, arbitrarily seized Canadian sealing vessels, contending that the Bering Sea was under American dominion. During the Harrison administration, after Secretary of State Blaine and British Foreign Secretary Lord Robert Salisbury had exchanged acrimonious diplomatic notes, Blaine finally agreed to submit the dispute to arbitration. In 1893 an international tribunal decided against the United States on every point of law, although it provided some rules for protection of the seal herds.

The Venezuelan Boundary Adjustment. Of all the disputes between the United States and Great Britain in the post–Civil War decades the one that brought the two nations closest to war was the controversy over the Venezuelan boundary. The long-contested line of demarcation between the republic of Venezuela and the British colony of Guiana came into lively controversy in the 1880s, when gold was discovered in the disputed region. Three times (in 1886, 1890, and 1894) the United States volunteered to act as mediator, but the offers were rejected by both Great Britain and Venezuela. Finally, in 1895, when it appeared that Great Britain was attempting to use the boundary controversy as a means to acquire substantial mineral-rich additional territory, Secretary of State Richard Olney sent several sharp notes to the British government in which he asserted (1) that the United States was bound under the Monroe Doctrine to protect the territorial integrity of Venezuela; (2) that the United States was "practically sovereign" on the South American continent and its decrees were "law upon the subjects to which it confines its interposition"; (3) that arbitration was the only way to settle the boundary line.

When Foreign Secretary Lord Salisbury denied the applicability of the Monroe Doctrine and refused to submit the disputed boundary to arbitration, President Cleveland in December, 1895, sent a message to Congress requesting approval of the appointment of a commission to draw the boundary line which it would be the duty of the United States to defend against any British aggression. This stirring presidential message roused the nation, although Lord Salisbury was correct in branding the Olney dispatches as a completely novel interpretation of the Monroe Doctrine. But the war spirit subsided when it became evident that responsible leaders in the American Congress and in the British Parliament desired peace. Through the efforts of the United States, representatives of Great Britain and Venezuela signed a treaty in 1897 providing for the boundary dispute to be submitted to an international board of arbitration. The decision, rendered in 1899, was in basic accord with the claims of Great Britain, making Venezuela regret its reliance on American support.

RELATIONS WITH LATIN AMERICA

One of the most serious defects in the foreign policy of the United States during the last third of the nineteenth century was the failure to establish enduring friendship with the independent republics of Latin America.

Mediation under the Monroe Doctrine. The interest of the United States in its neighbors to the south was based upon one of the Monroe Doctrine's principles—that European nations were not to interfere in the affairs of the republics of the Western Hemisphere. Since peace was often threatened by quarrels over international boundaries, the United States frequently offered its services as a mediator (its "good offices"). In 1876 the United States arbitrated a boundary dispute between Argentina and Paraguay; in 1880 its good offices were accepted by Colombia and Chile in all controversies that they could not settle by direct negotiations; in 1881 it helped Mexico and Guatemala, as well as Argentina and Chile, settle boundary disputes; the same year it intervened in the quarrel between Peru and Chile over the provinces of Tacna-Arica and earned the ill will of Chile by its efforts for compromise; it tried hard to bring to an end the War of the Pacific (1879 to 1884) between Bolivia and Peru on one side and Chile on the other. But in the hands of diplomats of the United States the Monroe Doctrine could be a two-edged sword. The gratitude of Latin American nations for such protection as the Doctrine provided against European interference in Western Hemisphere affairs was often overshadowed by their resentment against the position of superiority assumed by the United States.

Blaine's Pan-American Policy. No secretary of state since Henry Clay (who served in the 1820s) had worked harder than James G. Blaine to promote the interests of the United States in Latin America. But much of Blaine's effort was nullified by his aggressive insistence that commercial contracts be worked out along the lines laid down by the State Department. During his brief tenure as secretary of state under President Garfield, Blaine arranged for a conference of the nations of the Western Hemisphere at Washington, D.C., but his immediate successor, Frederick T. Frelinghuysen, abandoned the project. Later, during 1889–1890, the first International Conference of American States did meet at Washington, D.C., and as secretary of state under President Harrison, Blaine presided over deliberations. He gained little satisfaction from it, however, as the delegates refused to approve his proposals for a customs union.[2] The sole tangible result of the conference was the establishment of the International Bureau of American Republics (later called the Pan-American Union) to facilitate the exchange of commerical information.

Under Blaine's direction the State Department was eager to maintain order in the republics of Latin America. When its minister in Chile, Patrick Egan, assumed a truculent attitude toward a government that in 1891 had taken control by force, Blaine supported him. Later that year Blaine used an attack by a mob on American sailors on shore leave in Valparaiso, Chile, as a pretext for a tone of belligerency that brought the United States to the verge of war with the Latin American republic. Although Blaine secured an official apology from Chile, his attitude created among Latin Americans an impression of unrestrained aggressiveness on the part of the United States.

THE LURE OF THE PACIFIC

Into the early 1890s most Americans were little interested in the relations of their government with foreign nations, but a change in sentiment was already becoming evident. It was particularly noticeable in the favorable reaction throughout the nation to American expansion in the Pacific.

Emergence of the New Imperialism. Many forces gave strength to the growing desire on the part of the United States to acquire territory beyond its continental borders.

MARINERS AND MISSIONARIES. Although many Americans failed to realize it, there was much in the new wish for overseas possessions that was old. In the Pacific the reaching out was in large part the result of attitudes developed during the era of clipper ships and whaling vessels. The zeal of Christian missionaries who had for decades longed to reform the people of the Orient to the ways of their gospel was also a major factor. Mariners and missionaries, indeed, were the American pioneers in Samoa and Hawaii.

THE SETTLEMENT OF THE WEST. The westward advance on the

[2]An association of nations that have abolished restrictions on trade among themselves and have adopted a common trade policy toward other nations.

continental United States stopped with the close of the frontier in the early 1890s. Habits of pioneering were then transferred overseas. And those who had settled in the Far West maintained a great economic interest, if only because of geographic proximity, in the Pacific region.

THE SEARCH FOR MARKETS. Expansion into the Pacific was spurred by the growing industrialization of the United States. Every decade after 1870 brought an increase in its exports and, more significantly, an accompanying rise in the proportion of manufactured goods to agricultural products in its export totals. As the industrial system took hold, the need for markets for manufactured articles gave added impetus to the demand that American political control over areas in the Pacific be strengthened.

IMPORTANCE OF SEA POWER. Although the United States had never maintained a large standing army, its people had long cherished the tradition of the American navy. But naval strength was allowed to decline after the Civil War. In the 1880s work was begun to improve the navy by adding newly constructed steel vessels. This marked the acceptance by the government of the concept of a navy capable of meeting successfully any potential foe on the Atlantic or the Pacific. The new policy was being effected at a time when many Americans were reading books and articles on the importance of sea power, particularly in relation to a nation's commercial expansion, by Alfred Thayer Mahan, a career naval officer who became one of the world's leading authorities on the subject.

Samoa. An early example of the changed attitude of many Americans toward overseas imperialism was the peaceful penetration of the Samoan Islands. Contacts with the islanders, first stimulated by the pre-Civil War trade with China, passed through several stages.

TRADING CONCESSIONS. Casual relations established by American traders led in 1872 to the negotiation of a treaty, which the Senate failed to ratify, granting the United States a coaling station. In 1878, however, a treaty that gave to the United States certain trading rights and permitted it to establish a naval base at the harbor of Pago Pago was approved by the Senate.

POLITICAL CONTROL. During this time Germany and Great Britain also received trading rights in Samoa, and they and the United States entered into an often fierce competition for favored treatment by the Samoans. This rivalry aroused in the United States a nationalistic spirit that was only partially satisfied when in 1889 a joint protectorate[3] of the three nations was established over Samoa. In 1899 a treaty was signed by which Great Britain relinquished its claims in Samoa in return for concessions elsewhere; Germany took over two of the islands; and the United States retained the

[3]A relationship in which a nation, without having legal possession, exercises governmental powers over a smaller and weaker territorial unit, especially in the areas of defense and foreign relations.

rest, including Tutuila, with its fine harbor of Pago Pago, which provided an important naval base in the Pacific.

Hawaii. Acquisition of the Hawaiian Islands was the result of forces similar to those which brought to the United States colonial responsibilities in Samoa.

EARLY CONTACTS. As early as the 1820s New England missionaries had established themselves on several of the Hawaiian Islands, where their descendants were joined by traders with the Orient and sailors on the clipper ships and whaling vessels. All these groups steadily augmented the American population in the islands.

SUGAR PLANTERS. Within a generation, the production of sugar became the chief interest of Americans in Hawaii. Those sugar planters who were Americans—and a majority were—worked indefatigably for closer relations with the United States. In 1875 they secured a tariff agreement between the United States and the islands which greatly stimulated their sugar trade. However, the McKinley Tariff of 1890, while removing the duty on raw sugar imported into the United States, also provided to the domestic producers of raw sugar a bounty of two cents a pound on their product. Thus the Hawaiian sugar planters lost their favored position and began to seek annexation as their best prospect.

OVERTHROW OF THE MONARCHY. The government of Queen Liliuokalani, who ascended the throne in 1891, was determined in its opposition to foreigners, and the American minority in the islands became alarmed when the queen proclaimed that Hawaii was for the Hawaiians. In 1893 the foreign elements staged a revolution that succeeded swiftly after the American minister to Hawaii, John L. Stevens, gave his support to the temporary government of the revolutionists and American marines landed to "preserve order."

CLEVELAND'S REJECTION OF ANNEXATION. President Benjamin Harrison, who favored annexation, left office before a treaty could be acted upon. The incoming President, Grover Cleveland, withdrew the proposed annexation treaty from the Senate and appointed James H. Blount, a former representative from Georgia, who was known as an antiimperialist, as special commissioner to investigate the situation. After receiving Blount's report, which criticized American involvement in the recent uprising, Cleveland attempted to restore the government of Queen Liliuokalani on the condition that she pardon all the revolutionists. This the queen refused to do, and the revolutionary government continued in power. On July 4, 1894, this government proclaimed the Republic of Hawaii, and in the following month it was formally recognized by the United States.

VICTORY OF THE ANNEXATIONISTS. When William McKinley became president in 1897, sentiment in favor of annexation was running strong. Acquiring the Republic of Hawaii, said the expansionists, was highly desirable because (1) it might otherwise fall under the control of a foreign power; (2) it would provide a badly needed naval base in the Pacific; (3) it would offer opportunities for American commercial investment. These arguments were reinforced in the minds of many citizens by the belief that the United States was destined to control the Pacific and that the nation had a duty to take the Christian gospel and American democratic institutions to the people of that area. A formal protest by Japan against annexation also spurred on the move, and the war with Spain in 1898 gave it added impetus. All these considerations brought about the annexation of Hawaii by a joint resolution of Congress, which President McKinley signed on July 7, 1898.

The Far East. Upon acquiring island possessions in the Pacific, the United States was compelled to become much more actively interested in the course of events in the Far East.

THE "OPEN-DOOR" POLICY. Among the champions of overseas expansion was John Hay, who became secretary of state in 1898. Hay particularly wanted to maintain the stable relationship already established among the foreign powers in the Far East for the benefit of American trade. He was alarmed by the activity of a half-dozen foreign powers in a China that was weakened and dispirited after having been defeated in a recent war with Japan. Each of the powers assumed in China a sphere of influence.[4]

Hay asked Great Britain, Germany, Russia, France, Italy, and Japan to agree to an "open-door" policy—that no nation within its sphere of influence would interfere with the normal commercial and transportation activities of other nations. The foreign powers reluctantly agreed to Hay's doctrine, thus ensuring to American traders equal treatment with the citizens of the nations that had previously received economic concessions from China.

THE BOXER REBELLION. The expansionist activity in China was threatened by a society of ultrapatriotic Chinese known in English as Boxers. Early in 1900 the Boxers, fully committed to acts of terrorism, demanded that the "foreign devils" be driven from the nation. In June, 1900, the Boxers attacked members of the foreign community in the capital, Peking. The United States assumed the lead in organizing an international relief force which arrived in Peking in time to rescue the majority of besieged foreigners. When some of the foreign powers used the Boxer Rebellion as a pretext for discarding the open-door policy and partitioning China, Hay successfully argued for the preservation of China as a "territorial and administrative entity" with, however, certain restrictions on the nation's sovereignty.

---

[4]A geographic area more or less under the control of a nation considered to have paramount political or economic interests in the region.

WAR WITH SPAIN

The Spanish-American War caused the people of the United States to move rapidly along the path of empire already clearly defined by the more enthusiastic expansionists in the nation.

The Situation in Cuba. Throughout the nineteenth century the United States frequently showed its concern over the fate of its close neighbor Cuba, which was Spain's chief possession in the Caribbean.

THE AMERICAN POLICY. Early in the nineteenth century the American government expressed fear lest the control of the island by Spain should be replaced by that of a more formidable European power. In the 1850s there was much discussion of the United States' acquisition of Cuba either by purchase or seizure. In the last quarter of the century, as American commercial contacts and financial investments in Cuba increased, the government was inclined to support a policy which gave promise of maintaining stable political and economic conditions on the island.

THE CUBAN INSURRECTION. A rebellion of the Cubans against Spanish authority, lasting from 1868 to 1878, not only brought devastation to large areas of the island but also pushed the United States to the verge of war with Spain because of Spanish charges that Americans were aiding the rebels in violation of international law. The Spanish mistreated American citizens in Cuba and in 1873 summarily executed Americans (along with other nationals) who were crew members of the arms-running ship *Virginius*, which illegally flew the American flag. But since the United States at this time had no desire for war, it acted with moderation. The period following the insurrection left the Cuban leaders resentful over the Spanish government's unfulfilled promises of reform and sent many of them to the United States, where they disseminated propaganda for Cuban independence.

THE CUBAN WAR OF INDEPENDENCE. Continuing Cuban discontent with Spanish rule flared into revolt in 1895 when prices for Cuban sugar and tobacco sharply declined, as a result of two factors that affected the American market: the financial panic of 1893 and the Wilson-Gorman Tariff of 1894, with its high import duties. The island experienced widespread economic depression. Nevertheless, the wealthier classes in Cuba and most Americans with investments there were opposed to the revolutionists' demand for independence. The revolutionists therefore embarked on a campaign of widespread destruction of such property as sugar plantations, in which Americans had extensive investments, hoping by this action to induce the intervention of the United States. General Valeriano Weyler was sent by the Spanish government to suppress the uprising. Deciding that the revolutionists would never be defeated unless they were deprived of arms and other supplies from the population, Weyler began confining civilians in camps closely supervised by Spanish troops. Although Weyler's policy was misrepresented in sensational accounts in several American newspapers, there was some justification for his nickname "Butcher" because of the brutal effects of his concentration camps. Many noncombatants, including women and children, lacking proper food and sanitation, became victims of starvation and disease. Equally brutal, however, were the guerrilla tactics of the revolutionary forces.

American Demands for Military Intervention. The United States government endeavored to maintain a policy of strict neutrality regarding the situation in the Caribbean island, but an increasing number of citizens voiced their sympathy for the Cuban revolutionists.

CLEVELAND'S ATTITUDE. During the last months of his second term President Cleveland strove both to maintain genuine neutrality and to persuade the Spanish leaders that the granting of a measure of Cuban self-government was the surest way to establish political stability and economic order. Cleveland feared, however, that the growing demand in the United States for intervention would compel his successor, McKinley, to act accordingly.

THE WAR FACTION. American intervention in the Cuban situation was not desired by those holding the largest financial interests in the island, since they believed that Spain would eventually restore stability. The groups most enthusiastic for a war to secure Cuban independence were (1) humanitarians who believed that Spanish policy, as exemplified by the actions of Weyler, was both arbitrary and cruel; (2) "jingoes,"[5] who felt that Spain should be chastised; (3) certain Republican politicians who hoped that a successful struggle with Spain would increase support for the McKinley administration; (4) a few public officials, such as Assistant Secretary of the Navy Theodore Roosevelt and Republican Senator Henry Cabot Lodge of Massachusetts, who were nationalistic in spirit and eager to have the United States become a world power; (5) some newspaper publishers, notably William Randolph Hearst of the *New York Journal* and Joseph Pulitzer of the *New York World*, who to increase their papers' circulation printed exaggerated accounts of Spanish atrocities, while deemphasizing atrocities of the Cuban revolutionists. It has been argued by many that the single most important factor in pushing the United States into war with Spain was the activity of the "yellow press."[6]

THE DE LÔME LETTER. The position of the war faction was strengthened when, on February 9, 1898, Hearst's *New York Journal* printed a letter that the Spanish minister to the United States, Enrique

[5]Those who favor a belligerent foreign policy.

[6]Journalism that holds reader interest by dealing with sensational items or ordinary news sensationally distorted, so named after the "Yellow Kid," the first comic strip printed in color, which appeared in the *New York Journal* and the *New York World*.

Dupuy de Lôme, had written to a friend in Cuba. This private communication had been stolen from the mails in Havana by Cuban revolutionists who made it available to the Hearst organization. The letter contained slurs against President McKinley, referring to him as "weak and a bidder for the admiration of the crowd." To spare his government embarrassment, de Lôme promptly resigned. But the anger of the American people over the letter remained undiminished.

THE SINKING OF THE *MAINE*. On February 15, 1898, the United States battleship *Maine*, which had been ordered to Havana harbor to protect American life and property, blew up and sank with the loss of 260 of its crew. An American naval court of inquiry was unable to determine whether the explosion had been the work of hostile Spanish loyalists or of Cuban revolutionists who hoped that the destruction of the warship would induce American intervention, or had been entirely accidental. Although the Spanish authorities, desirous of preventing American military involvement in Cuba, had good cause for *not* committing such an act, those in the United States who were eager for war attributed the explosion to them. The war faction made "Remember the *Maine*" a popular slogan, which rapidly aroused sentiment throughout the nation for American intervention to liberate Cuba from Spain.

McKinley's War Message. Although personally desirous of averting war, President McKinley realized that a policy of "peace at any price" might split his party and wreck his administration. Therefore, on April 11, 1898, he sent a message to Congress charging that the Spanish government was unable to suppress the Cuban rebellion and calling for American military intervention to establish peace on the island. As a matter of fact, between the time McKinley wrote his message and the time he transmitted it to Congress, Spain had already capitulated to the United States demands that it proclaim an armistice, close the concentration camps, and enter into negotiations with the revolutionists. But the pressure for war was so great not only in Congress but throughout the nation that McKinley could resist it no longer. On April 19, 1898, Congress adopted a joint resolution for military intervention and McKinley signed it the next day. Attached to the document as its final clause was the Teller Amendment (sometimes called the Teller Resolution), sponsored by Republican Senator Henry M. Teller of Colorado, which disclaimed any intention by the United States to exercise control over Cuba, pledging that the government of the island would be left to its inhabitants as soon as peace had been restored.

Preparation for Hostilities. During the three decades following the Civil War the United States was negligent about maintaining an up-to-date and efficient military organization, primarily because no powerful foe was a threat to the nation. In the war with Spain the American people paid the price for this unpreparedness.

THE ARMY. For years Congress had been miserly in its appropriations for the Department of War. Furthermore, many high officials in the department had been appointed for political reasons rather than for administrative or technical skills. When the war with Spain began, department routine foundered. The necessary tasks of doubling the size of the regular army of 30,000 men and training 200,000 volunteers were not accomplished with the speed and efficiency that the war demanded. The performance of the War Department was distressing to the American people, who slowly learned that inferior equipment, spoiled food, improper clothing for a tropical climate, poor sanitation facilities, and inadequate medical services caused more deaths than did the fighting on the battlefield.

THE NAVY. Because of the nature of the war, the brunt of the fighting fell upon the navy of 26,000 men, which was far better prepared than the army. This was the first test of the new steel ships, construction of which had been going on since 1883. In addition to the North Atlantic Squadron under Rear Admiral William T. Sampson, the Flying Squadron under Commodore Winfield S. Schley, and the Asiatic Squadron under Commodore George Dewey, the Department of the Navy put into service more than 100 auxiliary ships. The number of naval personnel had already been doubled and contracts had been placed for munitions and other supplies—all with speed and efficiency.

War on Two Fronts. With the outbreak of war, Spain became vulnerable not only in its Caribbean colonies but also in its Pacific possessions. Despite serious blunders by both civil and military authorities, the United States won the war with a weak Spain with relative ease.

THE PHILIPPINE CAMPAIGN. The first United States blow for Cuban independence was struck not in the Caribbean but in the far distant Spanish colony of the Philippine Islands. Commodore Dewey's Asiatic Squadron had been on the alert for two months, as a result of secret orders sent by Assistant Secretary of the Navy Theodore Roosevelt to immediately engage the Spanish fleet in the Philippines should war break out. Dewey's fleet steamed from its base near Hong Kong to Manila Bay. There on May 1, 1898, it destroyed the Spanish fleet, which was ill-equipped and had poorly trained crews. Dewey then imposed a blockade until the arrival of army forces, which captured the city of Manila on August 13.

THE CARIBBEAN CAMPAIGN. Rear Admiral Sampson and Commodore Schley engaged in blockading Cuban ports but were not able to prevent the most important Spanish fleet, under the command of Admiral Pascual Cervera, from entering the harbor of Santiago, on Cuba's southeastern shore. There Cervera's ships took a position well protected by land batteries. American naval forces then blockaded the harbor and waited for the arrival of the army from the United States to begin a coordinated operation in the Santiago area. On June 22, 1898, 17,000 troops under the command of General William R. Shafter landed to the east of Santiago. The joint operation against the city was brief and decisive. It consisted of two phases—the action of the land troops to the north and east of the city and the action of the naval forces blockading the harbor.

In the battles of El Caney and San Juan Hill, both occurring on July 1, 1898, the American army gained control of the heights to the north and east of Santiago and began preparations for the bombardment of the Spanish fleet below. In a victorious charge led by Theodore Roosevelt during the battle of San Juan Hill, the First United States Volunteer Cavalry Regiment, nicknamed the "Rough Riders," achieved a large measure of fame. (The Rough Riders had been organized by Roosevelt, who had resigned as assistant secretary of the navy and became second in command of the volunteer regiment.)

Cervera made a desperate effort to break through the blockade. In the ensuing battle his entire fleet was destroyed. On July 17 Santiago surrendered. After the termination of the Santiago operation, American troops were dispatched to capture the nearby Spanish colony of Puerto Rico, which they did after meeting but feeble military resistance.

American War Costs. Of the approximately 275,000 men who served, 5,462 died and 1,604 were wounded in combat. Only 385 of the deaths were battle casualties, most of the remainder being caused by disease, attributed to improper food, poor sanitation, and inadequate medical attention. As for financial costs, the United States spent approximately $250 million in the conflict.

The Treaty of Paris. The terms of the peace settlement with Spain immediately impressed upon the American people how far and how fast they had traveled along the road of expansionism.

NEGOTIATIONS. Through the good offices of the French government, on August 12, 1898, representatives of the United States and Spain signed a protocol[7] calling for a peace conference in Paris in October. Appointed by President McKinley to the peace delegation were Secretary of State William R. Day, publisher Whitelaw Reid of the *New York Tribune,* Republican senators Cushman K. Davis of Minnesota and William P. Frye of Maine, and Democratic Senator George Gray of Delaware. Gray was the sole antiexpansionist of the group. Causing the most serious disagreement among the members of the American commission was the future status of the Philippines—whether all of the islands, some, or none should be retained by the United States.

PROVISIONS. McKinley settled the issue of the Philippines by becoming convinced that the nation favored the retention of all the islands and that humanitarianism (in the President's words, to "uplift and civilize" the

[7]A preliminary memorandum that serves as a basis for a final diplomatic action.

Filipinos), as well as economic and strategic considerations, justified doing so. The main provisions of the treaty, which was signed on December 10, 1898, were the following: (1) Cuba was granted independence and Spain agreed to assume the Cuban debt; (2) Puerto Rico, Guam, and the Philippines were ceded to the United States; (3) the United States paid $20 million to Spain for the Philippines.

RATIFICATION. The final realization of American expansion, which was implemented by the Treaty of Paris, was the result of varied motives: (1) to increase the prestige of the nation by having it play a larger role in world affairs; (2) to tap the expanding trade with the Far East; (3) to frustrate the naval and commercial designs of rivals Germany and Japan in the Pacific; (4) to "uplift and civilize" the people of the islands in the Caribbean and the Pacific. Nevertheless, the President encountered great difficulty in persuading the Senate to ratify the treaty. A determined antiexpansionist force was rapidly developing in the nation. Even before the treaty was signed, the influential Anti-Imperialist League had been organized. Its numbers, led by historian Charles Francis Adams, economist and sociologist William Graham Sumner, and liberally oriented Republican leader Carl Schurz, denounced the acquisition of colonial possessions as a policy which would have Americans control millions of people hostile to their rule and, in so doing, impose heavy burdens upon the national treasury. In the Senate some Republicans, under the leadership of George F. Hoar of Massachusetts, condemned any attempt to govern distant overseas possessions. The Democratic party sought to derive political gains out of the debate over ratification. Although he was opposed to overseas expansion, William Jennings Bryan, as the titular head of the party, persuaded some Democratic senators to vote for ratification, hoping to make the new imperialism an issue on which the Democrats might achieve victory in the election of 1900. Thus the McKinley administration got the treaty ratified with the aid of Democratic votes.

A COLONIAL EMPIRE

The administration of its new overseas possessions and relations with an independent Cuba presented the United States with kinds of constitutional, political, and economic problems that it had never before experienced.

Election of 1900. Imperialism was the paramount issue in the contest for the presidency.

DEMOCRATS. William Jennings Bryan was made the presidential nominee by acclamation. Selected to be his running mate was Adlai E. Stevenson, who had been vice-president during Cleveland's second term. A strong antiimperialist policy for the nation was recommended by the platform.

REPUBLICANS. The delegates to the Republican national convention renominated William McKinley for president with great enthusiasm. Theodore Roosevelt, who after returning from the Spanish-American War a dashing hero had been elected governor of New York, was chosen for second place on the ticket. The Republican platform praised the McKinley administration for its conduct of a "righteous war" against Spain and its assumption of a "moral duty" in the Philippines after the conflict.

THE CAMPAIGN. Bryan endeavored to spread the gospel of anti-imperialism. Denunciation of the trusts, condemnation of the protective tariff, and support of the unlimited coinage of silver received less attention from the Democratic candidate than did his demand that the nation repudiate the course of empire upon which the Republicans had embarked. Republican leaders assailed Bryan throughout the campaign as an impractical radical.

MCKINLEY'S VICTORY. McKinley received 292 electoral votes to Bryan's 155. Only four states outside the quarter-century-old Solid South were carried by the Democratic candidate. From the outset Bryan's cause had been hopeless. The nation was enjoying widespread prosperity at home and heightened prestige abroad. The voters were ready to assume the burdens of empire and to reward the party that had brought a revival of manufacturing and commercial activity.

The Insular Cases. A fundamental question regarding the status of the overseas dependencies was this: Does the Constitution follow the flag? Imperialistically inclined Americans asserted that the newly acquired territories did not become routinely incorporated into the United States and that the inhabitants of those possessions did not hold the same rights granted to the citizens of the United States by the Constitution. Antiexpansionist Americans, on the other hand, maintained that the very fact of acquisition made the possessions a fully integrated part of the United States and thus gave to their inhabitants all the constitutional benefits enjoyed by the citizens of the United States.

In a group of rulings from the Insular Cases of 1901–1903 the Supreme Court settled the status of the island possessions by laying down the principle that not all provisions of the Constitution need apply to those who lived under the American flag but outside the continental boundaries of the United States. Thus the Constitution did *not* follow the flag. In effect, Congress was virtually free to administer each particular island possession as it saw fit.

Puerto Rico. In the decades following the war with Spain the United States endeavored to lead the people of Puerto Rico toward self-government and stable economic conditions.

MOVEMENT TOWARD SELF-GOVERNMENT. In 1900 Congress passed the Foraker Act, making Puerto Rico an unincorporated territory—a position

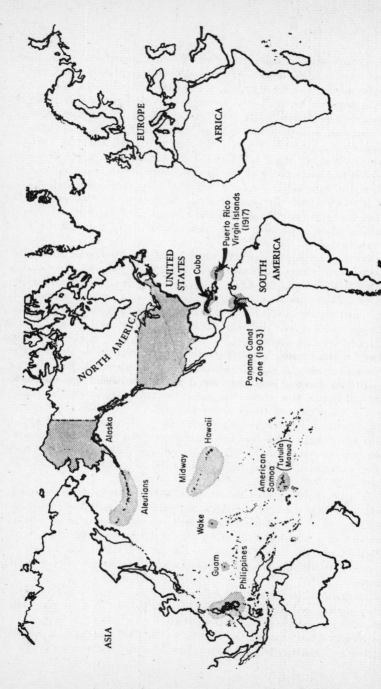

THE UNITED STATES AS A COLONIAL POWER, 1900

midway between that of a colony and a territory, with no provision for eventual statehood. The President of the United States was empowered to appoint the governor-general, who headed the executive branch of the island's government, and to name the members of the upper house of the two-house legislature, while Puerto Rican voters elected representatives to the lower house.

The Jones Act, passed in 1917, conferred American citizenship upon all Puerto Ricans and made the upper house of the legislature elective. In 1947 Congress passed a law granting Puerto Ricans the right to elect their own governor. The following year journalist and legislative leader Luis Muñoz Marín became the first elected governor. Muñoz Marín served four consecutive four-year terms and became very popular for his promotion of economic and social reforms.

In 1952 President Harry Truman signed a joint resolution of Congress which approved a new constitution drafted by the islanders themselves. Under it Puerto Rico became voluntarily associated with the United States as a commonwealth.[8] In 1967 the people of Puerto Rico in a special election expressed their preference regarding the future political status of the island: 60 percent of those voting favored retaining the commonwealth; 35 percent, statehood; 5 percent, independence.

ECONOMIC CONDITIONS. As Puerto Ricans moved toward self-government, they made efforts to improve their standard of living. Devoting itself almost entirely to the production of sugar in order to meet the tremendous demand from the United States, the island was unable to produce sufficient foodstuffs or other commodities for its fast-growing population. During the 1950s the Puerto Rican government made a determined effort, with assistance from the United States, to develop the production of agricultural commodities other than sugar and to stimulate industrial enterprise.

The Philippines. The most severe challenge to American colonial policy was that of devising procedures for governing the Philippine Islands.

THE AGUINALDO INSURRECTION. When the Spanish-American War began, Emilio Aguinaldo, a municipal official who had recently led an unsuccessful revolt against Spanish control of his homeland, formed a native army to aid the American forces sent there. He hoped that after the anticipated American victory was achieved, he would be installed as president of a new Philippine republic. When he realized that the United States would keep the islands, he organized an insurrection which was finally suppressed by American troops in 1902.

ESTABLISHMENT OF CIVIL GOVERNMENT. While the American army was

[8]A colony that achieves a self-governing, autonomous status but remains associated in a loose political federation with its former ruling power.

still fighting the Aguinaldo-led insurrectionists, President William Mc-Kinley appointed two commissions to report on political conditions in the islands. The first Philippine Commission, which was investigative in nature, affirmed that the ultimate goal for the islands should be independence. The second Philippine Commission, led by William Howard Taft, who was then a federal judge, set up civil government in the islands, and in 1901 Taft was appointed head of the executive branch, eventually receiving the title of governor-general. In 1902 Congress passed the Organic Act, which outlined the conditions under which the Filipinos were to participate in their government. The act provided for a two-house legislature, the upper house consisting of the members of the second Philippine Commission and the lower house consisting of representatives elected by Filipino voters.

THE JONES ACT OF 1916. Passed by a Democratic-controlled Congress and signed into law by Democratic President Woodrow Wilson in 1916, the Jones Act was in keeping with planks in the Democratic party's platforms since 1900 favoring a steady move toward ultimate independence for the Philippines. Under the act, although the head of the executive branch of the government was still to be an American governor-general, five of the executive departments were to be led by Filipinos. The upper house of the legislature was made elective, as the lower house had been for fourteen years.

REPUBLICAN POLICY. The governor-general who served throughout the eight years of the Wilson administration, Francis B. Harrison, pursued a notably liberal course, which gave impetus to the demand both in the islands and in the United States for immediate Philippine independence. But beginning in 1921 each of the three Republican Presidents of the next dozen years—Harding, Coolidge, and Hoover—exhibited his party's reluctance to grant early independence.

THE TYDINGS-McDUFFIE ACT. The overwhelming Democratic victory in the election of 1932 was a stimulus to the Philippine independence movement. In January, 1933, toward the end of the Hoover administration, the outgoing Congress passed over the President's veto the Hawes-Cutting Act, providing for the independence of the Philippines after a ten-year transition period. However, the Philippine legislature refused to ratify the act because of certain provisions on immigration and imports. In 1934 the Democratic-controlled Congress passed and the Philippine legislature unanimously ratified the Tydings-McDuffie Act. This measure established the Philippines temporarily as a commonwealth, with the provision that complete independence would be granted in 1946. Manuel Quezon, who had held a number of government positions, became president of the Philippines Commonwealth, and prepared the way for independence.

Despite a five-year occupation of the islands by Japan during World War II, there was no delay in bestowing independence, as promised, in 1946.

Manuel Roxas, who had served in various positions in the American-sponsored government in the islands, was elected the first president of the Republic of the Philippines.

Relations with Cuba. Although the United States withdrew its military forces from Cuba as soon as order had been restored, it imposed upon the newly established island republic certain conditions that kept it under American control.

THE PLATT AMENDMENT. The United States established in Cuba a military government headed by Major General Leonard Wood. In 1901, with American support, a convention of Cuban delegates wrote a constitution for the new nation. As a condition for the withdrawal of American forces, the delegates were compelled to accept provisions that had been passed by Congress as a rider to an army appropriations bill. These provisions, known collectively as the Platt Amendment after their sponsor, Republican Senator Orville H. Platt of Connecticut, stipulated that (1) Cuba would sign no treaty impairing its sovereignty without the consent of the United States; (2) Cuba would not incur a debt unless the interest could be met out of current revenues; (3) the United States could intervene to preserve the independence or the political and social stability of Cuba; (4) Cuba would grant to the United States land for the establishment of naval bases. (Under the terms of the last clause the United States built at Guantánamo Bay in the eastern part of the island a naval station which it continues to operate.)

In 1902 American troops sailed for home. The following year the Platt Amendment was incorporated into a treaty between the United States and Cuba. In 1934 the Platt Amendment was abrogated, as part of the policy of the Franklin D. Roosevelt administration to improve relations between the United States and Latin America.

MILITARY INTERVENTION. While the Platt Amendment was in effect the United States intervened in Cuba several times. Usually, diplomatic pressure was sufficient to bring compliance with American wishes. However, military forces were dispatched to the island on three occasions: in 1906 to quell disorderly protests by a political party that had suffered defeat in a recent election; in 1912 to restore order when blacks engaged in an insurrection against white control in one of the provinces; and in 1917 to put down a political revolt against the government.

ECONOMIC PENETRATION. After the Spanish-American War, commercial contacts between Cuba and the United States increased rapidly. By the early 1920s nearly three-fourths of Cuba's imports consisted of American goods while more than four-fifths of its exports went to the United States. Americans soon came to control a wide range of economic enterprises in the island republic, including sugar production and railroading. Thus Cuba, while in the strict sense politically independent, became in a full sense economically dependent upon its powerful neighbor to the north.

Chapter 8

THE ERA OF
THEODORE ROOSEVELT

The period made memorable by Theodore Roosevelt lasted for the almost-twelve years during which Roosevelt and Taft were in the White House. The era was one of vigorous effort to remodel the structure of government, to further democratize its processes, and to make it an arbiter of social justice. For close to eight years the exuberant style of Roosevelt gave a new meaning to the presidency. His hand-picked successor, William H. Taft, although possessing none of the Roosevelt style, did achieve many of the widely demanded reforms of the period. In foreign policy the era of Theodore Roosevelt was marked by the aggressive actions of the United States to expand its role as a world power.

THE PROGRESSIVE MOVEMENT

Progressivism was a widely accepted reform movement that held sway from about the time Theodore Roosevelt assumed the presidency in 1901 until the United States entered World War I in 1917. The adherents of the movement, called progressives whether their party affiliation was Democratic or Republican, endeavored to make government organization and processes on the federal, state, and local levels more democratic and to foster legislation that would directly benefit the people economically and socially.

Political Progressives. On all three levels of government—federal, state, and local—efforts by a number of committed and vigorous political leaders propelled the progressive movement forward.

THE FEDERAL LEVEL. In the group of politicians of progressive persuasion were all three Presidents of the period in which progressivism was in existence—Theodore Roosevelt, William H. Taft to a lesser degree, and Woodrow Wilson.

THE STATE LEVEL. Republican Governor Robert M. La Follette of Wisconsin was the first progressive chief executive on the state level. His program of reform, dubbed the Wisconsin Idea, was, among other things, leveled against the corruption of political bosses and the abuses of business interests, particularly the railroads. Other governors who drew nationwide attention as progressives were Republicans Hiram Johnson of California and Charles Evans Hughes of New York. Democrat Woodrow Wilson distinguished himself as a progressive governor of New Jersey before he was elected to the presidency.

THE LOCAL LEVEL. The most notable of the many progressive mayors across the nation were Democrat Tom L. Johnson of Cleveland and Republican Samuel M. ("Golden Rule") Jones of Toledo. Johnson worked ceaselessly to remove a gamut of political, economic, and social faults and abuses that existed in his city. He was widely considered the most competent person up to his time to serve as head of a municipality. Among the many reforms Jones implemented in Toledo were both an eight-hour workday and minimum wages for municipal employees.

The Muckrakers. The term "muckrakers" was applied to a group of writers who stirred public opinion to the point of action by exposing abuses in business and corruption in politics. The term originated with President Roosevelt, who, although concurring with the basic accusations of the crusading writers, criticized them for their focus on sensationalism. The President compared them with a character in John Bunyan's seventeenth-century allegory *Pilgrim's Progress* who was so intent on piling up the filth with his muckrake that the only direction in which he looked was downward.

Some of the best-known muckrakers were Frank Norris, whose novels *The Octopus* (1901) and *The Pit* (1903) attacked the Southern Pacific Railroad and the Chicago grain market respectively; Ida M. Tarbell, whose *History of the Standard Oil Company* (1904) condemned the practices of that monopolistic corporation; Lincoln Steffens, whose *Shame of the Cities* (1904) exposed corruption in various municipal governments across the nation; and Upton Sinclair, whose novel *The Jungle* (1906) decried conditions in the Chicago meat-packing plants. Several popular magazines of the period, including *Collier's*, *Cosmopolitan*, *Everybody's*, and *McClure's*, provided the muckrakers with a forum for some of their most sensational disclosures.

Although President Roosevelt was not always willing to recognize his indebtedness to the muckrakers, his own crusade for social justice was significantly aided by the work of such writers. One can trace to the efforts of the muckrakers such results as legislation for the protection of consumers and suits by the federal government against various trusts.

Direct Government. The charge by critics that American legislative bodies were dominated by privileged interests and therefore did not truly represent the people as a whole led to a demand that the will of the people be translated more directly into governmental action.

THE INITIATIVE. First adopted by South Dakota in 1898, the initiative permits a certain portion of the voters (usually about 10 percent) to initiate, or propose, by petition a law, which is then submitted to either the state legislature or the people for approval. Twenty-two states have at various times tested the initiative.

THE REFERENDUM. Like the initiative, the referendum was first used by South Dakota in 1898. It permits a certain portion of the voters (usually about 10 percent), by signing a petition, to have submitted to the voters for their acceptance or rejection a law that has passed the legislature. In some states the referendum procedure allows the state legislature to submit to the voters a proposed bill for their acceptance or rejection, and if accepted the bill becomes a law.

THE RECALL. This plan to make public officials more responsive to the people's will was first used in Los Angeles in 1903. The recall permits a certain portion of the voters (usually about 25 percent) by petition to remove an officeholder before the expiration of the term for which he has been elected or appointed. Its use in connection with the recall of judges, as provided in the constitution of Arizona, aroused bitter controversy, but there have been few examples of summary removal of officeholders in any of the three branches of government.

THE DIRECT PRIMARY. This system was introduced in Wisconsin in 1903 during La Follette's governorship. The direct primary is a preliminary election in which the voters directly nominate candidates of their own party to run in a general election. By 1933 some form of the direct primary was used in all but six of the states. But the hopes of the reformers that the device would break the power of the bosses at party nominating conventions proved overoptimistic.

THE SEVENTEENTH AMENDMENT. The champions of direct government were particularly insistent in their demand for the popular election of United States senators. Charging that selection by the state legislatures resulted in a Senate brought into being by an alliance between wealthy businessmen and unscrupulous politicians, they persuaded state after state to permit the voters to express a senatorial preference that the legislature was bound to accept. At the same time, the progressives worked hard to secure a constitutional amendment to implement their objectives. Passed by Congress in 1911 and ratified in 1913, the Seventeenth Amendment to the Constitution provided for direct election of senators.

Municipal Reform. The progressives' vigorous attack upon the structure and administration of municipal government led to reforms that broke the power of city political machines in various parts of the nation.

THE COMMISSION PLAN. In 1900 Galveston, Texas, following a destructive hurricane, experimented with a new form of government—the commission plan. The system spread rather fast. Under this plan all municipal functions are vested in a small group of elected persons, usually five, each of whom is responsible for the management of an administrative department. The commission, all of whose members theoretically hold equal power, determines policy as a body. One of the commissioners serves as ceremonial head of the municipal government. By 1914 more than 400 of the nation's smaller cities had tried the plan, some with such indifferent results that they abandoned it.

THE CITY MANAGER PLAN. In 1914 Dayton, Ohio, adopted the city manager type of municipal organization, a plan patterned after a system introduced six years earlier by Staunton, Virginia. The Dayton approach was widely followed. Under the city manager plan a commission of elected persons, acting in the capacity of a board of directors, appoints a nonpolitical city manager to administer the government as if it were a business concern. As in the case of the commission plan, the results did not prove uniformly satisfactory.

Woman Suffrage. The progressive era was marked by a notable extension of suffrage, as state after state gave women the right to vote.

STATE ACTION. The egalitarian philosophy of the far western frontier, the entrance of women into certain trades and professions, the opening of institutions of higher education to women—all these gave impetus to the campaign for woman suffrage after the Civil War. Wyoming was the first state to grant the ballot to women, having been admitted to the Union in 1890 with the provision already established by law. By the end of the Taft administration (1913) eight states—Kansas, Colorado, Idaho, Utah, Arizona, Washington, Oregon, and California—had given women the right to vote.

THE NINETEENTH AMENDMENT. Many advocates of women's rights believed that a constitutional amendment was the ultimate solution to the issue of equal political rights for men and women. Susan B. Anthony, a social reformer and leader in the woman suffrage movement, proposed such an amendment in 1869; nine years later it was introduced in Congress. There it languished for more than forty years. In 1919 Congress passed the Nineteenth Amendment to the Constitution, granting nationwide woman suffrage. Ratification in August, 1920, permitted women to vote in the presidential election of 1920. This result was a testimonial to the effective work of such feminists as Anthony, Elizabeth Cady Stanton, and Carrie Chapman Catt.

State and Municipal Welfare Action. The progressives were responsible for a good deal of state and municipal welfare legislation passed during the Roosevelt and Taft administrations.

THE STATE LEVEL. A number of states enacted laws that regulated hours and wages of workers; restricted the type and amount of labor performed by women and children; provided for workmen's compensation; granted public aid to widowed or deserted mothers with dependent children and to the needy aged; and set health and safety standards for industry.

THE MUNICIPAL LEVEL. Progressive reforms in the cities included the establishment of settlement houses to supply various educational, leisure, medical, and other services to congested urban communities; slum clearance; and the setting up of recreational facilities.

The Socialist Challenge. Although the socialist movement in the United States had its start immediately after the Civil War, Socialists attracted little attention until they began to offer alternative programs to those of the progressives.

The Socialist Labor party, established in 1876, and the Social Democratic party, founded in 1897, united in 1901 to form the Socialist Party of America, headed by Eugene V. Debs. The party set for its ultimate goal the establishment of public ownership and operation of the means of production and distribution, according to the principles of the German social philosopher Karl Marx. The Socialist Party of America advocated the following preliminary steps for achieving its goal: (1) reduction of workday hours; (2) enactment of unemployment insurance; (3) government ownership of railroad lines, telegraph companies, telephone firms, and other public utilities; (4) nationwide adoption of the initiative, referendum, and recall; (5) implementation of proportional representation.[1] The Socialists denounced the programs of the progressives as the futile "tinkering" of the bourgeoisie (the middle class engrossed in material interests).

The first substantial vote received by a Socialist Party of America candidate in a presidential election was in 1912, when Debs polled 897,000 ballots. In the election of 1920, with women voting for the first time, Debs secured 919,000 votes. From the election of 1928 on, although the party's candidate over and over again was its able head, Norman Thomas, the electoral strength of the organization declined.

THE SQUARE DEAL

The assassination of President William McKinley by a crazed anarchist, on September 6, 1901, threw the conservative Republican leaders into a panic. They feared that the young and dynamic Vice-President, now elevated to the presidency, might put into effect too many of his progressive ideas. Roosevelt manifested a lively concern that his administration should afford a "square deal" for all Americans—businessmen, laborers, farmers,

---

[1]An electoral system designed to represent in a legislative body each political group or party in optimum proportion to its actual voting strength in a community.

and consumers. The reason for Roosevelt's impact lay in his unusual ability to arouse his fellow Americans to an awareness of their civic duties, rather than in any measurable progress made under his leadership toward the ideal of social justice.

The Roosevelt Administration. Implicit in everything that Roosevelt did as president was his theory that the one who held that office should be the leader in the formulation of all governmental policies.

THE PRESIDENT. Roosevelt exuded a zest for living that perhaps none of his predecessors in the White House had ever matched. He was a person of varied talents—outdoorsman, writer, politician. By his fellow Americans the colorful Roosevelt was called, with affection, "Teddy."

FIRST STATE OF THE UNION MESSAGE. The new President's first State of the Union Message was transmitted to Congress in December, 1901, less than three months after he was thrust into office. Calculated to quiet the fear of his party associates, the message was nevertheless a blueprint for far-reaching reforms. Roosevelt called for (1) greater control of corporations by the federal government; (2) more authority for the Interstate Commerce Commission; (3) conservation of natural resources; (4) extension of the merit system in the civil service; (5) construction of an isthmian canal; (6) a vigorous foreign policy.

THE CABINET. Wanting to suggest continuance of the previous administration's policies, Roosevelt retained the McKinley cabinet intact. Thus the distinguished John Hay and Elihu Root remained as heads of the departments of state and war respectively. Eventually, however, he made changes in all of the posts except one. The members of the official family were, on the whole, men of ability, but the strong-willed Roosevelt dominated them all.

The Coal Strike. Roosevelt's concern for a "square deal" for all Americans prompted his actions in a strike that took place in the anthracite coal fields.

THE MINERS' GRIEVANCES. For many years miners in the anthracite coal districts of eastern Pennsylvania, unable to effect a satisfactory organization to protect their interests, had been exploited by the mine operators. They had grievances regarding (1) the forcing upon them of long hours; (2) their low wages; (3) being compelled to live in company houses and to trade at company stores; (4) the refusal of the operators to recognize the union and collective bargaining. When the mine owners refused to arbitrate grievances, the miners went on strike in May, 1902.

THE WHITE HOUSE CONFERENCE. With the strike dragging on, Roosevelt in October, 1902, invited the mine owners and John Mitchell, president of the United Mine Workers, to confer with him in the White House. But the President's attempt to mediate failed completely, as the mine owners still refused to make any concessions.

SETTLEMENT. Soon after the conference at the White House, Roosevelt quietly began exerting pressure in financial circles to resolve the conflict. He also threatened to use federal troops to run the mines. The operators were finally persuaded to agree, as the miners had already done, to Roosevelt's plan for a board of arbitration to review the issues in the dispute. In March, 1903, the board decided to grant a 10 percent wage increase and a nine-hour workday, but not to recognize the union. The decision became the basis of peace between management and labor in the anthracite coal districts for the next fifteen years.

Election of 1904. Having served three and a half years of McKinley's term, Roosevelt was eager to become president in his own right.

DEMOCRATS. The delegates to the Democratic national convention, turning aside from the "radicalism" of William Jennings Bryan and ignoring the claims of *New York Journal* publisher William Randolph Hearst for the nomination, selected a conservative New York jurist, Alton B. Parker. Chosen the vice-presidential nominee was Henry G. Davis of West Virginia, a merchant and former senator.

REPUBLICANS. For a time Roosevelt had feared that the ultraconservative wing of his party would oppose him for the presidential nomination and support Mark Hanna. But Hanna's death early in 1904 removed all likelihood of opposition, and Roosevelt was nominated by acclamation at the Republican national convention. Selected to be his running mate was Senator Charles W. Fairbanks of Indiana.

THE CAMPAIGN. At issue in the campaign was whether the people were in favor of a continuation of the policies and style of Theodore Roosevelt.

ROOSEVELT'S VICTORY. The President was elected by an electoral vote of 336 to 140 for Parker. He carried every state outside the Solid South. In popular votes, Roosevelt received 7,628,000 to Parker's 5,084,000.

Handling the Trusts. Roosevelt was opposed to any program of destroying the trusts, but he advocated close governmental regulation of industry under the terms of the Sherman Antitrust Act of 1890, which so far had not been vigorously enforced.

THE NORTHERN SECURITIES CASE. The first assault in the battle against business combinations in restraint of trade occurred when Attorney General Philander C. Knox filed suit in 1902 against the Northern Securities Company, a holding company that had a controlling share of stock in the Northern Pacific, the Great Northern, and the Chicago, Burlington, and Quincy railroads. The President, who had declared that the most powerful corporation, like the humblest citizen, would be compelled to obey the law, was pleased that the government won its case in the lower federal courts and that the Supreme Court, in 1904, upheld the decision.

FEDERAL LEGISLATION. Congress failed to undertake a comprehensive modification of the Sherman Antitrust Act, which Roosevelt had urged, but it passed several measures designed to facilitate enforcement of the act. The

Expedition Act of 1903 gave precedence on the calendar of the federal courts to cases arising from alleged nonobservance of the Sherman Antitrust Act or the Interstate Commerce Act. Within the Department of Commerce and Labor, established in 1903, was the Bureau of Corporations, which was authorized to investigate possible violations of antitrust prohibitions. Congress appropriated a special fund of $500,000 for bringing suit against illegal business combinations.

FEDERAL PROSECUTIONS. During the almost eight years of the Roosevelt presidency the Justice Department obtained twenty-four indictments against the trusts. The most significant of the judicial decisions were (1) the injunction (1905) forbidding the member firms of the beef trust to engage in certain practices designed to restrain competition; (2) the suit (1911) that resulted in the dissolution of the Standard Oil Company of New Jersey, a holding company which had a monopoly of the oil refining business; (3) the order (1911) requiring the reorganization of the American Tobacco Company, found to be an illegal combination. In the course of deliberating alleged violations of the Sherman Antitrust Act, the Supreme Court formulated what became known as the "rule of reason"—only "unreasonable" combinations in restraint of trade should be prohibited.

Regulating the Railroads. Roosevelt constantly recommended a more comprehensive regulation of the railroads by extending the power of the Interstate Commerce Commission, which had been crippled by judicial limitation of its functions.

THE ELKINS ACT. This measure, passed in 1903, struck at the practice of secret rebates, which had been declared illegal by the Interstate Commerce Act of 1877. According to the Elkins Act, the recipient, as well as the grantor of the rebate, was made liable to prosecution. Further, the agent or official of the railroad was held legally responsible for any deviation from regular published rates.

THE HEPBURN ACT. By increasing the power of the Interstate Commerce Commission the Hepburn Act, passed in 1906, made a great advance toward government regulation of the railroads. The act (1) raised the membership of the commission from five to seven; (2) extended the commission's authority over express companies, ferries, and pipelines; (3) gave the commission power to reduce unreasonably high and discriminatory rates, subject to judicial review; (4) placed the burden of proof in all legal disputes upon the carrier rather than the commission; (5) forbade the railroads to transport commodities in the production of which they were themselves interested; (6) established a uniform system of accounting to be used by the carriers. Although the Hepburn Act fell short of conferring upon the Interstate Commerce Commission the absolute power to fix rates, it made the commission an effective agency for the first time since its creation twenty years earlier.

SUPPORTIVE JUDICIAL DECISIONS. After the passage of the Hepburn Act the federal courts showed an increasing disposition to lend support to the decisions of the commission. In 1910 the Supreme Court laid down the principle that the railroads could expect protection from the federal courts only if they proved "beyond any reasonable doubt" that their property was being confiscated. At the same time, however, the judiciary as a whole refused to sanction extreme penalties imposed upon railroads or shippers found guilty of violating the law. In 1907 the higher courts set aside the decision of Judge Kenesaw M. Landis of the Second District Court imposing a fine of $29,240,000 on the Standard Oil Company of Indiana for accepting secret rebates from the railroads.

Conservation. No part of Roosevelt's program was carried forward more energetically or more successfully than his campaign for the conservation of natural resources.

EXPOSING NATIONAL WASTE. Roosevelt's outstanding achievement in the conservation movement was his arousal of widespread public interest in stopping the squandering of natural resources. The generosity of the federal government in transferring portions of the public domain[2] to private ownership had resulted in wasteful exploitation of the nation's riches of lumber, coal, petroleum, natural gas, and metals. Roosevelt, aided by such associates as Gifford Pinchot, chief of the Forest Service of the Agriculture Department, and James R. Garfield, secretary of the interior, undertook to educate the American people to support conservation and to secure legislative action for this purpose.

THE NEWLANDS ACT. Recommended by Roosevelt, the Newlands Act, passed in 1902, provided for the appropriation of most of the money received from the sale of public lands in the West and Southwest to finance the construction of irrigation projects. Within five years twenty-eight projects in fourteen states were under way.

NATIONAL PARKS AND FORESTS. Roosevelt was not the originator of the campaign for the establishment of national parks, but he gave vigorous support to those who were trying to preserve regions of great natural beauty. In addition, to prevent the forests from being virtually depleted, he set aside 148 million acres as timber reserves.

INTERNAL WATERWAYS. Conservation included also the utilization of the system of inland bodies of water to facilitate transportation, to promote irrigation projects, and to develop waterpower sites. To supervise such activities, Roosevelt appointed the Internal Waterways Commission.

NATIONAL CONSERVATION COMMISSION. In 1908 Roosevelt held at the White House a governors' conference to discuss the fundamental issues relating to conservation. The result of the conference was the appointment by Roosevelt of the National Conservation Commission, with Gifford Pinchot

[2]Land owned or controlled by the government.

as chairman, and the creation of thirty-six state boards that cooperated with the national body.

Consumer Protection Laws. The scandal arising from supplying spoiled canned meat to servicemen during the Spanish-American War and the works of muckrakers such as Upton Sinclair on the meat-packing industry resulted in legislation for the protection of consumers. The Pure Food and Drug Act, passed in 1906, forbade the adulteration or fraudulent labeling of foods and drugs sold in interstate commerce. The Meat Inspection Act, also passed in 1906, provided for the supervision of conditions of sanitation in meat-packing firms engaged in interstate commerce and for federal inspection of the meat they sold.

TAFT AND REFORM

Although Taft was much more conservative in temperament than Roosevelt, he nevertheless sympathized with the political reformers of his time and approved of many of their objectives. In listing the achievements of his four years in office his admirers included the vigorous prosecution of illegal combinations in restraint of trade, the extension of the merit system to new branches of the civil service, the adoption of the eight-hour workday for employees on government contracts, and the passage of legislation reserving additional public lands from private enterprise. But Taft frequently took issue with the methods of the political reformers and criticized the haste with which they attempted to put their progressive ideas into effect.

Election of 1908. At the end of his second term Roosevelt could have been nominated again for president, but he declined to be a candidate, basing his decision largely on a desire to observe the two-term tradition established by George Washington. Without the zestful "Teddy" in the running, the election was dull from start to finish.

DEMOCRATS. Once more dominant in Democratic circles, William Jennings Bryan was chosen by the national convention of the party to be its standard-bearer for the third time. Indiana lawyer and progressive state legislator John W. Kern was nominated for vice-president.

REPUBLICANS. The Republican national convention was a Roosevelt-dominated convention. The delegates were wildly enthusiastic over the President. At his behest they nominated Taft to be their standard-bearer and adopted a platform that had been drafted in the White House. Representative James S. Sherman of New York was chosen as Taft's running mate.

THE CAMPAIGN. The vigorous orator Bryan was unable to make any headway in the campaign against the easygoing Taft. Indeed, there was much in the Republican position on the various issues that met with Bryan's approval.

TAFT'S VICTORY. Taft won 321 electoral votes to Bryan's 162. The Democratic candidate had thus regained for his party some of the ground lost by presidential candidate Alton B. Parker four years earlier.

The Taft Administration.

Taft set himself a twofold task: to carry forward in his own right the policies that his predecessor had so effectively dramatized and to reconcile the progressives and the conservatives within the Republican party.

THE PRESIDENT. Taft was a hearty and placid 350-pound man whose judicial temperament made it impossible for him to assume the dynamic role that Roosevelt had played so successfully in the progressive movement. As a result, Taft seemed inclined to restrain the zealous liberals rather than to win over the conservatives to the cause of reform.

THE CABINET. Most of the members of Taft's official family were lawyers who emphasized the legal limitations on presidential prerogative and the difficulties of implementing the progressive program. Two influential cabinet members were Secretary of State Philander C. Knox of Pennsylvania, a former attorney general and United States senator, and Secretary of War Henry L. Stimson, a former United States attorney.

Tariff Revision.

The first significant test of Taft's leadership both as president of the United States and as leader of the Republican party arose out of attempts to revise the tariff.

PROTESTS AGAINST PROTECTION. In 1897 the Republican-controlled Congress passed and President McKinley signed into law the protective Dingley Tariff, with an average rate of 57 percent. The high tariff, which then had seemed reasonable to the Republican party, became the object of vigorous attacks as the prices of protected American manufactured goods advanced more rapidly than did workers' wages. In 1907 Roosevelt declared that the tariff needed revision, and in the 1908 campaign Taft pledged that he would interpret the plank on tariff revision in the Republican platform to mean a reduction in rates.

THE PAYNE-ALDRICH TARIFF. The House of Representatives passed the Payne Bill, which provided for a modest general lowering of rates and the placing of coal, iron ore, and hides on the free list. Through the sponsorship of protectionist Republican Nelson W. Aldrich of Rhode Island, the Senate added to the Payne Bill 847 amendments, almost all of which provided for increased rates. The amended bill was fought by a group of midwestern progressive Republican senators, ably led by Robert M. La Follette of Wisconsin. After a lowering of some duties in response to strong requests from Taft, Congress in 1909 passed the Payne-Aldrich Bill, which removed coal and iron ore from the free list and established rates that came to an average of approximately 40 percent. Thus the tariff remained decidedly protectionist.

Eager to persuade the progressive Republicans that the new tariff should be accepted in the interest of party harmony, Taft signed the Payne-Aldrich Bill into law, subsequently asserting that as a tariff it was "the best bill that the Republican party ever passed." This statement put the progressives immediately on their guard against the recently installed President.

The Ballinger-Pinchot Controversy. Conservationists were apprehensive over the plans of Richard A. Ballinger, whom Taft had promoted from superintendent of the General Land Office to secretary of the interior. The new secretary concluded that Roosevelt had exceeded his legal powers in reserving certain public lands, and he soon opened them once more to private leasing. Also, he restored to private operation waterpower sites in Wyoming and Montana and he approved the claims of private interests to valuable coal lands in Alaska. For those acts he was severely criticized in published articles by Louis R. Glavis, a special agent of the Field Division of the Interior Department, and Gifford Pinchot, head of the Forest Service.

Taft, distressed by the publicity attending the quarrel in the administration, dismissed Glavis in September, 1909, and removed Pinchot in January, 1910, after the latter had carried his charges to Congress. Pinchot was quick to rally Roosevelt's supporters and persuade them that Taft was a traitor to the former President's conception of conservation. The accusation was unjust to Taft, but he had to bear the brunt of public antagonism to Ballinger, who was permitted to resign in 1911.

Reform in the House of Representatives. Although Taft was not directly involved in the battle between conservatives and progressives in the House of Representatives, the revolt of the progressive Republicans, popularly called "insurgents," against Speaker Joseph G. Cannon's rule clearly indicated the President's inability to control his party.

"CANNONISM." Republican Joseph G. ("Uncle Joe") Cannon of Illinois, as Speaker of the House of Representatives, exercised enormous power in connection with the legislative process. He served on and appointed the other members to the significant Committee on Rules, which determined the routine procedures of the House; he chose the membership and designated the chairmen of all other standing (permanent) committees. Cannon wielded his considerable influence in such a way as to aid the conservatives and hinder the progressives.

THE REVOLT OF 1910. Republican insurgents rose in revolt against Cannon's dictatorial tactics in March, 1910. Through a coalition with the Democratic minority, they succeeded in having the House adopt an amendment to its rules of procedure (proposed by Republican George W. Norris of Nebraska), depriving the Speaker of the power to appoint members to the Rules Committee and barring him from serving on it. The Rules Committee was made elective. Further, the following year the Democrats, then in the majority, through the adoption of a resolution by the House, denied the

Speaker even the right to appoint standing committees. The success of the Republican insurgents was a defeat for Taft, who had given indirect support to Speaker Cannon in the struggle.

Further Regulation of the Railroads. The desire to strengthen and refine government regulation of the railroads was widespread. The Taft administration gave support to that end.

THE MANN-ELKINS ACT. Through the efforts of congressional progressives of both major parties, legislation was passed during the Taft administration that corrected certain defects in the Hepburn Act. Signed into law in 1910 by President Taft, the Mann-Elkins Act (1) extended the Interstate Commerce Commission's authority to supervise telephone, telegraph, cable, and wireless companies; (2) empowered the commission on its own to institute proceedings against carriers for violations of the law; (3) authorized the commission to suspend all new rates until it was satisfied of their reasonableness; (4) created a new Commerce Court (which was in existence for three years) to expedite the handling of rate cases.

THE PHYSICAL VALUATION ACT. Through the efforts of the progressive Republicans, under the leadership of Senator Robert M. La Follette of Wisconsin, Congress passed in 1913 (three days before the Taft administration came to a close) the Physical Valuation Act, empowering the Interstate Commerce Commission to make a study with the objective of determining the value of the property held by the various railroads. The purpose of the study, which took the commission eight years to complete, was to provide a basis for setting rates that would represent a reasonable profit to the lines on their investment.

Government Reorganization and Reform. The record of the Taft administration for progressive measures compared favorably with that of the Roosevelt administration. This could be readily seen in the area of government reorganization and reform.

THE POSTAL SAVINGS BANK ACT. Upon the recommendation of Taft, Congress in 1910 established the postal savings bank system, whereby certain post offices were authorized to receive deposited funds and pay interest on them.

THE SIXTEENTH AMENDMENT. Passed by Congress in 1909 and ratified in 1913, just as the Taft administration was coming to an end, the new amendment to the Constitution permitted the imposition of a graduated income tax without regard to apportionment among the states according to population.

DEPARTMENTS OF COMMERCE AND LABOR. From the Department of Commerce and Labor, Congress created in 1913 on Taft's last day in office two separate departments—the Department of Commerce and the Department of Labor, whose heads would both be cabinet members. The Department of Commerce was authorized to help supervise and advance the nation's commerce, domestic and foreign. The Department of Labor was set up to improve the status of wage earners in all aspects of their working conditions.

AN AGGRESSIVE FOREIGN POLICY

Roosevelt's conspicuously aggressive manner of conducting foreign relations increased the influence of the United States in world affairs. His style came to be called "big stick diplomacy," a phrase originating from a remark he made before becoming president: "I have always been fond of the West African proverb: 'Speak softly and carry a big stick; you will go far.' " When Taft succeeded Roosevelt as Chief Executive, he endeavored to enlarge American participation abroad by relying on business and financial pursuits.

The Panama Canal. Acquiring island possessions in both the Atlantic and the Pacific dramatically emphasized to Americans the desirability of an isthmian canal under the control of the United States between the two oceans.

THE HAY-PAUNCEFOTE TREATY. In 1850 the United States and Great Britain signed the Clayton-Bulwer Treaty, by which each nation agreed never to exercise exclusive control over or to fortify an isthmian canal, nor to colonize any part of Central America. But after adhering to the terms of the treaty for half a century, the United States was able to secure abrogation of the agreement in the Hay-Pauncefote Treaty. Signed in 1901, the new agreement permitted the United States exclusively to build and control a canal but stipulated that the use of the waterway should be accorded to all nations on equal terms. Although it was not written into the treaty, during negotiations the British in a written communication conceded the right of the United States to fortify the canal.

THE HAY-HERRÁN TREATY. As soon as the Hay-Pauncefote Treaty was concluded, Congress began considering where the waterway should be constructed—in the republic of Nicaragua or in the Isthmus of Panama, a province of the republic of Colombia. The proposed route through Panama was chosen and Congress paid to the New Panama Canal Company (a French firm that had tried to build a canal in the 1880s and still held the franchise for the project) $40 million for its rights. The next step was to negotiate with Colombia for a transfer of sovereignty over the strip of Panamanian territory containing the proposed canal route. In 1903 the Hay-Herrán Treaty was signed with Colombia, by which the South American nation granted the United States a ninety-nine-year lease over a canal zone six miles wide in return for $10 million and an annual payment of $250,000 beginning nine years after the treaty was ratified by both nations. Much to the disgust of President Roosevelt and many other Americans, the Colombian Senate rejected the treaty, hoping that an eager United States would then offer better financial terms.

THE PANAMANIAN REVOLUTION. Colombia's refusal to ratify the Hay-Herrán Treaty angered large numbers of Panamanians who envisaged loss to the province of prestige and income from not having the waterway located there. Panama had long felt that it was being misruled by Colombia; during the second half of the nineteenth century inhabitants of the province engaged in more than fifty uprisings against the national government. It was no surprise, therefore, when on November 3, 1903, Panama revolted against Colombia and declared itself a republic. The revolutionists were successful because of United States action. Roosevelt ordered a warship to Panama, ostensibly to maintain the free and uninterrupted right of way across the Isthmus guaranteed the United States by a treaty with Colombia in 1846. What the vessel accomplished in fact was to prevent Colombia from landing troops in the province to suppress the uprising.

THE HAY-BUNAU-VARILLA TREATY. Two weeks after the revolution the United States promptly negotiated with Panama, which Roosevelt had already formally recognized, the Hay-Bunau-Varilla Treaty. The agreement granted the United States the perpetual control of a canal zone in Panama ten miles wide. The new Latin American republic would receive from the United States $10 million and an annual payment of $250,000 beginning nine years after the treaty was ratified by both nations. On each side, ratification was easily achieved. In 1921, after Roosevelt's death and in a move to bring the United States and Colombia closer together after all that had transpired between them, the Senate approved a treaty which—without providing any reason—called for a payment of $25 million to Colombia.

CONSTRUCTION OF THE CANAL. Excavation for the canal was begun in 1904, but it was hampered by tropical diseases, particularly malaria and yellow fever, among workmen. Colonel William C. Gorgas, a physician in the Army Medical Department, was put in charge of a comprehensive sanitation program. He soon rid the canal zone of malaria and yellow fever. In 1907 Lieutenant Colonel George W. Goethals of the Army Corps of Engineers was appointed to direct the construction job as chief engineer. In 1914 the first ship passed through the Panama Canal.

The Monroe Doctrine Reinterpreted. The growing interests of the United States in the Caribbean, tremendously stimulated by the acquisition of the Panama Canal Zone, caused the Roosevelt administration to develop a theory of responsibility for the preservation of order in that area. Under Roosevelt's direction, the Monroe Doctrine was reinterpreted to justify the intervention of the United States in the domestic and foreign affairs of the Latin American nations.

THE VENEZUELAN DEBT DISPUTE. In 1902 Great Britain, Germany, and Italy, in an effort to force settlement of the debts owed their citizens by the government of Venezuela, dispatched warships to the South American nation and imposed a blockade of its ports. Roosevelt feared that the debt controversy might be the opportunity for a violation of the Monroe Doctrine by the foreign powers involved. By exercising diplomatic pressure behind the scenes, particularly against Germany, Roosevelt helped convince the European nations to decide to grant Venezuela's plea that the issue of the debts be submitted to arbitration. According to the final decision, rendered in 1904, the claims of the European nations were reduced collectively to one-fifth of what they had been, and Venezuela agreed to apply 30 percent of its customs receipts to pay the determined sums.

THE DRAGO DOCTRINE. The Venezuelan incident caused Argentine Minister of Foreign Affairs Luis M. Drago to formulate a doctrine that a European power must not resort to military intervention to achieve the payment of debts owed its citizens by a Western Hemisphere nation. At the Second International Peace Conference, held in The Hague in 1907, the United States delegation secured the adoption of a resolution supporting a modified version of the original Drago Doctrine: that a nation must not resort to force to collect debts owed its citizens by another nation unless the nation in default refused to submit the matter to arbitration, or having done so, failed to abide by the decision rendered.

THE ROOSEVELT COROLLARY. As had been the case with Venezuela, the Dominican Republic was heavily in debt to citizens of various European nations. In 1904 France, Italy, and Belgium threatened to use force to collect debts. To prevent such an action, Roosevelt in his fourth State of the Union Message to Congress (December, 1904) announced: "Chronic wrongdoing, or an impotence which results in a general loosening of the ties of civilized society, may in America" compel the United States "to the exercise of an international police power." This amplification of the Monroe Doctrine came to be known as the Roosevelt Corollary. A new direction in American foreign policy was begun.

The Roosevelt Corollary was to lead to intervention by its formulator or one of his successors in the Dominican Republic, Haiti, Nicaragua, and Cuba. The first application was in the Dominican Republic only weeks after its promulgation. In 1905 the Roosevelt administration negotiated with the Dominican Republic a treaty by which the United States would manage the Caribbean nation's customhouses and oversee the payment of its foreign debts. When the Senate refused to ratify the treaty, Roosevelt carried out the terms of the agreement by executive order. This manifestation of "international police power" was widely criticized in the United States and aroused grave apprehension throughout Latin America.

Relations with Japan. Japan's easy victories in wars with China and Russia, making it at the beginning of the twentieth century the dominant power in the Far East, convinced many Americans that the Japanese were a threat to the interests of the United States in the area.

ROOSEVELT AND THE RUSSO-JAPANESE WAR. Commercial and territorial rivalry between Russia and Japan in neighboring China and Korea resulted in 1904 in a war between the two powers. President Roosevelt realized that an overwhelming defeat of either belligerent would upset the balance of power in the Far East, and he was sure that such unrivaled strength on the part of one nation would adversely affect American interests in the region. He thus intervened to bring the war to an end by inviting the two nations to engage in discussions at which he would serve as mediator.

Representatives from Russia and Japan conducted their negotiations at the navy yard in Portsmouth, New Hampshire, and in September, 1905, signed a treaty terminating hostilities. Due largely to Roosevelt's opposition, Japan received neither the financial reparations nor the full territorial gains it had pressed for. In fact, the treaty negotiations began to undermine the friendship that had existed between the United States and Japan since the 1850s, when Japan was "opened" to the Western world by American Commodore Matthew C. Perry. In 1906 Roosevelt was awarded the Nobel Prize for Peace for his efforts as mediator.

THE TAFT-KATSURA MEMORANDUM. During the summer of 1905, while the President of the United States was bringing Russia and Japan together at Portsmouth, a secretly drafted document, the Taft-Katsura Memorandum, was signed by the United States and Japan. Under the terms of the memorandum, Japan acknowledged American sovereignty over the Philippines and the United States acknowledged Japanese control of Korea. Further, the two nations pledged to cooperate with each other to maintain peace in the Far East.

THE "GENTLEMEN'S AGREEMENT." Within a year after the Taft-Katsura Memorandum, resentment flared in Japan over discrimination in California against the large number of Japanese laborers who had gone to the state seeking better job opportunities. What rankled in particular was the recent action of the San Francisco School Board in ordering all Oriental students to attend a separate school. Anticipating a rupture in American-Japanese relations, President Roosevelt decided to intervene. He invited the entire school board of San Francisco to a conference in the White House. A formula was found. The school board agreed to rescind the segregation order, and Roosevelt pledged that Japanese immigration would, in some way, be limited. What followed was a series of diplomatic notes during 1907–1908 between the United States and Japan, embodying the "Gentlemen's Agreement." Japan promised to deny passports to Japanese laborers seeking to emigrate to the United States, while the United States agreed not to prohibit Japanese immigration completely. Although Japan observed the arrangement with care, the United States in 1924 unilaterally ended the agreement by a congressional act that totally prohibited Japanese immigration to the United States.

WORLD CRUISE OF THE UNITED STATES NAVY. Roosevelt was eager to prevent Japan from interpreting his role in the San Francisco school matter as indicating fear of Japanese power. Accordingly, he sent a major part of the United States fleet on a fourteen-month world cruise as a demonstration of naval strength.

THE ROOT-TAKAHIRA AGREEMENT. The effect of the American naval cruise upon relations between the United States and Japan was immediately realized. While the ships were still under way, Japanese leaders suggested that the United States and Japan attempt to achieve accord on the varied issues relating to the Far East. The result in 1908 was the Root-Takahira Agreement, by which the two nations agreed (1) to maintain the *status quo*[3] in the Pacific; (2) to respect each other's territorial possessions in the Pacific; (3) to uphold the open-door policy in China; (4) to preserve the political independence and territorial integrity of China.

Relations with Europe. Realizing that any upset in the balance of power in Europe could weaken American security, Roosevelt decided to play a role in the diplomatic affairs of the continent. This course of action meant a departure from the established American policy of noninvolvement in purely European concerns.

THE ALGECIRAS CONFERENCE. In 1905 French efforts to establish a protectorate over the North African nation of Morocco clashed with German commercial activity in the region. Fearing the conflict over Morocco might start the war in Europe that many had been expecting for years, President Roosevelt arranged for an international conference to settle Morocco's future status. In 1906 the United States and eight European nations, including France, Germany, Great Britain, and Russia, met in Algeciras, Spain. The outcome of the conference revealed the powerful influence of the United States; the formula the delegates accepted for the international regulation of trade, banking, and police in Morocco did not differ substantially from the American proposals.

THE SECOND HAGUE CONFERENCE. In 1899 twenty-six nations, including the United States, had participated in the International Peace Conference in The Hague. Known as the First Hague Conference, it had established for the adjudication of international disputes the Permanent Court of Arbitration, which came to be called the Hague Court. The Second International Peace Conference, which was suggested by Roosevelt, took place in The Hague in 1907, with forty-four nations in attendance. The accomplishments of the Second Hague Conference were disappointing. As in the First Hague Conference, the limitation of armaments was placed on the agenda with no settlement being reached in the matter. The American delegation pressed for the adoption of a court of international justice, which would be much more comprehensive in scope than the Hague Court. However, this pro-

---

[3]The existing state of affairs at the time in question.

posal did not succeed. The Second Hague Conference ended with a recommendation for a third conference, but preparations for it were halted when World War I broke out.

"Dollar Diplomacy." Unlike Roosevelt, who had used dynamic and sometimes flagrantly aggressive approaches in conducting foreign affairs, Taft was inclined to employ economic means to reach diplomatic objectives. Both supporters and critics of the Taft administration called this policy "dollar diplomacy."

THE CHINESE CONSORTIUM. In 1909 Taft's secretary of state, Philander C. Knox, persuaded American financiers to join with their British, French, and German counterparts in a consortium[4] to construct a railroad in China. Three years later Taft gave his approval to a more ambitious undertaking—a government loan to the newly proclaimed Republic of China in which American bankers were invited to participate.

THE EFFECTS OF ECONOMIC EXPANSIONISM. The investment of American money abroad, which so many called dollar diplomacy, was described by Taft as merely an effort "directed to the increase of American trade." He sincerely hoped that American dollars would help American diplomats maintain the balance of power in the Far East, thus perpetuating such foreign policy interests of the United States as the open-door principle in China and the preservation of the political independence and territorial integrity of China. During the first decade of the twentieth century the growth of American foreign investments seemed to follow the pattern of European economic imperialism, but the American interest in overseas trade rarely led to the attempt to impose political control over foreign lands.

[4]An international business combination created for the financial assistance of another nation or for the control of a particular industry in another nation.

Chapter 9

Wilsonian Liberalism

In 1913, after sixteen years of Republican rule, the nation had the Democratic Woodrow Wilson in the White House. Wilson had a strong sense of right and wrong, which he applied to the handling of domestic matters and international relations. In his first term he brought the progressive movement to its climax. In domestic affairs he supported a number of reforms relating to the tariff, banking and currency, trusts, labor, and agriculture. In foreign policy, he attempted to diminish American imperialism and promote the development of democracy in the smaller nations.

THE NEW FREEDOM

In his campaign for the presidency Wilson expressed a body of ideas that constituted a program of action he called the New Freedom. In essence, it sought to curb any business that enjoyed a monopoly and to restore an earlier condition of competition. To the American people Wilson conveyed a determination to bring much-needed reforms.

Election of 1912. A deep split in the Republican party had brought into being the new rival Progressive party and thus made certain the victory of the Democratic candidate for president.

DEMOCRATS. The Democratic national convention witnessed a spirited contest between the conservative and liberal forces within the party. Speaker of the House Champ Clark of Missouri was the front-runner, with both conservative and liberal delegates in his following. The extreme conservatives were favorably disposed toward Governor Judson Harmon of Ohio and Representative Oscar W. Underwood of Alabama. The liberals rallied behind Governor Woodrow Wilson of New Jersey, who described himself as a "progressive with the brakes on." It appeared that Clark was going to win the nomination. However, William Jennings Bryan dramatically denounced the "sinister influences" of the financial sector endorsing Clark and on the fourteenth ballot switched from Clark to Wilson, carrying many of his followers with him. Wilson was finally nominated on the forty-sixth ballot. The delegates chose Governor Thomas R. Marshall of Indiana for second place on the ticket. The party platform invited the support of those who were willing to enlist in the warfare against political and economic privilege.

REPUBLICANS. The Republican national convention was a scene of turmoil. After weeks of indecision, former President Theodore Roosevelt agreed to become a candidate for the nomination. Then came an unseemly scramble for delegates between the incumbent Taft and Roosevelt. Wherever the delegates were chosen by state conventions or hand-picked by the bosses, Taft had the advantage, but in states that permitted the voters to express their individual preferences, Roosevelt was clearly the choice. The convention was controlled by the Taft forces and proceeded amidst great confusion and wrangling to grant the occupant of the White House another nomination. Vice-President James S. Sherman was renominated for the position.

PROGRESSIVES. More than a year before the election liberal insurgent Republicans tried to mobilize the progressive sentiment of the country. In January, 1911, several Republican senators formed an organization called the Progressive Republican League, which announced the following political aims: (1) direct election of senators; (2) direct primaries; (3) direct election of delegates to national nominating conventions; (4) state adoption of the initiative, referendum, and recall. Initially the League merely advocated progressive principles, but in October, 1911, it endorsed Senator Robert M. La Follette of Wisconsin for the Republican nomination against President Taft. La Follette, who had won national fame for his successful battle against the power of large corporations in his own state, promptly started a vigorous drive to rouse the voters from their lethargy. Although former President Roosevelt had been supporting the liberal insurgent Republicans ever since the summer of 1910, he refused to join the League or to support La Follette.

Roosevelt charged that the Republican nomination had been "stolen" from him by irregular tactics. With evangelical fervor his followers undertook the task of helping to form a new party called the Progressive party. In August, 1912, the Progressive party held its first convention in Chicago, where two months earlier its hero La Follette had been rejected by the Republicans at their convention. La Follette was the logical leader of liberal insurgent Republicans openly at war with the party leadership. The revolt against Taft no longer appeared hopeless, but many of La Follette's supporters seized on a pretext to switch to Roosevelt at the convention and La

Follette was shunted aside. Roosevelt was nominated for president by acclamation, while Republican Governor Hiram Johnson of California was nominated for vice-president. The schism in the Republican ranks was complete. The Progressive party was nicknamed the "Bull Moose" party, from Roosevelt's frequent use of the term to describe someone full of strength and vigor.

THE CAMPAIGN. During the campaign the positions of all three presidential candidates were very much alike on a host of political, economic, and social reforms that were discussed. Where the three men differed was on the issues of the tariff and of the handling of trusts. In keeping with the traditional Republican position, both Taft and Roosevelt called for a protective tariff, although one with lower rates than the existing Payne-Aldrich Act; representing the traditional position of his party on the tariff, Wilson advocated the passage of a new tariff for revenue purposes only. As for government handling of trusts, Roosevelt presented views known collectively as the New Nationalism, which looked to even stricter federal regulation of trusts than had previously been exercised—but not an elimination of them. Although Taft used a different phraseology, he supported a policy of stricter trust regulation that was virtually indistinguishable from the one advocated by Roosevelt. Wilson, however, sought the elimination of business monopoly as an inherent evil.

WILSON'S VICTORY. Wilson captured forty states with a total of 435 electoral votes; Taft secured only Vermont and Utah with their 8 electoral votes; Roosevelt carried six states with 88 electoral votes. The House of Representatives and the Senate went Democratic by wide margins. The overwhelming nature of the Democratic victory was plainly due to the split of the Republican party.

The Wilson Administration.

Wilson viewed the presidency as a means of securing the legislation needed to make government responsive to the will of the people.

THE PRESIDENT. Wilson was a model of independence, firmness, and energy. He wrote and spoke with a rare eloquence. During his first term he used executive power creatively, notably in dealing with Congress.

INAUGURAL ADDRESS. After taking the oath of office, Wilson delivered a stirring inaugural address, summoning "all honest men, all patriotic, all forward-looking men" to join him in service to the nation. In his presentation he itemized "things that ought to be altered," including the tariff, banking and currency, and industry.

THE CABINET. Wilson felt compelled to select William Jennings Bryan to head the cabinet as secretary of state, in recognition of Bryan's considerable influence within the Democratic fold and also his significant support at the party's 1912 convention. Testimony to the power of the southern wing of the Democratic party was the fact that more than half of those chosen for the remaining cabinet posts had been born and reared in the South. The following cabinet members were to become well-known for particular competence: Georgia-born New York City businessman William G. McAdoo as secretary of the treasury; North Carolina newspaper editor Josephus Daniels as secretary of the navy; and former Texas representative Albert S. Burleson as postmaster general.

UNOFFICIAL ADVISER. Edward M. House, known as "Colonel" House, who had been active in the politics of his state of Texas, became the President's most trusted adviser. Wilson admired him for his combination of idealism and common sense and turned to him often for counsel, particularly in foreign affairs.

Revision of the Tariff.
The Democratic party's traditional opposition to the principle of the protective tariff was firmly supported by the new administration, alerting the nation to expect an early and strong attempt at tariff reduction.

WILSON'S ROLE. After Congress decided to deal with the tariff issue, Wilson presented himself a number of times at the Capitol to consult with leaders of his party on the strategy that would most effectively achieve a lowering of tariff duties. When it seemed that lobbyists representing special interest groups would be able to block some of the proposed reductions in rates, he took a variety of effective approaches, including a direct appeal to the American people for their moral support.

THE UNDERWOOD TARIFF. Passed in 1913, the Underwood Tariff provided for the first substantial lowering of duties in over half a century. Its distinctive features were (1) reduction of rates on close to 1,000 commodities considered no longer in need of protection against foreign competition; (2) increase of rates on almost 100 articles deemed luxury in nature; (3) expansion of the free items list to include such important products to American consumers as iron, steel, and wool; (4) imposition of a graduated income tax as permitted by the recently ratified Sixteenth Amendment to the Constitution (to compensate for anticipated loss of revenue from the new schedule of duties). Before the effect of the measure upon either foreign trade or governmental finances could be determined, the beginning of World War I brought about a period of abnormal economic activity.

Reorganization of Banking and Currency.
Wilson argued forcefully for the creation of a banking system capable of supplying currency that would expand and contract in amount according to the needs of business.

BACKGROUND TO ACTION. By the end of the nineteenth century the United States had experienced half a dozen financial panics. In 1907 another occurred. The brief, but sharp, Panic of 1907 demonstrated the inelasticity of the monetary system and the inflexibility of the credit structure in the United States. In 1912 the House Committee on Banking and Currency, through a subcommittee chaired by the Democratic Arsène Pujo of Louisiana, began investigating the extent of the concentration of financial power in a small group of banking firms. The report of the Pujo Committee, published early in 1913, declared that there existed a "money trust," consisting of a few Wall Street banking houses whose control of money and credit had serious ramifications throughout the manufacturing, trade, and transportation establishments of the nation. Both the effects of the Panic of 1907 and the findings of the Pujo Committee were used by Wilson as evidence in the case he made for banking and currency reform.

THE FEDERAL RESERVE ACT. From his White House office Wilson played an effective role both in the framing of the Federal Reserve Act and in the parliamentary maneuvering that secured its passage in 1913. In short, the act created a flexible credit structure so that funds could be transferred promptly from one section of the nation to another as the need arose, and instituted an elastic currency system so that the supply of money could be expanded and contracted according to the requirements of business. The act established the Federal Reserve System, which operated as follows: (1) the nation was divided into twelve districts, based upon economic and geographic considerations, with a Federal Reserve Bank in each; (2) a Federal Reserve Bank dealt not directly with the public but with the banks in its district that joined the system as member banks, serving those banks primarily by depositing their cash reserves and extending them loans; (3) the Federal Reserve Board, composed of a bipartisan group of financial experts, supervised the system; (4) the Federal Reserve Board could regulate the supply of credit available in every section of the nation by raising or lowering the interest rate each Federal Reserve Bank would charge member banks seeking loans from it, which action would in turn raise or lower the interest rate member banks charged private individuals for loans, thereby giving flexibility to the national credit structure; (5) each Federal Reserve Bank could issue into the money supply in circulation Federal Reserve notes, the amount of which could be expanded or contracted depending on the needs of business, thus providing an elastic currency system.

Regulation of Industry. Having expounded the proposition that "private monopoly is indefensible and intolerable," Wilson urged legislation to supersede the Sherman Antitrust Act, which, in large part due to the imprecision of its language, had never been adequately enforced. Somewhat reluctantly, Congress presented two measures to the President for his signature.

THE FEDERAL TRADE COMMISSION ACT. This act, passed in 1914, established a bipartisan commission of five members to prevent interstate businesses from using unfair methods of competition. Under the provisions of the measure, the Federal Trade Commission was authorized to (1) require annual and special reports from corporations; (2) conduct investigations of corporations reported to be engaged in unfair practices in interstate commerce; (3) issue orders to corporations to "cease and desist" from using those practices considered in violation of the law. Some unfair trade practices the commissioners were particularly alert to were deceptive advertising, mislabeling of containers, and adulteration of products.

THE CLAYTON ANTITRUST ACT. Designed to regulate the nation's monopolies, the Clayton Antitrust Act, passed in 1914, declared illegal the following business practices: (1) price discriminations in interstate trade to the extent that they were destructive of competition; (2) excessive acquisition of stock of one corporation by another corporation; (3) interlocking directorates in large-scale business enterprises engaged in interstate commerce. The act stipulated that exempt from its terms were agricultural associations and labor unions. The section on labor prohibited the use of injunctions in labor disputes, except in certain cases, and provided that strikes, peaceful picketing, and boycotts were not to be considered practices in restraint of trade and thus were not violations of federal law.

Aid to Labor. The leaders of labor exercised an influence on the Wilson administration that was reflected not only in the labor provisions of the Clayton Antitrust Act but also in several separate pieces of legislation.

THE LA FOLLETTE SEAMEN'S ACT. In addition to requiring high standards of safety and sanitation for the crews of American ships, this act, passed in 1915, also regulated the hours, food, and payment of wages of seamen.

THE KEATING-OWEN ACT. This act, passed in 1916, banned from interstate trade articles produced in factories employing children under fourteen years of age. In 1918, however, in *Hammer* v. *Dagenhart* the Supreme Court declared the act unconstitutional on the ground that it had the effect of regulating conditions of labor within the state and thus infringed upon powers reserved to the states by the Constitution.

THE ADAMSON ACT. This law, passed in 1916, established the eight-hour workday and the granting of time-and-a-half pay for overtime work for employees of railroads engaged in interstate commerce.

Aid to Agriculture. The Wilson administration lent its support to proposed legislation that would benefit farmers.

THE SMITH-LEVER ACT. This law, passed in 1914, provided for home instruction in farming methods under the joint supervision of the Department of Agriculture and the various state agricultural colleges.

THE FEDERAL FARM LOAN ACT. This measure, passed in 1916, established a Farm Loan Bank in each of twelve districts of the nation. Cooperative farm loan associations holding membership in a Farm Loan Bank were authorized to make available to farmers long-term loans for mortgages at a lower rate of interest than could be obtained at the commercial banks.

THE NEW DIPLOMACY

Wilson assumed the presidency determined that the basis of his foreign policy would be antiimperialism. He repudiated the pursuit by Presidents Theodore Roosevelt and William H. Taft of military intervention in the affairs of weak nations and the use of diplomatic relations to foster economic enterprise abroad. However, despite his declared moral and idealistic approach to diplomacy, realities both at home and abroad were such that Wilson eventually began to direct a foreign policy that was little different from that of his two immediate Republican predecessors.

Controversy over the Panama Canal. The moral tone Wilson attempted to inject into American diplomacy was evidenced in his solution to the spirited dispute between the United States and Great Britain concerning the use of the Isthmian waterway. The Panama Canal Tolls Act, passed in 1912, during the Taft administration, imposed a schedule of tolls upon vessels using the soon-to-be-completed canal, but provided that ships of the United States engaged in the coastwise trade were to be accorded free passage through the waterway. Great Britain protested, claiming that the Hay-Pauncefote Treaty stipulated that use of the canal would be made available to all nations on equal terms. Americans who defended the act asserted that the phrase "all nations" in the treaty should exclude the United States as the proprietor of the canal, that "all nations" signified, in effect, all *other* nations. Wilson strongly urged that Congress repeal the act on the ground that the British interpretation of the Hay-Pauncefote Treaty was correct. The legislators complied in June, 1914, and the Panama Canal was soon opened. The administration's success in settling the tolls controversy had the practical effect of winning the support of Great Britain for Wilson in his dealings with the then politically distressed Mexico.

Relations with Mexico. Since the Thomas Jefferson administration the United States had given *de facto* recognition[1] to any foreign government that came into being, whatever the circumstances that led it to power. Determined to replace this policy with one that used moral criteria for recognizing foreign governments, Wilson was given an opportunity to do so in dealing with revolution-torn Mexico.

THE REVOLUTION AGAINST DIAZ. In 1910 the long rule of Mexico's despotic President Porfirio Diaz was brought to a close by a revolution led by Francisco I. Madero. The liberal government established under Madero attempted to implement a program of reforms, a notable component of which was the breaking up of large estates and the parceling out of sections to the landless peasants. In 1913 Madero was assassinated in a counterrevolution

---

[1]Acceptance of a government as the controlling power in reality, although not yet permanently established.

on behalf of the landholders, led by General Victoriano Huerta, who set up
a reactionary regime with himself as provisional president.

THE QUARREL WITH HUERTA. Although more than twenty nations
promptly gave *de facto* recognition to the Huerta government, the Wilson
administration refused to do so, charging that it did not represent the will of
the people and that it was responsible for the murder of Madero. A revolution against Huerta started, led by Madero's former ally, Venustiano Carranza. Wilson announced he would pursue a policy of "watchful waiting."
Months later he decided to abandon that policy. He permitted American
arms to be shipped to the Carranza faction and set up a blockade of Veracruz to prevent European munitions from reaching Huerta. The Huerta
regime retaliated with acts of reprisal on United States citizens in Mexico,
culminating in the arrest of a group of American sailors at Tampico in April,
1914. Informed that a ship was approaching Veracruz with war matériel for
Huerta, American troops occupied the city. War between the United States
and Mexico seemed imminent.

MEDIATION BY THE ABC POWERS. To avert war, Argentina, Brazil, and
Chile (the "ABC Powers") volunteered to mediate the dispute, and their offer was accepted. The mediators proposed that Huerta relinquish his office
and a government be established that would implement political and
economic reforms. Although Huerta formally rejected the proposal, he
resigned within a month. In 1915 the United States and a number of Latin
American nations, including the ABC Powers, gave *de facto* recognition to a
government formed in Mexico with Carranza as president.

THE PURSUIT OF VILLA. Carranza was unable to restrain his former
associate Francisco ("Pancho") Villa, whose band began to attack resident
foreigners and finally (March, 1916) crossed the border and raided
Columbus, New Mexico. With Carranza's reluctant consent, Wilson sent
General John J. Pershing with 15,000 troops into Mexico to apprehend
Villa. This expeditionary force failed to capture Villa, and it was withdrawn
in January, 1917, as the likelihood of American entry into World War I
increased.

Relations in the Caribbean. Wilson's attitude toward the nations of
the Caribbean was less idealistic than it was toward Mexico because the
opening of the Panama Canal, with the attendant necessity of establishing
an appropriate defense of the interoceanic waterway, dictated an American
presence in the Caribbean. But the President was motivated more by a
desire to promote the political and economic stability of the nations close to
the canal than to carry out a program of economic imperialism.

THE DOMINICAN REPUBLIC. In 1907 the United States and the
Dominican Republic signed a treaty formalizing existing American control
of Dominican finances. In 1916 a revolution in the Dominican Republic
threatened the treaty arrangements and caused Wilson to engage in

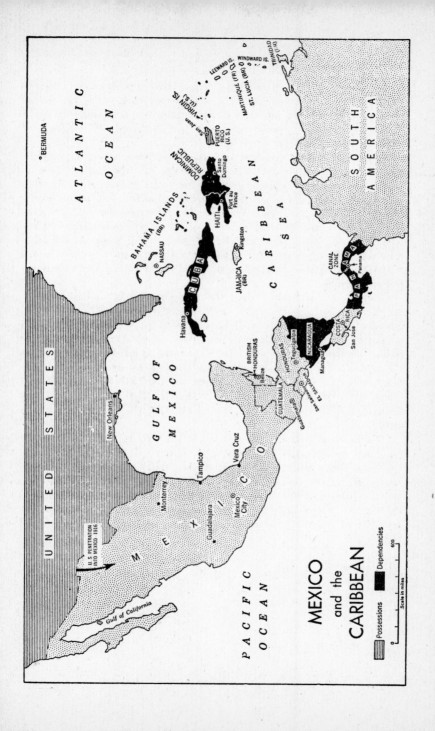

MEXICO
and the
CARIBBEAN

military intervention to maintain the peace. For a number of years a provisional government, supported by American troops, gave the Dominican people orderly rule, despite their protests against the occupation. In 1924 a new treaty on Dominican finances, superseding that of 1907, was signed and American military forces left the nation.

HAITI. After Haiti's creditors in Europe had pronounced the republic bankrupt and threatened to take drastic measures, the United States in 1915 imposed a military occupation and forced the Haitian government to sign a treaty that established American control of finances, public works, sanitation facilities, and the police force. The resistance of many Haitians to the occupation caused frequent disorders, but American officials went forward with instituting financial reforms, constructing buildings and highways for public use, and improving sanitation. Not until 1934 were the last of the American civilian administrators and military personnel withdrawn from the republic.

NICARAGUA. In 1912, toward the close of the Taft administration, American marines were landed in Nicaragua to put an end to political disorder. In the second year of the occupation the Wilson administration negotiated the Bryan-Chamorro Treaty with the Central American republic. Ratified by the Senate in 1916, the treaty granted the United States the exclusive right to construct a canal through Nicaragua, a renewable ninety-nine-year lease to the Great Corn and the Little Corn Islands, and permission to establish a naval base on the Gulf of Fonseca. The marines left in 1925 but returned in 1926 to quell civil disturbances and then stayed until 1933.

PURCHASE OF THE VIRGIN ISLANDS. In 1917 the Wilson administration purchased for $25 million the Danish West Indies, which the United States had been endeavoring to acquire from Denmark for more than a decade. The primary motive behind the acquisition was the desire to use the islands as a naval defense station for the Panama Canal. The United States renamed the territory the Virgin Islands and instituted a program of limited self-government. In 1927 the inhabitants were made citizens of the United States.

Chapter 10

World War I

In the summer of 1914 World War I broke out in Europe between the Allies, headed by Great Britain, France, and Russia, and the Central Powers, led by Germany and Austria-Hungary. President Wilson issued a proclamation of neutrality, warning his people not to be thrown off balance by a "war with which we have nothing to do." However, public sympathy with the Allies and opposition to the activity of the Central Powers eventually brought the United States into the war on the side of the Allies. American military and economic powers were swiftly mobilized to support the war effort and contributed greatly to the defeat of the Central Powers. In the ensuing treaty negotiations, Wilson's desire for a "peace without victory" was thwarted by the nationalistic demands of the leading Allies and by the failure of the United States Senate to agree on terms for participation in the League of Nations, the new organization created to maintain world security.

A NEUTRAL IN DIFFICULTY

Inspired by the hope that the United States might eventually be able to mediate in the European conflict, Wilson tried to maintain American neutrality—but in vain. An affinity existed between the United States and the principal Allies, based on ethnic and cultural, and to a degree, diplomatic factors. Bolstering the relationship were the sophisticated Allied propaganda and the ever-tightening financial and commercial links between the American people and the Allied governments. On the other hand, an intense aversion to Germany, the leading force of the Central Powers, was rampant in the United States. To many Americans the nation was the epitome of militarism and arrogance. But it was the activity of the Central Powers—chiefly Germany's pursuit of its submarine policy—that prompted the United States to relinquish its neutrality in favor of a declaration of war.

British Maritime Policy. The first difficulties of the United States as a neutral were with Great Britain, whose powerful navy attempted to prevent foreign supplies from reaching the Central Powers.

THE AMERICAN PROTEST. The State Department insisted on the following principles: (1) that a long-range blockade of Germany by Great Britain, the enforcement of which required the British fleet to engage in a wide range of restrictive activity, was not recognized in international law; (2) that the British extension of the internationally accepted list of contraband[1] included commodities, such as foodstuffs, that had been considered noncontraband[2] in the 1909 Declaration of London, which had codified the rights of belligerents and neutrals during war; (3) that the British navy intercepted American vessels and seized goods on board bound for neutral nations such as Sweden, Denmark, and the Netherlands.

THE BRITISH REPLY. Great Britain argued (1) that its definition of contraband should not be restricted by the Declaration of London, since the document had never been ratified by the leading naval powers, including Great Britain; (2) that the doctrine of continuous voyage,[3] which had been upheld in American courts during the Civil War, was being applied to stop shipments from the United States to neutral nations only when it was clear that the ultimate destination was Germany; (3) that the British government would compensate citizens of the United States for their noncontraband goods seized during a search.

German Maritime Policy. The dispute of the United States with Great Britain over maritime policy was quickly overshadowed by the aggressiveness of Germany's submarine policy, which threatened not only the property but also the lives of American citizens.

SUBMARINE ACTIVITY. In February, 1915, Germany declared that the waters surrounding Great Britain and Ireland constituted a war zone in which German submarines would destroy all enemy vessels. To avoid "unfortunate mistakes" the German government warned neutral ships to remain outside the zone and advised citizens of neutral nations to refrain from traveling on the Allies' ships. The United States protested vigorously against the use of submarines without observing the rule of visit and search.[4] Germany complained that the United States was allowing Great

---

[1] Goods directly useful in maintaining a nation's military force.

[2] Goods useful to the civilian economy of a belligerent nation but not essential to its military activity.

[3] The right of a belligerent vessel to stop a neutral ship bound for another neutral nation and seize contraband on board if the *ultimate* destination of the goods were to opposing belligerent territory.

[4] According to international law, a belligerent ship was allowed to stop a neutral ship so that personnel of the former could visit and search for contraband, and if none was found, the neutral ship was permitted to continue on its way.

Britain to violate its rights as a neutral with impunity, urged the United States to compel Great Britain to abide by the Declaration of London (which presented the Central Powers with a firm legal basis for extensive trade with neutral nations), and suggested that unrestricted submarine warfare would be abandoned if the United States would cease furnishing the Allies with munitions and other supplies.

THE SINKING OF THE *LUSITANIA*. The potential threat of submarines became actual in the sinking in May, 1915, of the British liner *Lusitania* off the Irish coast, with the loss of 1,198 persons, of whom 128 were American citizens. The ship was carrying contraband but was unarmed. Avoiding the clamor for war by many Americans, President Wilson strove by diplomatic pressure to persuade Germany to abandon unrestricted submarine activity. During May–July, 1915, Wilson sent three notes to the German government regarding the *Lusitania* sinking, insisting on the maintenance of neutral rights and demanding that Germany stop unrestricted submarine warfare. Fearing that the *Lusitania* notes might precipitate American entry into the war. Secretary of State Bryan resigned in protest. He was replaced by the well-known international lawyer Robert Lansing, who supported Wilson's policy. In September, 1915, Count Johann von Bernstorff, the German ambassador to the United States, informed the State Department that liners would not be sunk by his nation's submarines without protection of the lives of noncombatants.

THE *SUSSEX* AFFAIR. Despite the assurances from von Bernstorff, miscellaneous reports of submarine tactics caused a sense of distrust in the United States. In March, 1916, the French passenger steamer *Sussex* was torpedoed in the English Channel, injuring some on board, including two Americans. Wilson sent an ultimatum to Germany that unless it ceased engaging in its present methods of submarine warfare, the United States would sever diplomatic relations. The official reply to the United States ("the *Sussex* Pledge") gave assurances that Germany would not sink merchant vessels "without warning and without saving human lives." For the next nine months there was little cause for complaint regarding submarine activities.

The Preparedness Campaign. The struggle to defend American neutral rights was paralleled by a campaign to prepare the nation effectively for the possibility of war. Such persons as former President Theodore Roosevelt, Republican Senator Henry Cabot Lodge of Massachusetts, former secretary of war Henry L. Stimson, and General Leonard Wood campaigned vigorously for a comprehensive program of military preparedness. Their pleas were reinforced in molding public opinion by the activities of organizations such as the National Security League, the American Defense Society, and the American Rights Committee.

To counteract the pressure for increased armaments and military forces, peace organizations such as the American Union Against Militarism, the American League to Limit Armaments, the American Neutrality League, and the Women's Peace Party labored valiantly. Initially, President Wilson was sympathetic with the aspirations of the antimilitarist groups. As German submarine warfare developed, making the likelihood of war for the United States more apparent, the preparedness movement gained force. In the spring of 1916 Wilson abandoned his earlier position and appealed to the nation to support an increase in the land and sea forces.

Defense Legislation. The drive for preparedness brought tangible results in 1916 in the form of congressional legislation. The National Defense Act provided for the expansion of the regular army to 223,000 men and the National Guard to 450,000. The Army Appropriation Act established the Council of National Defense to formulate plans for the efficient use of the nation's resources in the event of war. The Shipping Act created the Shipping Board to build or buy vessels which in wartime might be operated by the government.

Election of 1916. In a relatively spiritless contest the voters endorsed the policy of neutrality and progressive domestic legislation that Wilson had sponsored. In winning votes, the President proved stronger than his party in almost every congressional district.

DEMOCRATS. The delegates to the Democratic national convention renominated Wilson by acclamation. Their choice for vice-president was the incumbent Thomas A. Marshall.

REPUBLICANS. In an attempt to reunite their party after the recent Taft-Roosevelt imbroglio, the Republicans gave the presidential nomination to Charles Evans Hughes, an associate justice of the Supreme Court and formerly a liberal governor of New York; Hughes had taken no part in the party disputes of 1912. Roosevelt's Vice-President, Charles W. Fairbanks, was chosen for second place on the ticket. When the national convention of the Progressive party nominated Roosevelt for president, as it had four years earlier, he declined, recommended that the party disband, and urged his followers to vote for Hughes—all in his determination to defeat Wilson.

THE CAMPAIGN. It soon became apparent that in his effort to please every faction of his party, Hughes was unwilling to take a firm stand on the direction of American foreign policy during this critical period. (He was portrayed by political cartoonists as the "Sphinx.") The most forceful argument of the Democrats was their repeated assertion that Wilson, through his efforts on behalf of neutrality and preparedness, had prevented the nation from becoming part of Europe's quarrel. Their slogan was: "He kept us out of war." The Democrats insisted that a vote for Hughes would mean American intervention in the war raging across the Atlantic.

WILSON'S VICTORY. Wilson carried the Solid South and the trans-Mississippi West, except South Dakota and Oregon, for a total of thirty states, while Hughes won all but two of the northeastern states. It was the region from which William Jennings Bryan had drawn his strength in three presidential elections that gave Wilson a margin of 277 to 254 in the electoral college.

Efforts at Mediation. Still hoping for a negotiated peace settlement in Europe rather than one imposed by the victors upon the vanquished, Wilson increased his efforts to become the mediator.

THE HOUSE MISSION. During January–February, 1916, Colonel House was in Europe on behalf of President Wilson to approach British, French, and German leaders regarding a negotiated peace. At that time, however, both the Allies and the Central Powers were confident that they could achieve military victory and were not receptive to the American efforts.

"PEACE WITHOUT VICTORY." In December, 1916, Wilson strongly urged both belligerent groups to state their war aims. The Allies presented their objectives in terms which meant, in essence, the complete defeat of the Central Powers. Germany, speaking for the Central Powers, merely indicated a willingness to discuss conditions for peace at some future time. Soon thereafter, in January, 1917, Wilson, in an address before the Senate, made an eloquent appeal to worldwide opinion for "peace without victory." The proposal found no favor with the belligerents.

UNITED STATES ENTRY INTO WAR

German leaders had come to the conclusion by 1917 that their nation was in a position to win the war before any military aid from the United States could reach the Allies. Based upon that assumption, the German government took a certain course of action, one effect of which was to prompt the United States to declare war.

Resumption of Submarine Activity. With a blatant disregard for its *Sussex* Pledge, Germany announced on January 31, 1917, that it would immediately resume unrestricted submarine warfare. In February the United States replied to the submarine threat by severing diplomatic relations with Germany and arming American merchant ships. Wilson, however, refused to give up his hopes for continued neutrality until he was certain that the Germans would carry out their intention. In March German submarines torpedoed five American merchant ships, killing, in all, thirty-six crewmen.

The Zimmermann Note. A few weeks after the German announcement of resumed submarine warfare, British intelligence agents intercepted, and made available to Wilson, a note written by German Secretary for Foreign Affairs Arthur Zimmermann to his government's minister in Mexico. Zimmermann suggested that in the event of war between the United States and Germany, a Mexican-German alliance might be arranged that would enable Mexico to recover Arizona, New Mexico, and Texas—

territory it had lost as a result of the 1840s war with the United States. Further, Mexico was to urge Japan to disassociate itself from the Allies and to side with the Central Powers. Wilson had the note released to the newspapers. The nation was shocked.

Wilson's War Message. The President called for a special session of Congress, which convened on April 2, 1917. In his address to the legislators, after characterizing the German submarine activity as "warfare against mankind," he asked for a declaration of war against Germany to make the world "safe for democracy." On April 4 the Senate responded by passing a resolution that a state of war existed between the United States and Germany; two days later the House of Representatives concurred.

"OVER THERE"

When the United States declared war, the size of its armed forces was extremely small. In answer to the requests from the civil and military leaders of the Allies for extensive troop reinforcements, the American government expended tremendous energy, and after some months the first contingent of soldiers sailed, in the phrase of the most popular American wartime song, "over there."

Military Mobilization. The difficult task of creating a large and effective fighting force was accomplished with notable success. There were approximately 200,000 men in the army when the United States entered the war. Embodying the principle of universal conscription, the Selective Service Act of 1917 required all men between the ages of twenty-one and thirty to register with locally established draft boards. Subsequent legislation lowered the minimum age to eighteen and raised the maximum to forty-five. More than 24.2 million men were registered for the draft, of whom some 2.8 million were inducted into the army. As for enlistments, about 2 million men voluntarily entered the regular army, National Guard, navy, and marine corps. For the first time in the history of the nation women were permitted to become members of the armed forces in fields other than nursing.

THE ARMY. Army draftees as well as regular army and National Guard enlistees were trained at thirty-two camps that were speedily constructed throughout the nation, mostly in the South where the climate was favorable for military maneuvers. General John J. Pershing, who had recently gained fame leading a punitive expedition into Mexico, was placed in command of the troops sent to Europe—called the American Expeditionary Force (AEF). By the end of the war more than 2 million men had gone overseas, of whom some 1.4 million had engaged in active fighting.

THE NAVY. By the end of the war the navy consisted of more than

500,000 men and approximately 2,000 ships. Admiral William S. Sims was in charge of all naval forces abroad. Two important achievements of the navy were aiding the British fleet in enforcing its blockade of Germany and attacking German submarines on the high seas. Probably the greatest service the American navy rendered was its participation in the convoy[5] system. Navy craft accompanied scores of convoys of both troop and freight ships across the Atlantic Ocean to protect them from German submarine attacks. In this way more than 2 million men and more than 5 million tons of supplies reached Europe.

THE "AIR FORCE." The United States did not possess an air force as a separate military unit. By the end of the war approximately 1,000 airplanes had been produced, but only about 200 actually reached Europe, so that American aviators were forced to rely heavily on British and French aircraft. Invented little more than a decade earlier, the airplane (in World War I it was canvas-covered, relatively slow-moving, and capable of holding only one or two fliers) was used mostly for observation of enemy movements and for light bombing raids. Squadrons of fighter pilots from each of the leading nations contended for supremacy of the air. The United States had more than twenty "aces" (pilots who brought down five or more enemy aircraft), including Captain Edward V. ("Eddie") Rickenbacker, who got the record among the American fliers by shooting down at least twenty-five German airplanes.

Land Campaigns. When in the spring of 1918 the Germans launched massive offensives on the western front, American troops engaged in a series of campaigns to push the German army back.

CHÂTEAU-THIERRY. In May, 1918, the Germans reached Château-Thierry, forty miles from Paris. American forces, aided by French colonial troops, stopped the Germans at this point.

THE SECOND BATTLE OF THE MARNE. The turning point of the war occurred in July–August, 1918, with the Second Battle of the Marne, in which the last great German offensive was repulsed decisively by the Allied armies. Approximately 85,000 American troops participated prominently in this fighting, which took place in the valley of the Marne River.

THE ST. MIHIEL SALIENT. Since the first year of the war the Germans had held the town of St. Mihiel and its surrounding region, called the St. Mihiel salient because the Germans controlled a deep projection into the Allied side of the trench system. In September, 1918, about 500,000 American troops, in their first basically independent action, engaged in four days of bloody fighting that flattened the bulge.

THE MEUSE-ARGONNE OFFENSIVE AND THE ARMISTICE. In September, 1918, American forces totaling about 1.2 million began a major offensive in

[5]A group of vessels sailing under the protection of an armed escort.

the Argonne Forest along the Meuse River, breaking the German lines. The Meuse-Argonne offensive was an important component of an overall advance launched by Marshal Ferdinand Foch of France, supreme commander of the Allied forces. It started the Germans on their last retreat. As it became evident that the Allies were headed for German territory, resistance collapsed and representatives of a newly established republican government in Germany signed an armistice on November 11, 1918, at the headquarters of Foch at Compiègne.

American War Costs. World War I was up to that time the nation's second most costly war in lives (the number of deaths in the Civil War was exceedingly high) and its most costly in money. About 54,000 Americans were killed in battle and about 63,000 died of disease. Some 200,000 men were wounded in combat. The United States spent an estimated $24.5 billion, approximately three times the amount disbursed on all of its previous wars combined.

THE HOME FRONT

During the war virtually all Americans cooperated in numerous ways to insure victory. Congress rose above the limitations of partisanship, conferring upon the President the powers that he requested. Representatives of both business and organized labor served on the various governmental units that were created in order to transform the economic activity of the nation into one great war machine. The Wilson administration successfully accomplished the difficult task of mobilizing matériel, labor, transportation, and money and dealt in the sensitive area of molding public opinion in support of the armed conflict.

Mobilizing National Resources. To mobilize effectively the resources of the nation in the prosecution of the war, Wilson fashioned the Council of National Defense. This body oversaw the function of several units, each of which managed a particular aspect of wartime effort.

THE WAR INDUSTRIES BOARD. With New York City financier Bernard M. Baruch as chairman, the War Industries Board coordinated the activities of all of the nation's industries engaged in the war effort. The agency had as its primary objectives the increase of production and the elimination of waste. Its functions included the conversion of many existing plants from peacetime to wartime operations, the purchasing of equipment, and the allocating of raw materials.

THE WAR LABOR BOARD. This body was established to arbitrate management-labor disputes in order to prevent work stoppages, which would impede war production. Since the War Labor Board was created not by a congressional act but by presidential proclamation, its decisions were not enforceable by law. Nevertheless, the cooperation of both employers and employees was generally easy to get because of the pervasive desire on the part of both groups to win the war.

THE FOOD ADMINISTRATION. Headed by Herbert C. Hoover, who had recently organized a successful relief program for war-ravaged Belgians, the Food Administration controlled production and distribution of, reduced waste of, and fixed prices of food, and promoted observance of wheatless and meatless days.

THE FUEL ADMINISTRATION. This agency was authorized to stimulate the production, regulate the distribution, and restrict the prices of various coal and petroleum products. The Fuel Administration encouraged civilians to practice voluntary conservation.

THE RAILROAD ADMINISTRATION. By proclamation Wilson placed the railroads under government control. The Railroad Administration, with Secretary of the Treasury William G. McAdoo as director general, operated the lines as a unified system. Coordination of rail transportation during the wartime period resulted in marked savings of time and energy.

THE EMERGENCY FLEET CORPORATION. Created by the Shipping Board, which had been established in 1916 during the preparedness campaign, the Emergency Fleet Corporation had as its goal the increase of merchant vessel tonnage for the war effort. Soon the United States was building two ships for each Allied vessel sunk by German submarines.

Financing the War. To raise the large amounts of money needed to conduct the war, the government used the traditional methods of taxation and borrowing. Personal income tax rates were revised upward; an excess-profits tax was imposed on corporations; sales taxes were levied on numerous luxury items. Through expanded taxation the government raised more than $11 billion. The bulk of the war expenses, however, was met by borrowing from the public through the sale of government bonds. There were four Liberty Loan drives and a final Victory Loan drive, which brought a total of approximately $20.5 billion into the government coffers.

Mobilizing Public Opinion. The government manifested considerable concern about solidifying public opinion in support of the war and suppressing criticism against the war.

THE COMMITTEE ON PUBLIC INFORMATION. Directed by George Creel, a Denver journalist, the Committee on Public Information presented the United States government position on the various aspects of the armed conflict to the people at home and abroad through news releases to the press, pamphlets, posters, films, and speakers.

MEASURES AGAINST DISSENT. Under the terms of the Espionage Act of 1917 and the Sedition Act of 1918 the government was authorized to suppress any form of dissent from its policy that it deemed a hindrance to winning the war. The Espionage Act imposed heavy penalties for spying, sabotage, obstructing military conscription, or encouraging insubordination in the armed forces. The measure also provided for the exclusion from the mails of materials considered by government authorities to be "treasonable." The Sedition Act imposed heavy penalties for speaking or writing about the American form of government or the American armed services in what the authorities considered a "disloyal" manner or for advocating the curtailment of war production.

Approximately 1,500 pacifists and antiwar socialists were imprisoned under these laws, which were criticized by civil libertarians as violations of the First Amendment to the Constitution, which prohibits Congress from interfering with freedom of speech, press, and assembly. However, the Supreme Court upheld the laws on the ground that the government had authority to prevent a "clear and present danger" to the nation and that free speech, press, and assembly had always been subject to some restraint, especially in time of war. The Court, however, reversed some convictions on the ground that the defendants' acts had not been proved a "clear and present danger." The Department of Justice acted aggressively in ferreting out persons considered obstructionist, while the postal authorities exercised rigorous censorship over material sent through the mails.

THE LOST PEACE

During the war each Allied government prepared its own list of financial and territorial demands to be imposed upon the Central Powers after the anticipated victory was achieved. (The United States was never officially a member of the Allies, insisting that it be identified as the "Associated Power" of the body of belligerents formally known as the "Allied and Associated Powers.") A spirit of seeking a nonpunitive settlement, personified by President Wilson, pervaded the United States. The misfortune of the peace negotiations that took place in Paris was that the collective position of the Allied leaders and the position of the American President were never wholly reconciled. Subsequently, the Senate of the United States refused to ratify the settlement that had been reached, the punitive Treaty of Versailles—and in so doing failed to adopt the document's section containing the idealistic Covenant of the League of Nations. Thus the United States withheld its support from the world organization that had been conceived as the means of ensuring that the peace would not be lost.

The Background to a Peace Settlement. After the entry of the United States into the war President Wilson became by general consent the spokesman for the cause of the Allies. While his pleas for a war to make the world "safe for democracy" and for a "peace founded upon honor and justice" stirred people everywhere, he did not succeed in eradicating the spirit of selfish nationalism.

NATIONALISTIC AMBITIONS. Many Allied leaders who had been pleased during the fighting with the idealistic case that Wilson presented against the Central Powers found it difficult when the time came for a peace settlement to reconcile their nationalistic objectives with his altruistic pronouncements. Prime Minister David Lloyd George of Great Britain asserted that Kaiser Wilhelm II of Germany should be hanged and that the Germans should be compelled to pay the Allies for all damages sustained as a result of military aggression. Premier Georges Clemenceau of France demanded for his nation not only financial reparations but also territorial concessions. French security could be accomplished, he insisted, only by keeping Germany stripped of military strength so that it could never again wage war. During the war several Allied nations entered into secret treaties under which they would divide among themselves territory taken from the Central Powers. These agreements contained specific pledges of the precise territorial gains to be realized by Great Britain, France, and Russia and by such other nations as Italy, Japan, and Rumania as an inducement to entering the war on their side.

THE FOURTEEN POINTS. In an address to Congress on January 8, 1918, Wilson presented as the "only possible program" for maintaining peace following the war a set of fourteen proposals, which was immediately dubbed the Fourteen Points. The first five points, covering a broad range of relations that nations have with one another, were in essence as follows: (1) abolition of secret diplomacy; (2) freedom of the seas in peace and in war; (3) removal of international economic barriers and establishment of equality of trade; (4) reduction of armaments; (5) impartial adjustments of colonial claims. The next eight points pertained to specific cases of political or territorial readjustments concerning Russia, Belgium, Alsace-Lorraine, Italy, Austria-Hungary, the Balkan states, the Turkish Empire, and Poland. The fourteenth point was the crowning proposal: "a general association of nations" must be formed to afford "mutual guarantees of political independence and territorial integrity to great and small states alike." Although Allied leaders appreciated the Fourteen Points as an aspect of propaganda, the ambitious postwar plans those leaders had for their nations kept them from formally adopting the proposals as a basis for peace.

The Peace Conference. During January–June, 1919, the victorious nations met in Paris and sometimes in nearby Versailles to draw up a peace settlement that would be dictated to the defeated nations.

ORGANIZATION. More than sixty delegates from twenty-seven Allied and Associated Powers participated in the negotiations. Russia was not represented, for under the Bolsheviks it had withdrawn from the war and had signed a separate peace treaty with the Central Powers. Germany and the other defeated nations were denied participation in the conference. Major matters were submitted for consideration to the Council of Ten, consisting of two representatives from each of the leading powers in attendance—the United States, Great Britain, France, Italy, and Japan. Ultimately, however, most issues were settled by four men, who were soon known as the "Big Four": Wilson, Lloyd George, Clemenceau, and Premier Vittorio Orlando of Italy. Wilson's expansive idealism came into immediate conflict with the narrow nationalism of the other three leaders.

WILSON'S DIFFICULTIES. Wilson faced the enormous task in Paris of making the Fourteen Points the foundation of the peace negotiations. The people of Europe to an astounding degree relied upon him to satisfy their nationalistic aspirations and to meet their deep economic and social needs. Wilson was handicapped from the very beginning of the conference. The American people repudiated the Wilson administration by sending a Republican majority to both the Senate and the House of Representatives in the congressional elections held but a month before the President's departure for Paris. Wilson's choice of fellow members for the American delegation—Secretary of State Lansing, Colonel House, former chief of staff of the army General Tasker Bliss, and retired career diplomat Henry White— shocked and angered Republicans, for Wilson had failed to select an influential member of their party to go to Paris. (White was merely a recognized Republican.) Further, in the selection of the peace commission Wilson engendered particular ill will in the Senate, the body that under the Constitution must ratify any treaty to which the nation is to become a party, for not only had he failed to choose one of their number to serve on the delegation but he had not even consulted that body on the appointments he did make. Wilson's disinclination to cultivate the support of the press led to bad relations between the President and reporters when he most needed favorable news coverage. Finally, Wilson failed to reach a preconference agreement with the other leaders regarding the disposition of the secret treaties.

The Treaty of Versailles. The lengthy document, which was a punitive instrument of peace imposed by the victors, pertained solely to Germany. To complete the settlement officially ending the war a separate treaty was framed for each of the nations that along with Germany had constituted the Central Powers.

PROVISIONS. The treaty compelled Germany to assume the responsibility of having caused the war. By its provisions Germany was committed to (1) surrender Alsace-Lorraine to France and border areas to three other surrounding nations; (2) transfer all of its colonies to a mandate system, under which they would be administered by various Allied powers, subject to the general supervision of the newly established League of Nations; (3) reduce its army to 100,000 men; (4) relinquish all warships of a substantial size, all military airplanes, and all heavy guns; (5) make reparations for the entire cost of the war, which was subsequently fixed at approximately $56.5 billion.

GERMANY'S REACTION. Germany insisted that the burden of the terms imposed upon it was crushing. Furious protests by the nation's leaders over the treaty provisions brought no modification in them, and in June, 1919, representatives of Germany, in a sullen mood, signed the document.

The League of Nations. It was anticipated that in the matter of future peace the framework of the newly created association of nations would compensate for the deficiencies of the Treaty of Versailles. All countries except the Central Powers and Communist-controlled Russia were asked to affiliate with the world organization.

DRAFTING THE COVENANT. At the conference Wilson achieved his supreme goal of having the Covenant of the League of Nations written into the Treaty of Versailles. To gain support for this objective, he was compelled to compromise with the British, French, Italian, and Japanese delegates, who pressed vigorously their particular nationalistic claims. Although Wilson was the chief designer of the League of Nations, he received valuable contributions from a number of people, notably David Hunter Miller of the United States, a lawyer and writer on foreign affairs; Lord Robert Cecil of Great Britain, a holder of a succession of cabinet posts; Leon Bourgeois of France, a former premier and a social philosopher; and Jan Christiaan Smuts of South Africa, a general and a minister of defense. Also, Wilson incorporated into the Covenant several suggestions made by leading Republicans William H. Taft, Charles Evans Hughes, and Elihu Root.

AIMS. Member nations of the League agreed upon the following aims: (1) to respect and preserve the political independence and territorial integrity of one another; (2) to employ military and economic sanctions against nations resorting to aggression; (3) to present to the League for inquiry all controversies which threatened war; (4) to reduce armaments; (5) to establish a Permanent Court of International Justice (soon known as the World Court), which would arbitrate disputes submitted to it by contending nations.

STRUCTURE. The final form of the Covenant provided for the following structure: (1) an Assembly, composed of delegates from all the member nations, each of which had one vote; (2) a Council, composed of representatives from the five leading powers—the United States, Great Britain, France, Italy, and Japan—and representatives from four other nations elected periodically by the Assembly; (3) a Secretary-General to manage the routine affairs of the League. The League headquarters were at Geneva, Switzerland.

Senate Rejection of the Treaty. After winning his fight at the peace conference in Paris to have the Covenant of the League of Nations incorporated into the Treaty of Versailles, Wilson was to lose his struggle with the Senate of the United States over ratification of the treaty.

WILSON'S APPEAL TO THE NATION. Failing to persuade the Senate Committee on Foreign Relations, which Republican Henry Cabot Lodge of Massachusetts chaired, to recommend ratification of the treaty, President

Wilson decided to carry his case in person to the American people. In September, 1919, he undertook a speaking tour of the Middle and Far West. But his trip was cut short when his health broke and he was compelled to return to Washington, there suffering a stroke that paralyzed the left side of his face and body. Although Wilson had gained larger and more enthusiastic audiences as the tour proceeded, there was no indication that his appeal had aroused the public to demand ratification.

THE LODGE RESERVATIONS. There was criticism of many sections of the treaty, such as those that dismembered the Austro-Hungarian Empire, allotted most of the German colonies under the mandate system to Great Britain and its dominions, and granted to Japan rights in the Shantung province of China. But the hostility to the document was primarily toward the Covenant of the League of Nations. In September, 1919, a few days after Wilson had begun his speaking tour, the treaty was reported out of the Senate Committee on Foreign Relations with more than forty amendments and four reservations to the League Covenant. After weeks of debate the treaty came to the actual voting stage, with fourteen reservations (called the Lodge Reservations after the chairman of the Committee on Foreign Relations) having already been passed and added to it. The Lodge Reservations included, among other things, the following: (1) the United States reserved the right of withdrawal at any time from the League of Nations; (2) American military forces could not be used to carry out Article X of the Covenant of the League (in which member nations pledged to defend the political independence and territorial integrity of one another against aggression) except by an act of Congress; (3) purely domestic questions were to be excluded from consideration by the Assembly and the Council of the League; (4) a mandate could be accepted by the United States only by congressional consent; (5) the Monroe Doctrine was wholly outside the jurisdiction of the League. President Wilson asserted that the Lodge Reservations had the effect of nullifying the treaty, and urged his supporters in the Senate to vote against the treaty if it were coupled with the reservations.

SENATE DIVISIONS. Members of the Senate divided on the League issue into four groups: (1) the Democratic supporters of Wilson, who favored the ratification of the treaty without changes, led by Senate Minority Leader Gilbert M. Hitchcock of Nebraska; (2) the mild reservationists, who were willing to accept the treaty with minor changes; (3) the strong reservationists, who favored the ratification of the treaty with the Lodge Reservations to insure the protection of American interests, led by Henry Cabot Lodge; (4) the "irreconcilables," a faction of fifteen ultraisolationists who advocated full rejection of the treaty, led by Republicans William Borah of Idaho, Hiram Johnson of California, and Robert M. La Follette of Wisconsin.

THE FINAL VOTE. On November 19, 1919, the Senate voted on the

Treaty of Versailles, rejecting ratification either with or without the Lodge Reservations. A combination of Wilson supporters and irreconcilables had defeated the treaty with reservations. In the spring of 1920 the Senate returned to a consideration of the treaty and the Lodge Reservations. (At this time a fifteenth reservation was adopted, expressing sympathy for self-government for Ireland.) The final test came on March 19. Some Democrats disregarded Wilson's instructions to vote against the treaty with the Lodge Reservations. Even so, the treaty with reservations received fifty-seven ayes and thirty-nine nays, less than the two-thirds vote necessary under the Constitution for ratification.

AFTERMATH. In May, 1920, Congress passed a joint resolution declaring the war with Germany at an end, but Wilson vetoed it. On July 2, 1921, Wilson's successor, Warren G. Harding, signed a similar resolution. Subsequently, treaties that did not provide for a League were negotiated with Germany, Austria, and Hungary (the latter two nations had been newly created from the former Austro-Hungarian Empire) and were promptly ratified by the Senate. After his inauguration, Harding had said bluntly: "The Administration which came into power in March, 1921, definitely and decisively put aside all thoughts of entering the League of Nations. It doesn't propose to enter now, by the side door, back door, or cellar door."

Chapter 11

THE 1920s:
PEACETIME PURSUITS

In the decade following World War I the Republican party and its new-found conservatism held the loyalty of most Americans. The people of the United States desired to return to the quest of peacetime pursuits. However, serious economic and social problems had to be solved: achieving a balance among the demands of business, labor, and agriculture; coping with imminent large-scale immigration; controlling the prohibition experiment; and combating radicalism without destroying civil liberties. Tired of war and disillusioned by the treaty-making that followed, the people attempted to withdraw from international commitments. Even so, the three Republican administrations did not withdraw the United States into full isolationism. The unprecedented prosperity that characterized the 1920s proved insecurely founded. And the decade ended with the stock-market crash—prelude to the worst depression in the history of the nation.

RETURN TO "NORMALCY"

Politics in the 1920s saw the old issues go. Progressive reform, imperialism, war, treaty-making—all were forgotten. The vast majority of voters, desiring to escape from the challenge of Wilsonian idealism and the responsibilities of world leadership, believed that they were returning to "normalcy" (a campaign term used to good effect by the Republican presidential candidate in 1920) by putting the Republican party back in power.

Election of 1920. The issue dealt with most extensively in the 1920 campaign was American entry into the League of Nations, but the essence of the election was an expression of disapproval of the Wilson administration, arising out of the animosities of the war years and the disappointments of the postwar period.

DEMOCRATS. At the Democratic national convention there were three front-runners for the presidential nomination: Secretary of the Treasury William G. McAdoo; Attorney General A. Mitchell Palmer; and Governor James M. Cox of Ohio. On the forty-fourth ballot the delegates chose Cox to be the party's standard-bearer. Selected as his running mate was the young Franklin D. Roosevelt of New York, who had achieved distinction during World War I as assistant secretary of the navy. The platform advocated the ratification of the Treaty of Versailles, thus providing for American entry into the League of Nations.

REPUBLICANS. In order to prevent a deadlock between the two leading aspirants to the presidential nomination, General Leonard Wood, who had served in the Caribbean and Philippines, and conservative Governor Frank O. Lowden of Illinois, the convention settled upon a little-known party regular, Senator Warren G. Harding of Ohio. For vice-president the delegates named Governor Calvin Coolidge of Massachusetts, who had recently gained fame by breaking a police strike in Boston. The platform straddled the League of Nations issue.

THE CAMPAIGN. President Wilson had stated that if the Treaty of Versailles were rejected by the Senate, the issue would be submitted to the people at the next national election in a "great and solemn referendum." Cox made it clear that if elected his first duty would be to press for the ratification of the treaty. As the campaign progressed, Harding vacillated on the League issue even more than his party's platform did.

HARDING'S LANDSLIDE VICTORY. Harding received 16,152,000 popular votes to Cox's 9,147,000. He captured every state outside the Democratic Solid South; he even cracked that by taking Tennessee. As one prominent Democrat remarked: "It was not a landslide, it was an earthquake." Harding's great victory signified the people's disapproval of the Wilson administration and their desire to have power transferred to the Republican party.

The Harding Administration. Believing that the Constitution meant to keep presidential power within certain prescribed bounds and fully aware of his own limited ability, Harding allowed the Congress and his cabinet to give the nation the leadership it needed.

THE PRESIDENT. Warren Gamaliel Harding was a handsome man of amiable disposition. He enjoyed hugely the ceremonial functions of the presidency, but he found making decisions on the myriad of matters that demanded his attention to be torture.

THE CABINET. While campaigning for the presidency, Harding announced that if elected he would turn to the "best minds" in the Republican party. Considered by contemporaries to be the most distinguished appointees to the cabinet were Secretary of State Charles Evans Hughes, who was a former governor of New York, a former associate justice of the

Supreme Court, and the Republican candidate for president in 1916; Secretary of the Treasury Andrew Mellon, the Pittsburgh industrialist and financier; and Secretary of Commerce Herbert C. Hoover, a mining engineer who had successfully directed a program for the relief of the Belgians during World War I. In contrast, Albert B. Fall of New Mexico was made secretary of the interior and Harry M. Daugherty of Ohio was made attorney general—both were friends of the President and both were to bring disgrace to the administration.

The Scandals. Harding placed great confidence in his personal friends and political associates. Some of them betrayed that trust.

THE VETERANS BUREAU. In 1925 Charles R. Forbes, the recently resigned director of the Veterans Bureau, received a two-year prison sentence and a $10,000 fine for bribery and conspiracy. He and his associates had made about $200 million in graft by granting to private interests government contracts connected with the care of disabled veterans.

THE ALIEN PROPERTY CUSTODIAN. Thomas W. Miller, the Alien Property Custodian, accepted a $50,000 bribe in a transaction involving the sale for much less than its value of German property confiscated during World War I. In 1927 Miller was sent to prison for eighteen months and fined $5,000 for conspiracy to defraud the government.

TEAPOT DOME. The major disgrace associated with the Harding administration was known as Teapot Dome. In 1921 Secretary of the Interior Albert B. Fall, after gaining the support of Secretary of the Navy Edwin Denby, convinced President Harding to transfer from the Navy Department to the Interior Department control of naval oil-reserve land at Teapot Dome in Wyoming and Elk Hills in California. Fall then, secretly and without asking for bids, granted drilling rights to private companies operated by oil producers Edward L. Doheny and Harry F. Sinclair, but not until he had received a "loan" of $100,000 from Doheny and three times that much in cash and World War I bonds as a "gift" from Sinclair. An investigation was begun in 1923 by a Senate committee headed by Democrat Thomas J. Walsh of Montana. Fall resigned from the cabinet, and was soon "lent" $25,000 by Sinclair. The Senate investigation led to an indictment of Fall, Doheny, and Sinclair. Their cases dragged on for a number of years. Meanwhile, the government canceled the leases to the oil-reserve land. Finally, in 1929 Fall was convicted of bribery, sentenced to one year in prison, and fined $100,000. He became the first cabinet member in the nation's history to go to jail for dishonoring his office. Both Doheny and Sinclair were acquitted of bribery, although the latter received a prison sentence and fine for contempt of court.

CHARGES AGAINST DAUGHERTY. Evidence was produced disclosing that Attorney General Harry M. Daugherty had received sums of money from liquor dealers who were evading the prohibition statutes. Also, it was discovered that he had not taken the proper course of action to prosecute Forbes and others in the Veterans Bureau for graft. Further, he was implicated in the matter involving Alien Property Custodian Miller. In 1924 Daugherty was forced by President Coolidge to resign. Two years later he was tried in connection with the Miller case for conspiracy to defraud the government, but was acquitted.

Harding's Death. On August 2, 1923, President Harding died suddenly of a stroke in San Francisco, as he was returning from an official visit to Alaska. The last months of his life had been darkened by his awareness that a few of his close advisers had betrayed him and their public trust. Shortly before his death he realized that evidence of gross political corruption would soon be revealed.

Coolidge's Succession. Thrust into office by Harding's unexpected death, Calvin Coolidge insisted that his associates should help in the investigation of corrupt political acts committed during his predecessor's administration; he thus quickly won the confidence of the American people, who admired his courage and personal integrity.

Election of 1924. Coolidge sought the presidency in his own right. With prosperity at its height and the Democrats choosing a compromise candidate who was as conservative as Coolidge, a Republican victory seemed assured.

DEMOCRATS. Trouble developed in the Democratic ranks over a proposed plank in the platform denouncing by name the Ku Klux Klan, an organization designed to maintain the political supremacy of native-born white Protestants. After prolonged and acrimonious debate the convention rejected by one vote the inclusion of an anti-Klan plank. The platform that was adopted lashed out at the corruption in the Harding administration and proposed a referendum to decide the issue of United States membership in the League of Nations. When it came to choosing a presidential nominee, the convention was once more split by the Klan issue. The candidate of the anti-Klan delegates was Governor Alfred E. Smith of New York; the candidate of the pro-Klan delegates (although he repeatedly denied any Klan affiliation) was William G. McAdoo of California, who had been Wilson's secretary of the treasury. After the longest deadlock in the history of national political conventions, the delegates chose on the 103rd ballot John W. Davis, originally from West Virginia, who had become a prominent New York City corporation lawyer. For vice-president the liberal Governor Charles W. Bryan of Nebraska, brother of William Jennings Bryan, was nominated.

REPUBLICANS. So successful had Coolidge been in removing the stigma of corruption from his party that he was the virtually unanimous choice of the delegates to the Republican national convention. Chosen as his running mate was Charles G. Dawes, a Chicago Banker who had served as first director of the budget. The platform was an appeal to the nation's conservative business interests, already feeling the stimulating influence of more prosperous times.

PROGRESSIVES. The dissatisfaction of the eastern laborers and the western farmers with the two major parties resulted in the formation of a new Progressive party. The third party nominated for president the reform-minded Republican Senator Robert M. La Follette of Wisconsin. He selected for second place on the ticket Democratic Senator Burton K. Wheeler of Montana. The platform, drafted by La Follette himself, was largely an expression of labor unrest and agrarian discontent.

THE CAMPAIGN. Davis castigated the Republican party for allowing the recently exposed graft in the Harding administration. In Coolidge's few speeches he did not deign to reply to the Davis indictment. La Follette, whose candidacy was endorsed by the American Federation of Labor and the Socialist party, provided what spirit there was in a rather listless campaign. The strategy of each of the major parties was to frighten the voters with the charge that La Follette was a dangerous radical and to proclaim that the best way to defeat him was to vote for its candidate.

COOLIDGE'S LANDSLIDE VICTORY. In popular votes, Coolidge received 15,725,000; Davis, 8,386,000; La Follette, 4,822,000. Coolidge captured the electoral vote of every state in the East, Midwest (except for Wisconsin), and Far West, while Davis secured only the Solid South and Oklahoma, and La Follette won the electoral vote of his home state alone. The big advantage to the Republicans was that the times were so prosperous that most people were uninterested in Davis's attacks on the party in power or La Follette's recommendations for reform.

The Coolidge Administration. The executive branch under Coolidge achieved a reputation for rectitude as under Harding it had earned a reputation for wrongdoing. But in terms of policy the Coolidge administration accommodated itself as much as the Harding administration had to the needs of American industry and commerce.

THE PRESIDENT. Coolidge was unpretentious and laconic. While not a creative person, he did possess a respectable amount of common sense.

THE CABINET. Wanting to suggest that there would be a smooth transition from the previous administration to his, Coolidge had retained the Harding cabinet intact. Two members who proved a discomfort because of their involvement in Harding administration scandals were Secretary of the Navy Denby and Attorney General Daugherty; both were let go before the 1924 election.

Election of 1928. The Republican candidate represented the Protestant middle class, while the Democratic nominee was an antiprohibitionist Catholic from the city. With continued prosperity a help, the Republican standard-bearer achieved an easy victory.

DEMOCRATS. The Democratic national convention was quite different from the factious one four years earlier. The delegates, with merely token opposition, nominated Governor Smith of New York on the first ballot. For his running mate they selected Joseph T. Robinson of Arkansas, the Senate minority leader, who as a southerner, Protestant, and prohibitionist, balanced the ticket. The Democratic platform pledged the party to international cooperation (American membership in the League of Nations was not mentioned) and an "honest" attempt to enforce the Eighteenth (Prohibition) Amendment.

REPUBLICANS. A year before the Republican national convention, Coolidge issued a short public statement: "I do not choose to run for President in 1928." This made inevitable the nomination of the highly efficient Secretary of Commerce Herbert C. Hoover. The Republicans chose Hoover on the first ballot and selected for his running mate Charles Curtis of Kansas, the Senate majority leader. The platform, adopted amid much accord, declared against American entry into the League of Nations and demanded full enforcement of the Eighteenth Amendment.

THE CAMPAIGN. In a number of speeches throughout the nation, Smith urged revision of the prohibition laws and accused the Republican party of giving undue attention to the interests of the business community. Compared with the energetic campaign waged by Smith, Hoover's was rather easygoing.

HOOVER'S LANDSLIDE VICTORY. In popular votes, Hoover received 21,392,000 to Smith's 15,016,000. Hoover won the electoral vote of forty states, including his opponent's home state of New York and five states— Virginia, Tennessee, North Carolina, Florida, and Texas—of the half-century-old Solid South. Smith's race for the presidency seemed doomed from the outset; he was handicapped in the South and Midwest by his antiprohibition views, his Catholic faith, and his connection with Tammany Hall (the Manhattan Democratic political machine). But more important, the American people were experiencing great prosperity and were in no mood to break the spell that appeared to have been induced by Republican rule.

The Hoover Administration. Upon his inauguration, Hoover was hailed as a person who would run the complicated machinery of government with skill and efficiency. Four years later he was rejected by a nation consumed by economic despair.

THE PRESIDENT. Hoover was among the most conscientious of all who have ever occupied the White House. A man of scrupulously correct behavior, he became stiff in dealing with others during the difficult days of his presidency.

THE CABINET. The Hoover cabinet thoroughly reflected the conservative philosophy of the man who selected it. Members of the official family implemented policies that won the appreciation of the business community. As a matter of fact, more than half the men in the cabinet were millionaires, including Secretary of the Treasury Andrew Mellon.

DOMESTIC ISSUES

In the post-World War I decade there were many persistent economic and social problems that Americans were reluctant to face. Among them were those regarding business, agriculture, immigration, prohibition, and radical thought and action.

The Mellon Fiscal Policy. Andrew Mellon headed the Treasury Department from 1921 to 1932, holding that position longer than any other person in the nation's history. Hailed by his conservative Republican supporters as the "greatest Secretary of the Treasury since Alexander Hamilton," Mellon was given more and more freedom to set the fiscal policies of the three Republican administrations of the 1920s, until the depression hit at the end of the decade.

BUDGETARY REFORM. In order to reduce government expenditures, Secretary Mellon advocated a reform of the national budget system. The Budget and Accounting Act, passed in 1921, established the Bureau of the Budget, with a director appointed by the President, and required the President to submit to each session of Congress an estimate of federal income and expenditures. Named the first director of the budget was Chicago banker Charles G. Dawes, who became the supervisor of the government's economy campaign.

TAX REDUCTIONS. Mellon and the three Presidents under whom he served won the acclaim of businessmen for their efforts to decrease tax rates both on corporations and on individuals in the higher personal income brackets. Although taxes were lightened, the increasing prosperity of almost the entire 1920s enabled the government to collect more than enough revenue to meet current expenses and to apply the surplus to the steady reduction of the national debt.

CONGRESSIONAL REACTION. Mellon's tax program did not meet with full success in Congress, where a combination of Democrats and rebellious Republicans compelled the Harding administration and the early Coolidge administration to accept higher rates on large personal incomes than the Treasury Department had proposed. This political dissent centered in the farm bloc, representing constituencies of the midwestern "corn belt," which insisted that agriculture receive governmental favors equivalent to those conferred upon industry. However, as prosperity reached unprecedented heights from 1924 until the onset of the depression five years later, the people, through their choice of federal legislators, permitted Mellon to pursue his policy as he saw fit.

Aid to the Railroads. The placing of rail transportation under government control during World War I stimulated the demand in some quarters for government ownership and operation of the railroads. However, after the war the Wilson administration recommended the return of the railroads to private control, while warning against the reestablishment of "the old conditions unmodified." During the 1920s the operators of railroads, as hostile as ever to government regulation, nevertheless turned to the federal government for relief.

THE PLUMB PLAN. A plan formulated by Glenn E. Plumb, counsel for the Railroad Brotherhoods (a combination of four railway unions), called for the purchase of the railroads by the government and operation by a corporation composed of government representatives, rail officials, and rail employees. Although the Plumb plan was considered in Congress in 1919, hostility among many legislators prevented it from coming to a vote.

THE ESCH-CUMMINS ACT. Congressional discussion of numerous proposals for the revamping of the rail system finally resulted in the passage in 1920 of the Esch-Cummins Act, which provided for the return of the lines to private control. The main provisions of the act were (1) increased regulation of the railroads by the Interstate Commerce Commission, which was empowered to issue railroad stocks and bonds, set minimum and maximum rates, and consolidate lines for the purpose of eliminating unnecessary competition; (2) the guarantee by the government of a "fair" return (5½ percent) of profits to the owners for a period of two years; (3) compulsory arbitration of wage disputes by a newly created Railroad Labor Board composed of three members from the owners, three from the employees, and three from the public.

NEW FORMS OF COMPETITION. After 1920 the railroads were alarmed over competition from improved internal waterways, trucking firms, expanding pipeline facilities, and airlines. From railroad executives came insistent demands that Congress place their competitors under governmental regulation.

CONSOLIDATION. The solution implicit in the Esch-Cummins Act of the overriding railroad problem was the unification of independent lines into great systems based upon a careful analysis of the nation's needs. The Interstate Commerce Commission and the railroad executives alike explored the difficulties and possibilities of consolidation, but action was slow. Between 1920 and 1929, when the depression began, hundreds of short lines were acquired by the larger rail systems. Not until 1931 did the northeastern roads submit a plan for unification, which the Interstate Commerce Commission approved with certain changes in details. There were to be four great networks in the Northeast: (1) the New York Central, with almost 13,000 miles; (2) the Pennsylvania, with more than 16,000 miles; (3) the Baltimore and Ohio, with over 11,000 miles; (4) the unified Van

Sweringen holdings, which included such subsidiary lines as the Erie and the Chesapeake and Ohio, with approximately 12,500 miles. In 1933 Congress passed legislation providing for a scheme of railroad coordination which would effect savings in the transportation system.

The Power Issue. During the postwar decade the increasing demand for governmental regulation of public utilities, especially those producing and distributing electric power, brought action from state and federal officials.

STATE REGULATION. The public utility companies, which had greatly expanded their activities through mergers and holding companies, were gradually brought under some kind of state supervision. By 1930 almost every state had created a public service commission, but the various commissions were handicapped in their ability to regulate by the modest character of their authority. Further, the large utilities firms were engaged in enterprises that crossed state lines, thus taking those operations outside the jurisdiction of an individual state.

THE WATER POWER ACT. This measure, passed in 1920, created the Federal Power Commission to issue licenses to water power facilities, such as dams and hydroelectric plants, on public lands and navigable waterways. The commission had regulatory authority over its licensees affecting rates in cases where electricity was sold across state lines. After the Water Power Act had been in effect for ten years, only 5 percent of the nation's hydroelectric power was produced under the commission's supervision.

The Labor Movement. Quickly succumbing to the pleasant features of the higher standard of living that the prosperous 1920s made possible, the core of organized labor lost much of its militancy.

MODERATE UNIONISM. Before 1920 organized labor had grown steadily, but in the post–World War I decade it declined both in activity and prestige. The conservative American Federation of Labor reported more than 4 million members in 1920 and fewer than 3 million in 1930. Several circumstances explain the decline in moderate unionism: (1) it clung to its commitment to the craft-type labor organization in an ever-more industrialized society; (2) it failed to come to grips with the problem of technological unemployment; (3) it was still disinclined to enroll blacks, who in larger numbers were entering into important trades; (4) it developed nothing to offer unskilled laborers; (5) it had difficulty making union benefits attractive in the face of increasing company programs of health protection, unemployment insurance, recreational facilities, and profit sharing.

RADICAL UNIONISM. The activities of the radical wing of American labor were curbed by the anti-Communist campaign of the federal and various state governments during the post–World War I period. The leftist Industrial Workers of the World never recovered from this onslaught, and by 1925 had virtually disappeared. In labor circles, workers who were Communists at first strove to capture moderate unions by a policy of boring from within, but by the end of the decade they had begun a concentrated drive to form new industrial unions committed to the intensification of the class struggle. In 1928 radical workers were responsible for the establishment in the United States of the Communist party, which, however, was never able to pull more than 60,000 votes for its presidential candidate.

Aid to Agriculture. The perennial problem of the relation of agriculture to the industrial order became acute immediately after World War I. Because farmers did not share with businessmen and laborers the great prosperity of the 1920s, the government decided to take steps to help them.

WARTIME PROSPERITY. The demands for food during World War I brought unprecedented good times to American farmers, who were tempted by the phenomenal rise in the prices of their staples to strive for an increase in the productivity of acreage already under cultivation and to buy more acres for new cultivation. The mechanization of agriculture, which went forward rapidly in response to the needs of the warring nations, brought increasing returns to farmers who chose to use the new methods.

PEACETIME REVERSAL. The farmers' prosperous years were few. Peace brought a quick descent to the prewar price level. From 1919 to 1921 the value of farm products was cut in half. The farmers' plight, to which foreclosed mortgages bore mute witness, was the result of (1) the expanding use of land for agricultural purposes, much of it submarginal; (2) the increased productivity per acre due to improved machines and methods; (3) the decline of agricultural prices in the world market, where the farm surplus of the United States competed with those of other nations.

THE FARM BLOC. Like the Grangers and the Populists of earlier periods, the farmers, through their organizations, turned to Congress for relief from their economic hardships. The pressure exerted by agrarian groups such as the American Farm Bureau Federation and the Farmers' National Council caused the formation in Congress of a bipartisan farm bloc that worked for legislation providing agrarian relief. As a result, Congress passed the Grain Futures Trading Act (1921) to prevent manipulation of the grain market; the Cooperative Marketing Act (1922) to exempt agricultural cooperatives from the antitrust laws; and the Intermediate Credit Act (1923) to extend agricultural loans on easier terms.

THE MCNARY-HAUGEN BILL. The basic problem of agricultural surpluses was treated by the McNary-Haugen Bill, which passed Congress in 1927 only to be vetoed by President Coolidge. Its sponsors, Republican Senator Charles L. McNary of Oregon and Republican Representative Gilbert N. Haugen of Iowa, modified some of the bill's provisions and secured passage of the revised bill the following year, but again Coolidge vetoed it. The central feature of the plan was that the federal government would purchase at relatively high prices farm surplus staples, such as wheat, corn, and cotton, and sell them in the world market, with whatever losses the government might incur to be made up by an equalization fee (the difference between the fixed domestic price and the unfixed world price) imposed upon producers. It was asserted that the fee plan would operate automatically to curb excessive production of any staple. In vetoing the bill Coolidge gave as reasons that it sanctioned unwarranted price-fixing and was, in fact, an incentive to agricultural overproduction.

THE AGRICULTURAL MARKETING ACT. Upon the recommendation of President Hoover, Congress passed in 1929 the Agricultural Marketing Act, which attempted through the storage of surplus crops to prevent the already low farm prices from falling to ruinous levels. The act created a Federal Farm Board authorized to extend low-interest loans to agricultural cooperatives, enabling them to purchase and store surplus farm commodities and then to sell those surplus crops at a time when the market supply was low. The act was criticized by many for not providing incentives to farmers to limit their production. Within four years the not-very-successful Federal Farm Board was disbanded.

The Tariff Issue. Despite the growing realization of the interdependence of manufacturing, agriculture, and trade among the nations of the world, there was a significant increase in tariff barriers after World War I.

THE FORDNEY-McCUMBER TARIFF. This measure represented a decisive return by the United States government to protectionist principles, in keeping with the traditional position of the Republican party, which had recently come to power. The Fordney-McCumber Tariff, enacted in 1922, was an elaboration of the emergency tariff of 1921, which had reversed the notably low rates of the Wilson administration's Underwood Tariff. It (1) reduced the number of commodities on the free list; (2) increased the rates on agricultural products; (3) charged the Tariff Commission, established six years earlier, with investigating for purposes of comparison production costs at home and abroad; (4) empowered the President to revise rates up to 50 percent in either direction whenever it seemed advisable on the basis of the commission's report. In general, the act restored the level of duties of the Payne-Aldrich Tariff of the Taft administration.

THE SMOOT-HAWLEY TARIFF. This tariff provided for the highest rates in the nation's history. The average duty was approximately 60 percent. In May, 1930, Hoover had received a petition signed by more than 1,000 prominent economists, opposing the passage of the Smoot-Hawley bill and urging a presidential veto if the Congress approved the measure. The petition argued that the rates would sharply reduce American trade, a situation particularly harmful during the recently begun depression. Hoover signed the bill in June, 1930. Within three years, thirty-three foreign countries retaliated against the high rates by increasing their rates on American products.

Restriction of Immigration. As a direct consequence of World War I, the United States during the 1920s reversed its traditional immigration policy.

THE DEMAND FOR LIMITATION. Before 1914 the United States permitted unrestricted immigration from Europe, barring only those aliens considered likely to affect adversely public health, safety, or morals. The United States, representing in the minds of many the epitome of the New World, was proud to be an asylum for the oppressed of the Old World. In addition, the nation needed cheap labor to exploit its abundant mineral wealth, to build its railroads, and to operate the machinery in its factories. Yet there was a growing demand for a selective immigration policy.

THE LITERACY TEST ACT. Bills providing for a literacy test for immigrants had been vetoed by Cleveland in 1896, Taft in 1913, and Wilson in 1915. Finally, in 1917 Congress succeeded in passing over Wilson's veto an act requiring immigrants to be able to read and write a language, whether English or another.

THE EMERGENCY QUOTA ACT OF 1921. When it appeared to many at the close of World War I that "the world was preparing to move to the United States," Congress rather hastily adopted a policy of restriction. The Emergency Quota Act of 1921 limited immigration from Europe in any one year to 3 percent of the number of each nationality resident in the United States according to the census of 1910. The total number of immigrants who would be permitted to enter the United States was set at approximately 357,000 annually.

THE QUOTA ACT OF 1924. This measure further restricted the number of people settling in the United States by limiting immigration from Europe in any one year to 2 percent of the number of each nationality resident in the United States according to the census of 1890, with the total number of immigrants set at approximately 164,000 annually. The changing of the census base from 1910 in the act of 1921 to 1890 in the act of 1924 drastically reduced the quotas of the "new immigrants" (those coming from eastern and southern Europe beginning in the 1880s) and automatically increased the proportion of the "old immigrants" (those arriving from northern and western Europe before the 1880s). Members of the former group, because of language barriers, their relatively poor education, and their tendency to cluster together in large cities, were considered by many to be more difficult than those of the latter group to assimilate into the dominant American culture. As for the non-European nations, the act exempted the Western Hemisphere from its terms but totally prohibited immigration from Asia.

THE NATIONAL ORIGINS PLAN. The Quota Act of 1924 called for a set of permanent regulations to take effect three years later, but the calculations for establishing new quotas proved so difficult that the regulations did not become operative until 1929. According to the National Origins Plan, the total number of immigrants from outside the Western Hemisphere was restricted to approximately 150,000 annually, with each country given a quota based on the proportion that the number of persons of that "national origin" residing in the United States bore to the total American population in 1920. But each European country was permitted to send at least 100 people a year. All immigration from Asia was still prohibited. Although the quota system did not apply to Canada or the independent nations of Latin America, so wide was the latitude for administrative discretion that State Department and Labor Department officials were able to restrict selectively even nonquota groups by requiring certain qualifications, such as the holding of property. Mexican immigration, for example, was greatly reduced as a result of this administrative action. The National Origins Plan remained in effect until 1965.

Prohibition. Probably no public issue was so widely discussed during the 1920s as the prohibition of the manufacture and sale of intoxicating beverages.

BACKGROUND. National prohibition was the culmination of a long campaign against the liquor traffic. From its inception in the early nineteenth century, the movement rested upon the conviction of an increasing portion of the American people that intoxicants (1) had an injurious effect upon the mind and body; (2) led users into vice and crime, thus constituting a menace to the life and property of others; (3) sent many to asylums and prisons, the maintenance of which required heavy taxes; (4) reduced workers' efficiency, thus increasing management problems. The organizations particularly effective in the prohibition movement were (1) the Prohibition party, formed in 1869, which in its platform placed destruction of the liquor traffic above every other issue; (2) the Woman's Christian Temperance Union, established in 1874, which undertook a spirited educational campaign; (3) the Anti-Saloon League, organized in 1893, which mobilized the sentiment of evangelical Protestantism so that it wielded great political influence.

THE EIGHTEENTH AMENDMENT. So successful were the tactics of the Anti-Saloon League that by the fall of 1917 the legislatures of more than half the states had banned the liquor traffic and fully two-thirds of the people of the nation were living in areas that were "dry" by either state or local legislation. In December, 1917, Congress passed the Eighteenth Amendment to the Constitution, prohibiting the manufacture, sale, or transportation of intoxicating liquors. It was not surprising to the American people that ratification by the required number of states was achieved by January, 1919, with ease.

THE VOLSTEAD ACT. This act, passed over President Wilson's veto in October, 1919, provided the machinery for implementing the Eighteenth Amendment. It defined as intoxicating any beverage containing more than

one-half of 1 percent alcohol. Administration of the act was assigned to the
Bureau of Internal Revenue, a division of the Treasury Department.

There were major obstacles to successful enforcement of the Volstead
Act, including (1) the opposition of some communities, especially larger
cities, to national prohibition; (2) the lack of cooperation between federal
and local authorities; (3) the corruption of some enforcement agents, who
accepted bribes from bootleggers earning large profits from the illicit liquor
traffic; (4) the failure of the Treasury Department and the Justice Department to centralize control of the enforcement services. The difficulties of
making the Volstead Act effective caused opponents of prohibition to
denounce the Eighteenth Amendment as a failure, the chief result of which
had been an increasing disrespect for law, as evidenced in the rise of
bootlegging and hijacking.

THE WICKERSHAM COMMISSION. In 1929 President Hoover appointed the
National Commission on Law Observance and Enforcement, with former
attorney general George W. Wickersham as chairman, to conduct an investigation of prohibition and related problems of law enforcement. In 1931
the Wickersham Commission submitted its report, which declared that prohibition was not being effectively enforced but recommended further trial
of the Eighteenth Amendment and the Volstead Act.

THE TWENTY-FIRST AMENDMENT. In February, 1933, Congress passed,
and by December, 1933, the required number of states had ratified, the
Twenty-first Amendment, which repealed the Eighteenth Amendment.
Thereupon, control of the liquor traffic reverted to the states. All but eight
promptly permitted the manufacture and sale of intoxicating liquors under
various types of regulation.

Antiradicalism. During the 1920s fear pervaded the nation that radicalism might destroy American traditions. Even the moderate reforms of
the recent progressive era came under suspicion. As a result, some who had
been reformers in their younger years now gained prominence as defenders
of the existing economic and social order.

THE "RED SCARE." The success of the 1917 Communist revolution in
Russia convinced many Americans that the Communists ("Reds") and their
sympathizers were using the postwar turmoil to secure political power
elsewhere in the world, including the United States. Law enforcement
agencies, both federal and state, were put on their guard against radical
uprisings. In 1919 almost 250 aliens whose views were regarded as dangerously radical were deported to Russia. Early in 1920 Attorney General
A. Mitchell Palmer authorized raids on both acknowledged and alleged
Communists, resulting in the arrest of more than 4,000 persons, many of
whom were apprehended and held in violation of their constitutional rights.
In the fall of 1920 a bomb exploded on Wall Street, killing 38 people, sending a wave of fear across the nation, and contributing greatly to the

antiradical fervor. Palmer asserted that the "Reds" were ready to "destroy the government at one fell swoop." By the beginning of 1921, however, the "Red Scare" had abated.

THE BOSTON POLICE STRIKE. A dispute in Boston between the police commissioner and members of the police force over the latter's right to affiliate with the American Federation of Labor led to a strike in the fall of 1919 of about three-fourths of the force. To prevent the collapse of law enforcement, Calvin Coolidge, then governor of Massachusetts, dispatched the state militia to the city. Although Coolidge had taken action after Boston was already under control, he won widespread approval by his statement: "There is no right to strike against the public safety by anybody, anywhere, anytime."

THE SACCO-VANZETTI CASE. Fear of radicalism was evident in the handling of the case against two acknowledged anarchists, Nicola Sacco and Bartolomeo Vanzetti. In 1921, despite inconclusive evidence, the men were found guilty of murdering a paymaster and a guard in the course of a robbery at a shoe factory in South Braintree, Massachusetts. They received the death sentence, which was stayed for a number of years by appeals from many people both in the United States and abroad who felt that the two men had been convicted because of their anarchist beliefs rather than the evidence presented. They were finally executed in 1927. As a *cause célèbre*, the Sacco-Vanzetti case forced large numbers of Americans to reappraise their fears of radical views and those who held them.

THE SCOPES TRIAL. Conservative alarm over radicalism had a counterpart in the area of religion, as many were apprehensive that the changing mood of the nation would weaken traditional religious beliefs. The liberals among Protestant clergy and laymen feared that a fundamentalist (literal) acceptance of every Biblical idea and a denial of the discoveries of science would separate the Christian churches from any interaction with modern culture. At times the liberals were inclined to test traditional religious beliefs by the standards of the twentieth century. The conservatives, or fundamentalists, feared that the liberal interpretation of the Scriptures would destroy the power of Protestantism to maintain its evangelical influence in human affairs. Among conservative Protestant laymen none defended their position more forcefully than William Jennings Bryan, who urged state legislatures to prohibit teaching the theory of evolution in the public schools. When John T. Scopes, a young teacher in Dayton, Tennessee, was indicted in a test case for presenting the evolutionary theory in his high school biology class, Bryan himself served on the prosecution staff. Scopes's defense attorney was Clarence Darrow, the most famous trial lawyer of the period. The arguments of the two distinguished counselors focused the attention of the world on the trial in 1925. Scopes was found guilty of violating the state law and fined $100. Bryan's strenuous efforts for the conservative point of view and the severe cross-examination to which he was subjected by the skillful Darrow probably were factors in shortening his life. The fundamentalist cause steadily declined thereafter.

THE KU KLUX KLAN. In the United States during the 1920s fear created intolerance. The most notorious manifestation of organized hatred was the Ku Klux Klan. Founded in 1915 by a former itinerant preacher, William Joseph Simmons, in Atlanta, Georgia, the organization spread rapidly throughout the nation after 1920. Although the secret order was to be a memorial to the Ku Klux Klan of the post–Civil War period, it had a wider program than the antiblack one of its precursor. To the original Klan's attacks on blacks, the Klan of the 1920s added anti-Catholicism, anti-Semitism, and antiforeign-bornism. Under a burning wooden cross and clad in white hoods and robes, Klansmen would listen to their officers (holding such titles as "Imperial Wizard," "Grand Dragon," and "Exalted Cyclops") preach an intolerance seldom matched in the history of the nation. Looking upon their organization as a nationwide vigilance committee, some Klansmen engaged in "night riding," the culmination of which could be tar and feathering, whipping, branding, emasculation, hanging, or burning at the stake. At the height of its activity in the mid-1920s the Klan had an estimated 4 million members. But as a result of the nation's increasing wrath toward the organization, by the beginning of the 1930s the membership had withered away to scarcely 50,000. Since then the Ku Klux Klan has been revived a number of times, existing, however, as a multiplication of splinter groups, as government on all three levels—federal, state, and local—took action against the order.

The Speculative Mania. From 1919 to 1929 the people of the United States experienced a rise in their standard of living more remarkable than any change that had taken place in any previous decade. The vast expansion of business enterprise concealed from many economists the highly speculative nature of this period of unprecedented prosperity, which ended in 1929 with the collapse of the stock market.

THE BUSINESS SCENE. The prosperity of the nation was marked by significant changes in the production, distribution, and sale of goods. Business statistics during the 1920s showed the following conditions: (1) a decline in manufacturing costs resulting from the use of standardized methods of operation and the making of uniform goods; (2) a greatly increased number of stockholders; (3) a proliferation of chain stores; (4) an extension of credit to customers through the use of the installment buying plan; (5) a significant increase of wages in most industries.

SIGNS OF DANGER. Several disquieting features of those boom years were becoming alarming at the beginning of the Hoover administration: (1) agricultural profits were lagging far behind industrial profits; (2) wages of factory workers were increasing, but not nearly so rapidly as the prices of manufactured goods; (3) the nation's factories and farms were producing more than American and foreign consumers were able to buy, while the high tariff was curtailing the overseas market; (4) consumers were buying an ever-increasing amount of goods on installment, thereby raising the total of outstanding private debts; (5) an extremely large proportion of the annual national income was being invested in highly speculative manufacturing, mining, and transportation enterprises.

THE STOCK-MARKET CRASH. Hundreds of thousands of Americans, for the first time, were buying securities (stocks and bonds) on the stock exchange; and many were acquiring their shares on credit. In late October, 1929, panic developed in the New York stock market. Prices of securities dropped with startling rapidity to low levels. Over 13 million shares were traded on October 23, soon to be known as "Black Thursday." By November 14 approximately $30 billion in the market value of listed stocks had been wiped out. At no previous period had so many Americans been directly involved with corporate securities. The collapse of the New York Stock Exchange, therefore, was the prelude to economic disaster.

FOREIGN AFFAIRS

The United States in the 1920s found it difficult to cooperate with other nations in any form of collective action to promote peace, for the feeling among Americans of political isolationism and economic nationalism was exceedingly strong. Nevertheless, the United States did engage in some worthwhile international projects.

Participation in International Conferences. During the 1920s the United States gradually abandoned its earlier decision to have no dealings with the League of Nations, and increasingly cooperated in the nonpolitical aspects of the League's activities. American delegates participated in such League-sponsored conferences as those on opium traffic control in 1924 and on tariff reform in 1927. By the beginning of the 1930s the United States had participated in more than thirty-five League conferences and was retaining a permanent corps of "unofficial observers" at League headquarters in Geneva, Switzerland.

The World Court. The Harding, Coolidge, and Hoover administrations all favored having the United States join the World Court that had been established by the League to arbitrate disputes submitted to it by contending members. In 1926, at the prompting of President Coolidge, the Senate approved the protocol of membership with five reservations, but not all these reservations were acceptable to the Court's member nations. In 1929 former secretary of state Elihu Root led in the formulation of a revised protocol that seemed more satisfactory, but the Senate refused to ratify the

Root formula. Although the United States never became a member of the World Court, during the 1920s the League of Nations Assembly appointed as judges to the Court two Americans, Columbia University professor John Bassett Moore and former secretary of state Charles Evans Hughes, both of whom served with distinction. After World War II the functions of the World Court were assumed by the International Court of Justice established under the United Nations. American membership in this court was promptly ratified by the Senate.

War Debts and Reparations. Relations with European nations during the 1920s were seriously affected by efforts to collect the sums which the United States had lent to the Allied governments during and immediately after World War I.

THE FOREIGN DEBT COMMISSION. Many Americans believed that the United States should cancel the war debts, since the Allies had used most of the money to buy war matériel from American firms in order to achieve victory not only for themselves but also for the United States. Congress, however, in 1922 created the Foreign Debt Commission, which negotiated agreements with the various nations on the basis of each debtor's ability to pay. The total indebtedness of seventeen nations was set at approximately $10.3 billion. Payments on the loans and accrued interest were spread over a period of sixty-two years.

THE DAWES PLAN. In 1921 the Allied Reparations Commission, set up under the Treaty of Versailles, had fixed Germany's obligation at approximately $33 billion. Although the United States refused to admit that payment of war debts was contingent upon collection of reparations from Germany to the Allies, this was in fact the case. After Germany defaulted on reparations payments, the United States in 1924 proposed, and the European governments accepted, the Dawes Plan. Named after Chicago banker Charles G. Dawes, it substantially reduced the German obligation, set up a new schedule of reparation payments, and advanced a loan to Germany.

THE YOUNG PLAN. As a result of eventual German objections to the operation of the Dawes Plan, revision of the reparations agreement became necessary. In 1929 a commission of experts, headed by American lawyer and businessman Owen D. Young, arranged new terms partially contingent upon the American policy concerning the reduction of Allied war debts. Called the Young Plan, it reduced the German obligation to $8 billion payable over a period of 58½ years. Further, it established a Bank for International Settlements to facilitate reparations payments and other processes of international finance.

THE HOOVER MORATORIUM. So alarming was the financial weakness of Germany in the worldwide depression that in 1931 President Herbert Hoover proposed a year's postponement on all war debts and reparations.

This moratorium was not extended in 1932, but several Allied nations failed to make payments on their debts to the United States, and after two more years all but one nation, Finland, defaulted. As for reparations, after 1931 Germany repudiated the remainder of the amount due. What with defaulting and repudiation, the United States ultimately collected approximately $2.3 billion in war debts and the Allies received about $4.5 billion in reparations from Germany.

The Antiwar Movement. After World War I there was among many nations a spirited crusade against war. Despite its isolationist attitude, the United States participated in several conferences designed to limit armaments and one conference called to outlaw war.

THE WASHINGTON CONFERENCE. At President Harding's invitation, representatives from Great Britain, France, Italy, Japan, China, Belgium, the Netherlands, and Portugal met in Washington from November, 1921, to February, 1922, to discuss reduction of naval armaments and issues relating to the Pacific. The conference drafted nine treaties, three of which were particularly significant. A five-power treaty was signed by the United States, Great Britain, Japan, France, and Italy, the world's leading naval powers, whereby they agreed to observe a ten-year "naval holiday" in the construction of capital ships (those over 10,000 tons) and to fix the tonnage of their capital ships at a ratio of 5 : 5 : 3 : 1.67 : 1.67 respectively. In order to conform to this ratio some ships already built or in construction by the signatories had to be scrapped. A four-power treaty bound the United States, Great Britain, France, and Japan as signatories to respect one another's possessions in the Pacific and to confer in the event that any issue threatened to disrupt harmonious relations in the area. A nine-power treaty, signed by all participants at the conference, guaranteed the political independence and territorial integrity of China and reaffirmed support of the open-door policy in that nation.

THE GENEVA NAVAL CONFERENCE. President Coolidge suggested that the signatories to the five-power treaty of the Washington Conference meet in Geneva, Switzerland, to consider limiting the construction of cruisers, destroyers, and submarines. France and Italy, however, declined to participate. In 1927 delegates from the United States, Great Britain, and Japan spent six weeks deliberating without coming to agreement on restricting these smaller vessels.

THE KELLOGG-BRIAND PACT. Developing from a suggestion of French Foreign Minister Aristide Briand that was supported by American Secretary of State Frank B. Kellogg, the pact was signed by fifteen nations in Paris in 1928. Ultimately forty-seven other nations became signatories. The covenant declared that the subscribers renounced war as an instrument of national policy and agreed to settle all disputes among themselves by peaceful means. Since no machinery was provided for its enforcement, the Kellogg-Briand Pact proved ineffective.

THE LONDON NAVAL CONFERENCE. The danger of a new race in naval armaments caused Great Britain to invite the United States, Japan, France, and Italy to participate in a naval disarmament conference in London in 1930. Soon France and Italy withdrew from the proceedings, dissatisfied. The United States, Great Britain, and Japan signed a treaty fixing ratios among themselves for cruisers, destroyers, and submarines, and extending to 1936 the naval holiday in the construction of capital ships as set by the Washington Conference.

THE GENERAL DISARMAMENT CONFERENCE. Representatives of thirty-one nations, including the United States, began meeting in Geneva early in 1932 to discuss general disarmament. An American proposal for the abolition of all offensive armaments failed to be adopted. After prolonged negotiations interspersed by two long adjournments, the conference came to an end in 1934, having achieved no success.

The Manchurian Crisis. Defying the Covenant of the League of Nations, treaties concluded at the Washington Conference, and the Kellogg-Briand Pact, Japan engaged in a military operation to secure control of Manchuria. The United States denounced the Japanese move but was unwilling to apply force to halt it.

JAPANESE AGGRESSION. In September, 1931, Japanese troops marched into and then occupied the Chinese province of Manchuria, using as a reason an explosion on the South Manchurian Railroad. Within a year Japan established there a puppet state called Manchukuo.

THE STIMSON DOCTRINE. In January, 1932, Hoover's secretary of state, Henry L. Stimson, in identical notes to Japan and China, declared that the United States would not recognize any agreement that impaired the political independence or territorial integrity of China or that adversely affected the open-door policy. This declaration of nonrecognition soon came to be known as the Stimson Doctrine.

THE LYTTON REPORT. Hoover announced that he would cooperate with the League of Nations in the Manchurian crisis, although he was opposed to the use of economic sanctions against Japan then being considered. In December, 1931, the League appointed the British Earl of Lytton chairman of a commission, which included an American representative, to investigate the whole matter. The commission's report condemned Japan but also proposed that Manchuria become an autonomous state under Chinese sovereignty but Japanese control. In February, 1933, the League adopted the Lytton Report, and the following month Japan gave notice of its withdrawal from the organization.

Relations with Latin America. Presidents Coolidge and Hoover tried to promote a better understanding between the republics of Latin America and the United States.

MEXICO. In the early 1920s first the Álvaro Obregón and then the Plutarco E. Calles adminstrations in Mexico made efforts to enforce a provision of the 1917 constitution that all mineral resources belonged to the people. American firms operating oil fields or mines in Mexico became alarmed. President Calles's decision in 1925 to dispossess all foreign oil and mining companies brought a warning from Secretary of State Frank B. Kellogg that "the government of Mexico is now on trial before the world." As tensions mounted, President Coolidge named his close friend, New York City banker Dwight W. Morrow, to be ambassador to Mexico. Morrow served from 1927 to 1930. His sympathetic and skillful handling of a sensitive situation won him acclaim both in the United States and Mexico, and he succeeded in securing satisfactory modifications of the Mexican Petroleum Law, which restricted foreign corporations. In addition, Morrow mediated a dispute between the Roman Catholic hierarchy in Mexico and the government arising out of legislation nationalizing church property.

PAN-AMERICAN CONFERENCES. At conferences of the American republics the United States engaged in conciliatory diplomacy toward its neighbors to the south. In 1923 a Pan-American Conference at Santiago, Chile, adopted a resolution that any dispute between republics of the Western Hemisphere should be settled by peaceful means, a principle the United States formally endorsed. In 1928 President Coolidge in an address opening a Pan-American Conference at Havana, Cuba, stated: "All nations here represented stand on an equal footing." The participating countries signed a treaty providing for the arbitration of virtually all types of disputes in the Western Hemisphere.

THE CLARK MEMORANDUM. In 1928 Under Secretary of State J. Reuben Clark drafted a memorandum that clarified the current American interpretation of the Monroe Doctrine. Approved by both the Coolidge and Hoover administrations, the Clark Memorandum declared that the United States would not again claim the right to intervene in the internal affairs of a Latin American country through "the exercise of an international police power," thus repudiating the Roosevelt Corollary to the Monroe Doctrine. The Clark Memorandum, which was published by the Hoover administration in 1930, was greeted with much satisfaction throughout Latin America.

RECOGNIZING NEW GOVERNMENTS. In 1931 Secretary of State Stimson declared that the United States would no longer use the criterion of moral basis, first employed by President Wilson, as a test for the diplomatic recognition of a new Latin American government.

Chapter 12

THE NEW DEAL

The economic expansion of the 1920s with its increasing production of goods and high profits culminated in an orgy of speculation that collapsed with disastrous results in 1929. It gradually became apparent that strong measures would be necessary to combat the depression that resulted. In accepting the presidential nomination of the Democratic party in 1932, Franklin D. Roosevelt pledged that if elected he would give the nation what he called a New Deal. Roosevelt assumed the presidency, and the New Deal attempted to cope with the emergency situation by engaging in experimental programs of relief and recovery. The New Deal also enacted long-range reform programs to promote the economic security and social welfare of the American people. In many ways the New Deal represented a continuation of the reform movement begun toward the end of the nineteenth century. But in one sense it did constitute a new direction in government policy; during the 1930s the government turned from a primarily restrictive and coercive philosophy to one of bold activism on behalf of the people.

In the realm of foreign affairs the Roosevelt administration immediately indicated it was eager to adopt a new policy toward Latin America—that of the "good neighbor."

THE GREAT DEPRESSION

The stock-market crash in late October, 1929, marked the beginning of the worst depression in the nation's history. It is commonly referred to as the Great Depression.

Hoover's Response. It was President Hoover's misfortune that his years in the White House coincided with the most difficult phase of the depression.

The President took the traditional American view that the surest and quickest way out of a depression was to rely mainly on individual initiative. He clung to the hope that self-help and private charity, with a minimum of governmental intervention, would restore more prosperous times. The federal government was not, however, entirely inactive. The Hoover administration tried several limited remedies which it believed would help businessmen, workers, and farmers.

THE RECONSTRUCTION FINANCE CORPORATION. Hoover finally accepted a plan to "pump" government funds into private business enterprise. In February, 1932, he signed the bill passed by Congress establishing the Reconstruction Finance Corporation (RFC) to provide government loans to banks, railroads, insurance companies, building and loan associations, and agricultural credit organizations. Former Vice-President Charles G. Dawes was appointed the chairman of the RFC, which lent $1.2 billion during its initial six months of operation.

THE RELIEF AND CONSTRUCTION ACT. Hoover and Congress yielded to the pressure for legislating funds for emergency relief. The Relief and Construction Act, signed into law in July, 1932, enlarged the range of activity of the RFC by authorizing it to grant approximately $2 billion to states and municipalities for construction of public buildings, aid to agriculture, and emergency relief.

THE FEDERAL HOME LOAN BANK ACT. This measure, passed by Congress in July, 1932, provided for the creation of eight to twelve home loan banks established in different sections of the nation to make loans to mortgage-lending institutions, permitting them in turn to encourage the purchase of private dwellings, thus stimulating construction and increasing employment.

The Effects of the Depression. The reversal in 1929 of the economic trend was at first regarded as merely temporary, but the nation slowly realized that it would be many years before the damage caused by excessive speculation could be repaired.

BUSINESS FAILURES. From 1929 to 1932 approximately 85,000 businesses failed, with assets totalling about $4.5 billion. A great number of the nation's industrial plants stood idle, their machines in disrepair and rusting.

UNEMPLOYMENT. Factories by the thousands locked their doors. By the end of 1931 almost 10 million workers were unemployed. During 1932 more than 4 million more were looking for jobs.

DECLINING INCOMES. The scope of the nation's suffering could be seen in the statistics of national income. In 1929 the total was $81 billion; in 1931 it fell to $53 billion; in 1932 it dropped to $41 billion. Savings in 9 million bank accounts were wiped out to meet current family expenses.

THE "BONUS ARMY." In late May, 1932, approximately 1,000 unemployed ex-servicemen of World War I converged on Washington, declaring that they would remain there until Congress authorized the immediate cash payment of the twenty-year bonus voted in 1924 for World War I veterans. Other veterans arrived in the city, bringing the total number to more than 15,000 by mid-June. By mid-July most of them had departed, but some 2,000 refused to disband. Believing that the "Bonus Army" might eventually resort to some kind of violence, President Hoover ordered the use of infantry, cavalry, and tank corps to drive it from the capital.

THE NADIR OF NATIONAL MORALE. Perhaps the most serious injury sustained by the American people was spiritual rather than material. In the descent from "riches to rags" many of them lost self-confidence and felt that the old values had been destroyed. Throughout the nation homeless men built shacks for themselves of flattened tin cans, cardboard, tar paper, and waste lumber, or they lived in abandoned factories or idle freight cars. In New York City homeless men slept in subway stations. A few in the nation died from starvation, but in every community voluntary charitable agencies tried to care for the hungry by setting up soup kitchens and bread lines. Churches and synagogues, community centers, welfare societies, the Red Cross, and the Salvation Army all attempted to help people. An apple shippers' association devised a plan to market their surplus fruit and at the same time to help the jobless. Soon thousands of apple vendors took charge of the organization's stands on the sidewalks of large cities. The operation brought a pittance to a few, but it chiefly became a symbol of the will of the people to survive on their own and of their reluctance to turn to the government for direct relief.

Election of 1932. With the Republican party handicapped by the generally accepted view that it was responsible for the depression, the Democratic candidate for president appeared a certain victor.

DEMOCRATS. The powerful drive by Governor Franklin D. Roosevelt of New York to become the Democratic presidential nominee had made such an impact that the only question in the minds of the delegates to the national convention was whether a combination could be effected to prevent him from securing the two-thirds vote required by the party's rules for the nomination. When the "stop Roosevelt" movement, led by former Democratic presidential candidate Alfred E. Smith collapsed, the New York governor was chosen on the fourth ballot. For second place on the ticket the delegates named Speaker of the House John N. Garner of Texas. The platform, which was an unusually brief and specific one, committed the party to the repeal of the Eighteenth (Prohibition) Amendment and to the principle of "continuous responsibility of government for human welfare."

REPUBLICANS. President Hoover controlled the proceedings of the Republican national convention. His nomination on the first ballot was quickly made unanimous, and in accordance with his wishes, Vice-President Charles Curtis was also renominated. The platform, drafted by Hoover and his aides, was adopted after a spirited battle over the prohibition plank, which as finally approved called for a referendum on the issue.

THE CAMPAIGN. Both Hoover and Roosevelt carried out extensive programs of speechmaking. Hoover defended his party's policies on the tariff, agricultural relief, and general economic recovery, and denounced the proposals of the opposition as demagogic appeals. Roosevelt stressed a "new deal" for the "forgotten man" without clearly indicating the specific measures of his program. He accused the Republicans of seeking prosperity by conferring favors on special interests and emphasized that the Democrats believed it the responsibility of government to promote the well-being of the great masses of the people.

ROOSEVELT'S LANDSLIDE VICTORY. The result at the polls was an unprecedented majority for the Democrats. In popular votes, Roosevelt won 22,830,000 to Hoover's 15,761,000. Roosevelt captured forty-two states with 472 electoral votes while Hoover carried four of the New England states, Pennsylvania, and Delaware, with a total of 59 electoral votes. The victory represented not so much a vote of confidence in the Democratic party and its leaders as a measure of resentment, engendered by the depression, against the Hoover administration.

THE FIRST NEW DEAL

On March 9, 1933, Congress met in a special session called by President Roosevelt to deal with what seemed to be the impending collapse of the American banking system. After Congress passed an emergency act on banking it remained in special session, upon Roosevelt's request, to treat a variety of economic ills, including unemployment among laborers and falling prices for farmers. This session came to a close on June 16, 1933, after enacting a host of measures deemed essential by the Roosevelt administration. The March 9 to June 16 special session of Congress, soon called the "Hundred Days," was a remarkable period of cooperation between the executive and legislative branches of government. The Hundred Days launched the First New Deal, which had as its objective the relief and recovery, and then the reform, of the various economic sectors of the nation.

The Roosevelt Administration. Roosevelt was an unabashed activist in the office of the presidency. He believed deeply in the government's responsibility to insure to the utmost the economic and social well-being of the people of the United States.

THE PRESIDENT. Roosevelt was an extraordinarily adroit politician. Over the radio on many an evening he spoke in a relaxed style to the American people in "fireside chats." As an orator he had few equals. He was not the first president to agree to press conferences, but he held them more often and, through his masterful give-and-take with reporters, used them more skillfully than had any of his predecessors to present his views to the American people. Although confined to a wheelchair since 1921 as a result of an attack of polio (wearing heavy leg braces he was able to take a few steps and stand to deliver an address), he exhibited striking self-assurance and unlimited mental and physical energy.

INAUGURAL ADDRESS. Between Roosevelt's election in November, 1932, and his inauguration in March, 1933, economic conditions had steadily worsened. His inaugural address, however, sounded a high note of confidence. He declared in ringing tones that "the only thing we have to fear is fear itself," and pledged strong executive leadership to resolve the grave economic conditions.

THE CABINET. Roosevelt chose the members of his cabinet with considerable care and skill. Democratic Senator Cordell Hull of Tennessee, a powerful legislative leader, became secretary of state. Henry Morgenthau, Jr., of New York, a specialist in agriculture and a close friend of the President's, soon joined the cabinet as head of the Department of the Treasury. Harold L. Ickes of Illinois, a former liberal Republican who had become a Democrat, was appointed secretary of the interior and immediately began to bring reforming zeal into his department. Frances Perkins, who had been an adviser to Roosevelt on social legislation when he was governor of New York, became secretary of labor; she was the first woman to hold a cabinet post.

THE "BRAIN TRUST." During his early years in office Roosevelt consulted on matters of economic and social reform a group of unofficial advisers that newspaper reporters dubbed the "Brain Trust" because its members were academicians. Particularly influential in the Brain Trust were Columbia University professors Raymond Moley, Adolph A. Berle, Jr., and Rexford Tugwell.

The New Deal Philosophy. Much of Roosevelt's approach to the difficult problems of the depression was pure experimentation, but the experiments he tried convinced him that the best course for the nation was away from traditional principles of economic individualism toward a planned economy. Roosevelt and his associates in the administration maintained that by such planning it was possible to establish an enduring balance in the economic system among conflicting sectors of the nation.

The watchwords of the New Deal were *relief, recovery, reform*. The mission of the New Deal lay in, first, relief to persons in need by providing them with money, loans to make mortgage payments, or jobs; second, recovery to the nation as a whole by passing legislation to assist business, labor, and agriculture to reestablish themselves in strength; third, reform of institutions, such as banking, to make for economic and social stability.

Relief for the Unemployed. Any attempt to remedy the fundamental economic and social weaknesses within the nation had to wait until emergency measures could meet the immediate needs of a discouraged people, many of whom were destitute.

CIVILIAN CONSERVATION CORPS (CCC). A dramatic relief measure was the Unemployment Relief Act, passed in March, 1933, that created the Civilian Conservation Corps to provide work for men between the ages of eighteen and twenty-five. They were employed in such projects as reforestation, soil conservation, flood control, and road construction throughout the nation. By the end of 1941 more than 2 million young men had been employed by the CCC.

FEDERAL EMERGENCY RELIEF ADMINISTRATION (FERA). This agency was established by the Federal Emergency Relief Act in May, 1933, to assist states and cities in caring for the unemployed. Under the direction of Harry L. Hopkins, an adviser and close friend of Roosevelt's, the FERA matched the funds expended by state and municipal governments in administering their relief projects for the jobless.

CIVIL WORKS ADMINISTRATION (CWA). Created in November, 1933, the Civil Works Administration, headed by Hopkins, provided jobs for approximately 4 million men in such undertakings as road repair and park improvement. The CWA was disbanded the following year and its functions were assumed by the Federal Emergency Relief Administration.

Recovery in Business. The Roosevelt administration made strong legislative moves to help business.

THE NATIONAL INDUSTRIAL RECOVERY ACT (NIRA). Passed in June, 1933, the National Industrial Recovery Act (NIRA) was intended to help business revival by means of self-regulation and in so doing lessen unemployment. The act created the National Recovery Administration (NRA), which supervised the preparation of codes of fair competition by employers, employees, and consumers in each industry. After the codes received the approval of the President, they became binding upon every segment of the industry in question, and were to be enforced by law. The codes accomplished such objectives as the abolition of child labor, the limiting of production, the control of prices, and the establishment of minimum wages and maximum hours for workers. Hundreds of these codes were administered by the NRA under the chairmanship of the iron-willed former brigadier general Hugh Johnson, but few proved effective. Participating firms within each industry displayed the Blue Eagle (symbol of the NRA) and used the motto of the agency, "We do our part." Organized labor achieved a long-standing goal through the NIRA, for Section 7a of the act guaranteed workers the right to bargain collectively. Approximately 500 industries had adopted fair competition codes and were operating under them when in 1935 the Supreme Court declared the NIRA unconstitutional on the grounds that it granted the President too much power and that it dealt in commercial activities that were intrastate in nature.

PUBLIC WORKS ADMINISTRATION (PWA). The NIRA established the Public Works Administration (PWA) for the construction of roads, school buildings, hospitals, dams, bridges, and a variety of other projects to stimulate the economy. The agency cooperated with state and local governments in the granting of contracts to private firms. Under the direction of Secretary of the Interior Ickes, from 1933 to 1939 the PWA spent approximately $5 billion on close to 35,000 construction projects, employing more than 500,000 people.

Recovery in Agriculture. Legislation was sponsored by the Roosevelt administration to strengthen the status of agriculture and to prevent the loss of farms by debt-ridden owners.

THE AGRICULTURAL ADJUSTMENT ACT. This measure, passed in May, 1933, was designed to help farmers gain higher profits by encouraging them to reduce their production, which would in turn decrease their surpluses and thus raise the prices of their goods. It was hoped that through this action the farmers' purchasing power would be restored to parity with that of the prosperous and relatively stable five-year period before the outbreak of World War I. The act created the Agricultural Adjustment Administration (AAA), which was authorized (1) to control production of such commodities as wheat, cotton, corn, rice, tobacco, and hogs by paying cash subsidies to farmers who voluntarily restricted acreage planted in such crops or reduced the numbers of such livestock; (2) to impose taxes upon the processors of agricultural commodities—such as flour millers and meat packers—in order to secure funds to pay the subsidies; (3) to pay farmers to sow grasses on untilled land that would provide cover for top soil and prevent dust storms. The act remained in operation until 1936, when it was declared unconstitutional by the Supreme Court.

THE FARM CREDIT ACT. This act, passed in June, 1933, set up the Farm Credit Administration (FCA) to provide loans to farmers for production and marketing, with the object of enabling them to refinance farm mortgages that were in jeopardy of being lost through foreclosures. Within the first two years of its existence the agency helped refinance approximately 20 percent of the farm mortgages in the nation.

THE FRAZIER-LEMKE FARM BANKRUPTCY ACT. This measure, passed in June, 1934, provided for a five-year postponement on the foreclosure of farm mortgages, during which time a farmer in default of his payments could repurchase his property at a reappraised price. When the Supreme Court invalidated the act the following year, Congress passed (August, 1935) the second Frazier-Lemke Act, which allowed for only a three-year moratorium on farm mortgage foreclosures and for a more precise guarantee of the rights of the lending institutions.

Recovery in Housing. The Roosevelt administration sponsored legislation to prevent the loss of homes by financially distressed owners, to encourage the building of new homes and the improvement of existing ones, and to establish a stable procedure for home financing.

HOME OWNERS LOAN CORPORATION (HOLC). This agency, created in June, 1933, was provided with more than $2 billion to refinance the mortgages of nonfarm homeowners who were threatened with losing their properties through foreclosures. The HOLC was in existence for three years, during which time it aided approximately 1 million homeowners.

FEDERAL HOUSING ADMINISTRATION (FHA). This agency was established by the National Housing Act in June, 1934, to insure mortgages made by private lending institutions for the building of new homes and the improvement of existing homes. By 1941 the government had insured $3.5 billion in mortgages.

Reform in Banking. While Congress was enacting the various measures that constituted a program of relief for the unemployed and recovery in business, agriculture, and housing, it was also considering legislation to bring about long-range reforms in banking.

THE EMERGENCY BANKING ACT. Numerous demands upon banks for the payment of money had forced thousands to suspend operations by the time Roosevelt assumed office. Fearful that the banking system was on the verge of collapse, Roosevelt, on March 5, 1933, declared an immediate four-day bank holiday which closed all national banks and financial institutions affiliated with them. All on the single day of March 9, 1933, there was introduced, passed, and signed into law the Emergency Banking Act, empowering the President to reorganize insolvent national banks. Under the terms of the measure a majority of the banks soon reopened.

THE GLASS-STEAGALL BANKING ACT. Passed in June, 1933, this significant reform law, among other things, (1) separated commercial banking from investment banking;[1] (2) increased the authority of the Federal Reserve Board to prevent member banks of the Federal Reserve System from engaging in excessive speculation; (3) created the Federal Deposit Insurance Corporation (FDIC) to guarantee bank deposits up to $5,000 each (subsequent legislation increased the sum) in the event of the failure of the institution.

THE SECURITIES EXCHANGE ACT. This measure, passed in June, 1934, provided for the regulation of securities exchanges in order to protect the purchasers of stocks and bonds against fraudulent practices. The Securities Exchange Act set up the five-member Securities Exchange Commission (SEC) to register and supervise the sale of new issues of stocks and bonds and authorized the Federal Reserve Board to control the buying of stocks and bonds on margin.[2]

[1] A specialization primarily in the buying and selling of large blocks of securities.
[2] Making partial payment of the purchase price.

THE BANKING ACT. This measure, passed in August, 1935, strengthened government control of the banking system of the nation through a revision of the Federal Reserve Act of 1913. The new law, among other things, (1) changed the title of the Federal Reserve Board to the Board of Governors of the Federal Reserve System, increased its bipartisan membership of financial experts from six to seven, and enlarged its power over the twelve Federal Reserve Banks; (2) required that all state banks with deposits of $1 million or more join the Federal Reserve System within seven years in order to have their deposits guaranteed by the Federal Deposit Insurance Corporation; (3) permitted the Federal Reserve Banks to purchase government bonds only in open-market transactions.

The Government as Regional Developer. An earlier demand for a relatively simple plan of government production of electric power led eventually to a rather complex program of government participation in regional development.

BACKGROUND. In the 1920s the advocates of government ownership and operation of electric power facilities concentrated their efforts upon Muscle Shoals, a gigantic project on the Tennessee River that had been built by the government during World War I to produce hydroelectric power and extract nitrate for the manufacturing of explosives. In 1928 liberal Republican Senator George Norris of Nebraska guided a bill through Congress that provided for the creation of a government-owned corporation to work the nitrate plants for the production of fertilizer and to sell the surplus power generated at the hydroelectric station. President Coolidge vetoed the bill on the ground that the government operation would compete with private enterprise. In 1931 a virtually identical bill passed Congress, only to be vetoed by President Hoover on the same ground.

THE TENNESSEE VALLEY AUTHORITY ACT. In May, 1933, President Roosevelt signed into law with much enthusiasm the Tennessee Valley Authority Act, marking the triumph of Senator Norris's attempt to place the power resources of the Tennessee River at the disposal of the people. The act established the Tennessee Valley Authority (TVA), an independent public corporation created not only to work the power project at Muscle Shoals but also, much more important, to develop fully a region embracing parts of seven states—Tennessee, Virginia, Kentucky, North Carolina, Georgia, Alabama, and Mississippi—for the economic and social well-being of the people. Through the construction of dams, power plants, and transmission lines, many villages and farms in the Tennessee River Valley were supplied with electric current at low rates. TVA electric rates served as a "yardstick" to measure the reasonableness of rates charged by utilities companies. Some other important projects of TVA were the implementation of a program of flood control, the improvement of navigation on the Tennessee River and its tributaries, and the production of nitrate fertilizer. The standard of living of the approximately 3 million inhabitants of the Tennessee

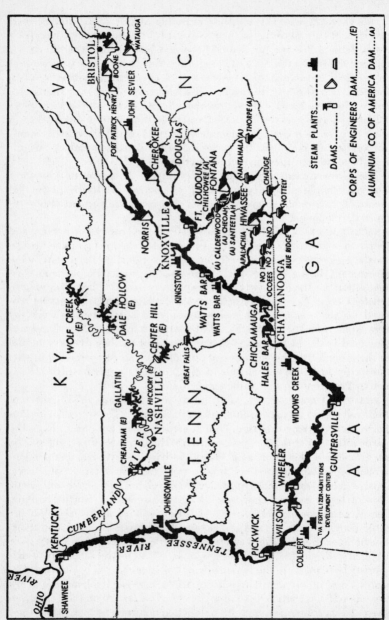

Tennessee Valley Authority—1959

River Vally was quickly raised. During World War II TVA generated hydroelectric power for the production of the atomic bomb at the government installation in Oak Ridge, Tennessee. Since the establishment of TVA representatives of big business and conservative politicians have called for the disbanding of the agency on the ground that it competes with private enterprise, but to no avail.

The Tariff Issue. As American exports increased rapidly, exceeding imports, nations in debt to the United States as a result of borrowing during World War I found it difficult to make payments for goods bought on credit.

TARIFF WARS. When the Smoot-Hawley Tariff, with an average duty of approximately 60 percent, was signed by President Hoover, there were protests from all parts of the world. More than thirty nations struck back at the excessively high rates by increasing their rates on goods from the United States. Many nations passed acts placing all sorts of restrictions on the passage of American-made goods through their customhouses.

THE TRADE AGREEMENTS ACT. Secretary of State Cordell Hull feared not only the economic but also the political effects of tariff wars. He therefore proposed the adoption of reciprocal trade agreements with those nations that traded most extensively with the United States. In 1934 Congress passed the reciprocal Trade Agreements Act, empowering the President, with the advice of economic experts, to negotiate with other nations agreements that revised tariff rates up to 50 percent in either direction without the consent of Congress. By 1950 agreements had been reached with some fifty nations in Europe, Asia, and Latin America. By the time the United States next engaged in extensive tariff legislation, in 1962, the average duty was approximately 10 percent.

THE SECOND NEW DEAL

Shortly after the Roosevelt administration received a tremendous vote of confidence from the American people in the congressional elections of 1934, it indicated that it was intent upon sponsoring a group of new projects to help the underprivileged throughout the nation. In his State of the Union Message to Congress, delivered in January, 1935, President Roosevelt declared that his administration was ready to implement a comprehensive program of social reform, having as its basic objective to provide security against unemployment, illness, the cares of old age, and the uncertainty of dependency upon family or friends. This plan of action soon became known as the Second New Deal.

New Directions. Whereas the First New Deal had instituted projects to help businessmen, laborers, and farmers, the Second New Deal gave assistance almost exclusively to laborers and farmers. In attempting to realize a fuller program of social action, the Second New Deal was decidedly more to the left in spirit than the First New Deal had been.

CRITICISM OF THE NEW DEAL. That many businessmen by mid-1934 began to resist what they considered the "radical" policies of the New Deal was an indication that the economy was heading in the direction of normality. Complaints increased that the Roosevelt administration was undermining the capitalist system with its bold experimentation. Conservatives charged that the government was destroying private enterprise through interference in every phase of business activity.

POLITICAL ENDORSEMENT OF THE NEW DEAL. Whatever the effects of New Deal acts, they were approved by the labor and farm vote in the congressional elections of 1934. In the new Seventy-fourth Congress the Roosevelt administration increased a dominant strength it already enjoyed in the legislative branch. In the Senate the Democratic majority went from 59 to 69 out of 96 members, while in the House of Representatives the number of Democrats rose from 313 to 323 out of 435 members. Although the administration sometimes experienced difficulty in maintaining unity of action among the Democrats, it met with no serious reversals in guiding the presidential program of legislation through the new session of Congress.

The Seventy-fourth Congress was the first to meet under the terms of the Twentieth Amendment to the Constitution, passed by Congress in 1932 and ratified in 1933. The amendment stipulated that Congress convene each year on January 3, thus abolishing the previous short session of Congress, in which "lame duck" legislators (those defeated for reelection and those choosing to retire) would remain in Congress for the special session that began in December and lasted until the following March 4. The amendment also specified that the president and vice-president take office on January 20 following their election rather than, as had previously been the practice, on March 4.

Election of 1936.
In a campaign marked by a vigorous defense and a bitter denunciation of the New Deal, Roosevelt won a strong reelection victory.

DEMOCRATS. There were no surprises at the Democratic national convention. President Roosevelt and Vice-President Garner were renominated without opposition.

REPUBLICANS. The delegates to the Republican national convention began their proceedings with little confidence that their candidate for president, whoever he might be, could beat Roosevelt in the coming election. The convention chose for its standard-bearer the rather liberal Republican Governor Alfred M. Landon of Kansas. Chicago newspaper publisher Frank Knox was named Landon's running mate.

THE CAMPAIGN. The candidates avoided such deep basic issues separating their parties as the philosophy underlying direct federal benefits, the centralization of power in the national government, the delegation of unusual authority to the President, and the relation of a heavily unbalanced budget to the economy of the nation. The Democrats were content to defend their record. The Republicans denounced the Roosevelt administration for reckless experimentation, extravagant spending, unbridled use of patronage, and failure to suppress communism. The conduct of the campaign by the Republicans was hesitant and inept, sharply contrasting with the assurance and proficiency of the politicians who managed the Democratic campaign. Roosevelt skillfully carried the brunt of the battle for his party, while Landon proved a dull campaigner both in his personal appearances and in his radio speeches.

ROOSEVELT'S LANDSLIDE VICTORY. The vote for the President cut across party lines. He was reelected with 27,757,000 popular votes to Landon's 16,684,000. Roosevelt carried every state except Maine and Vermont, thus capturing 523 out of 531 electoral votes.

Relief for the Unemployed.

On the basis of the experience secured from the Civil Works Administration of 1933–1934, the Roosevelt administration put a more comprehensive plan into operation early in 1935 to overcome persistent unemployment.

WORKS PROGRESS ADMINISTRATION (WPA). In April, 1935, Congress passed the Emergency Relief Appropriation Act, which signified a turning by the federal government from direct relief to work relief alone. The act established the Works Progress Administration (WPA), a name that was changed to the Works Projects Administration in 1939. Harold L. Ickes of the Public Works Administration and Harry L. Hopkins of the Federal Emergency Relief Administration each wanted to administer the new agency; Roosevelt chose Hopkins, in large part because he was more inclined to spend large sums and less heedful of stringent rules. Within six months of its creation the WPA was employing approximately 2.5 million manual laborers on such projects as the construction or improvement of roads, school buildings, hospitals, power plants, bridges, and parks. The WPA also provided work for the skilled and educated—artists, musicians, people of the theater, writers, teachers—by creating the Federal Art Project, the Federal Theater Project, and the Federal Writers' Project. For example, under the auspices of the Federal Art Project murals were painted in public buildings and under the auspices of the Federal Writers' Project state and local histories were written. By the time the WPA was terminated in 1943, it had spent approximately $11 billion on close to 1.5 million projects and in so doing had given temporary jobs to about 8.5 million persons. In spite of its achievements, the WPA was criticized by many conservative Americans as being wasteful and inefficient.

NATIONAL YOUTH ADMINISTRATION (NYA). Established by executive order in June, 1935, under the provisions of the Emergency Relief Appropriation Act, the National Youth Administration (NYA) gave part-time employment to needy persons between the ages of sixteen and twenty-five in high schools, colleges, and universities so that they could continue their education. More than 4 million unemployed young people had been helped by the time the NYA was disbanded in 1943.

Recovery in Labor. The Roosevelt administration was extremely supportive of organized labor's aspirations for a higher status in American society. The New Deal gained some of its most substantial victories in the field of labor legislation. Changes within the labor movement itself had great influence on the principles written into that legislation.

THE CONGRESS OF INDUSTRIAL ORGANIZATIONS. The activity of labor organizers in the early 1930s raised anew the issue of bringing into organized labor unskilled industrial workers. Within the American Federation of Labor certain unions sponsored industrial unionism as opposed to craft unionism. The most notable of those unions were the United Mine Workers under John L. Lewis, the Amalgamated Clothing Workers of America under Sidney Hillman, the International Ladies' Garment Workers Union under David Dubinsky, and the International Typographical Union under Charles Howard.

At the 1935 national convention of the AFL the organization's president, William Green, and his associates blocked Lewis's attempt to commit the AFL to industrial unionism. A majority of the delegates favored the traditional structure based upon representation of the skilled crafts. However, eight unions that were affiliated with the AFL formed the Committee for Industrial Organization (CIO). Under the leadership of Lewis and his mine workers, the CIO defied the executive committee of the AFL and proceeded to organize along industrial union lines the automotive and steel industries. The CIO soon secured partial recognition from the General Motors Corporation and several subsidiaries of the United States Steel Corporation. In 1937 the AFL expelled the ten unions that were by then within the CIO, which was reorganized the following year as the Congress of Industrial Organizations. (In 1955, after years of discussion, the AFL and the CIO merged into a powerful 15 million-member ogranization.)

MANAGEMENT-LABOR STRIFE. The vigorous efforts of the CIO to organize workers in the automobile and steel industries brought strikes marked by violence. In the automobile industry dissatisfied workers used a new weapon—the sit-down strike. They refused to leave plants against which their unions had called a work stoppage. The use of the sit-down strike spread rapidly to workers in many other industries. When employers began to use force to evict workers engaged in sit-down strikes, the labor organizers condoned meeting force with force. (In 1939 the Supreme Court declared the sit-down strike illegal.) The firing by police upon union demonstraters in front of a steel plant in South Chicago in May, 1937, led to a pitched battle between the two groups in which ten men were killed.

SECTION 7a OF THE NATIONAL INDUSTRIAL RECOVERY ACT. Despite outbursts of violence, organized labor made great gains in winning public support and in the recognition of its rights by employers. According to Section 7a of the National Industrial Recovery Act of 1933, labor was guaranteed the right "to organize and bargain collectively through representatives of their own choosing." This provision stimulated the growth of unions, greatly increasing their membership.

THE NATIONAL LABOR RELATIONS ACT. After the NIRA was declared unconstitutional by the Supreme Court in 1935, Senator Robert F. Wagner of New York initiated legislation to guarantee labor's right to bargain collectively. The result was the National Labor Relations Act (also called the Wagner-Connery Act), passed by Congress in July, 1935. The act created the National Labor Relations Board (NLRB), composed of three members, which was authorized to determine suitable units for collective bargaining, to conduct elections for the choice of labor's representatives, and to prevent interference with such elections. The NLRB was empowered to investigate complaints of unfair labor practices, to issue orders that such practices be stopped, and to petition federal courts to enforce its restraining orders. The NLRB's work was made difficult by the hostility of employers, who felt that the National Labor Relations Act benefited the working class unfairly over the business class, and by the quarrel within the ranks of labor between the AFL and the CIO.

THE FAIR LABOR STANDARDS ACT. This act, passed by Congress in June, 1938, was designed as a substitute for the codes of the disbanded NRA as they concerned fair labor standards. For each industry engaged in interstate commerce, a committee composed of employers and employees was to recommend a minimum wage—not less than twenty-five cents an hour, to be raised to forty cents by 1945—compatible with economic conditions in that industry and to establish over a period of time a forty-hour workweek. The act required payment for work over forty hours in a week at the rate of time and a half, prohibited the labor of children under sixteen years of age, and restricted the labor of those under eighteen to nonhazardous jobs.

Recovery in Agriculture. The problem of farmers trying to make a living on inferior land was a constant concern of the Roosevelt administration.

RESETTLEMENT ADMINISTRATION (RA). Established in May, 1935, under the provisions of the Emergency Relief Appropriation Act, the Resettlement Administration (RA) assisted farm families to move from submarginal to fertile land and extended loans at low interest rates to enable particularly needy farm families to purchase new land and equipment. Within four years almost 800,000 families had received rehabilitation aid. Also, under the auspices of the RA a few suburban communities were built for low-income city families.

THE SOIL CONSERVATION AND DOMESTIC ALLOTMENT ACT. This act was passed in February, 1936, soon after the Agricultural Adjustment Act of 1933 was declared unconstitutional. It attempted to curtail agricultural production not through a program of crop control (as under the Agricultural Adjustment Act) but through one of soil conservation. The act authorized the payment of cash subsidies to farmers for planting crops, such as alfalfa and clover, that would conserve the soil. This would curtail production of staple crops, such as wheat, cotton, corn, and tobacco, which deplete the soil, and would have the ultimate result of raising agricultural prices.

THE BANKHEAD-JONES FARM TENANT ACT. The work of the Resettlement Administration was assumed by the Farm Security Administration (FSA), established by the Bankhead-Jones Farm Tenant Act, passed in July, 1937. The FSA granted loans at low interest rates to tenant farmers, share croppers, and farm laborers so that they could purchase their own land. In addition, the FSA carried out a program of aid to migrant workers and experimented with the resettlement of rural groups in cooperative communities.

THE AGRICULTURAL ADJUSTMENT ACT. With the Agricultural Adjustment Act of 1933 declared unconstitutional by the Supreme Court and with the Soil Conservation and Domestic Allotment Act proving ineffectual, Congress passed in February, 1938, a second Agricultural Adjustment Act in another attempt to decrease agricultural surpluses and thus increase agricultural prices. The secretary of agriculture was authorized (1) to set acreage quotas for staple crops and pay farmers cash subsidies for planting in their stead soil-conserving crops; (2) to set marketing quotas for export crops that were in surplus to such a degree that the prices for them might be adversely affected. The act also implemented the "ever-normal granary" plan, sponsored by Secretary of Agriculture Henry A. Wallace, which operated as follows: a Community Credit Corporation would store crops that were in surplus to prevent a decline in prices and at the same time grant loans to farmers on the stored crops as a substitute for the profits that would have been realized by selling them, the loans to be repaid when the price of the crops rose and the farmers removed them from storage and sold them at a satisfactory profit. The financing of the various aspects of the program was to be derived from the federal treasury, rather than from taxes imposed upon the processors of farm commodities as in the act of 1933.

Security for the Needy. In what was to be one of its most far-reaching enterprises, the Roosevelt administration launched the government into assuming a duty (for all time to come) to insure the security of the needy people of the nation.

EXTREMIST PROPOSALS. One of the reasons for Roosevelt's strong support of attempts to give the people greater security was the appeal of several extremist proposals by groups that were hostile toward the Roosevelt administration. The Share-Our-Wealth movement, led by Democratic Senator Huey P. Long of Louisiana, advocated that the federal government guarantee to every family of the nation a homestead worth $5,000 and a minimum annual income of $2,000. The Old Age Revolving Pension plan, originated by Dr. Francis E. Townsend, a California physician, recommended that the federal government pay $200 a month to persons sixty years of age and over, who would be obligated to spend the entire sum within the month. The National Union for Social Justice, headed by the Reverend Charles E. Coughlin, a Michigan Roman Catholic priest who made effective use of the radio to spread his views, urged that the currency be extensively inflated through the use of silver.

THE SOCIAL SECURITY ACT. This act, passed by Congress in August, 1935, upon the recommendation of President Roosevelt, provided for (1) a federal program of benefits to retired workers beginning at the age of sixty-five and of benefits to the dependent survivors of deceased workers, based on the employees' earnings before the age of sixty-five, to be paid out of funds derived from a tax on employees and their employers; (2) a program of unemployment compensation administered by the state with grants from the federal government and financed by a similar payroll tax; (3) federal aid to the states for various projects, such as maternity and infant care services and assistance to crippled children and the blind.

Other Reform Measures. Among the wide range of acts passed during the New Deal were some measures that were designed to benefit consumers and reform the workings of government.

THE FOOD, DRUG, AND COSMETIC ACT. This measure, passed in 1938, extended the provisions of the Pure Food and Drug Act. It forbade manufacturers of foods, drugs, and cosmetics (1) to misbrand products; (2) to sell products without listing their ingredients on the containers' labels; (3) to engage in false advertising.

THE CIVIL AERONAUTICS ACT. This act, passed in 1938, created the Civil Aeronautics Authority, which two years later was renamed the Civil Aeronautics Board (CAB), composed of five members appointed by the President with the approval of the Senate. The CAB was authorized, among other things, to (1) regulate the economic aspects of American aviation service, including the charging of fares; (2) advise the State Department in its negotiations with foreign countries for the establishment of international standards of aviation activities; (3) investigate aviation accidents.

THE ADMINISTRATIVE REORGANIZATION ACT. This measure, passed in 1939, was designed to regroup the many independent units of the federal government in order to improve the efficiency of the executive branch. An executive order established the Federal Security Agency, the Federal Works Agency, and the Federal Loan Agency, the three of which along with the Executive Office of the President, assumed control of most of the independent units of the government.

THE HATCH ACT. This act, passed in 1939, forbade federal officeholders who were not on the policy-making level to participate in political campaigns or solicit contributions from people on work relief.

Roosevelt and the Supreme Court. The executive and legislative branches of the government seemed to be in substantial agreement regarding the need for the laws that comprised the recovery and reform programs of the New Deal. It remained for the Supreme Court to decide the constitutionality of the legislation sponsored by the Roosevelt administration.

INVALIDATION OF NEW DEAL LAWS. Decisions of the Supreme Court from the last third of the nineteenth century on indicated that most justices were opposed to the government's increasing its role in economic affairs and were reluctant to sanction government-fostered social improvements that restricted individual initiative. The Court soon showed its hostility toward much of the New Deal reform legislation. In 1935 in *Schechter* v. *United States* (the "Sick Chicken Case") the Court declared the National Industrial Recovery Act of 1933 unconstitutional on the grounds that it delegated too much power to the President and that it dealt in intrastate commerce. The Court held that a Brooklyn poultry dealer could not be prosecuted for violating National Recovery Administration codes governing the quality of chickens he sold and the level of wages he paid. The justices agreed unanimously that since the retail poultry business was not interstate commerce, Congress had no jurisdication over it. Roosevelt angrily retorted that this was a "horse-and-buggy" definition of interstate commerce. In 1936 in *United States* v. *Butler* the Court by a 6 to 3 vote declared the Agricultural Adjustment Act of 1933 unconstitutional on the grounds that Congress possessed no authority to tax for the benefit of a particular segment of society and that the regulation of agriculture was within the jurisdiction of the state governments. In addition, the Court invalidated two other pieces of legislation, the Frazier-Lemke Farm Bankruptcy Act of 1934 and the Guffey-Snyder Bituminous Coal Stabilization Act of 1935, which dealt with the recovery of the bituminous coal mining industry.

THE "COURT PACKING" PLAN. Despite his anger and his fear that the judicial branch would invalidate much New Deal legislation, Roosevelt postponed action until after the 1936 election. He then chose to interpret his overwhelming victory, which cut across party lines, as a blanket endorsement of his policies and quickly made plans to circumvent the Supreme Court. Because six of the nine justices were over seventy, the President struck at them as too old to remain on the bench. He also charged that the Court was violating the Constitution by acting as a "policy-making body." But he avoided a careful analysis of the basis of its decisions.

In February, 1937, Roosevelt submitted to Congress a bill called the Reorganization Plan, which was quickly labeled by its foes as the "Court Packing" Bill. It proposed the appointment of additional judges in the various federal courts where there were incumbent judges of recommended retirement age who did not choose to resign. In the case of the Supreme Court the recommended retirement age was to be seventy years, and the President was to appoint not more than six additional members to supplement nonretiring justices. The storm over the Reorganization Plan so agitated the Senate that the administration could not persuade conservative Democrats to support the measure in that body. This marked the first clear division between the conservative and liberal wings of the party since Roosevelt took office. After the sudden death of Democratic Senator Joseph T. Robinson of Arkansas, who had been directing parliamentary tactics on the Reorganization Plan, Roosevelt reluctantly abandoned the contest.

REVERSAL OF THE COURT. In the end the President won the fight with the Supreme Court. In the spring of 1937 the Court sustained several major New Deal laws, among them the Social Security Act of 1935 and the National Labor Relations Act of 1935. Also in 1937 the Court overruled earlier decisions by upholding a state minimum wage law. From 1937 to 1939 retirements from and deaths on the Court enabled Roosevelt to appoint four well-known supporters of the New Deal, bringing about such a change in the Court's membership that a reversal occurred in its interpretation of congressional powers over economic and social matters. By 1941 Roosevelt had named seven of the nine justices. With the retirement that year of the moderate Chief Justice Charles Evans Hughes, the President elevated the liberal Associate Justice Harlan F. Stone to the position. Among the legislation sustained by the Court with its new members were the Fair Labor Standards Act of 1938 and the Agricultural Adjustment Act of 1938.

EVALUATION OF THE NEW DEAL

The years of the New Deal constituted one of the most controversial periods in the nation's history. The ardent supporters of the New Deal thought it could do no wrong, while its critics believed that it was destroying the traditional American way of life.

The Financial Cost. The New Deal's elaborate spending programs to bring about relief and the granting of extensive loans to private enterprise to promote recovery placed an extraordinary financial burden upon the federal government. The Roosevelt administration tried to increase the annual tax revenues. Congress reluctantly yielded to presidential insistence and passed the Revenue Act of 1935, which increased the rates of taxation on individual incomes over $50,000, on gifts, on estates, on corporate earnings, and on excess profits. But taxation did not provide sufficient revenue to pay for the experiments of the New Deal. In 1933 the debt of the United States had stood at approximately $22.5 billion. Six years later it had increased to almost $40.5 billion. Thus deficit financing[3] had almost doubled the national debt in six years. However, later defenders of the New Deal pointed out that this rapid increase of the national debt was slight in comparison to the crushing burden of debt piled up during World War II.

A Continuation of Reform. In many ways Roosevelt's program was a continuation of the reform movement that had been interrupted by the outbreak of World War I. There were precedents from both Democratic and Republican administrations. The New Deal regulation of business extended some of the principles laid down in the Interstate Commerce Act of 1887, signed into law by a Democratic president, and the Sherman Antitrust Act of 1890, signed by a Republican president. Much of the New Deal farm relief program was foreshadowed by proposals to aid agriculture during the Wilson administration. There were borrowings from the Populists of the latter part of the nineteenth century and the progressives of the early twentieth century. Roosevelt's attacks on the leaders of industry as "economic royalists" were reminiscent of those conducted against the "money power" by the Populists and the progressives, and a number of New Deal reforms had first been demanded by those groups.

A New Direction in Government Policy. To most citizens the New Deal revealed the federal government in an entirely new role; government policy was not merely a restrictive and coercive force but an instrument to enable a democracy to solve its problems with speed and decision. Many believed that the New Deal was primarily a vital agency in providing economic security for all the people.

The Interruption of Reform. Roosevelt was still urging further reforms to strengthen the nation when war was thrust upon Europe by the Nazi dictatorship in 1939. Whether the voluminous legislation of the New Deal would have solved the economic and social problems exposed by the Great Depression was never determined, for recovery and reform programs were interrupted by World War II.

TOWARD SOLIDARITY WITH LATIN AMERICA

The Roosevelt administration used its influence in Latin America to promote greater understanding among all the American republics. It did so with a realization that the defense of the United States against increasing German, Italian, and Japanese aggression was linked with that of the rest of the Western Hemisphere.

[3]The financing of government expenditures by taking loans rather than by levying taxes.

The Good Neighbor Policy. In his first inaugural address Roosevelt indicated that his administration was eager to adopt a new policy toward Latin America. Said the President: "In the field of world policy I would dedicate this nation to the policy of the good neighbor—the neighbor who resolutely respects himself and, because he does so, respects the rights of others."

In 1933 Secretary of State Cordell Hull, with the full support of Roosevelt, declared that "no state has the right to intervene in the internal or external affairs of another."

NICARAGUA. In 1933 the American marines, who had occupied Nicaragua since 1912 except for a brief period during 1925–1926, were finally withdrawn.

HAITI. In 1934 the American military occupation of Haiti that had been in effect since 1915 was ended. Three years later, in order to forestall overtures by German financial interests, the United States agreed to purchase almost the entire $5 million worth of bonds issued by Haiti for a public works program.

CUBA. In 1934 the State Department announced the abrogation of the Platt Amendment as far as the provisions regarding the intervention of the United States in Cuban affairs was concerned.

MEXICO. The experiments in socialism undertaken by the Mexican government beginning in 1934 disturbed the United States, but the State Department refrained from interference. When in 1938 Mexico expropriated foreign-owned property, Secretary Hull admitted the right of a sovereign nation to do so and then reminded the Mexican government that it must compensate the dispossessed owners at "fair, assured, and effective values." Mexico rejected Hull's suggestion that the matter be arbitrated and insisted that it would reimburse the owners in its own way and at its own convenience. In 1941 a settlement was reached that proved satisfactory to American investors.

PANAMA. In 1939 the Senate ratified a treaty with Panama that modified the Hay-Buneau-Varilla Treaty of 1903, granting the United States control of a canal zone in Panama. The new treaty settled some of the long-standing grievances of Panama that had stemmed from the former treaty.

THE DOMINICAN REPUBLIC. In 1940 Roosevelt terminated the management of the Dominican Republic's customhouses that the United States had exercised since 1905.

Hemispheric Defense. Through a series of conferences among the nations of Latin America and the United States leading to a system of common defense, the Roosevelt administration hoped to deal with any possible threat to the Western Hemisphere from aggressive Germany, Italy, and Japan.

THE BUENOS AIRES CONFERENCE. In 1936 the American nations, including the United States, adopted the Declaration of Buenos Aires, pledging to consult with one another whenever the peace of the Western Hemisphere was threatened by the action of a non-American nation.

THE LIMA CONFERENCE. In 1938 the twenty-one American republics approved the Declaration of Lima, announcing their solidarity and affirming that any threat to peace in the Western Hemisphere from a foreign nation would lead to immediate consultation among all the signatories to the pact.

THE PANAMA CONFERENCE. With the outbreak of war in Europe in September, 1939, the American nations undertook to define their neutral position. The following month at a conference in Panama City, in keeping with the desire of the Roosevelt administration to prevent the war from reaching the Western Hemisphere, the American nations approved the Declaration of Panama, proclaiming the establishment of a safety zone extending for 300 miles around the Western Hemisphere south of Canada and warning belligerent nations to refrain from military action within the designated zone.

THE HAVANA CONFERENCE. In 1940 representatives of the twenty-one American republics adopted the Act of Havana, declaring that an act of aggression by a foreign nation against any one of them would be considered an attack on all of them. The act also provided, in the interest of hemispheric defense, for the taking over by the American republics of a European possession in the Western Hemisphere that was in danger of aggression.

Chapter 13

WORLD WAR II

In the 1930s the military aggression of the Axis nations—Germany, Italy, and Japan—brought war to Europe and Asia, turning the American people from a policy of neutrality to one of aiding victims of that aggression. In late 1941 the United States was brought into World War II as a result of a Japanese attack on Pearl Harbor. American manufacturing, agriculture, labor, and transportation were mobilized to support the armed forces sent to war against the Axis powers. By early 1942 representatives from twenty-six Allied nations, including the United States, had signed a declaration pledging joint military action until victory over the Axis was achieved. The strategy of the Allied nations was to defeat Nazi Germany first and then turn to destruction of the Japanese empire.

Administering the defeated Axis partners of the war, Germany and Japan, and helping both to establish themselves within the world community of nations were formidable tasks for the victorious powers. The postwar reconstruction of Germany and Japan was impeded by an ever-worsening disintegration in relations between the Western Allies on one side and the Soviet Union on the other.

During the war the Allied leaders attended a number of conferences to discuss, in addition to war strategy, their design for international cooperation after the anticipated peace was attained. The latter discussions resulted in the formation of the United Nations.

THE APPROACH OF WAR

Despite elaborate neutrality legislation, the Roosevelt administration moved steadily, although at times hesitantly, to prepare the nation for what might become a world war.

Unrest in Europe. Some Americans believed that the Treaty of Versailles had been too severe in the penalties imposed upon Germany. But observing the dictatorship established in 1933 by Adolf Hitler of the National Socialist (Nazi) Party, most Americans came to regard the regime as uncompromisingly despotic in its domestic policies and unjustifiably aggressive in its foreign relations. Italy, since 1922 under the dictatorship of Benito Mussolini of the Fascist Party, was also a threat to world peace.

ITALIAN AGGRESSION. In 1935 Italy, defying the opposition of the League of Nations, successfully invaded Ethiopia. The following year it joined Germany, which had withdrawn from the League of Nations in 1933, to form an alliance called the Rome-Berlin Axis.

GERMAN AGGRESSION. Germany violated the Treaty of Versailles in 1936 by sending troops into its demilitarized Rhineland area to the west. In March, 1938, Germany forcibly annexed Austria. The following September, at the Munich Conference, Great Britain and France, in the hope of averting a general war, agreed to German annexation of the western part of Czechoslovakia called the Sudetenland, a region inhabited by German-speaking people. (The Munich Conference soon came to symbolize appeasement.) The following, March Germany took over the rest of Czechoslovakia except for one region that was annexed by neighboring Hungary. In August, 1939, Germany and the Soviet Union announced the conclusion of a nonaggression pact. The conditions were now set for World War II. It began on September 1, 1939, when Germany invaded Poland, the independence of which the British and the French had guaranteed. Two days later Great Britain and France declared war on Germany.

Attempt at Neutrality. With Germany and Italy acting ever more aggressively, the United States Congress tried constantly to minimize the possibility of the nation's becoming involved again in a war in Europe.

THE JOHNSON ACT. Sponsored by Republican Senator Hiram Johnson of California, this act, passed in 1934, forbade the sale in the United States of bonds issued by any government that had defaulted in the payment of its obligations to the United States. Since every European nation that had incurred a World War I debt except Finland belonged in this category as a result of failure to repay its debt, the law was regarded as an effective device to prevent American financial involvement in the plans of a European nation seeking to acquire loans for the conduct of war.

THE NYE COMMITTEE. During 1934–1936 a Senate investigating committee, headed by Republican Gerald P. Nye of North Dakota, revealed that enormous profits had been made during World War I by American financiers and munitions makers, and suggested that pressure from those groups had forced the nation into the war. Congress was prompted by the findings of the Nye Committee into passing a series of neutrality acts.

NEUTRALITY LEGISLATION. In an effort to prevent American involvement in war should it occur anywhere in the world, Congress passed neutrality acts in 1935, 1936, and 1937. The acts varied mainly in the provisions affecting the discretionary powers of the President. Each succeeding act indicated a growing inclination on the part of Congress to keep foreign policy in its control. The Neutrality Act of 1935 authorized the President, after proclaiming the existence of a state of war, to prohibit the export of implements of war to belligerents and to forbid American citizens to travel on belligerent vessels except at their own risk. The Neutrality Act of 1936, which extended the Neutrality Act of 1935 until mid-1937, added a clause prohibiting loans to belligerents. The Neutrality Act of 1937, which was designed to be permanent, compelled the President to take certain actions, and permitted him to take other actions, whenever he determined the existence of a state of war. Among the compulsory prohibitions were (1) export of implements of war to belligerents; (2) travel by Americans on belligerent ships; (3) extension of loans to belligerents. In addition, the President could prohibit (1) the transport of any type of commodity on American vessels to belligerents; (2) the use of American ports as supply bases for belligerent warships. With these acts the United States relinquished its claims to a neutral's rights at sea during war, which it had so vigorously defended at the start of World War I.

When war broke out with the German invasion of Poland in September, 1939, the Roosevelt administration urged Congress to reconsider certain of the mandatory provisions of the 1937 Neutrality Act. The point at issue was the compulsory embargo on implements of war to belligerents. After a spirited debate Congress passed the Neutrality Act of 1939, which amended the act of 1937 to permit the export of arms and munitions to belligerents on a "cash and carry" basis. To satisfy the strongly isolationist congressional bloc, the act contained a provision authorizing the President to designate war zones from which American merchant ships would be barred.

Roosevelt's Policy. In opposition to the isolationist basis of the neutrality legislation, President Roosevelt delivered an address (October, 1937) in which he suggested that the United States take the lead in persuading all peace-loving nations that in the event of international strife they should "quarantine" the aggressor through economic boycott. Finding little support for this policy in Congress, Roosevelt undertook to persuade Germany and Italy that any just demands could be satisfied around the conference table rather than on the battlefield. When his pleas to the dictators for peaceful negotiations brought no results, he advised Congress that there were a variety of means "short of war" to curb the spread of totalitarian power.

Isolationists versus Interventionists. The policy advocated by Roosevelt was severely criticized by those called isolationists, who recommended that the nation refrain from words as well as deeds which might involve it in a struggle for power overseas. By the spring of 1941 the isolationists were exerting an enormous amount of effort to keep the United States out of World War II. Their spokesmen in Congress were Republican senators Gerald P. Nye of North Dakota, Arthur H. Vandenberg of Michigan, and Robert A. Taft of Ohio; Democratic Senator Burton K. Wheeler of Montana; and Republican Representative Hamilton Fish, Jr., of New York. The most effective pressure group working on behalf of an isolationist policy was the America First Committee, headed by Chicago businessman Robert E. Wood. The famous aviator Charles A. Lindbergh, who was an active member of the committee, won a considerable following by urging a negotiated peace between Great Britain and the Axis powers. On the other hand, those known as interventionists were convinced that the best security for the United States lay in assisting the Allies, through all measures "short of war," to make certain of German defeat. The most influential organization espousing interventionist sentiment was the Committee to Defend America by Aiding the Allies, led by Kansas newspaper editor William Allen White.

Preparedness and Defense. With the German attack upon Scandinavia in April, 1940, and invasion of the Low Countries the following month, Americans were shocked into a realization of the implications for them of total war. Their earnest endeavor to take steps to ensure full preparedness and defense began at that time.

ARMAMENTS APPROPRIATIONS. During 1940 Congress appropriated approximately $1.8 billion for armaments. The sum was used for the creation of a two-ocean navy superior to the combined naval power of nations unfriendly to the United States and for the purchase of munitions and other supplies for an army that was being rapidly increased in size to 1.2 million men. These two branches of the service were to be supported by a fleet of 35,000 airplanes.

THE SELECTIVE TRAINING AND SERVICE ACT. In September, 1940, Congress authorized the first peacetime conscription in the nation's history. Under the terms of the Selective Training and Service Act, all men between the ages of twenty-one and thirty-five were required to register for possible military service. From the 16.4 million registrants 800,000 were selected by lot for one year's military training. Also, National Guard enlistees were given intensive instruction in modern warfare.

WESTERN HEMISPHERE STRATEGY. German conquests in Europe raised questions in the United States concerning the fate of Dutch, French, and possibly British possessions in the Western Hemisphere. Acting upon a statement he made in 1938 that the United States would not permit a foreign power's domination of Canada (a self-governing autonomous state within the British Commonwealth of Nations), President Roosevelt joined Canadian Prime Minister William. L. Mackenzie King in creating in 1940 the Permanent Joint Board on Defense to study the defense needs of the

Atlantic and Pacific coasts of both nations. Further, Congress passed in 1940 a joint resolution declaring that the United States would not recognize the transfer of title of any territory of the Western Hemisphere from one non-American nation to another.

Election of 1940. The close advisers of President Roosevelt asserted throughout the campaign that his reluctance to run for a third term had been overcome by his conviction that it would be detrimental to the nation to change administrations in the midst of worldwide war.

DEMOCRATS. The delegates to the Democratic national convention, in a rather sullen mood over the possible adverse effects of the third-term issue upon their party's success in the election, permitted the administration leaders to persuade them that the ticket should consist of Roosevelt and his secretary of agriculture, Henry A. Wallace. The platform defended the New Deal record of social legislation and the party's recent achievements in the area of defense.

REPUBLICANS. The national convention of the Republican party passed over such well-known aspirants to the presidency as Senator Robert A. Taft of Ohio and racket-busting district attorney Thomas E. Dewey of New York. The delegates nominated a newcomer to politics, Wendell L. Willkie, who had recently transferred from the Democratic to the Republican party. As head of the Commonwealth and Southern Corporation, a utility holding company, Willkie had been a cogent critic of New Deal policies. His big-business connections were balanced by the nomination for vice-president of Senator Charles L. McNary of Oregon, a noted advocate of farm legislation. As for the platform, it supported many New Deal reform measures but attacked New Deal methods as wasteful, bureaucratic, and dictatorial.

THE CAMPAIGN. There had been forecasts that the campaign would revolve around foreign policy, but the two candidates offered the voters strikingly similar positions. Each favored a strong national defense, all aid to Great Britain "short of war," and protection of the Western Hemisphere against aggression. Both promised to keep the United States out of the European conflict. The Democratic candidate virtually repudiated conservative support and promised to extend social legislation, while the Republican candidate accused the Roosevelt supporters of stirring class antagonism for political advantage.

ROOSEVELT'S THIRD VICTORY. The balloting resulted in a third victory for Roosevelt; his success, however, was not so widespread as that four years earlier. The popular vote was 27,313,000 for Roosevelt and 22,348,000 for Willkie. Roosevelt captured thirty-eight states with 449 electoral votes. Although Willkie secured almost 45 percent of the popular vote, he received only 82 votes in the electoral college, representing ten states chiefly in the farm belt of the Midwest. The Democrats carried both houses of Congress. After the election Willkie promptly called for national unity despite differences of opinion on domestic issues. He was especially insistent that political partisanship play no part in modifying the nation's decision to aid Great Britain and to resist to the utmost totalitarian aggression.

Aid to the Allies. Although a large majority of Americans were anxious to avoid any involvement in World War II, they were eager for Great Britain and France to win. In 1941 the issue of giving aid to the Allies precipitated a bitter debate between the isolationists and interventionists which was finally won by the latter.

TRANSFER OF DESTROYERS. The British were sorely in need of additional destroyers to fight the German submarines that were attacking their merchant ships in the Atlantic. In September, 1940, President Roosevelt by executive agreement transferred fifty "over-age" destroyers to Great Britain in exchange for ninety-nine-year leases on eight naval and air bases on British possessions in the Western Hemisphere, ranging from Newfoundland to British Guiana. Amidst a furor from the isolationists over the destroyer-base deal, President Roosevelt defended his action on the sole ground of Western Hemisphere defense.

THE LEND-LEASE ACT. In March, 1941, Congress, over the protests of the isolationist leaders, passed the Lend-Lease Act, authorizing the President to sell, lend, lease, transfer, or exchange arms and other supplies to or with any nation whose defense he considered vital to the defense of the United States. The amount of aid that could be given was limited, but the President was allowed considerable discretion in placing a value upon such goods and in arranging the terms of the delivery. In June, 1941, in violation of their 1939 pact, Germany invaded the Soviet Union. American lend-lease aid was promptly extended to the Soviet Union. By 1942 thirty-five countries, in addition to the British Commonwealth of Nations, had received assistance under the terms of the act. The total in lend-lease aid during the course of World War II amounted to more than $50 billion.

Occupation of Greenland and Iceland. In an extensive agreement signed in April, 1941, with the Danish minister to Washington, the United States promised to defend the Danish possession of Greenland against invasion in exchange for the right to establish a base there. By agreement with Iceland, which had proclaimed its independence from Denmark after the German occupation of that nation, the United States in July, 1941, established a military base in Iceland to prevent its invasion by Germany. By taking such actions the United States made certain that the control of the Atlantic would not pass to any hostile nation.

The Atlantic Charter. In August, 1941, President Roosevelt and British Prime Minister Winston Churchill set forth in a joint statement the postwar objectives of their nations, a step that caused the Axis powers to insist that the United States and Great Britain were already in alliance.

Known as the Atlantic Charter, this statement was the result of conversations between Roosevelt and Churchill at secret meetings aboard their respective warships off the coast of Newfoundland. The document stated that both nations (1) renounced territorial aggrandizement; (2) opposed territorial changes contrary to the wishes of the people concerned; (3) respected the right of all people to choose their own form of government; (4) would assist in arranging for all nations equal access to the trade and raw materials of the world; (5) favored cooperation among the nations to improve the economic status and social security of all people; (6) hoped that the peace settlement would enable people throughout the world to "live out their lives in freedom from fear and want"; (7) supported freedom of the seas; (8) advocated disarmament of aggressor nations.

Combat in the Atlantic. The delivery of lend-lease goods from the United States depended upon the ability of Great Britain to get its merchant vessels back and forth across the Atlantic safely. Those vessels were convoyed by British warships and warships that had escaped from the ports of nations occupied by German forces. The American navy itself increasingly participated in protecting lend-lease shipments in the Atlantic through the convoy system. Germany tried to prevent the United States from continuing its lend-lease aid by submarine attacks on the ships moving across the Atlantic. In September, 1941, President Roosevelt ordered all American naval commanders to "shoot on sight" any Axis submarine entering Western Hemisphere defensive waters, including waters surrounding Greenland and Iceland. In October, 1941, a German submarine attacked and sank the American destroyer *Reuben James* on convoy duty in Icelandic waters, with the loss of seventy-six of its crew. The following month Congress passed an act authorizing the arming of American merchant ships and permitting them to carry goods directly to the ports of belligerent nations.

Strained Relations with Japan. In the 1930s Japan attempted by military aggression to secure control of the Far East. The government of the United States denounced the Japanese actions but was unwilling to apply force to prevent them. In July, 1937, Japan began an invasion of China, soon controlling the coastal areas of the nation. Although the American people became strongly anti-Japanese, their leaders were too much concerned over the threatening situation in Europe to take punitive action in the Far East. A crisis occurred between the United States and Japan when Japanese planes in China bombed the American gunboat *Panay* on the Yangtze River, killing two and wounding thirty. But the matter was resolved when the Japanese government issued a formal apology. In late 1938 Japan felt strong enough to warn the world that there would be a "new order" in Asia and it would not include adherence to the decades-old open-door principle of equality of opportunity for trade in China. The American State Department refused to accept any such unilateral abrogation of Japan's previous agreements on the open-door policy.

By 1939 the United States and Japan were carrying on a war of words. Japanese purchases in the United States of such materials usable in war as aviation gasoline and scrap iron continued, but the control over their sale became increasingly vigorous. Resentment against Japan served to quicken American sympathy for China. Contributions to the relief of Chinese war victims were but one evidence of that sympathy. By 1940 the American government had lent almost $70 million to the Chinese government for the purchase of badly needed supplies. To make such aid possible President Roosevelt refrained from invoking the provisions of the Neutrality Act of 1937 forbidding the extension of loans to belligerents, basing his position on the ground that there had been no declaration of war.

In late 1940 Japan became a member of the Axis, when it signed a ten-year pact with Germany and Italy pledging to assist one another in case war should occur with a nation not then a belligerent. Beginning in 1941 Japan became ever more truculent toward its neighbors in Asia. The war against China was ruthlessly pressed. Japanese forces occupied Indochina, the southeast Asian possession of France, now that the latter country had been defeated by Germany. Unprepared and unwilling to fight Japan in the Pacific while the fate of Europe was still undecided, the United States continued a policy of appeasement until the summer of 1941, when it finally forbade the export to Japan of aviation gasoline, scrap iron, and other war matériel.

THE KURUSU MISSION. Japan maintained that it desired to reach a peaceful settlement of all its outstanding differences with the United States. After the leader of the prowar party, General Hideki Tojo, became Prime Minister (October, 1941), Saburo Kurusu was sent to the United States as a special envoy to join the Japanese ambassador to Washington, Kichisaburo Nomura, in proposing a settlement of the two nations' disagreements in the Pacific. Nomura and Kurusu demanded, among other things, that the United States abandon its support of China, resume trade with Japan in all commodities, and halt its naval expansion program in the Pacific. Secretary of State Cordell Hull made counterproposals for the United States, including the signing of a multilateral nonagression pact for the Far East and the withdrawal of Japanese forces from China and Indochina.

The Attack on Pearl Harbor. While Nomura and Kurusu were engaged in discussing with Hull the possibilities for a peaceful settlement of differences in the Pacific, Japan struck the United States. On December 7, 1941, Japanese airplanes made a surprise attack on the American naval base at Pearl Harbor in Hawaii that began at 7:55 A.M. (local time) and continued for almost two hours. Of the eight battleships at Pearl Harbor, three were sunk, one was grounded, and four were damaged. A small number of lesser warships were disabled and approximately 175 planes were destroyed. In the attack 2,335 American soldiers and sailors were killed and 1,178 were wounded. On the same day Japanese forces assaulted the Philippines, Guam, the British crown colony of Hong Kong, and the British-controlled Malay Peninsula, including its port city of Singapore.

UNITED STATES ENTRY INTO WAR

The day after the attack on Pearl Harbor President Roosevelt addressed a joint session of Congress. Asserting that December 7, 1941, was "a date which will live in infamy," he asked for a declaration of war against Japan. Within hours Congress passed a resolution to that effect, with but one dissenting vote in the lower house. On December 11 Germany and Italy declared war on the United States, which in turn adopted war resolutions against them. The attack on Pearl Harbor quickly ended the debate between isolationists and interventionists over foreign policy and united the American people in a solemn determination to meet successfully one of the greatest crises in the nation's history.

"G.I.'s"

As in World War I, the difficult task of providing people to serve in the armed forces was accomplished with gratifying success. For the second time in less than a quarter-century, young men of the United States were compelled to perform military duty. Popularly called "G.I.'s" (from an unofficial abbreviation for "government issue"), they did not fail their nation.

Conscription and Enlistment. In December, 1941, Congress amended the 1940 Selective Training and Service Act by lowering the minimum draft registration age to twenty and raising the maximum to forty-four. More than 31 million men were registered, of whom some 9.8 million were conscripted into the various branches of the armed forces. Approximately 5 million men enlisted voluntarily for military service. By the end of the war there were over 11.2 million in the army (including its air force, numbering about 3 million), close to 4.2 million in the navy, approximately 675,000 in the marine corps, and about 250,000 in the coast guard. Almost 260,000 women enlisted for noncombatant duty in all the branches of the armed forces. In the army they were popularly known as WACs (for Women's Army Corps) and in the navy, WAVEs (for Women Appointed for Voluntary Emergency Service).

Training and Transport of Troops. The draftees and enlistees were quite speedily and rather effectively trained at scores of bases, of which some were expanded and others newly built, throughout the nation. By the end of the war approximately 12 million men had gone overseas, of whom about 4.7 million had engaged in combat duty.

American War Costs. World War II was for the United States its second (after the Civil War) most costly war in loss of life and by far its most costly in expenditure of money. Approximately 293,000 men were killed in battle, while some 116,000 died of other causes (disease or accident). About 670,000 men were wounded in combat. Financial expenditures of the United States amounted to an estimated $315 billion, about ten times the amount disbursed on all of its previous wars combined.

THE HOME FRONT

Modern warfare requires the participation of a nation in its totality. Those who go to meet the enemy must be buttressed materially as well as spiritually by those they leave at home. When the United States entered the war against the Axis powers, it needed to quickly mobilize national resources—manufacturing facilities, food, labor, transportation. To raise the huge sums necessary to pay for the war, the old methods of collecting revenue—taxation and borrowing—had to be refined.

Mobilizing Production. By the middle of 1943 the American people had converted their peacetime industrial establishment into the mightiest wartime arsenal that the world had ever seen.

THE WAR PRODUCTION BOARD. The nine-member War Production Board, headed by Donald Nelson, supervised the staggering tasks of constructing many new plants for the manufacture of war commodities and switching many existing plants from peacetime to wartime production. Within a year after the Pearl Harbor attack the nation produced under the War Production Board more than $47 billion worth of war matériel, including 32,000 tanks, 49,000 airplanes, and merchant ships totaling 8 million tons. By the end of the war the nation had produced under the War Production Board 85,000 tanks, 295,000 airplanes, and 70,000 warships and 5,500 merchant ships. Although the manufacture of many peacetime commodities was either curtailed or prohibited in order to facilitate the manufacture of war items, the total industrial production of the nation almost doubled during the war.

THE FOOD ADMINISTRATION. Despite the bumper crops during World War II, it was difficult to meet the extraordinary demand for foodstuffs. The entire problem of the production and distribution of food was placed directly under the supervision of the Food Administration, whose members were appointed by the President. To continue the program of helping the Allies and supplying the American armed services required careful planning, especially since farmers were handicapped by a dwindling work force and shortages of new agricultural machinery and parts to repair old machinery. The armed forces were taking approximately 30 percent of the American meat supply. Within fifteen months after the United States entered the war, it shipped to Great Britain, the Soviet Union, and China more than 7 billion pounds of food.

THE OFFICE OF PRICE ADMINISTRATION (OPA). Domestic consumption was partly controlled through the rationing imposed by the Office of Price Administration (OPA) on such foods as sugar, coffee, meat, and butter. The OPA also fixed prices and rationed other scarce commodities, such as tires and gasoline. The agency's complicated tasks were generally well handled.

Mobilizing Labor. Although the activities of workers were more strictly supervised by the government than at any other time in the nation's history, American laborers escaped the kind of regimentation experienced by workers of most other countries then at war.

Organized labor generally refrained from strikes and other forms of job action during the first years of the war. American workers were spurred to great efforts. Their record of output from 1942 to 1945 surpassed by far any previous record for a comparable period of time. At the same time, average weekly earnings rose from approximately twenty-five dollars to about forty-five dollars, while the length of the workweek increased from approximately thirty-eight to about forty-five hours.

THE WAR MANPOWER COMMISSION. The utilization of labor resources was placed under the nine-member War Manpower Commission, with Paul V. McNutt as chairman. The commission handled the task of apportioning the work of approximately 50 million men and about 20 million women in the labor force.

THE NATIONAL WAR LABOR BOARD. Within a month after the United States entered the armed conflict the twelve-member National War Labor Board was established to settle management-labor disputes through mediation and arbitration. When management-labor strife flared up in 1943, Congress passed over Roosevelt's veto the War Labor Disputes Act (also called the Smith-Connally Anti-Strike Act), which, among other things, authorized the President to seize plants where labor disturbances threatened to impede war production. An unsuccessful attempt was made to stabilize wages through the rulings of the National War Labor Board.

Mobilizing Transportation. If the United States had any "secret weapon" during the early years of the war, it was the marvelous efficiency of its transportation facilities.

THE OFFICE OF DEFENSE TRANSPORTATION. During World War I it had been necessary for the government to assume control of the railroads. During World War II, however, railroad operators and employees, working with the temporarily established Office of Defense Transportation, carried unprecedented numbers of troops and amounts of arms and equipment. In 1942 the railroads transported 40 percent more passengers and 30 percent more freight than they had the previous year. This was done with 20,000 fewer locomotives and 600,000 fewer freight cars than they had possessed during World War I.

THE WAR SHIPPING BOARD. The Allies had two countermeasures to the threat of the German submarines: first, improved methods of the Allied navies in seeking and destroying underwater vessels; second, the tremendous output of American shipyards. Under the supervision of the War Shipping Board, prefabricated vessels were built within the amazing time of 2½ months or less. This speed made it possible for the American fleet to maintain a supply line from the United States to the Allies in Europe that, after the first few months of the war, was more than adequate.

AIRWAYS. The commercial airlines, although subordinating their activities to war needs, managed to keep many of their normal schedules. Virtually all airplane construction by private firms was for military purposes. In 1943 the output was over 5,500 airplanes a month, compared with approximately 200 a month in 1939.

Financing the War. Between January, 1940, and January, 1943, the appropriations first for national defense and then for war itself amounted to approximately $220 billion—slightly more than the cost of government from the inauguration of George Washington in 1789 to 1940. During World War II the national debt rose from approximately $47 billion to about $247 billion.

TAXES. By the second year of the war it was estimated that the daily cost of the conflict to the American people was $1.15 for every man, woman, and child, while revenue to the government from taxes was scarcely forty cents per person. Successive tax bills were designed and passed to increase the proportion of the cost of the war to be met through taxation as opposed to borrowing. This was accomplished by (1) adding millions of taxpayers to the rolls through lowering the minimum tax-exempt income; (2) revising upward the personal income tax rates; (3) imposing on corporations a virtual confiscation of income that represented excess profits from the war. In 1943 Congress accepted a plan to place collection of personal income taxes on a withholding ("pay-as-you-go") basis.

WAR BONDS. Despite increased revenue from taxes, the federal government relied upon borrowing through the sale of war bonds and small denomination war stamps to meet the bulk of the war costs. By July, 1945, the government had conducted seven highly successful war-bond drives, which raised approximately $61 billion in all.

Election of 1944. Not since 1864 had the American people been forced to turn aside from the various pursuits involved in conducting a war to engage in the procedure of choosing a president.

DEMOCRATS. When the Democratic national convention began its proceedings, the delegates knew that President Roosevelt desired a fourth term. He was nominated on the first ballot, although the opponents of a fourth term, most of whom were in southern delegations, cast some ninety votes for Senator Harry F. Byrd of Virginia. The drama of the convention came in the fight of ultraliberal Vice-President Wallace for renomination. Although Wallace led on the first ballot, he was finally defeated by an alliance between certain conservative leaders from the South and the leaders of several powerful political machines in northern cities. As a result of a decision to choose a compromise vice-presidential candidate, and thus avoid a rupture between the liberal and conservative wings of the party, Senator Harry Truman of Missouri became Roosevelt's running mate.

REPUBLICANS. During the preconvention primaries Wendell Willkie, who had been defeated by Roosevelt in 1940, came to the conclusion that he could not again secure the Republican nomination for president. His position among Republicans was still strong, however, and he used his influence to counteract the power of the isolationist wing of the party. Those who were reluctant to make commitments concerning an activist role of the United States in the postwar period probably would have preferred Senator Robert A. Taft or Governor John Bricker, both isolationists from Ohio, as the presidential nominee. But the delegates to the Republican national convention yielded to the apparent popularity of the mildly liberal and internationalist Governor Thomas E. Dewey of New York and nominated him with only one dissenting vote. To balance the ticket Bricker was then chosen for the second slot.

THE CAMPAIGN. As soon as the campaign got under way, it became clear that it would not revolve around the issues; Roosevelt and Dewey held quite similar views on the domestic programs the government should pursue to bring economic security to the American people and on the foreign policy that it should conduct after the war. Week after week Dewey reiterated that after a dozen years of the New Deal it was time for the voters to retire the "tired old men" from the executive branch. Only as the campaign entered its latter stage did Roosevelt become actively involved by giving some "tough" speeches in his familiar dynamic style.

ROOSEVELT'S FOURTH VICTORY. Out of 47,969,000 popular votes cast, Roosevelt received a plurality of 2,357,000. In the electoral college he carried thirty-six states with 432 votes to twelve states with 99 votes for Dewey. The regard for Roosevelt had held strong.

THE WAR IN EUROPE

The German conquests in Western Europe, once they got under way, were swift and devastating. Then the German attack upon the Soviet Union quickly brought stunning military success. But the Allied invasions of North

Africa and of Italy prepared the way for the 1944 landings in France that began the defeat of Germany. Although the Germans fought stubbornly, their resistance was crushed within a year by the might of the Allied military forces.

German Conquests. During the winter of 1939–1940 there was little military action in Western Europe. The Soviet Union took advantage of the situation to invade and conquer the Baltic states: Estonia, Latvia, Lithuania (each of which in 1918 had achieved independence from the newly established Soviet Union), and Finland. But once the German offensives began, first in Western Europe and then against the Soviet Union, they were overpowering.

SCANDINAVIA AND THE LOW COUNTRIES. In April, 1940, German seaborne troops invaded Denmark and Norway. The former nation fell quickly, while the latter, aided by British and French forces, resisted for two months. Early in May the highly mechanized German army overran, simultaneously, Belgium, Luxembourg, and the Netherlands. In the face of overwhelming German military power Luxembourg fell in one day, the Netherlands in five, and Belgium in nineteen. The ruthless German invasion of the neutral Scandinavian nations and Low Countries aroused the people of the United States.

THE FALL OF FRANCE AND THE RESISTANCE OF GREAT BRITAIN. Early in June, 1940, Italy entered the war on the side of Germany. France surrendered less than two weeks later, after having been exposed to a punishing new offensive by German forces. The British expeditionary army was then forced to evacuate the continent. Great Britain fought on alone despite extensive and severe bombings by the Luftwaffe (German air fleet). The American people were quick to applaud the British heroism.

INVASION OF THE SOVIET UNION. In June, 1941, Germany began a huge surprise invasion of the Soviet Union. For months, approximately 3 million German troops drove deep into Soviet territory. By December, 1941, they were nearing Moscow. But with the bitter winter of 1941–1942 the German advance came to a halt, and the Soviets began a powerful counteroffensive.

German Setbacks. By the fall of 1942 the Germans controlled an empire that was at its height, extending from Norway to North Africa and from France to the western reaches of the Soviet Union. In less than two years it collapsed.

THE NORTH AFRICAN CAMPAIGN. In August, 1940, Italian troops attacked British territory in North Africa. Six months later German forces were sent to the area to assist in the Italian military operation. For almost two years British troops fought German and Italian troops back and forth across North Africa. In November, 1942, an armada of American and British forces landed on the coast of Morocco with the objective of driving the German and Italian troops out of North Africa. Within three days General Dwight

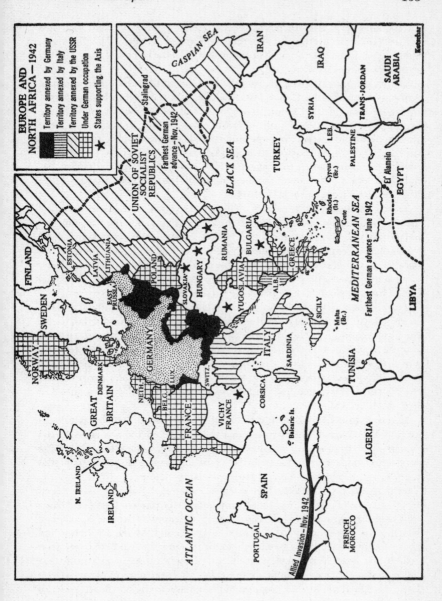

D. Eisenhower had so disposed the forces under his command that they controlled all Morocco and its neighbor to the east, Algeria. The Germans, aided by the Italians, fought stubbornly for six months before they yielded to superior forces in May, 1943.

THE ITALIAN CAMPAIGN. During the summer of 1943 the Fifth American Army, commanded by General Mark Clark, and the Eighth British Army, under General Bernard Montgomery, occupied several islands in the Mediterranean, including Sicily, off the south coast of Italy. The invasion of the Italian mainland began in September, 1943, more than a month after the Italian people had ousted Mussolini and his Fascist regime. Despite this revolt, the campaign in Italy against the German forces in the nation was long and costly. Not until the beginning of June, 1944, did the Allies liberate Rome from German control.

THE BOMBING OF GERMANY. During 1943 Germany was bombed massively by American and British airplanes. The Luftwaffe was knocked out of the sky; German production facilities were repeatedly demolished; the industrial centers of the Ruhr Valley and the Rhineland were all but paralyzed; the cities of Berlin, Hamburg, Munich, and Cologne suffered even more destruction than the terrible damage English cities had sustained from German air assaults earlier in the war.

THE SOVIET OFFENSIVE. In 1943, while the American Air Force and the British Royal Air Force (RAF) were attacking Germany's production areas, the Soviet forces launched large-scale offensives all along the eastern front from the Baltic Sea on the north to the Black Sea on the south. The primary aim of the Soviets was the destruction of the German forces, and in the process they had regained by the summer of 1944 all of their territory that the Germans had occupied and were able to establish routes into the Danube River Valley.

Coming to a Close. During 1943 the American and British navies conquered the German submarine menace and opened the sea lanes to the transport of troops and supplies. By June, 1944, more than 2 million American troops were in Great Britain awaiting the time for invasion of that part of Europe which lay behind Hitler's Atlantic defense.

THE BATTLE OF FRANCE. In the early hours of June 6, 1944, Allied troops, on orders from Supreme Commander Eisenhower, left their bases in Great Britain and crossed the English Channel to storm the French beaches in the vicinity of Cherbourg. Preceded by paratroopers and protected by an awesome bombardment from a huge naval fleet, they soon established beachheads and, with the aid of the air force, connected their individual landings into one battle front. Within three months of these landings, the Allied armies had conquered Normandy to the northeast, overrun Brittany to the west, chased the Germans north of the Seine River, and assisted the Free French forces of resistance in liberating Paris from the

Germans. In August, 1944, new landings were made, with slight losses, on the Mediterranean coast of France near Marseilles. On August 26 General Eisenhower announced the destruction of the German Seventh Army. The Battle of France had been won.

UNCONDITIONAL SURRENDER. German counteraction just west of the Rhine River proved to be surprisingly determined but was overcome by Allied military power. In December, 1944, the Germans mounted an offensive that created a huge bulge in the Allied lines, from which came the name Battle of the Bulge. After yielding some valuable ground, the American and British troops stood firm. One young American officer, Brigadier General Anthony McAuliffe, when the Germans pressed him to surrender, gave the simple but memorable reply: "Nuts!" While incessant bombing pounded much of the western reaches of Germany into rubble, the American First Army reached the Rhine River. In March, 1945, the first troops crossed the river southeast of Cologne and moved into the interior of Germany. For the next two months the Allied armies in the west advanced steadily, while the Soviet forces cut through Austria and closed in on Berlin. Hitler, aware that the end was near, took his own life, and other high Nazi officials either committed suicide or went into hiding. On May 7, 1945, at Reims, France, a representative of the German General Staff, which had taken over after Hitler's death, accepted the terms of unconditional surrender. May 8 was proclaimed to an expectant world as V-E (Victory in Europe) Day.

THE WAR IN THE PACIFIC

As with the German territorial victories, the Japanese conquests were massive. But a few months after the surrender of Germany in May, 1945, there followed the defeat of Japan—hastened by the dropping of the atomic bomb.

Japanese Conquests. The first half of 1942 was marked by a series of major victories for Japan in the Pacific.

ENGLISH AND DUTCH POSSESSIONS. The world was astonished at the speed of the Japanese military advance after the attack on Pearl Harbor in December, 1941. Within two months Japan had secured the entire British-controlled Malay Peninsula, with its great naval base at Singapore. Three weeks later the Japanese overran the Netherlands East Indies. Early in May Great Britain retreated from its possession of Burma into India. Japanese bases that had been established to the north on Dutch-owned New Guinea and to the east in the Bismarck and Solomon Islands, which had been under an Australian mandate, were growing in strength.

FALL OF THE PHILIPPINES. Under the command of General Douglas

MacArthur, American and Filipino troops heroically defended the Bataan peninsula and the fortress on the island of Corregidor until resistance was no longer possible. At the order of President Roosevelt, MacArthur transferred his headquarters to Australia in February, 1942, but his troops under General Jonathan Wainwright held Corregidor until the following May.

THE ALEUTIAN ISLANDS. Soon after Japan secured the Philippines, its forces far to the north moved into the American-owned Aleutians, a chain of islands that extends westward from the tip of the Alaska Peninsula. Japanese troops occupied the islands of Attu, Agattu, and Kiska for more than a year before American forces ousted them in the spring of 1943.

Japanese Setbacks. By the late summer of 1942 the Japanese had occupied 1 million square miles in their triumphant advance, but there it ended. Their retreat was humiliating and costly in life and material resources.

THE BATTLES OF THE CORAL SEA AND MIDWAY. In April, 1942, American airplanes commanded by General James Doolittle dropped tons of bombs on Tokyo, Yokohama, and Kobe. This was the first bombing of the Japanese home islands. A few weeks later American naval and air forces in the Coral Sea stopped an invading force aimed at Australia to the west. The first real defeat for Japan took place in June, 1942, with the rout of a strong Japanese naval force proceeding toward the American-owned Midway Islands, to the northwest of Hawaii.

FROM ISLAND TO ISLAND. In August, 1942, the Allies launched their counteroffensive in earnest, when American marines, buttressed by air and naval forces, landed on Guadalcanal in the Solomon Islands. For the next two years the trend in the western Pacific was of the Japanese avoiding battle and suffering costly defeats as island after island fell to Allied forces. Americans, under General MacArthur and admirals Chester W. Nimitz and William F. Halsey, played a major role in these victories, but they were ably supported by their allies. From the Solomons they moved into the Marshalls (which had been held by Japan under a League of Nations mandate), the British-owned Gilberts, and the Carolines and Marianas (both also held by Japan under a League mandate). They took Guam and then prepared for the reconquest of the Philippine Islands.

THE BOMBING OF JAPAN. In the spring of 1944 American airplane factories began to produce special bombers called "superfortresses," which were designed for long flights with heavy bomb loads. Based on airfields in China, which Chinese labor had built almost without tools, these airplanes effectively destroyed the industrial centers of Japan.

CHINA. While the Allied forces moved northward and westward across the islands of the Pacific, ever closer to Japan, the Chinese kept up a heroic resistance to the Japanese occupation of their homeland. They were

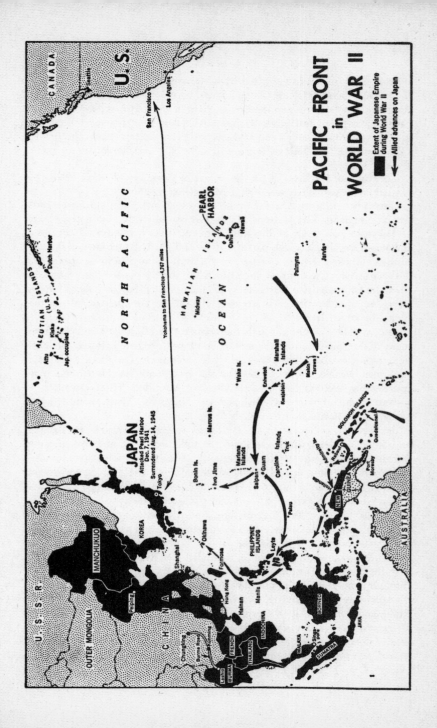

heartened by increasing support from American air forces in China commanded by General Claire Chennault and by the campaign of Chinese and American troops to reopen the Burma Road, a highway first used in 1938 to carry war supplies to Chinese troops and captured by Japanese forces during the war. At the same time forces of various countries within the British Commonwealth of Nations were gradually clearing the Japanese out of Burma.

Coming to a Close. With the defeat of Germany in May, 1945, the United States strove to speed up the war against Japan.

PREPARING FOR THE ASSAULT ON JAPAN. During the spring of 1945 troops commanded by General MacArthur continued to eliminate pockets of Japanese resistance in the Philippines and cooperated with the Australians in the attack on the partly British- and partly Dutch-owned Borneo to the southwest. To the north of the Philippines the combined operations of the army along with its air force, the navy, and the marine corps won Iwo Jima and Okinawa, two islands close to Japan proper. Bases on those islands were prepared by the early summer of 1945 for the final assault on the Japanese home islands.

THE ATOMIC BOMB. Through the cooperative efforts of scientists from many of the Allied nations the atomic bomb was perfected. It was the most devastating weapon that the world had ever seen. On August 6, 1945, American airmen dropped the first atomic bomb on Hiroshima. Approximately 180,000 people were killed or wounded. Three days later a second atomic bomb was dropped on Nagasaki. There were 80,000 casualties. Both cities were virtually obliterated.

UNCONDITIONAL SURRENDER. During a conference of American, British, and Soviet leaders, which assembled in mid-July, 1945, at Potsdam, near Berlin, Germany, the United States and Great Britain sent Japan an ultimatum demanding unconditional surrender. At the same time Soviet Premier Joseph Stalin informed President Harry S. Truman that the Soviet Union would soon enter the war against Japan. Two days after the atomic bomb was first used, the Soviet Union moved against the Japanese in Manchuria. Promptly the official Tokyo radio broadcasted an appeal for peace. After an exchange of notes between the United States and Japan, President Truman announced, on August 14, that hostilities had ceased. It was agreed that the Supreme Commander for the Allied Powers would rule Japan through Emperor Hirohito until militarism was eliminated and democratic reforms were implemented. General MacArthur was appointed Supreme Commander for the Allied Powers. On September 2, aboard the battleship *Missouri* in Tokyo Bay, members of a Japanese delegation signed the surrender documents before the representatives of nine of the Allied nations. President Truman proclaimed that September 2 was to be celebrated as V-J (Victory Over Japan) Day.

THE DEFEATED NATIONS

In dealing with Germany and Japan the victorious powers concerned themselves with three major tasks: occupying the conquered territories; conducting trials of war criminals; and drafting peace treaties.

Germany. The job of occupying defeated Germany proved long and difficult. On one point the wartime Allied powers could agree—the punishment of German war criminals. As tensions increased between the Western Allies and the Soviet Union it became impossible to frame a peace treaty with Germany.

THE OCCUPATION. A month after Germany surrendered, the nation was divided into four zones of occupation, with the military forces of the United States, Great Britain, France, and the Soviet Union each in charge of a specific zone. The United States commanded the southern sector, Great Britain the northwestern, France the southwestern, and the Soviet Union the eastern. Berlin, which lay within the Soviet sector, was itself divided by the Allies into four occupation zones. General Lucius D. Clay served as military governor of the American zone of occupation. The United States, Great Britain, and France pursued a policy of allowing German officials to assume increasing authority. In 1949 the three western zones were combined to form the Federal Republic of Germany with Bonn as the capital and the Soviet zone was transformed into the German Democratic Republic with the Soviet sector of Berlin as its capital. Military occupation then ended in the western zones, but it continued in the three western sectors of Berlin since no peace treaty uniting all Germany had been concluded.

WAR CRIMES TRIALS. Six months after the Germans surrendered, an International Military Tribunal at Nuremberg, Germany, brought to trial as war criminals civil and military leaders of the Nazi regime. Judges and attorneys from the four nations occupying Germany participated in the first of a series of trials. Associate Justice Robert H. Jackson of the United States Supreme Court served as one of the chief prosecutors. Among the twenty-two defendants taken into custody were Reich Marshal and Commander of the Air Force Hermann Goering, Deputy to the Führer Rudolf Hess, and Foreign Minister Joachim von Ribbentrop. The crimes the defendants were variously charged with included planning a war of aggression, using slave labor, and exterminating Jews. Twelve of the accused were sentenced to death, seven received prison terms, and three were acquitted. Trials of lesser figures were conducted in each of the four occupation zones. In the American zone approximately 500,000 former Nazis were convicted of war crimes.

THE PEACE TREATY. The drafting of a peace treaty with Germany was impeded by the increasingly deteriorating relations between the Western Allies and the Soviet Union. Finally, in 1955, the Western Allies signed a treaty with the six-year-old Federal Republic of Germany, by then known as West Germany. According to the treaty provisions, West Germany was granted complete independence, authorized to develop its own military force, and required to accept the stationing of Western Allied troops. Later in 1955 the Soviet Union declared the six-year-old German Democratic Republic, by then called East Germany, to be fully independent. Thus a general peace treaty with Germany was never concluded. The result was the establishment of two Germanys.

Japan. As was the case with Germany, the victorious powers had to deal with the difficult problems of occupying territory, conducting war crimes trials, and framing a peace treaty.

THE OCCUPATION. A commission based in Washington, D. C., and consisting of representatives from thirteen Allied nations, including the United States, Great Britain, France, and the Soviet Union, was to direct the occupation of Japan. However, the commission's activities were hampered by increasing animosity between the Western nations and the Soviet Union. General Douglas MacArthur was appointed Supreme Commander for the Allied Powers. In that capacity he ruled Japan. With the exception of a small number of military forces from the British Commonwealth of Nations, the troops were American. The primary goals of the occupation were to demilitarize and democratize Japan. The occupation ended in 1952. While it lasted, most Japanese were cooperative with MacArthur and his associates.

WAR CRIMES TRIALS. Early in 1946 the International Military Tribunal for the Far East, consisting of representatives from eleven Allied nations, convened in Tokyo to try twenty-five Japanese civil and military leaders for planning an aggressive war and committing crimes against humanity. Seven of the defendants, including former prime minister Hideki Tojo, were hanged; the others received prison sentences. In addition, numerous Japanese army and navy officers were brought to trial for violating the rules of war. Of those accused, approximately 6,000 were found guilty.

THE PEACE TREATY. In 1951 in San Francisco a peace treaty with Japan, which had been drafted under the direction of John Foster Dulles, a New York lawyer and foreign affairs adviser to the Truman administration, was signed by forty-nine nations. The Soviet Union, objecting to various provisions of the document, refused to become a signatory. The treaty ended the military occupation and recognized the full sovereignty of Japan. The nation was permitted to maintain armed forces for purposes of self-defense. Japan agreed to divest itself of its overseas holdings. At the San Francisco conference the United States and Japan concluded a defense treaty providing for the stationing of American armed forces in Japan. Finally, in 1956, Japan signed a separate peace treaty with the Soviet Union.

Italy, Austria, and the Axis Satellites. Hostilities were formally ended with Italy and the Axis satellites—Hungary, Bulgaria, Rumania, and Finland—before relations between the Western powers and the Soviet Union began to worsen. The postwar status of Austria, however, was affected by Western-Soviet tensions.

THE OCCUPATION. Italy and the minor Axis nations were occupied by Allied troops. The occupations did not last long, however, since peace treaties signed soon after the war provided for the prompt withdrawal of military forces from these nations. As for Austria, after its liberation from Germany it was divided for a number of years into four occupation zones, with the military forces of each of the Big Four—the United States, Great Britain, France, and the Soviet Union—in command of a particular zone.

THE PEACE TREATIES. In 1947 the Allied nations signed peace treaties with Italy and the Axis satellites. The United States did not participate in the treaty-making with Finland, since the two nations had not been at war. The treaties were quite similar in requiring Italy and each of the Axis satellites to surrender territory, to demilitarize, and to make reparations. In 1955 the Big Four signed a treaty with Austria, restoring that nation to full sovereignty and prohibiting a political union with Germany such as had occurred before World War II.

THE UNITED NATIONS

During World War II the leaders of the principal nations that were fighting the Axis powers attended a number of conferences. They discussed not only pressing military affairs but also the nature of the peace they desired and how it could be achieved. Many viewed those wartime meetings as steps in reaching the goal of permanent postwar international cooperation for peace. And many hoped that goal had been attained when in 1945 representatives of fifty nations signed the Charter of the United Nations Organization. In 1952 the permanent headquarters of the world body were finally established in New York City.

International Planning for a Peaceful World. The leaders of five Allied nations—the United States, Great Britain, the Soviet Union, France, and China—met in formal conferences over a period of three years, discussing plans for international cooperation after the war.

THE CASABLANCA CONFERENCE. In January, 1943, President Roosevelt and Prime Minister Churchill met at Casablanca in French Morocco, where after agreeing on a number of military matters, they declared that the war would continue until the "unconditional surrender" of the Axis nations.

THE MOSCOW CONFERENCE. Secretary of State Cordell Hull, Foreign Secretary Anthony Eden of Great Britain, and Foreign Minister Vyacheslav M. Molotov of the Soviet Union conferred in Moscow in October, 1943. The three men issued a statement, which came to be known as the Moscow Declaration, that a world organization for the maintenance of peace would be established after the war.

THE CAIRO CONFERENCE. In November, 1943, Roosevelt and Churchill met in Cairo with Generalissimo Chiang Kai-shek, the political and military leader of China. There they formally promised to deprive Japan of all territory it had acquired since the latter part of the nineteenth century, with the areas taken from China restored to that country.

THE TEHERAN CONFERENCE. It was in Teheran, Iran, in November, 1943, two days after the Cairo Conference was concluded, that Roosevelt, Churchill, and Premier Stalin met for the first time. In a joint declaration issued at the close of the conference the three leaders pledged that their nations would work together to win not only the war but also the peace after the war. The concluding sentence of their declaration was: "We leave here, friends in fact, in spirit, and in purpose."

THE YALTA CONFERENCE. The most fateful of all the wartime conferences took place in February, 1945, at Yalta, in the Crimea, the Soviet Union. There Roosevelt, Churchill, and Stalin met for the second and final time. They were accompanied by their most important diplomatic and military advisers. It was decided to call a special conference of all the Allies the following April in San Francisco to draft a charter for an association of nations to maintain peace. Further, Roosevelt, Churchill, and Stalin publicly agreed: (1) to divide postwar Germany into American, British, Soviet, and French occupation zones; (2) to readjust the boundaries of Poland, with that nation relinquishing a portion of its eastern area to the Soviet Union and receiving German territory to the north and west as compensation; (3) to guarantee free elections in Poland; (4) to insure the establishment of a democratic form of government for all liberated European nations.

A number of agreements made at Yalta were not made public immediately. One secret clause granted the Ukraine and Byelorussia (two of the fifteen historically and ethnically cohesive republics constituting the Soviet Union) membership in the projected postwar association of nations equal to that of independent countries. Other secret provisions pertained to the Far East. The Soviet Union promised to enter the war against Japan after Germany's anticipated surrender. In return for this pledge, the Soviet Union, according to additional secret clauses, would regain the sphere of influence it had enjoyed in Manchuria before the Russo-Japanese War of 1904–1905 and receive an occupation zone in Korea. Additionally in secret, the United States and Great Britain agreed to self-government for Outer Mongolia, which had been Chinese territory but under Soviet influence.

In the years after the Yalta Conference, the American delegation was attacked for having conceded too much to the Soviet Union. Critics argued, for example, that although the Soviet Union did enter the war against Japan, the use of the atomic bomb precluded the need for Soviet military aid in achieving Allied victory in the Far East. Counterarguments were offered in support of the American delegation. Defenders pointed out, for example, that in the matter of Soviet aid in the war in the Far East, it was widely believed that such assistance would save the lives of many American servicemen in the final offensive against Japan, that those few American leaders who knew of the atomic bomb were unsure about its potential.

THE POTSDAM CONFERENCE. The last meeting during World War II of the leaders of the three principal Allied nations took place during July–August, 1945, at Potsdam, Germany. In attendance were Harry S. Truman, who a few months earlier had become president; Churchill, who was replaced while the conference was in progress by his successor as prime minister, Clement R. Attlee; and Stalin. Germany, but not Japan, had surrendered before the conference began. A declaration was issued at the Potsdam Conference calling upon Japan to surrender unconditionally. The conferees agreed on a policy for the occupation of Germany and Japan, which included plans for both the decentralization and democratization of the two Axis nations. At Potsdam the American delegation began to perceive elements of noncooperation by representatives of the Soviet Union that had not been in evidence at the previous wartime conferences.

Drafting the United Nations Organization Charter. In 1944 and 1945 countries fighting the Axis engaged in drawing up a charter for a postwar association of nations to preserve world peace.

THE DUMBARTON OAKS CONFERENCE. Upon Secretary of State Cordell Hull's invitation, representatives of Great Britain, the Soviet Union, and China met with delegates from the United States during August–October, 1944, at Dumbarton Oaks, outside Washington, D. C., for a series of discussions concerning an international association after the war. Proposals were drafted that were to serve as the basis for the charter of the hoped-for world organization.

THE SAN FRANCISCO CONFERENCE. During April–June, 1945, approximately 300 representatives from fifty countries met in San Francisco to draw up the charter of the international association. The American delegation was headed by Secretary of State Edward R. Stettinius, Jr. At some of the sessions there were bitter exchanges between the American and Soviet representatives. After weeks of deliberation, the delegates adopted the Charter of the United Nations

Structure of the United Nations. The Charter of the United Nations established six major bodies and provided for the setting up of such specialized agencies as might be deemed useful.

GENERAL ASSEMBLY. This body was composed of all member nations, each of which had one vote. The General Assembly had the power to discuss any issue that came under the Charter and to recommend a course of action. In addition, it was granted power to supervise the specialized agencies.

SECURITY COUNCIL. This body was composed of five permanent members—the United States, Great Britain, the Soviet Union, France, China—and six (later increased to ten) members elected for overlapping two-year terms by the General Assembly. The Security Council was entrusted with the maintenance of international peace and security, being empowered to take military action for this purpose. Each permanent member was granted the right to veto a decision of the Security Council.

SECRETARIAT. This body was composed of a Secretary-General and a large staff to manage the routine affairs of the United Nations. As chief administrator of the organization, the Secretary-General was charged with implementing decisions reached by the General Assembly and the Security Council.

ECONOMIC AND SOCIAL COUNCIL. This body consisted of eighteen (later increased to twenty-seven) member nations that were elected by the General Assembly for overlapping three-year terms. The Economic and Social Council was to investigate all economic, social, cultural, educational, and health problems and then to recommend solutions.

INTERNATIONAL COURT OF JUSTICE. This body consisted of fifteen jurists elected for nine-year terms by the General Assembly and the Security Council. The Court had its headquarters at The Hague. (It replaced the Permanent Court of International Justice, known as the World Court, of the League of Nations.) The Court was to be the principal judicial organ of the United Nations.

TRUSTEESHIP COUNCIL. This body consisted equally of member nations administering and member nations not administering trust territories.[1] The trust territories included lands previously held under the mandate of the League of Nations and colonies taken from the Axis powers at the end of World War II.

SPECIALIZED AGENCIES. Subsidiary bodies, eventually totaling more than a dozen, were set up to deal with a broad range of economic and social problems. These specialized agencies included the United Nations Education, Scientific, and Cultural Organization (UNESCO), the Food and Agricultural Organization (FAO), the International Labor Organization (ILO), and the World Health Organization (WHO).

---

[1]Colonial areas not prepared for independence that the United Nations assigned to certain member nations for administration.

Chapter 14

THE QUEST FOR STABILITY AT HOME AND PEACE ABROAD

On April 12, 1945, Franklin D. Roosevelt died of a massive cerebral hemorrhage. For Harry S. Truman and then Dwight D. Eisenhower to take on the presidency following Roosevelt, who had performed brilliantly in the office for a dozen years, was exceptionally difficult. Although foreign affairs unquestionably dominated the Truman and Eisenhower administrations, many important domestic issues presented themselves. These included government reorganization and reform, the advance of civil rights, the implementation of social legislation, the regulation of labor, and the question of internal security. The conferences among Allied leaders during World War II, followed by the establishment of the United Nations, inspired hope for a lasting peace based on worldwide cooperation. In the postwar period, however, tensions increased between the Western Allies, led by the United States, and the Communist bloc of nations, led by the Soviet Union. Armed conflict between the two sides finally broke out in Korea.

TRUMAN AND THE DOMESTIC SCENE

The Truman administration faced many important issues—some of them bitterly controversial. Upon congressional acceptance of portions of his comprehensive program of social legislation, known as the Fair Deal, Truman witnessed some improvements in the general condition of the American people. The domestic issue making for the greatest controversy was that of internal security. The extent of Communist infiltration into every sector of society was examined and argued.

The Truman Administration. Truman was fully aware of his strengths and weaknesses. As president, he capitalized on the former and refused to be troubled by the latter.

THE PRESIDENT. Truman projected the image of the common man. But he was truly uncommon at bearing up under long and hard work, at grasping the various aspects of a problem, at engaging in courageous decision-making, and at being determined to help those in need.

THE CABINET. In office during a period of deep political strife, Truman kept changing cabinet members in order to find skillful administrators who could also be politically helpful. Concerned over the grave international situation, the President paid particular attention to finding a secretary of state. James F. Byrnes, who had long represented South Carolina in Congress, was appointed to the post. When Byrnes resigned for reasons of health, he was succeeded by General George C. Marshall, who had been army chief of staff during World War II. Marshall was also forced to resign because of failing health, and he was replaced by Dean Acheson, who had been serving in the State Department for a number of years. Of all the members of the cabinet, Truman's closet advisers, in addition to Byrnes, were Fred M. Vinson and John W. Snyder, each of whom served as secretary of the treasury.

Government Reorganization and Reform. In order to cope with the tremendous expansion of the federal bureaucracy that developed out of the New Deal and World War II and to deal with the difficult domestic and foreign issues stemming from the postwar period, reorganization and reform measures were deemed necessary.

THE HOOVER COMMISSION. In 1947 Congress authorized the establishment of the Commission on Organization of the Executive Branch of Government. Known as the Hoover Commission after its chairman, former President Herbert Hoover, the body was charged with recommending ways to streamline the structure of the executive branch and to economize on its operations. Acting upon the commission's findings, Truman submitted to Congress thirty-six proposals leading to reorganization of the executive branch. All were adopted by Congress except a plan for the creation of a department of welfare to consolidate government programs in health, education, and welfare.

DEPARTMENT OF DEFENSE. Rivalry among the various armed forces during World War II produced an appreciation of the need for a unified system of defense. In 1947 Congress created the Department of Defense by merging the Department of War and the Department of the Navy. A secretary of defense holding cabinet rank was to have three assistants: secretaries for the army, navy, and air force. Appointed by Truman as the nation's first secretary of defense was James V. Forrestal, who had previously served as secretary of the navy. The act of Congress creating the Department of Defense also established the Central Intelligence Agency, whose responsibility was to gather and evaluate information concerning national security.

THE PRESIDENTIAL SUCCESSION ACT. This measure revised the line of succession to the presidency that had been provided by an 1886 act of

Congress. The new act, passed in 1947, placed in line of succession to the office of chief executive after the vice-president, the Speaker of the House of Representatives and then the president pro tempore of the Senate.[1] They would be followed by the members of the cabinet, according to rank.

THE TWENTY-SECOND AMENDMENT. Passed by Congress in 1947 and ratified in 1951, the new amendment to the Constitution prohibited election to the presidency for more than two full terms or the election of a president for more than one term if he had served more than two years of an unfinished term. The amendment stemmed from the view that with the Franklin D. Roosevelt administration, presidential power so greatly increased that there should no longer be the possibility of having a multitermed chief executive. Many considered the new addition to the Constitution to have been instituted by a Republican-controlled Congress merely as a reproach to Truman's immediate predecessor.

Labor. An epidemic of strikes brought about a great deal of antilabor feeling throughout the nation, culminating in the passage of legislation by a conservative Republican-controlled Congress to curb "unfair" labor practices.

MANAGEMENT-LABOR UNREST. In the immediate post-World War II period relations between management and labor were troubled. As is usually the case, war had caused inflation. When wages lagged behind spiraling prices, workers made demands for wage increases and turned to the strike to compel employers to meet their demands. In 1946 close to 1.75 million persons were on strike. Both the United States Steel and the General Motors corporations were struck by the unions for months. A strike by maritime workers closed the nation's ports for two weeks. Railroad workers went on strike but cut short their job action when Truman threatened to have the government seize and operate the railroads. When the United Mine Workers went on strike against the bituminous coal mine companies, Truman seized the mines. The government retained control of the mines after some operators rejected a contract that had been negotiated between the union and government representatives. John L. Lewis, president of the United Mine Workers, then called on the bituminous coal miners to strike again, this time against government operation of the mines. Lewis soon ordered the miners to resume work while the Supreme Court wrestled with the legal issues. The decision was in favor of the government, and Lewis agreed to a compromise contract with the mine owners.

THE TAFT-HARTLEY ACT. In an attempt to reduce the number of management-labor disputes and to curb what the conservative Congress believed were "unfair" labor practices, the legislative branch in 1947 passed

[1]The senator selected to preside over that body in the absence of the vice-president of the United States, who normally presides.

the Labor-Management Relations Act over President Truman's veto. Commonly referred to as the Taft-Hartley Act after its two Republican sponsors, Senator Robert A. Taft of Ohio and Representative Fred A. Hartley, Jr., of New Jersey, the measure, in amending and superseding the National Labor Relations Act of 1935, removed some restrictions upon management and added a number of restrictions upon organized labor. Specifically, the Taft-Hartley Act (1) prohibited the closed shop; (2) permitted employers to sue unions for breaking contracts or for damages incurred as a result of a strike; (3) required employers and unions to give sixty days notice of a decision to modify or terminate a contract; (4) authorized the federal government to take legal action to delay for eighty days a strike that threatened public health or safety; (5) required unions to divulge their financial statements; (6) forbade unions to make contributions to political campaigns; (7) prohibited the paying of union dues by the "check-off" system;[2] (8) compelled union leaders to sign oaths that they were not members of the Communist party; (9) declared illegal the secondary boycott[3] and the jurisdictional dispute.[4]

Unions assailed the Taft-Hartley Act as a "slave labor" measure. However, by making organized labor feel a vulnerability it had not recently experienced, the act had the effect of unifying labor. In the following years President Truman repeatedly urged Congress to repeal—or at least modify—the Taft-Hartley Act, but without success.

Election of 1948. The Republican party entered the campaign certain of victory; the Democratic party, virtually with the sole exception of its nominee, began the campaign prepared for defeat. The election resulted in the most surprising political upset in the nation's history.

DEMOCRATS. The national convention of the Democratic party was a factious affair, beginning with a movement to deny Truman the nomination in favor of someone less controversial. Many party leaders turned to General Dwight D. Eisenhower, then president of Columbia University, while others turned to William O. Douglas, associate justice of the Supreme Court. After both men had made it clear that they were not available, the delegates somewhat reluctantly selected Truman as their candidate. Senator Alben W. Barkley of Kentucky was named for second place on the ticket. The platform, which praised the Truman administration for its commitment to increased social legislation and for its foreign policy, was most notable for the strong civil rights plank, adopted amid a bitter struggle.

[2] A method whereby the employer collects dues for the union from the workers' pay.

[3] A boycott of an employer in order to induce him to bring pressure upon another employer to come to terms with his workers.

[4] A dispute involving two or more unions over which one has the right to exclusive control over certain work.

REPUBLICANS. By the time the Republican national convention began its proceedings, there were three leading aspirants to the presidential nomination: Governor Thomas E. Dewey of New York, who, though he had been the party's unsuccessful standard-bearer in 1944, was the acknowledged favorite; Senator Robert A. Taft of Ohio; and former governor Harold E. Stassen of Minnesota. The convention chose Dewey on the third ballot. Governor Earl Warren of California was nominated for the vice-presidential slot. In addition to recommending such measures as civil rights protection, aid to housing, and tax reform, the platform advocated a bipartisan foreign policy.

DIXIECRATS. Following the Democratic convention a rupture occurred in the party. Some conservative southern Democrats formed the States' Rights Democratic ("Dixiecrat") party, nominating Governor J. Strom Thurmond of South Carolina for president and Governor Fielding L. Wright of Mississippi for vice-president. The platform they adopted focused on condemning the Democratic party's civil rights program.

PROGRESSIVES. Some members of the ultraliberal wing of the Democratic party also held a separate convention, where they organized the Progressive party and selected former Vice-President Henry A. Wallace for first place on the ticket and Democratic Senator Glen Taylor of Idaho as his running mate. The platform advocated a host of economic and social reforms and called for a redirection of American foreign policy toward friendship with the Soviet Union.

THE CAMPAIGN. The schisms within the Democratic party made the Republicans confident of victory. Happy with the predictions of the pollsters that he was certain to win, Dewey conducted an easygoing campaign; in an effort to avoid offending any particular group of voters, he refrained from being specific on the issues confronting the nation. Truman, on the other hand, was an energetic campaigner. Exuding plucky optimism, he traveled to all sections of the country, giving informal speeches in simple, direct language. He dwelt on the Republican-controlled "do-nothing" Eightieth Congress, assailing it for not being interested in the welfare of the people.

TRUMAN'S UPSET VICTORY. In a political upset that confounded the commentators, Truman carried twenty-eight states with 304 electoral votes; Dewey, sixteen states with 189 votes; and Thurmond, four states with 38 votes. Wallace did not win a single state. In popular votes, Truman received 24,179,000; Dewey, 21,991,000; Thurmond, 1,176,000; and Wallace, 1,157,000. The surprising outcome of the election was due to a number of reasons—in addition, of course, to Truman's courageously masterful campaigning. The overconfident Republican party conducted its campaign in too sluggish a fashion. Farmers in normally Republican states of the Midwest voted the Democratic ticket because the Democratic—but not the Republican—party was committed to fuller price-support aid to the recently declining farm prices. In several northern states attractive Democratic candidates for gubernatorial and congressional offices ran ahead of Truman and helped him carry those states. The anticipated siphoning off of millions of votes from the Democratic party by Wallace never materialized, as many people abandoned the Progressive party because of its increasing domination by radical political elements.

The Fair Deal. Truman recommended to Congress a comprehensive program of social legislation that he regarded as an extension of Franklin D. Roosevelt's New Deal; to emphasize the relationship between the two, Truman referred to his own program as the Fair Deal. Congress passed bills on housing, minimum wages, and the extension of Social Security, which the President signed into law.

THE HOUSING ACT OF 1949. This law provided approximately $2.8 billion for slum clearance and low-rent housing projects.

THE MINIMUM WAGE ACT OF 1949. This measure, by amending the Fair Labor Standards Act of 1938, increased the minimum wage from forty to seventy-five cents an hour.

SOCIAL SECURITY AMENDMENTS OF 1950. The Social Security Act of 1935 was amended to extend coverage to new groups of wage earners, to provide pensions for some who were self-employed, and to increase benefits to retired workers.

Truman's Unachieved Goals. Ahead of his time in believing that the federal government must commit itself to policies that would advance civil rights, health, and education, Truman pushed for enabling legislation. But a coalition of conservatives in Congress, composed of many Republicans and most southern Democrats, prevented the passage of these progressive and controversial portions of the Fair Deal.

CIVIL RIGHTS. Truman experienced the most disappointing failure in the area of civil rights. In 1946 the President appointed a Committee on Civil Rights, which made a number of recommendations, including the establishment of a permanent commission to enforce fair employment practices; the denial of federal subsidies to health, education, and housing facilities that practiced racial discrimination; the prohibition of segregation of the races in interstate transportation facilities; and the designation of lynching as a federal crime. Early in 1948 Truman urgently requested Congress to pass legislation embodying the proposals of the committee. When Congress failed to do so, Truman issued an executive order against segregation of the races in all government departments and another abolishing it in the armed services. After his surprising election in the fall of 1948, Truman appealed to Congress to enact measures based on the civil rights planks of the platform he had campaigned on. But the conservative southern wing of his own party was able to block the civil rights proposals. Disappointed and discouraged, Truman resorted to the only course open to him to achieve some limited gains—executive action. For example, in 1951 he appointed the first black as a judge in the federal court system and in 1951 he appointed a committee to oversee the awarding of federal defense contracts, with a charge to bar contracts to companies that practiced racial discrimination in their employment policies.

NATIONAL HEALTH INSURANCE. Congress rejected Truman's proposal for a compulsory health program, in which people would receive medical and dental care through a system of payroll deductions and matching government funds.

FEDERAL AID TO EDUCATION. Although there was strong bipartisan congressional support for Truman's plan for federal aid to the states to increase and equalize educational opportunity, the proposal foundered on the issue of whether assistance should go to parochial schools as well as to public schools.

Internal Security. As in the post-World War I era, the United States in the years following World War II was convulsed by fear of widespread Communist infiltration. In the latter period, however, there was greater justification for believing in the existence of Communist subversion, prompting the American people themselves to be more receptive to taking drastic measures against anyone suspected of it.

TRUMAN'S EXECUTIVE ORDER. As postwar relations between the United States and the Soviet Union rapidly deteriorated, the American people became increasingly suspicious that there were employees within the government who were betraying the nation to the Soviet Union. In 1947, in an effort to ferret out Communists, Truman issued an executive order inaugurating a comprehensive investigation of the loyalty of all federal employees. By the end of the probe, which lasted four years, over 3 million government employees had been cleared, approximately 2,000 had resigned, and 212 had been dismissed on the basis of a reasonable doubt as to their loyalty. Further, in what were described as "sensitive" areas of government, Truman consented to the dismissal of persons who were deemed to be not disloyal but—for one reason or another—security risks. The execution of Truman's loyalty probe was severe and thorough. However, this did not prevent the Republican party from exploiting the issue of Communists in government through allegations that the Truman administration was too "soft" on Communist infiltrators.

THE HISS CASE. In 1948 Whittaker Chambers, an editor of *Time* magazine, while giving evidence regarding a Communist cell to which he had belonged in the 1930s, named as a fellow member Alger Hiss, a former official in the Department of State. Chambers admitted to having been a messenger for the Soviet espionage system, asserting that Hiss had passed on to him State Department classified documents. Hiss denied this charge under oath before a federal grand jury. After Chambers produced evidence to corroborate his charge, Hiss was found guilty of perjury and sentenced to five years in prison.

THE ROSENBERG CASE. With the public already alarmed by the Hiss case, another episode took place that lent some credence to the wildest charges of Communist infiltration. In 1950 Klaus Fuchs, a naturalized British physicist engaged in atomic research during World War II, confessed that he had supplied the Soviet Union with data on the making of the atomic bomb. Fuchs provided information that led to the arrest of his accomplices in the United States. Julius Rosenberg, a civilian employee in the United States Army Signal Corps during World War II, and his wife Ethel were arrested and tried for passing information on atomic weapons, as well as standard military equipment, to Soviet agents. The Rosenbergs were found guilty and executed in the electric chair. Three other Americans were convicted of being members of this atomic spy ring and received long prison terms.

THE TRIAL OF COMMUNIST LEADERS. The Alien Registration Act of 1940, called the Smith Act after its congressional sponsor, among other things, declared it illegal to advocate the overthrow of the United States government by force or to belong to a group dedicated to that end. Put aside during World War II when the United States and the Soviet Union were allied against a common enemy, the act was made use of during the postwar period of American-Soviet tensions. In 1949 a dozen leaders of the American Communist party, including national chairman William Foster and national secretary Eugene Dennis, were indicted for violating the Smith Act provisions on subversive activities. Because of ill health Foster did not go on trial, but before the year was over the eleven others were tried, found guilty, and sent to prison.

THE McCARRAN ACT. Determined to strike at Communism even harder, Congress in 1950 overrode Truman's veto to pass the Internal Security Act. Known as the McCarran Act after its sponsor, Democratic Senator Pat McCarran of Nevada, it required the registration of Communist and Communist-front organizations, compelled the internment of Communists during declared national emergencies, and prohibited the employment of Communists in defense work. The McCarran Act also contained a provision forbidding immigration to the United States of anyone who had been a member of a totalitarian organization. This was amended in 1951 to permit exceptions for those who had been forced to belong to such groups.

THE McCARRAN-WALTER ACT. In 1952 Congress passed over Truman's veto an act sponsored by Senator McCarran and Republican Representative Frances E. Walter of Pennsylvania that revised existing statutes on immigration and naturalization. The McCarran-Walter Act retained from the Quota Act of 1924 the quota system that favored immigration from northern and western European countries and repealed that portion of the Quota Act that prohibited the immigration and naturalization of people from Asia.

The new act gave preferential treatment to would-be immigrants who possessed occupational skills deemed useful to American society or the economy and to relatives of American citizens. The act barred entry into the United States of anyone who had been a member of a Communist or Communist-front organization, and it provided for the deportation of any immigrant or naturalized citizen who, once in the United States, participated in a Communist or Communist-front organization.

EISENHOWER AND MODERATE REPUBLICANISM

In 1953, after twenty years of Democratic rule, the nation had a Republican Chief Executive. However, the new President, Dwight D. Eisenhower, disappointed those conservative members of his party who wanted a frontal attack on the laws passed during Roosevelt's New Deal and Truman's Fair Deal. The moderates of both major parties at the time of the Eisenhower administration accepted the principle that the federal government was responsible for the welfare of its citizens.

Election of 1952. "Time for a change" proved to be an effective slogan for the Republican party, which, without alienating its liberal and internationalist wing, succeeded in winning the votes of the conservative and isolationist-oriented Americans in the Middle and Far West.

DEMOCRATS. The Democratic national convention was wide open because Truman refused to become a candidate—thus there was a host of contenders. The leading aspirants to the presidential nomination were Vice-President Alben W. Barkley; Governor Adlai E. Stevenson of Illinois; foreign affairs specialist and former secretary of commerce W. Averell Harriman; and senators Estes Kefauver of Tennessee, Richard B. Russell of Georgia, and Robert S. Kerr of Oklahoma. On the third ballot the nomination went to Stevenson, who insisted that he was being drafted. For second place on the ticket the convention named Senator John J. Sparkman of Alabama, hoping thus to overcome the disaffection of some of the southern Democratic leaders.

REPUBLICANS. By the time the Republican national convention began its proceedings, there were two front-runners for the presidential nomination: General Dwight D. Eisenhower (who had just relinquished his position as Supreme Commander of NATO) and Senator Robert A. Taft of Ohio. The former was supported by the party's liberal and internationalist wing; the latter was the candidate of the more conservative and isolationist "Old Guard" Republicans. After a spirited revolt of many delegates against the Taft supporters, who seemed to have control of the convention committees, the convention gave a first–ballot nomination to Eisenhower. Selected to be his running mate was Senator Richard M. Nixon of California, who was presented as a fighter against Communist infiltration in the civil service.

THE CAMPAIGN. Governor Stevenson, with his rare philosophical and literary skill, tried to convince the voters that the nation was threatened by poverty at home and tyranny and war abroad—and that the struggles against those menaces were costly but necessary. But Stevenson could not overcome the personal popularity of General Eisenhower. Perhaps the most effective piece of oratory of the campaign was Eisenhower's simple promise regarding the war that for 2½ years had been going on in Asia between United Nations and Communist forces: "I will go to Korea." The American people hoped he could thus end the armed conflict.

EISENHOWER'S VICTORY. Eisenhower received 33,936,000 popular and 442 electoral votes to Stevenson's 27,314,000 popular and 89 electoral votes. However, the size of this victory did not carry over to the congressional vote. The Republicans won control of the House of Representatives, but by a slim margin; the Republican margin in the Senate was dependent upon liberal Senator Wayne Morse of Oregon, who had supported Stevenson in the election as an "Independent Republican." To have his legislative program passed by Congress, Eisenhower would thus be compelled to solicit support from conservative Democrats as well as Republicans.

The Eisenhower Administration.

Eisenhower did not believe in exercising strong presidential leadership, expressing concern that such a practice did damage to the important—and delicate—balance among the executive, legislative, and judicial branches of government. As president he delegated much authority to his subordinates and relied heavily upon the recommendations of his advisers.

THE PRESIDENT. Eisenhower was a sincere, unpretentious, and kind man. His winning smile topped off an affable manner. He did not possess the gift of eloquence. Finding partisan conflict distasteful, he made a conscious effort to shun it, thus appearing to be "above" politics. Fond of leisure activities, he devoted much time to playing golf, painting, and reading stories about the Old West.

THE CABINET. It was clear from the beginning that the Eisenhower cabinet was industrially and commercially oriented. More than half the appointees were businessmen; all except one were millionaires. Chosen secretary of state was John Foster Dulles, a New York lawyer who had been a consultant on foreign affairs to the Truman administration. George M. Humphrey, head of an Ohio-based firm with extensive interests in shipping and steel, became secretary of the treasury. Charles E. Wilson, president of General Motors Corporation, was named secretary of defense. These three became the most powerful figures in the cabinet. In the conduct of American foreign affairs Eisenhower permitted Dulles more control than had been exercised by any previous secretary of state.

ASSISTANT TO THE PRESIDENT. Sherman Adams, former governor of New Hampshire, was appointed Assistant to the President. As head of

Eisenhower's personal staff, the extraordinarily hard-working and efficient Adams wielded enormous power in executing the many and varied duties assigned to him. In 1958 he felt compelled to resign after being widely criticized for accepting gifts from a businessman whose operations were being investigated by the government.

Government Reorganization and Reform. The Eisenhower administration made a commitment to continue the work of government reorganization and reform that had been successfully started by the preceding administration.

THE SECOND HOOVER COMMISSION. In 1953 Congress authorized the establishment of the Commission on Organization of the Executive Branch of the Government. Known as the Second Hoover Commission after its chairman, former President Herbert Hoover, it was charged with proposing methods to streamline the structure of the executive branch, a task similar to that of the 1947 Hoover Commission. Most of the commission's recommendations were approved by Congress.

DEPARTMENT OF HEALTH, EDUCATION, AND WELFARE. In 1947 President Truman's proposal for the establishment of a department of welfare to coordinate government-sponsored social programs was defeated by a coalition of congressional conservatives. A few years later the legislative branch took positive action. In 1953 Congress created the Department of Health, Education, and Welfare, the head of which would be a cabinet member. The new department was established to consolidate and supervise the various government agencies that dealt with the health, education, and social and economic welfare of the American people. Appointed by Eisenhower as the first secretary of health, education, and welfare was Oveta Culp Hobby, who had commanded the Women's Army Corps during World War II.

Social Legislation in Eisenhower's First Term. Although Eisenhower was elected comfortably to the presidency in 1952, his party carried the House of Representatives by a narrow margin and, with the support of Independent Wayne Morse, tied the Democrats in the Senate. The President thus needed and sought bipartisan support to enact his legislative proposals into law.

SOCIAL SECURITY AMENDMENTS OF 1954. Congress amended the Social Security Act to provide coverage to new occupational groups, including farmers and state and local government employees, and to increase the amount of pensions to retirees.

THE MINIMUM WAGE ACT OF 1955. This measure increased the minimum hourly wage from seventy-five cents to one dollar.

McCarthyism. There were many politicians who exploited the deep anti-Communist feeling in the nation, but no one did so with such vehemence and initial success as Republican Senator Joseph R. McCarthy of Wisconsin. And because of his activities his name entered the English language. The term McCarthyism soon came to denote the making of indiscriminate and unsubstantiated charges of subversive activities.

THE SENATOR AND HIS TACTICS. McCarthy first achieved national prominence when he charged in a speech delivered in West Virginia in February, 1950, that he had in his possession a list of "card-carrying" Communists in the State Department. But he was never able to prove his case. Over the next few years he alleged that a number of government agencies were infiltrated by Communists, Communist sympathizers, and "security risks." Anyone who took issue with him he characterized as disloyal or obtuse. He charged with treasonable conduct such persons as General George C. Marshall and Secretary of State Dean Acheson.

THE McCARTHY-ARMY DISPUTE. In 1954 the army accused McCarthy of attempting to obtain preferential treatment for an assistant who had been drafted. McCarthy, who chaired both the Senate Committee on Government Operations and its permanent Subcommittee on Investigations, countered that the army was trying to embarrass him for his investigations of spying at Army Signal Corps facilities at Fort Monmouth, New Jersey. During April–June, 1954, televised hearings were held on the two sets of charges. In many confrontations with army counsel Joseph B. Welch, McCarthy's bullying methods were revealed to an estimated 20 million American viewers, with the result that the senator's reputation among his supporters was severely damaged.

CONDEMNATION BY THE SENATE. The public exposure during the hearings of McCarthy's long-standing methods convinced the Senate to take action. In December, 1954, the upper house by a vote of 67 to 22 decided to "condemn" his conduct as "unbecoming a member of the United States Senate." His influence was precipitately destroyed.

Election of 1956. The result of the election was a triumphant victory for Eisenhower, who sought a second term, but it was not a success for his party as a whole.

DEMOCRATS. On the first ballot the delegates to the Democratic national convention nominated for president their 1952 standard-bearer, Adlai E. Stevenson. Senator Estes Kefauver of Tennessee was selected for second place on the ticket.

REPUBLICANS. The national convention of the Republican party was a harmonious affair. Neither a heart attack in the summer of 1955 nor an operation for an intestinal ailment in the summer of 1956 could deter Eisenhower from seeking a second term, and he was nominated by acclamation on the first ballot. Chosen as his running mate was Vice-President Nixon.

THE CAMPAIGN. With Eisenhower and Stevenson again competing for the presidency, the campaign was in many ways a recapitulation of the one conducted four years earlier. Stevenson, however, shied away from the profundity of thought and eloquence of wit that he had exhibited in 1952, having been convinced by some of his advisers that it had all been too "heavy" for most of the voters.

EISENHOWER'S VICTORY. Eisenhower polled 35,580,000 popular votes to Stevenson's 26,031,000 and received 457 electoral votes to Stevenson's 73. Eisenhower took seven of the states in the Solid South, one more than the number the Republican had carried in the region four years earlier. The voters' overwhelming endorsement of the President did not, however; apply to his party. The Democrats captured both houses of Congress.

Social Legislation in Eisenhower's Second Term. After his reelection, Eisenhower began to exert pressure on Congress for his legislative program. Since both houses of that body were Democratic-controlled, the President sought—as he had been forced to do during his first term—bipartisan support to enact those measures into law. He was, to a degree, successful.

SOCIAL SECURITY AMENDMENTS OF 1956. The Social Security Act was extended to cover new vocational groups, such as physicians and those in the armed services. Also, the eligibility age for receiving pensions was lowered for women to sixty-two and the eligibility age for receiving benefits was lowered for disabled workers to fifty.

THE NATIONAL DEFENSE EDUCATION ACT. Alarmed by Soviet achievements in space, Congress authorized the expenditure of $887 million over a four-year period for the improvement of American education. The act, passed in 1958, among other things, provided funds for (1) long-term, low-interest loans to undergraduate college students, with half the loan to be canceled for those who after receiving their degrees taught in elementary or secondary schools for at least five years; (2) fellowships for graduate students who agreed to enter college or university teaching; (3) matching grants with state governments to public schools for the purchase of textbooks and laboratory equipment to improve the teaching of mathematics, science, and modern languages. Later congressional action extended the measure for two more years at a cost of $500 million.

SOCIAL SECURITY AMENDMENTS OF 1958. Further amendments to the Social Security Act provided for a substantial increase in benefits to those receiving old-age, survivor's, and disability assistance.

Civil Rights. The issue of extending equality of public treatment to black Americans divided the nation along sectional rather than party lines. The Truman administration was supported by many Republicans and the Eisenhower administration by many northern Democrats in the effort to broaden the application of civil rights. Encouraged by a basic sympathy on their behalf by the Truman and Eisenhower administrations, blacks became increasingly more active in attempting to improve their status.

BROWN V. BOARD OF EDUCATION OF TOPEKA. By the middle of the twentieth century most public schools in the South were racially segregated by state or local laws, whereas in the North a number of public schools were segregated because of custom or the separation of the white and black races through neighborhood housing patterns. The Supreme Court in the *Plessy* v. *Ferguson* case of 1896 had decided that a Louisiana law requiring "separate but equal" facilities for whites and blacks on railroad cars was constitutional. The "separate but equal" doctrine for segregation was soon extended in the South to other kinds of public accommodations, including educational institutions. But schools for whites were almost without exception superior to those for blacks. On May 17, 1954, the Supreme Court, presided over by Chief Justice Earl Warren, handed down a momentous decision on the issue of segregation in the public schools that reversed the Court's earlier position. The *Brown* v. *Board of Education of Topeka* case involved a Kansas law requiring segregated classrooms in the public elementary and secondary schools of the state. In this case the Court held unanimously that segregation in the public schools was unconstitutional. The justices declared that maintenance of "separate but equal" school facilities for blacks (which was the practice in seventeen states) was a denial of the guarantee of equal protection of the laws established by the Fourteenth Amendment to the Constitution. Writing the opinion for the Court, Chief Justice Warren stated that separating black children from others solely because of their race "generates a feeling of inferiority as to their status in a community that may affect their hearts and minds in a way unlikely ever to be undone" and therefore concluded that "separate educational facilities are inherently unequal." In 1955 the Supreme Court ordered that the desegregation of public schools should begin "with all deliberate speed."

THE MONTGOMERY BUS BOYCOTT. In December, 1955, a Montgomery, Alabama, black woman, Rosa Parks, refused to give up her seat on a bus to a white man and was arrested. The black community decided to call a boycott of the buses as a protest against segregated seating on public transportation in the city. Car pools among blacks were organized. Under the skillful leadership of the Reverend Dr. Martin Luther King, Jr., a Baptist minister, the bus boycott was extraordinarily successful. Enduring intense hostility from many whites of the city, the black community persevered in the boycott month after month. In November, 1956, the Supreme Court declared segregated seating in local transportation unconstitutional. Soon thereafter the blacks of Montgomery began using the city buses once more—and sat where they pleased. The Montgomery bus boycott had become the first direct community action by blacks to achieve national prominence.

THE CIVIL RIGHTS ACT OF 1957. Influenced both by the ruling of the Supreme Court for school desegregation and by the increasing activism of blacks to improve their condition, Congress passed a civil rights act—the first since the Reconstruction period. After long and hard debate, during which many conservative white southern legislators voiced strenuous objections to a civil rights measure, Congress passed an act creating a Civil Rights Commission, composed of six members. The commission was to investigate the denial of voting rights and the violation of the equal protection of the laws and to make recommendations for new legislation as it saw the need. The attorney general was authorized to obtain court orders to secure the right to vote anywhere in the nation.

THE CIVIL RIGHTS ACT OF 1960. After the Civil Rights Commission appointed by President Eisenhower under the Civil Rights Act of 1957 had declared that the act was in itself ineffectual in protecting the voting rights of blacks, Congress passed another measure. The Civil Rights Act of 1960 empowered federal judges to appoint referees to assist blacks in registering and voting. Further, in order to halt a spate of recent bombings of buildings, such as churches and schools, used by blacks, the act made it a federal crime to transport explosives across a state line in order to bomb a building or to cross a state line in order to escape prosecution for having bombed a building.

CONFRONTATION IN LITTLE ROCK. Implicit in the ruling in the *Brown* v. *Board of Education of Topeka* case of 1954 was the Supreme Court's understanding that enforcement of desegration would require careful planning over a considerable period of time. The Eisenhower administration encouraged the states to work out their own plans. At hundreds of schools in the South integration was accomplished peacefully. But there were scattered incidents of violent opposition, the most prominent occurring in Little Rock, Arkansas. In September, 1957, the Board of Education of Little Rock was prepared to admit to one of the city's high schools nine carefully selected black students. Governor Orval Faubus of Arkansas, insisting that violence would break out if the students were admitted to classes, used the Arkansas National Guard to bar them from the school building. President Eisenhower declared that Faubus's action violated the law of the nation. Obeying a federal court injunction, Faubus withdrew the National Guard. When a taunting, riot-prone mob prevented the black students from going into the high school, Eisenhower responded by ordering federal troops to Little Rock. During the entire academic year of 1957–1958 the troops protected the nine black students.

New States. The admission of Alaska and Hawaii to the Union put an end to the issue of whether the United States must be composed of contiguous land on the North American continent.

ALASKA. In January, 1959, after Congress had approved the necessary enabling legislation, President Eisenhower issued a proclamation declaring Alaska the forty-ninth state of the Union. The new state ranked first in area and last in population. Alaska's importance to the rest of the nation was due to its vast natural resources, particularly mineral wealth.

HAWAII. Bringing Alaska into the Union gave impetus to a half-century-old movement for granting statehood to Hawaii. In August, 1959, after Congress had passed the required bill, President Eisenhower proclaimed Hawaii the fiftieth state of the Union. Reflecting the ethnic diversity of Hawaiian society, the first elected congressional delegation was composed of one senator of white mainland ancestry, one of Chinese ancestry, and a representative of Japanese ancestry. Hawaii provides the naval base at Pearl Harbor, the most important American naval station in the Pacific.

THE COLD WAR

One year after World War II ended, relations began to deteriorate between the Western Allies, under the general leadership of the United States, and the Communist bloc, which was strictly led by the Soviet Union. According to the phrase used by Winston Churchill in 1946, an "iron curtain" had been dropped by the Soviets across Europe from north to south, thus establishing a barrier between Soviet-controlled Eastern Europe on one side and Western Europe plus the Western Hemisphere on the other. The persistent hostility between the Western and Communist nations was soon called the Cold War.

Checking Communism in Europe. Underlying the struggle for power between the Western Allies and the Communist bloc was the knowledge that if the Cold War were to become "hot" over an issue on the European continent, it could possibly turn into an atomic war—and bring doom to humankind.

THE TRUMAN DOCTRINE. Early in 1947 Greece experienced attacks by native Communist guerrilla bands that were receiving aid from Communist nations to the north. In the same year demands were made upon Turkey by the Soviet Union for the granting of military bases and for concessions in the Dardanelles, the strait that is part of the waterway connecting the Black Sea and the Mediterranean Sea. Truman reacted to the situation by delivering an address to Congress in March, 1947, requesting an appropriation of $400 million for economic and military aid to bolster the governments of Greece and Turkey. Congress complied and the assistance proved effective. Truman's message was, however, more far-reaching than a request for aid to Greece and Turkey. The President called for the containment of Soviet expansion and pledged the use of American economic and military resources to help the "free peoples" of Europe resist Communist aggression, whether by direct attack or subversion. This policy became known as the Truman Doctrine. In providing the ground for the principle of containment, the Truman Doctrine can be regarded as the basis for the American position in the Cold War.

THE MARSHALL PLAN. After Congress had provided assistance to Greece and Turkey, Secretary of State George C. Marshall recognized the need for the United States to support the economic and social recovery of Europe from the effects of World War II in order to preserve governments established on that continent. In June, 1947, in an address at Harvard University, Marshall pointed out that the United States was anxious to cooperate with Europe, if the nations of the continent were ready to formulate a program for mutual reconstruction. By declaring that American policy would be directed "not against any country or doctrine but against hunger, poverty, desperation, and chaos," Marshall made it clear that the Communist nations were welcome to participate in the program.

This offer was accepted by sixteen Western and Western-oriented nations, including Great Britain, France, Italy, Greece, and Turkey. In July, 1947, the participatory nations sent representatives to a conference in Paris, where details were worked out for international cooperation along economic lines. The Soviet Union and its allies refused to send representatives, charging that the entire program was an American imperialist plot for the economic enslavement of Europe. In December, 1947, Truman submitted to Congress a proposal entitled the European Recovery Program, which incorporated much from the report of the conference in Paris on Europe's needs. A few months later, and after much discussion, Congress approved a modified version of the Truman administration's European Recovery Program. Popularly called the Marshall Plan, the program was in existence from 1948 to 1951. Under the Marshall Plan the American government provided Europe with aid totaling approximately $15 billion, most of which was spent in the United States for foodstuffs, raw materials, and machinery. The impact of the Marshall Plan on the European nations was soon noticeable. It accomplished the following: (1) promoted strong economic recovery, permitting many nations to surpass prewar levels of production; (2) spurred cooperative economic enterprises among Western European nations, such as the customs union established by Belgium, the Netherlands, and Luxembourg; (3) promoted political stability; (4) stiffened the resistance of European nations to Communist expansionism.

THE BERLIN AIRLIFT. In 1948 the Soviet Union refused to consider a Western proposal on the status of Berlin and also insisted that Soviet currency be the sole medium of exchange not only in the Soviet occupation zone of the city but also in the American, British, and French zones. The increasing tension precipitated strong Soviet action. In June, 1948, the Soviet Union imposed a blockade on all surface traffic (road, rail, and canal) moving from the three western occupation zones of Germany through the Soviet occupation zone to the three western sectors of Berlin, which lay within the Soviet zone. The Western powers, led by the United States, responded by establishing an air corridor between their zones in western Germany and their respective sectors of Berlin, along which they could fly supplies into the city. For more than ten months about 1,000 planes a day flew cargoes of food, fuel, and other basic necessities to the more than 2 million people of the western zones of Berlin. The massive airlift strikingly demonstrated the determination of the Western Allies not to be forced into a policy of appeasing the Soviet Union. The only option available to the Soviet Union to thwart the airlift was to attack the planes, but it was disinclined to do so since such action could very well have precipitated war. Finally, in May, 1949, the Soviet Union announced that it would terminate the blockade if the three Western Allies would lift the counterblockade that they had set up and if the foreign ministers of the four occupying powers would meet soon to enter into discussions on the future of Germany in general and of Berlin in particular.

THE NORTH ATLANTIC TREATY ORGANIZATION (NATO). A number of Western observers felt that the Soviet announcement in May, 1949, of willingness to negotiate on the status of Germany had been induced in part by the success of the Western nations in achieving a treaty among themselves. In April, 1949, twelve nations on both sides of the North Atlantic—including the United States, Canada, Great Britain, France, Italy, Belgium, the Netherlands, and Norway—signed the North Atlantic Treaty, by which they would consider an attack upon any one of them as an attack upon all. The signatories pledged that they would go to the defense of an attacked member of the pact, if necessary with armed force. The membership of the alliance was increased to fifteen when it admitted Greece and Turkey in 1952 and West Germany in 1955. For the United States, becoming a party to the North Atlantic Treaty was a momentous decision, marking the nation's first military alliance with Europe during peacetime.

To implement the defensive pact the original signatories formed in 1950 the North Atlantic Treaty Organization (NATO), which integrated the military forces of member nations for optimum defense. NATO differed from previous alliances in that it provided not only for joint action in wartime but also for joint military and economic action in peacetime. The headquarters of NATO were established in Paris, and various regional military commands were set up. The command headquarters in Europe, named Supreme Headquarters, Allied Powers in Europe (SHAPE) is led by the Supreme Allied Commander in Europe, who has thus far been an American general. The first to occupy the post was General Dwight D. Eisenhower. As a counterforce to NATO, the Communist nations adopted the Warsaw Pact, a military alliance of seven Eastern European Communist countries (East Germany was admitted in 1955), led by the Soviet Union.

Since NATO was established there have been a number of disputes among the member nations. Many difficulties were precipitated by France. In 1966 French President Charles de Gaulle, an ardent nationalist and archcritic of American influence in NATO, withdrew French military forces from NATO and demanded that NATO troops in France be put under that country's control or be removed. However, he pledged that France would still honor its commitments as a signatory to the original North Atlantic Treaty of 1949. The following year the other nations withdrew the NATO troops from France and transferred NATO and SHAPE headquarters from in and near Paris to in and near Brussels, Belgium.

THE GENEVA SUMMIT CONFERENCE. In an attempt to ease Western-Soviet tensions the heads of the American, British, French, and Soviet governments met in July, 1955, at Geneva, Switzerland, for the first summit conference.[5] The United States was represented by President Dwight D. Eisenhower, Great Britain by Prime Minister Anthony Eden, France by Premier Edgar Faure, and the Soviet Union by Premier Nikolai A. Bulganin and First Secretary of the Soviet Communist Party Nikita S. Khrushchev. (Bulganin headed the Soviet government in name only; Khrushchev held the real power.) The participants rejected war as an instrument of national policy and agreed to increase economic and cultural contacts between the Western Allies and the Soviet Union. They discussed the issues of political unification of Germany and disarmament by the leading powers, but failed to reach an agreement on either matter. The discussion on disarmament prompted the participating nations to hold subsequent meetings on that issue; these also brought no conclusion. Although the conferees at Geneva settled only some of the important issues, they did conduct themselves in a strikingly affable manner, which generated for a brief time a spirit of good will between the Western Allies and the Soviet Union.

THE HUNGARIAN REVOLT. In the post–World War II period the Soviet Union's allies—Poland, Czechoslovakia, Hungary, Rumania, Bulgaria, and Albania—came under the control of Moscow. Yugoslavia also had a Communist regime, but under Premier Josip Tito it frequently followed an independent line and consequently secured economic aid from the Western powers. In October, 1956, a revolt against Soviet domination took place in Hungary. Hungarian Premier Imre Nagy, a nationalistic Communist and follower of Tito, demanded the immediate removal from Hungary of Soviet troops and announced his nation's withdrawal from the Warsaw Pact, the alliance of Communist countries. The Soviet Union stated that it would make concessions. President Eisenhower publicly described these developments as the beginning of a wonderful new era for Eastern Europe. However, Secretary of State John Foster Dulles had let it be understood regarding an earlier uprising against Soviet domination in Poland that the

[5]A meeting attended by two or more heads of state, usually representing both Western and Communist nations; the term was originated by Winston Churchill in his post–World War II appeal for an international meeting "at the summit."

United States would not give military assistance to the insurgents. In November Soviet troops entered Hungary and crushed the revolt. A puppet government was set up under Janos Kadar, secretary of the Hungarian Communist party. Soon after this successful Soviet retaliation, Eisenhower felt compelled to declare that American policy did not advocate uprisings within the nations allied to the Soviet Union. The final action taken by the United States concerning the short-lived revolt was to give asylum to thousands of Hungarians who fled their homeland.

THE U-2 INCIDENT. In September, 1959, Nikita S. Khrushchev, who was then premier of the Soviet Union as well as first secretary of the Soviet Communist party, made a tour of the United States upon President Eisenhower's invitation. The two leaders used the occasion to engage in some face-to-face negotiations and to lay plans for a new summit conference, the first since the 1955 Geneva meeting, to be held the following spring in Europe. On May 1, 1960, two weeks before the summit conference was to take place in Paris, an unarmed American U-2 reconnaissance plane was shot down deep within Soviet territory. On May 7 Khrushchev announced that the pilot, Francis Gary Powers, was alive and had confessed to high-altitude photographing of Soviet military installations. (Powers was subsequently tried in the Soviet Union for espionage, found guilty, and sentenced to ten years in prison, of which he served a year and a half before being exchanged for a Soviet agent.) After Powers's admission Eisenhower stated that he himself had authorized the U-2 flights, which he defended as the only means of gathering certain information vital to the security of the United States. Nevertheless, he ordered future U-2 flights canceled. Such an admission of espionage activity by a head of government was unprecedented. By May 16 Eisenhower and Khrushchev, along with Prime Minister Harold Macmillan of Great Britain and President Charles de Gaulle of France, had assembled in Paris to begin the summit conference. But Khrushchev vilified Eisenhower and declared that he would not participate in the summit conference unless the President apologized for the U-2 flights. Eisenhower refused to do so, and Khrushchev left for the Soviet Union in anger. The summit conference never took place.

The Korean War. An unprovoked assault upon South Korea by North Korean forces was regarded by many in the United States and in Western Europe as a signal that the Cold War was moving into the stage of widespread military hostilities.

THE DIVISION OF KOREA. At the end of World War II, Japan was divested of Korea, which had long been its protectorate. Korea was divided at 38° north latitude into two zones of occupation; the northern part of the peninsula was commanded by Soviet troops and the southern part by American troops.

THE REPUBLIC OF KOREA. The United States and the Soviet Union failed to agree on the unification of Korea. After having trained and equipped a strong native army, the Soviet Union in 1948 established a Communist government in North Korea. Soviet troops then left. In the same year South Korean elections under the supervision of the United Nations resulted in the establishment of the Republic of Korea with Dr. Syngman Rhee as head of an anti-Communist government. President Rhee was an ardent nationalist who hoped eventually to incorporate North Korea into the Republic of Korea. In 1949 the last American occupying forces were withdrawn.

NORTH KOREAN AGGRESSION. In June, 1950, without warning, North Korean troops, led by Soviet-trained officers and supplied with Soviet equipment, crossed the 38th parallel and invaded South Korea.

UNITED NATIONS ACTION. The United Nations Security Council, with the Soviet delegate absent, declared North Korea an aggressor and recommended that member nations of the world organization render military aid under its auspices to South Korea. The United Nations forces consisted of units from seventeen Western and Western-oriented nations, with the bulk of combat personnel furnished by the United States and South Korea. The United Nations forces in Korea were commanded by General Douglas MacArthur. In the course of their military drive the North Korean forces had enjoyed tremendous success, occupying within three months all of South Korea except for a small enclave in the southeast. The United Nations forces under MacArthur then launched a counterattack that drove the enemy back across the 38th parallel and deep into North Korea close to the border of the Chinese region of Manchuria until, by November, 1950, three-fourths of North Korea was occupied by United Nations troops.

CHINESE INTERVENTION. In November, 1950, the new Communist regime in neighboring China sent its troops across the Manchurian border into North Korea, apparently with the determination to defeat the United Nations forces and drive them from the entire Korean peninsula. The United Nations General Assembly voted, with opposition only from the Soviet Union and its allies, to declare Communist China guilty of aggression.

DISMISSAL OF MacARTHUR. General MacArthur wanted to launch an all-out counteroffensive against Communist Chinese troops, even to the point of carrying the war into Communist China itself by attacking in Manchuria. Committed to conducting a limited war in Asia, President Truman felt certain that an invasion of Manchuria would precipitate war with the Soviet Union and Communist China. Frequent disagreements between Truman and MacArthur over the way in which the Korean war should be conducted caused an open rupture between the two. In April, 1951, President Truman relieved the general of his command for disobeying an order to refrain from making foreign policy statements that were counter to the government's official foreign policy position. MacArthur was replaced in Korea by General Matthew B. Ridgway. On returning to the United States, MacArthur was hailed by some as a hero, but many agreed with the President that the real issue in the Truman-MacArthur dispute was the subordination of the military to civil authority and that drastic action was needed in order to prevent the fighting in Korea from developing into a third world war.

THE ARMISTICE. In June, 1951, after the North Korean and Communist Chinese troops had been checked by the United Nations forces just north of the 38th parallel, the Soviet Union suggested that discussions between the antagonists in Korea could lead to a cease-fire. Negotiations between the North Korean and Communist Chinese team on the one hand and the United Nations team on the other began promptly, but dragged on month after month with each side trying to check the other's diplomatic moves. The truce talks took place mainly at Panmunjom at the 38th parallel. The issue on which the negotiations were deadlocked was that of repatriation of prisoners of war. The United Nations team insisted that each prisoner should be free to choose whether or not he wished to return to the nation for which he had been fighting, while the Communist team demanded the compulsory repatriation of all. In December, 1952, Eisenhower as President-elect put into effect a campaign promise he had made to visit the Korean front. Although not directly related to the truce negotiations at Panmunjom, his military inspection signified the great desire of Americans to end the war. An armistice was finally signed in July, 1953, fixing the line of demarcation between North Korea and South Korea and providing for repatriation of prisoners of war on a voluntary basis.

AMERICAN WAR COSTS. In Korea about 55,000 American men died and some 104,000 were wounded in combat. The United States spent an estimated $18 billion on the war.

Combating Communist Expansion. While the leading nations of the Western Allies continued to give full support to the United Nations, they formed new alliances in efforts to limit indirect as well as direct Communist expansion.

THE CIVIL WAR IN CHINA. In the post–World War II period the Nationalist Chinese government under Generalissimo Chiang Kai-shek lost the people's support. The regime was widely criticized as being inefficient, corrupt, and unconcerned about much-needed economic and social reforms for both rural peasants and urban workers. The Chinese Communists, led by Mao Tse-tung, exploited the deep anti-Nationalist feelings throughout the nation. Supplied with equipment from the Soviet Union, they concentrated in the northern part of the nation, and engaged in military action, achieving victory after victory over the Nationalist troops and in the process broadening their territorial base.

While in no way sympathetic toward the Communists, the United States was reluctant to become enmeshed in what appeared to be a long civil war on the side of the Nationalist Chinese government, a World War II ally now held in disrepute. At the end of 1945 General George C. Marshall, who had recently retired as army chief of staff, was sent to China by President Truman to attempt to bring about a settlement between the Communist and Nationalist factions. Marshall tried unsuccessfully to convince Chiang Kai-shek to introduce reforms, not only because they were needed but also because they would counteract Communist propaganda. After six months of frustrating activity, Marshall managed to arrange a truce between the Communists and Nationalists, but it was broken as soon as he returned to the United States.

When Marshall became secretary of state early in 1947 he argued successfully for the withdrawal of all American military forces from China, maintaining that support of Chiang Kai-shek's regime would require more men and matériel than the American government could, in practical terms, supply. American economic aid to the Nationalist forces, however, never stopped. During the next three years the Communist troops continued to make steady and striking gains of territory. Ultimately, in December, 1949, Chiang Kai-shek and his followers fled the Chinese mainland and set up the Nationalist government on the offshore island of Formosa (so named by early Portuguese explorers; called Taiwan by the Chinese). The Communists immediately proclaimed the establishment of the People's Republic of China with Mao Tse-tung as chairman and Chou En-lai as premier.

Although many nations, including a number from the Western bloc, recognized the Communist rule, the United States promptly accepted the regime on Taiwan as the true government of China. The United States viewed Taiwan with its 10 million original inhabitants and the 2 million Nationalist (military and civilian) refugees from the mainland as an important American military base in the Pacific, and the Nationalist army as a dependable military force to be used in case of need. Consequently, the United States extended economic and military aid to Taiwan and pledged to defend it against aggression. As for the People's Republic of China, with its population of 800 million, over the next two decades the United States consistently refused recognition to it, prevented its admission to the United Nations, and maintained an embargo on trade with it.

THE POINT FOUR PROGRAM. President Truman in his 1949 inaugural address advocated four major courses of action for the nation to take in its quest for international peace. The fourth point called for technical assistance to underdeveloped nations to raise their living standards. Congress responded to this recommendation by authorizing the Technical Assistance Program, known as the Point Four Program. Large sums of money were subsequently appropriated to meet the needs of the peoples of

Asia, as well as of Africa and Latin America. In so doing, the United States hoped to make less attractive to those people the economic and social principles of Communism.

THE ANZUS PACT. In 1951 Australia, New Zealand, and the United States signed a mutual defense treaty. Called the ANZUS Pact from the first letters of the member nations' names, it declared that an attack upon one of the signatories constituted a danger to all. Each nation pledged to act within its constitutional processes to meet the common danger.

SEATO. In 1954 eight nations—the United States, Great Britain, France, Australia, New Zealand, the Philippines, Thailand, and Pakistan—signed a collective defense treaty, forming what came to be called the Southeast Asia Treaty Organization (SEATO). The member nations pledged to act jointly against aggression toward any one of them. The United States became a signatory on condition that the aggression in question be considered to mean only that from the Communist bloc of nations.

THE TREATY WITH NATIONALIST CHINA. In 1954 the United States signed a treaty with Nationalist China providing for mutual aid in the defense of Taiwan and the Pescadores, a group of islands belonging to Taiwan and lying in the strait between it and Communist-held mainland China. Four years later Quemoy and Matsu, two offshore island groups that were occupied by the Nationalist government, were shelled from the mainland. Although the 1954 mutual defense treaty did not cover islands just off mainland China, such as Quemoy and Matsu, the United States chose to become involved in the shelling incident to the degree that it dispatched warships to escort through nearby international waters the Nationalist vessels carrying supplies to Quemoy.

The Middle East. After World War II both Great Britain and France, weakened by the effects of the recent armed conflict, steadily lost their influence in the Middle East. As a consequence, the United States found itself with increasing responsibilities in the area. The Arab nations, which had been so long under Western European domination, learned quickly how to play the United States against the Soviet Union and thus gain concessions from both powers.

THE SUEZ CANAL CRISIS. In 1955 Egypt began receiving military and technical aid from the Soviet Union and its allies. In attempting to forestall Soviet influence in the region, Secretary of State Dulles promised Egypt financial assistance to build a dam on the Nile River at Aswan. But with Egyptian President Gamal Abdel Nasser exhibiting increasing friendship for the Communist bloc of nations and hostility toward the Western bloc, the Eisenhower administration, upon Dulles's strong recommendation, in 1956 abruptly withdrew its offer of aid. Thereupon Nasser announced that the Suez Canal, operated by a company of mostly British and French stockholders, would be nationalized, making it clear that the tolls collected from operation of the waterway would be used for the construction of the Aswan Dam.

In October, 1956, Egypt was invaded by Great Britain and France in an effort to reestablish their control of the Suez Canal and also by Israel in an attempt to stop periodic Egyptian guerrilla attacks upon its borders. The Soviet Union threatened to give military aid to Egypt. President Eisenhower declared that although Nasser's actions had been provocative, the invasion was wrong, a position that angered Great Britain, France, and Israel as long time allies of the United States. When action on the crisis by the United Nations Security Council was blocked by Great Britain and France in their capacity as permanent members of that body, the General Assembly—with the United States and the Soviet Union playing key roles—moved promptly, securing the withdrawal of the invading troops and the stationing of a United Nations Emergency Force in Egypt to patrol the area.

THE EISENHOWER DOCTRINE. As a result of the Suez Canal crisis, Soviet influence in the Middle East was enhanced. Aware that the region's political and economic instability made it vulnerable to the spread of Communism, Eisenhower acted quickly. In January, 1957, he asked Congress both to appropriate funds for economic and military assistance to Middle Eastern nations to help them preserve their independence and to permit the use of American armed forces if necessary to resist open Communist aggression. Two months later Congress approved this policy, which came to be called the Eisenhower Doctrine. Although some nations, including Egypt and Syria, denounced the Eisenhower Doctrine as an attempt by the United States to dominate the region, many welcomed it, and it remained an integral part of American foreign policy.

LEBANON AND JORDAN. In 1958 both the Lebanese and Jordanian regimes were threatened by internal subversion from dedicated followers of the staunchly pro-Soviet Nasser. Upon the request of President Camille Chamoun of Lebanon for American military assistance, the United States sent troops. At the same time Great Britain dispatched forces to Jordan upon the request of its King Hussein. The American and British moves were condemned as aggression by both the Soviet Union and Egypt. The United States and Great Britain insisted that the United Nations Security Council deal with the crisis. When a Soviet veto prevented action by that body, the General Assembly was called into special session. In an address to the General Assembly in August, 1958, Eisenhower presented a basic plan for the political and economic stabilization of the Middle East under the supervision of the United Nations. A compromise resolution sponsored by the Arab nations was finally passed. American and British troops were withdrawn from the region after calm had been restored.

Chapter 15

THE NEW FRONTIER AND
THE GREAT SOCIETY

In 1961 the elderly and staid Republican, Dwight D. Eisenhower, vacated the White House for the young and vigorous Democrat, John F. Kennedy. From the beginning, the Kennedy administration captivated the American people with its distinctive verve. In accepting the presidential nomination Kennedy stated that Americans faced many domestic and foreign challenges constituting what he referred to as a New Frontier. As the geographic frontier of the past had afforded Americans many opportunities, this spiritual New Frontier offered them opportunities to effect economic and social reforms at home and to exercise moral and humane leadership abroad.

After Kennedy was assassinated, Lyndon B. Johnson assumed the presidential office and firmly guided the nation. In seeking to become president in his own right, Johnson spoke with emotion of achieving what he referred to as the Great Society. He promised a renewed attack by all the forces of government against poverty, disease, ignorance, and racial discrimination. When Kennedy assumed the presidency the civil rights movement had not long before entered a new stage, which came to be called the Black Revolution. During the Johnson administration the Black Revolution reached its startling climax.

As for foreign affairs, both Kennedy and Johnson were forced to contend with the constant perplexities of the Cold War. During the Kennedy administration the hostilities between the United States and the Soviet Union brought the two powers close to armed conflict. During the Johnson administration the United States became deeply immersed in a morass of fighting in Vietnam.

KENNEDY AND THE NEW FRONTIER

After his inauguration, Kennedy attempted to persuade Congress to implement the domestic goals of the New Frontier, but the conservative coalition of Republican and southern Democratic legislators was able to thwart the full expectations of the executive branch. In dealing with the economy, the efforts of the administration were directed at halting spiraling inflation. As for civil rights, Kennedy, who had previously shown little interest in the trying status of the blacks, as president became more and more committed to their struggle for equality.

Election of 1960. The result of the election turned out to be the closest in over seventy-five years.

DEMOCRATS. There were two aspirants to the presidential nomination who were notably able and aggressive—Senator John F. Kennedy of Massachusetts and Senate Majority Leader Lyndon B. Johnson of Texas. The delegates chose Kennedy to run for president and Johnson for vice-president, and in so doing presented the voters with a geographically balanced ticket.

REPUBLICANS. By the time the Republican national convention began its proceedings, Vice-President Nixon's nomination as standard-bearer appeared inevitable. As expected, he captured the prize on the first ballot. Henry Cabot Lodge, Jr., of Massachusetts, a former Republican senator and the current ambassador to the United Nations, was chosen as his running mate.

THE CAMPAIGN. An innovative feature of the campaign was a series of four one-hour televised "debates," in which Kennedy and Nixon answered questions put to them by panels of news reporters. An estimated 75 million Americans watched. In the opinion of most political commentators Kennedy probably won the debates by a slight margin. What was certain was that the senator, much less known than the Vice-President, received valuable exposure to a national audience. Throughout the campaign Kennedy made two basic charges regarding the state of the nation as a result of the preceding seven and a half years of Republican rule: first, the United States was experiencing economic stagnation (he appealed for measures to "get the country moving again"); second, the United States was witnessing a decline in its power and prestige abroad. Nixon made vigorous efforts to refute both points.

KENNEDY'S NARROW VICTORY. Kennedy won 303 electoral votes; Nixon carried 219. In a total of approximately 69,000,000 ballots, Kennedy received a plurality of 111,957 over Nixon. This represented less than two-tenths of 1 percent of the votes cast—the smallest percentage difference between the popular votes of two major presidential candidates since the election of 1884.

The Kennedy Administration. Kennedy was determined to be a dynamic president. He cherished the idea that it was the obligation of his office to help both the people of the United States and the people of the rest of the world.

THE PRESIDENT. Kennedy was a handsome, intelligent, and charming man. Once having chosen politics as his profession, he practiced it with deep purpose and extraordinary daring. He made certain that nothing, including the heavy duties of the presidency, would curtail his intellectual and cultural growth.

INAUGURAL ADDRESS. Kennedy delivered a widely acclaimed inaugural address that focused on the sacrifices needed to insure individual freedom and world peace. To the people of the United States he entreated: "Ask not what your country can do for you—ask what you can do for your country." To the people of the rest of the world he pledged that Americans would "pay any price, bear any burden, meet any hardship, support any friend, oppose any foe to assure the survival and the success of liberty."

THE CABINET. During his campaign Kennedy promised the voters that if elected he would name as his cabinet a "ministry of talent." His appointees were on the whole strong-willed men possessing administrative experience. Two of the leading posts were given to Republican businessmen: C. Douglas Dillon, a New York banker who had been ambassador to France during the Eisenhower administration, was named secretary of the treasury; Robert S. McNamara, president of the Ford Motor Company, became secretary of defense. Chosen secretary of state was Dean Rusk, president of the Rockefeller Foundation, an organization that aids projects to advance welfare and culture. Robert F. Kennedy, younger brother of the President, was appointed attorney general and soon became the leading figure in the cabinet.

New Frontier Legislation. Congress rejected Kennedy's most progressive legislative recommendations. It did, however, pass bills on housing, minimum wages, and the extension of social security. The Peace Corps, which was established by executive order, soon received support from Congress.

THE HOUSING ACT OF 1961. This act provided approximately $5 billion for slum clearance and housing projects.

THE MINIMUM WAGE ACT OF 1961. This measure increased the existing minimum wage to $1.25 an hour for close to 25 million workers. By the end of four years more than 3 million new workers would be included under the provisions of the law.

SOCIAL SECURITY AMENDMENTS OF 1961. Congress amended the Social Security Act to provide such benefits as aid to the children of unemployed workers, and retirement funds, although in reduced amounts, to workers who chose to leave their jobs at the age of sixty-two rather than at sixty-five.

THE PEACE CORPS. Early in 1961 Kennedy issued an executive order creating the Peace Corps. This was an organization of persons who volunteered to serve as teachers and technicians to help raise the standard of living in underdeveloped countries of Africa, Asia, and Latin America. Six months later Congress appropriated funds to put the Peace Corps on a permanent basis. Appointed to direct the program was R. Sargent Shriver, Jr., an administrator of a Chicago commercial center and a brother-in-law of the President. Peace Corps volunteers lived among the people of the countries they were serving, and received modest allowances for their work.

Kennedy's Unachieved Goals. Kennedy failed to persuade Congress to accept the entire domestic program that he regarded as essential for improving the general condition of the American people. His proposals for aid to education, Medicare, and a department of urban affairs were all defeated by the coalition in Congress of Republicans and southern Democrats that had existed since the late 1930s. The coalition received help from various special interest groups.

FEDERAL AID TO EDUCATION. Kennedy's proposal for federal aid to education included giving financial assistance for constructing school buildings, increasing teachers' salaries, and granting scholarships to students. The proposal failed in Congress, largely because of the negative effects of the Kennedy administration's inability to come to terms with the demand by Roman Catholic church leaders that parochial schools as well as public schools be given aid.

MEDICAL CARE FOR THE AGED. The Kennedy administration presented to Congress a plan known as Medicare to provide hospital and nursing care for the aged. Congress twice rejected the proposal. An important factor in the measure's defeat was the antipathy of the nation's largest organization of physicians, the American Medical Association, which repeatedly and vigorously characterized the plan as a step toward "socialized medicine."

DEPARTMENT OF URBAN AFFAIRS. Kennedy submitted a plan for the creation of a department of urban affairs. The proposal was defeated in Congress by the conservative coalition.

The Economy. From the beginning the Kennedy administration faced the problem of a stagnant economy. In order to stimulate economic growth it strove to foster stable prices for products sold at home and an increase in the volume of goods sold abroad.

CONFRONTATION WITH STEEL MANAGEMENT. The price of such a widely used commodity as steel has always had a significant effect upon numerous industrial costs. To help curb inflation, Kennedy in the fall of 1961 extracted from the steel managers a tacit agreement not to increase prices. Then in April, 1962, the United States Steel Corporation suddenly announced an increase in the price of steel. Five other steel firms promptly did the same. An enraged Kennedy intervened immediately to divert the awarding of government contracts for the purchase of steel to firms that had not raised their prices. This step compelled the "offending" companies to cancel the increase. The Kennedy administration was careful to explain that its action did not arise from any hostility to business enterprise but was an attempt to halt inflation.

THE TRADE EXPANSION ACT. This law, passed in 1962, gave to the President a great deal of flexibility in negotiating with the newly established European Economic Community (known as the Common Market), an economic union of six (later increased to nine) Western European nations formed to stimulate within each of them both industrial enterprise and employment. The Trade Expansion Act gave the United States an opportunity to compete for trade in a freer market than had previously existed by empowering the President to lower tariff duties by as much as 50 percent over a five-year period and to abolish tariff duties on a number of products exported by both the United States and the member nations of the Common Market.

The Black Revolution. Although in the 1950s measurable progress had been made toward school integration and safeguarding the right to vote, blacks became more and more forceful in their efforts to put an end to their "second-class citizenship." Early in 1960 a new direction in the civil rights movement began.

SIT-INS. Throughout the South black college students began to defy local laws and customs of racial segregation. The form of that protest was based on the principle of nonviolent resistance that the Reverend Martin Luther King had expounded from the time of the highly successful Montgomery bus boycott during 1955–1956. On February 1, 1960, four black students from the Agricultural and Technical College of North Carolina in Greensboro sat at a nearby Woolworth's "whites only" lunch counter, requested service, and refused to leave when they were denied it. The use of the sit-in was taken over by many college students, both black and white, and spread quickly throughout the South. The young people received a great deal of moral and financial support from such civil rights organizations as the National Association for the Advancement of Colored People (NAACP), directed by Roy Wilkins; the Southern Christian Leadership Conference (SCLC), under King; and the Congress of Racial Equality (CORE), led by James Farmer. In April, 1960, at Shaw University in North Carolina the Student Non-Violent Coordinating Committee (SNCC) was formed to bring into concerted action the efforts of the sit-in demonstrators. During 1960–1961 eating facilities were desegregated in scores of southern towns and cities. By the end of 1961 approximately 75,000 students, both black and white, had made use of the sit-in. The sit-ins prompted kneel-ins at churches, read-ins at libraries, and wade-ins at beaches. Segregation as a way of life in the South was slowly disappearing.

FREEDOM RIDES. In May, 1961, CORE began a campaign against the "whites only" facilities of bus terminals in the South. An integrated group known as Freedom Riders set out by bus from Washington to New Orleans to put to the test the observance of the existing federal integration orders. The Freedom Riders were attacked by hostile mobs at several stops, with a number of serious incidents occurring in Alabama. Since the bus company drivers would not subject themselves to further danger, the Freedom Riders were compelled to complete their trip by airplane. Soon more Freedom Riders took to buses throughout the South. In September, 1961, the Interstate Commerce Commission, in response to a request by the Justice Department, issued an order prohibiting segregation on buses and in terminals used in interstate commerce. Not long afterwards railroads and airlines voluntarily desegrated all their facilities.

DESEGREGATION OF UNIVERSITIES. Beginning in the 1950s a small number of black students were admitted to some white colleges and universities in the South. But black Americans were dissatisfied with the slow pace of this desegregation. In September, 1962, James Meredith, a black air force veteran, obtained a federal court order that he be admitted to the University of Mississippi. But when he attempted to enroll, he repeatedly found his way barred, on two occasions by Governor Ross Barnett. Finally Meredith was accompanied to the campus by several hundred armed federal marshals. President Kennedy, in a television address, implored all those affected by the situation to comply with the law. But to no avail. Rioting by students and local citizens erupted on the campus. Two persons were killed and scores were injured. Kennedy then ordered federal troops into the area and calm was restored. The troops protected Meredith first as he enrolled and then as he pursued his studies until his graduation at the end of the academic year.

A repetition of the Mississippi incident threatened to occur at the University of Alabama. In June, 1963, Governor George C. Wallace of Alabama personally barred the way of two black students when they tried to enroll for the summer session. But the governor immediately backed down when President Kennedy federalized units of the Alabama National Guard and dispatched them to the campus.

MASS DEMONSTRATIONS. A new level in the demand by blacks for equality of treatment became evident in the spring of 1963 when they held mass demonstrations throughout the South. City after city felt the demand for a complete end to segregation in all public facilities, including schools, libraries, stores, and restaurants. Many black leaders, following the philosophy of Dr. King, advocated to their followers the use of persistent pressure for civil rights by nonviolent methods, such as petitions, boycotts, sit-ins, and orderly street demonstrations. However, nonviolent protests, in the North as well as the South, degenerated into violent clashes between blacks and their white sympathizers on the one hand and police authorities who claimed they were complying with local laws on the other. The attention of the nation was drawn to Birmingham, Alabama, where King himself was leading mass demonstrations to effect desegregation in the city. In May, 1963, there was violence in Birmingham as the police resorted to the use of high-pressure fire hoses, electric cattle prods, and dogs against the demonstrators. Soon leaders of the black and white communities reached an agreement on a plan to desegregate the city. But in September violence erupted once more in Birmingham; a bomb was thrown into a black church, and killed four girls attending a Sunday school class.

THE MARCH ON WASHINGTON. Believing that black protests could be better served if they were moved off the streets and into the courts, President Kennedy in June, 1963, submitted to Congress for its consideration a civil rights bill. The proposed legislation prohibited a number of common discriminatory practices and granted the Civil Rights Division of the Department of Justice increased authority to deal with instances of discrimination. Conservative white southern members of Congress began to block the measure. In August, 1963, while legislators were debating the bill, black civil rights leaders organized the "March on Washington for Jobs and Freedom" to dramatize the need for such a measure. The civil rights groups received notable support from numerous service, religious, and labor organizations. More than 200,000 people (about 60,000 of whom were white) took part in what was the largest demonstration ever to take place in the nation's capital. The participants proceeded in orderly fashion from the Washington Monument to the Lincoln Memorial, where they listened to speeches by such prominent black leaders as the longtime civil rights activist and head of the Brotherhood of Sleeping Car Porters A. Philip Randolph, executive secretary of the NAACP Roy Wilkins, and Dr. King. Among the whites who spoke was the head of the United Auto Workers of America, Walter Reuther. In a memorable address King described his "dream" that his children might one day live in a nation where they would be judged not "by the color of their skin but by the content of their character."

The Assassination of Kennedy. The young and vigorous Kennedy joined the three previous presidents who had met death from an assassin's bullet.

TRAGEDY IN DALLAS. Kennedy traveled to Texas in November, 1963, to help reconcile the sharp differences between the conservative and liberal wings of the state's Democratic party before the 1964 election, in which he was planning to seek a second term as president. On November 22, while riding alongside his wife in a motorcade in Dallas, Kennedy was shot in the head and neck by a sniper. He died shortly afterward, without regaining consciousness. Less than two hours later Vice-President Lyndon B. Johnson, who had accompanied Kennedy on the political mission, took the presidential oath of office. Charged with the murder was Lee Harvey Oswald, a former marine who had established a reputation for participation in various Communist causes. Two days after the assassination, as Oswald was about to be moved from one jail to another, before a national television audience, he was shot to death by Jack Ruby, a Dallas nightclub owner who had been a voluble admirer of the stricken President.

THE WARREN COMMISSION. Four days after Kennedy's funeral President Johnson appointed a commission of seven men, composed of past and current members of the three branches of government, to conduct a thorough investigation of the assassination. Known as the Warren Commission after its chairman, Chief Justice Earl Warren, the body received from more than 500 persons an amount of testimony that filled twenty-six volumes. In an 888-page report issued in September, 1964, the Warren Commission concluded that Oswald had killed President Kennedy and that Oswald and Ruby had each acted solely on his own. However, in the following years many called for a new inquiry, contending that the commission had not delved enough into the possibility of a conspiracy.

JOHNSON AND THE GREAT SOCIETY

In a number of addresses beginning in mid-1964 and culminating in his State of the Union Message to Congress in January, 1965, President Lyndon B. Johnson outlined the goals he cherished for the nation—goals that would bring about what he referred to as the Great Society. Johnson asserted that the federal government should assume a role more commanding than it had ever before played in improving the quality of life in the United States. In the Great Society no one would suffer from poverty, controllable diseases, lack of education, or racial injustice. The President's ability to transform his hopes into reality depended upon the approval by Congress of a program capable of being implemented in a practical way.

The Johnson Administration. Johnson assumed the duties of the presidency with a striking determination and intensity. His ability to get a job done, which he had exhibited brilliantly as the majority leader of the Senate, served him to good advantage in his new role.

THE PRESIDENT. Johnson was filled with shrewdness and a spirit of compromise that made him one of the most successful politicians of his time. With those who worked under him he could be savagely demanding. He was a southwesterner through and through, with a drawl he seemed to take delight in.

THE CABINET. Wanting to indicate that he was anxious to continue the policies of the previous administration, Johnson asked the members of the Kennedy cabinet to remain in office. But within a year Attorney General

Robert F. Kennedy, who had personal differences with the new President, resigned to run for the Senate and by the end of the following year Secretary of the Treasury C. Douglas Dillon had relinquished his post.

Election of 1964. Contemporary political analysts agreed that the meaning of the election was as follows: since the beginning of the New Deal the voters, when given a clear-cut choice between a liberal and a conservative course for the nation, would make an overwhelming commitment to the former.

DEMOCRATS. The Democratic national convention acceded to virtually every wish of President Johnson. His nomination as the party's standard-bearer was inevitable. The liberal Senator Hubert H. Humphrey of Minnesota was chosen as his running mate.

REPUBLICANS. The delegates to the Republican national convention nominated Senator Barry Goldwater of Arizona for president and Representative William Miller of New York for vice-president. Both were ultraconservative. The choice of Goldwater was a hard-fought and quite satisfying victory for the right wing over the usually strong internationalist left wing of the party.

THE CAMPAIGN. Goldwater maintained that his candidacy meant that for the first time since the 1932 Hoover-Roosevelt campaign the Republican party was offering the voters "a choice not an echo" of the Democratic candidate. On the domestic level, Goldwater recommended a rapid diminution of federal economic and social programs and a relaxation of government activity in the civil rights area. As for foreign affairs, he called for an extreme "get tough" policy toward the Communist bloc. Johnson extolled the benefits that would accrue to all from the implementation of the Great Society, without ever describing precisely the various components of the program. He assumed a moderate position on how to deal with the Communist nations.

JOHNSON'S LANDSLIDE VICTORY. Johnson received 43,167,000 popular votes to Goldwater's 27,146,000. The Democratic candidate was chosen president by the largest popular vote in the history of the nation. His 61.2 percent of the total vote topped Franklin D. Roosevelt's 60.8 percent in 1936 and Warren G. Harding's 60.4 percent in 1920. In the electoral college Johnson carried 486 votes against Goldwater's 52. Of the fifty states and the District of Columbia,[1] Goldwater carried only five states of the South plus his home state of Arizona.

Social Legislation. For a time after he entered the White House, Johnson had little difficulty in securing from Congress the legislation he

[1]As a result of the Twenty-third Amendment to the Constitution, passed by Congress in 1960 and ratified in 1961, the eligible residents of the District could now vote in presidential elections.

requested. Bill after bill was passed almost in the precise form that the President's advisers had suggested. But the spirit of cooperation began to wear thin in 1965, and Congress paid less attention to legislative proposals from the White House.

THE ECONOMIC OPPORTUNITY ACT. This measure, passed in 1964, provided close to $1 billion to undertake a "war on poverty." It established, among other things, a number of community action projects to improve health and housing conditions and a Job Corps to train persons between the ages of sixteen and twenty-one in a variety of occupations. Created under the act to supervise the antipoverty program was the Office of Economic Opportunity. Peace Corps director R. Sargent Shriver, Jr., was chosen to head the new agency.

THE APPALACHIAN REGIONAL DEVELOPMENT ACT. This act, passed in 1965, authorized the expenditure of approximately $1 billion to provide relief to the people in the distressed areas along the Appalachian mountain range, which covers eleven states east of the Mississippi River from Pennsylvania to Alabama.

THE ELEMENTARY AND SECONDARY SCHOOL EDUCATION ACT. As a result of the provisions of this act, passed in 1965, students in elementary and secondary schools, including parochial and other private ones, received governmental assistance indirectly through loans and grants to their schools. The act settled the controversy that had existed during the Kennedy administration over whether the federal government should grant such financial assistance to parochial educational institutions.

THE MEDICARE ACT. Despite widespread questioning of the role of the federal government in providing medical care and the outspoken opposition of many of the nation's physicians, Congress finally, in 1965, enacted the plan called Medicare to provide hospital and nursing care for those sixty-five and over, to be financed from payments under Social Security. Medicare became operative on July 1, 1965.

Government Reorganization and Reform. The need for the government to reorganize and reform itself was a continuing one. The Johnson administration directed some of its energy toward that end.

DEPARTMENT OF HOUSING AND URBAN DEVELOPMENT. In 1965 Congress created the Department of Housing and Urban Development. The new department was authorized to administer programs for the improvement of housing and community life in cities and their adjacent areas. Appointed by Johnson as the first secretary of housing and urban development was Robert C. Weaver, who had held a variety of administrative posts in federal and state government. Weaver became the first black cabinet member in the nation's history.

DEPARTMENT OF TRANSPORTATION. In 1966 Congress established the Department of Transportation to develop the policies and to supervise the programs of the federal government in the field of transportation. Johnson appointed Alan S. Boyd, who had served with distinction on the Florida Railroad and Utilities Commission, as the first secretary of transportation.

THE TWENTY-FIFTH AMENDMENT. The facts of President Eisenhower's three serious illnesses and the shooting of President Kennedy made the American people keenly aware that the Constitution provided no procedure for replacing a disabled president. Passed by Congress in 1965 and ratified in 1967, the Twenty-fifth Amendment to the Constitution provided means for the vice-president to assume the office of acting president in case the president should become incapacitated, and the method whereby the president would resume his office if he recovered. It also authorized the president, whenever the office of vice-president should become vacant, to appoint a new vice-president who would take office when confirmed by a majority of both houses of Congress. Thus a constitutional gap, which had troubled the nation for almost two hundred years, was filled.

The Climax of the Black Revolution. The upsurge of the Black Revolution that had begun early in 1960 reached its climax during the Johnson administration, which was sympathetic to all but the violent aspects of the new direction in activism.

THE TWENTY-FOURTH AMENDMENT. Since the end of the nineteenth century many of the southern states had adopted, as one method of keeping blacks from voting, the poll tax (see page 11). The result was that poor blacks—as well as poor whites—were kept from participating in elections. By 1960 five southern states still retained the poll tax. Passed by Congress in 1962 and ratified in 1964, the Twenty-fourth Amendment to the Constitution prohibited the use of the poll tax as a requirement for voting in federal elections.

THE CIVIL RIGHTS ACT OF 1964. Largely as a result of pressure from President Johnson, a filibuster by conservative white southerners in the Senate was finally overcome and Congress passed in July, 1964, a new civil rights act. The measure, among other things, (1) strengthened voting rights protection; (2) prohibited discrimination in places of "public accommodation," such as stores, restaurants, hotels, and theaters; (3) required the federal government to withdraw financial assistance from any state or local program permitting discrimination in its operation; (4) authorized the attorney general to institute suits to desegregate schools; (5) established the Equal Employment Opportunity Commission to foster compliance with the law forbidding discriminatory practices by employers and labor unions.

CONFRONTATION IN SELMA. It was soon evident that the Civil Rights Act of 1964 would be effective only if the American people decided to carry out its provisions in good faith. Crucial in the minds of many blacks was the issue concerning registration of voters. The act specifically forbade election officials to apply standards to black voting applicants that differed from those applied to white applicants. In 1965 Selma, Alabama, a community where black voters were few (approximately 350) in proportion to blacks who were of voting age (about 15,000), was chosen as a place to test the willingness of state and local officials to abide by the federal law. Voter registration among blacks was ferociously opposed by many whites, led by the county sheriff, who readily ordered the use of whips and clubs against demonstrators for black rights. What happened was a travesty, arousing Americans to the brutal ways in which the right to assemble, the right to petition, and the right to register were being denied to white citizens as well as black. The killing first of a black civil rights worker and then of a white one, a young minister from the North, attracted the attention of the nation.

THE VOTING RIGHTS ACT OF 1965. The events at Selma spurred President Johnson to address the Congress in March, 1965, as he submitted legislation which he believed would give the federal government power to insure nondiscriminatory procedures in all elections—federal, state, and local. The measure was necessary, the President insisted, in order to enforce the Fifteenth Amendment to the Constitution, which ninety-five years before had conferred on blacks the right to vote. Congress responded positively and a new civil rights act was signed into law in August, 1965. It contained the following provisions: (1) literacy tests were to be suspended in any county where less than 50 percent of the population eligible by age to vote was registered or had cast ballots in 1964 (five southern states and portions of two others were affected by this); (2) federal examiners would be dispatched to register prospective voters in any county practicing voting discrimination; (3) the attorney general was empowered to institute suits against the use of poll taxes (four southern states were affected by this).

MODERATE ORGANIZATIONS AND LEADERS. There was disagreement among the major black organizations and their leaders, especially after 1965, concerning the best strategy to use in the battle for equal treatment for blacks in a predominantly white society. The National Association for the Advancement of Colored People (NAACP), founded in 1909 by a group of blacks and whites to combat racial discrimination, employed a variety of methods, such as lobbying and educational programs, but concentrated on the use of legal action in the courts. The NAACP consistently rejected the use of violence. Roy Wilkins, executive secretary of the organization, ably presented the views of the moderates. The National Urban League, organized in 1910 by blacks and whites to help blacks who migrated to the cities from the rural South adjust to a new way of life, had A. Whitney Young as its executive director. Young was an articulate spokesman for vigorous but nonviolent black community action. Established in 1957, the Southern Christian Leadership Conference (SCLC) sought to end segregation in the use of public facilities and to end discrimination in employment and in voting. The founding president of the SCLC, the Reverend Martin Luther King, had difficulty reconciling his nonviolent methods with the demands of those blacks who advocated force to get results. In April, 1968, King was assassinated in Memphis, Tennessee. His death deepened the sense of bitterness and hostility among all blacks, whether moderate or militant.

MILITANT ORGANIZATIONS AND LEADERS. The Black Muslims, whose organization, the Nation of Islam, was founded in 1930, continued into the 1960s as a religious body that declaimed the inherent superiority of the black over the white race and advocated the complete separation of the two. Although Elijah Muhammad was the revered spiritual leader of the Black Muslims, his most prominent follower, the ardent Malcolm X, was the leading spokesman of the body. In the mid-1960s both the Congress of Racial Equality (CORE) and the Student Non-Violent Coordinating Committee (SNCC) became radicalized. Founded in 1942 by James Farmer, the Congress of Racial Equality, which had always encouraged the membership of whites, sought through nonviolent means to do away with racial discrimination. In 1966 Farmer resigned as head of CORE, and under such leaders as Roy Innes the organization became increasingly separatist in its philosophy. By 1967 the Student Non-Violent Coordinating Committee had renounced its original commitment to nonviolent methods and began to force white members out of the organization. The fiery Stokely Carmichael, the new chairman of SNCC, popularized the slogan "Black Power," which the moderate NAACP, National Urban League, and SCLC rejected as being hate-fomenting. The Black Panther Party for Self-Defense, founded in California in 1966 by Huey Newton and Bobby Seale, espoused a program leading to total political, economic, and social betterment of the black race. The most articulate spokesman of the group was Eldridge Cleaver. The Black Panthers advocated that blacks arm themselves in preparation for the direct violent confrontation with whites that they believed was certain to occur in the struggle for black liberation. As the years went by there were numerous violent encounters between the Black Panthers and the police. Emerging during the mid-1960s as a forceful intellectual leader in the black nationalist movement was the author LeRoi Jones, who assumed the African name Imamu Amiri Baraka.

URBAN GHETTOS. Germane to the black fight for an improved status was the fact that most black Americans had moved into the cities. By the mid-1960s close to 70 percent were living in metropolitan areas. Although they shared on a small scale in the national prosperity, their income level steadily fell behind that of white city dwellers. Because of their separation from whites through neighborhood housing patterns, schools that black children attended were segregated, not by law but in reality. A powerful theme running through all black objectives in the 1960s was the desire to break out of the restrictions of the ghetto. Each summer from 1964 to 1967 riots erupted in the black sections of many northern cities. At times looting and gun battles between blacks and police were rampant in the streets. Of the approximately fifty affected cities, those that suffered the most severe violence were Newark, Detroit, and Los Angeles. When the destruction finally came to an end, hundreds of people had been injured and scores had been killed.

A DIVIDED NATION—WITH HOPE. President Johnson appointed a biracial and bipartisan eleven-member Advisory Commission on Civil Disorders, headed by former governor Otto Kerner of Illinois. The unanimous report of the commission, issued in 1968, declared that the primary cause of the riots was the existence of a set of intolerable economic, social, and psychological conditions among urban blacks resulting from widespread and long-standing white racism. The report went on to state that some of the disturbances had been accentuated by the inefficiency of local police and of the National Guard units called in to help restore order. "Our nation is moving toward two societies, one black and one white—separate and unequal," the commission concluded. Most Americans seemed to accept the fact that the problem existed. But there was hope. During the 1960s blacks had made considerable gains in achieving status—politically, economically, and socially. Symbolic of their new pride of race was that in schools and colleges across the nation black students emphasized the importance of their own heritage by insisting on courses in black history and culture. And, as never before, black Americans fought for and won acceptance by white Americans.

The Continuing Plight of the Indians. With the arrival of white people from the European continent centuries ago the Indians began suffering tragic unhappiness at their hands. For the past several decades the particular problems marking the existence of the Indians have been poverty, inadequate education, and unemployment. In the 1960s the Indians exhibited a resurgence of militancy that fitted into the pattern of the period.

TRENDS IN GOVERNMENT POLICY. The philosophy underlying both the Dawes Act of 1882 and the Burke Act of 1906 that Indians should adapt themselves completely to American society was reversed in 1933 when Indian Commissioner John Collier began to stress government interest in a revival of tribal arts and crafts. In 1934 Congress passed the Wheeler-Howard Act, fostering the efforts of tribes to govern themselves and to preserve their customs and traditions. Individuals could still seek a place outside the reservation, but tribal Indians were encouraged to cherish the heritage of their people.

INDIAN SELF-RELIANCE. In 1966 the Bureau of Indian Affairs of the Department of the Interior began to allow tribal councils greater independence and authority and also began implementing plans to improve the education of Indian youth. Many Indian tribes showed a militancy that rivaled that of the blacks. By the early 1970s most Indian leaders were determined that the affairs of the tribal Indians on their reservations should be controlled not by the government but by the Indians themselves. For most Indians the primary decision was the choice that each had to make between life on the reservation and entrance into the larger society dominated by whites.

The Cause of Mexican-Americans. The long and hard struggle by blacks for equality of public treatment had a deep influence upon another group that was the victim of prejudice—Mexican-Americans.

PAST DISCRIMINATION. In the Southwest, where most of them lived, Mexican-Americans were the last to be employed in good times and the first to be dismissed in bad times. And when they worked, their pay was generally lower than that of others who performed the same jobs. Mexican-Americans were also subjected to discrimination in housing.

A NEWFOUND MILITANCY. In the mid-1960s Mexican-Americans, who as a group had tended to refrain from drawing attention to their economic and social condition, began to organize in an effort to improve their status. They strove to acquire all those elements—good education, well-paying jobs, decent housing—that constitute having "arrived" in American society. Important to the movement was the emphasis on the worth and beauty of Mexican-American culture. Militant members of the movement called themselves Chicanos (probably derived from *Mexicano,* the Spanish word for Mexican). The best-known Chicano was Cesar Chavez, who left social work among fellow Mexican-Americans to become a labor organizer in California and the Southwest among farm workers, many of whom were Mexican-Americans.

The Uprooted Puerto Ricans. The most recent major group to settle in the United States was the Puerto Rican. Choosing to be uprooted, they tried to make their sacrifice worthwhile.

ECONOMIC CONDITIONS IN PUERTO RICO. During the 1950s the government of Puerto Rico made a concerted effort, with aid from the United States, to develop production of agricultural commodities other than its principal crop, sugar, and to promote the growth of industry. It was hoped that such a policy would make for material prosperity, and in so doing provide support for cultural opportunities, including a better school system, for the island's people.

MIGRATION TO THE UNITED STATES. As a result of the new economic program the Puerto Ricans' income rose significantly in the 1950s. Nevertheless, their standard of living was far below that of Americans in the continental United States. Consequently, Puerto Ricans, as was their right as American citizens, began to move freely to the mainland, settling for the most part in and near New York City. By the end of the 1960s approximately 1 million Puerto Ricans were living in New York City itself, constituting approximately 12 percent of the population. As with every migrating group that had preceded them, they experienced culture shock and were subjected to various forms of discrimination in employment and housing. And as with every other migrating group, the Puerto Ricans took the initiative in order to achieve full equality. By establishing self-help organizations such as Aspira (meaning, in Spanish, "aspire") they sought to acquire for themselves, among other things, better employment and good housing. Of particular importance to them was the establishment of bilingual and bicultural educational programs for Puerto Rican and other Hispanic-American students.

Women's Liberation. The term "women's liberation" was applied to a surge of activity, beginning in the 1960s, in the women's rights movement, which had started in the nineteenth century and achieved a major goal with the granting of the suffrage to women in 1920.

OBJECTIVES. The basic objectives of the new feminists were full legal equality with men and the removal of discrimination between the sexes in American economic and social life, particularly in employment and home duties. Given high priority among specific measures they called for were the availability of an abortion without charge for any woman who requested it and the establishment of government-supported child care centers that would be put at the disposal of any mother.

METHODS. Particularly active in the leadership of the women's liberation movement were writers Betty Friedan and Gloria Steinem, and Bella Abzug and Shirley Chisholm, both Democratic congressional representatives of New York. To a large degree the movement was decentralized, with little conventional organizational makeup. Nevertheless, there did exist some organizations created for the cause of women's liberation. The largest of these was the National Organization for Women (NOW), formed in 1966 largely through the efforts of Friedan, whose widely read *Feminine Mystique* (published in 1962) analyzed how society had assigned to women the role of unthinking followers of men. In order to achieve its goals, NOW (which did not bar men from joining its ranks) concentrated on legal and political action. The National Women's Political Caucus was founded in 1971 to coordinate efforts toward acceptance of the cause of women's rights by both the Democratic and Republican parties.

The women's liberation movement influenced Congress to pass in 1972 the proposed "Equal Rights" Amendment to the Constitution, which declared that "equality of rights under the law shall not be denied or abridged on account of sex." Five years later ratification by the required number of states had not yet been achieved; the approval of three more states was needed.

In 1975 factional disputes hurt the women's liberation movement. Friedan and a dozen other past and current leading members of NOW formed a splinter organization named Womensurge, asserting that NOW had become too radical in its philosophy and tactics and was thereby alienating most of the women of the nation.

CONTINUANCE OF THE COLD WAR

The foreign policy of the Kennedy and Johnson administrations was controlled by the same factor that had regulated the diplomacy of the Truman and Eisenhower administrations—the Cold War. The conflict between the Western and Communist nations forced Kennedy and Johnson to couple hard-headedness with the moral idealism that they said they would bring to American foreign policy. American-Soviet tensions were fierce. Kennedy expended massive energy to prevent Soviet challenges to the United States, both in Latin America and Europe, from erupting into armed conflict. On the other hand, Johnson led the nation deeper and deeper into the morass of fighting between the Communist and anti-Communist forces in Vietnam.

Latin America. From the beginning of the Cold War the diplomacy of the United States was focused upon Europe and Asia. But the Kennedy administration did turn its attention to Latin America as a result of its interest in helping neighboring nations and its concern about the unrestrained activities of the Fidel Castro regime in Cuba.

THE ALLIANCE FOR PROGRESS. In March, 1961, Kennedy proposed the creation of the Alliance for Progress to improve the quality of economic and social life in Latin America. Five months later, at a conference in Punta del Este, Uruguay, the charter of the new organization was adopted by the United States and all the Latin American nations except Cuba. The United States agreed to supply most of the funds for the projects under consideration for raising living standards in the area. But the Alliance for Progress eventually foundered, partly because private investors in the program became uneasy over the political instability of several of the republics that were to be assisted.

THE BAY OF PIGS. After Fidel Castro had seized power in Cuba in 1959 and established himself as premier, he used repressive measures against his countrymen, grew more and more virulently anti-American, and turned to the Communist nations for economic and military support. Relations between Cuba and the United States deteriorated. Castro exacerbated the situation by demanding that the United States reduce the size of its embassy staff in Havana. In 1960 the Eisenhower administration responded by severing diplomatic relations. With full authorization from Eisenhower and somewhat reluctant approval by his successor, Kennedy, the Central Intelligence Agency secretly trained and equipped a group of Cuban refugees for an anti-Castro military operation. In April, 1961, about 1,400 CIA-prepared Cuban refugees launched an invasion of their homeland at Bahia de Cochinos (Bay of Pigs) on the southern coast. The operation ended in utter failure, primarily because promised air support was withheld by the Kennedy administration. Many nations, including several in Latin America, condemned the role of the United States in the Bay of Pigs affair. President Kennedy publicly assumed responsibility for the debacle and resolved that in the future he would be much more careful in the execution of foreign policy.

Europe. As Presidents Truman and Eisenhower before them, Kennedy and Johnson had to recognize the salient fact that after World War II the Soviet Union had emerged as the most powerful nation in Europe.

THE BERLIN WALL. In June, 1961, Soviet Premier Nikita S. Khrushchev asserted that before the year's end his nation would sign a separate peace treaty with Communist East Germany and make a demilitarized "free city" of West Berlin, which although lying within East Germany was still divided into American, British, and French occupation zones. The primary reason for the Soviet Union's desire to force the Western powers out of West Berlin and then to absorb it into East Germany was that West Berlin had been serving as a haven for many dissatisfied people fleeing from East Germany and other Eastern European Communist countries. Kennedy's response was prompt. In July, 1961, he asserted that the Western powers had a right to remain in West Berlin and began to increase the American armed forces in Europe. The next month, in reply to Kennedy's action, the government of East Germany—supported by the Soviet Union—built a wall of concrete blocks and barbed wire between East Berlin and West Berlin, a construction that came to be called the Berlin Wall. Tension eventually eased since the Soviet Union made no move to force the Western powers out of West Berlin and Khrushchev declared in October, 1961, that he had decided not to sign a separate treaty with East Germany that year.

THE CUBAN MISSILE CRISIS. In the summer of 1962 Cuba began receiving from the Soviet Union large supplies of arms that both Castro and Khrushchev maintained were purely defensive in nature. However, American aerial photographs over Cuba indicated the existence in the Caribbean nation of offensive missile bases being constructed by experts from the Soviet Union. In a television address on October 22 Kennedy announced that he was ordering an immediate naval "quarantine" (forced stoppage) of all offensive military equipment on its way to Cuba and demanded the prompt removal of the Soviet-installed missile bases. Some Soviet ships heading for Cuba altered their courses, while two Soviet ships bound for Cuba were stopped by American warships, searched for offensive military equipment, and then allowed to continue on their way after none was found. After several days of suspense, Khrushchev began to yield. The premier ultimately offered to dismantle the missile bases and remove the offensive weapons if the United States would pledge not to invade Cuba. On October 26 Kennedy accepted the proposal. The American-Soviet crisis was at an end. The two nations had come perilously close to war. In the entire history of post–World War II Western-Soviet confrontations, this one was the most serious.

THE NUCLEAR TEST BAN TREATY. Soon after the Cuban missile crisis, relations between the United States and the Soviet Union began to improve. The Soviet leaders started to see new worth in a policy of peaceful coexistence between the Western and Communist camps. For one thing, the Soviet Union wanted a respite from the difficulties with the Western nations in order to give attention to a serious rift between itself and the other power in the Communist bloc, the People's Republic of China. Through the initiative of President Kennedy, representatives of the United States, Great Britain, and the Soviet Union met in Moscow during July–August, 1963, to discuss the control of nuclear weapons testing. A treaty was signed by which the three nations pledged not to conduct nuclear tests in the atmosphere and under water. More than 100 nations eventually signed the nuclear test ban treaty. Refusing to become signatories were two recent nuclear powers, France and China.

The Middle East. The persistent hostility between Israel and the Arab nations was a constant threat to world peace, with, of course, serious consequences for the United States.

THE "SIX-DAY WAR." After months of accusations and recriminations between the governments of Israel and Egypt, an Arab-Israeli war broke out in June, 1967. Israel's victory within six days over Egypt and its allies, Syria and Jordan, resulted in a conquest of Arab territory that led to a bitter quarrel over the new boundaries and an accelerated arms race between the Arab nations and Israel.

A CHANGE IN AMERICAN-SOVIET RELATIONS. The Arab-Israeli war could have been a prelude to a new world war, but the United States and the Soviet Union quickly indicated that they would not intervene in the conflict. Both powers had supplied arms and other war matériel—the Soviet Union to the Arab nations and the United States to Israel—and neither could hold its allies in the Middle East to a peaceful course. Israel's swift victory over Egypt, Syria, and Jordan gave an important diplomatic advantage to the United States over the Soviet Union.

The Vietnam War. Native Communist parties became more active in almost every Asian country after the victory of the Communists in China in 1949. By 1960 Communist pressure in Southeast Asia had made Indochina a danger spot, and ensuing warfare there continued through the next twelve years.

THE DIVISION OF VIETNAM. In the mid-nineteenth century France took over Vietnam, Laos, and Cambodia in Southeast Asia, combining them to form the colony of French Indochina. During World War II Japan conquered the region. Of the many native groups that conducted guerrilla warfare against the Japanese occupation, the most effective was the military arm of the Communist-supported independence movement called the Viet Minh, which was led by Ho Chi Minh. In 1945, at the end of World War II, Ho, as spokesman for the Viet Minh, declared Vietnam an independent republic, soon affiliating it with the French Union, the association of France and its various overseas territories. In 1946, however, war erupted between the returning French and the Viet Minh. Most of the people of Vietnam who were non-Communist declined to aid the French, being even more antagonistic to them than to the Viet Minh. The fighting lasted until May, 1954, when the French forces suffered a serious defeat at Dien Bien Phu. The following month the foreign ministers of nineteen nations, including the United States, held a conference in Geneva to consider the situation in Indochina. The conference agreed to divide Vietnam into two parts and settled upon 17° north latitude as the line between the Communist-based Republic of North Vietnam, under the presidency of Ho, and the Western-oriented Republic of South Vietnam. The agreement at Geneva also included a provision for the holding of elections two years later for the purpose of reuniting the two Vietnams. However, South Vietnam, supported by the United States, refused to conduct elections, in its concern that the immense popularity of Ho would result in the reunification of the two Vietnams under Communist control.

AID UNDER KENNEDY. In South Vietnam, Communist guerrillas, who were called Viet Cong, strongly backed by Communist North Vietnam, infiltrated the jungles, determined to overthrow the anti-Communist government in the capital, Saigon. When South Vietnamese President Ngo Dinh Diem in 1961 asked President Kennedy for assistance, an American advisory mission was sent to South Vietnam to bolster the government and strengthen the military forces fighting against the guerrilla tactics of the Viet Cong. Although American aid at first was limited to military equipment and supplies plus civilian and military advisers, the United States under Kennedy steadily became more deeply involved as North Vietnam, China, and the Soviet Union supplied more and more arms and ammunition to the guerrilla forces.

THE JOHNSON POLICY. Early in 1965 President Johnson approved the first air raids by American planes on strategic bases in North Vietnam, usually in support of the South Vietnamese air force. American policy was twofold: first, to destroy the sources of Soviet and Chinese aid to the Viet

Cong that were located in the northern reaches of South Vietnam and the neighboring nations of Cambodia and Laos; second, to help change the corrupt and dictatorial government of South Vietnam into one that was popularly based.

By 1967 there were 464,000 American soldiers in Vietnam. Meanwhile, in the United States there was a fiercely rising opposition to American participation in the Vietnamese war. In March, 1968, President Johnson directed the cessation of American and South Vietnamese bombing of approximately 90 percent of North Vietnamese territory. The North Vietnamese government responded in May by sending representatives to a conference in Paris to discuss with American delegates the possibilities of a peaceful settlement of the Vietnamese conflict. Not until President Johnson ordered the cessation of all American bombing of North Vietnamese territory in October, 1968, did the North Vietnamese delegates seriously begin to discuss proposals for peace. By that time there were delegates at the conference representing the United States, South Vietnam, North Vietnam, and the Viet Cong.

The United Nations. The Western bloc and the Communist bloc were drawn into the difficult struggle for power in the Congo in late 1960, after the ninety-year Belgian colonial rule came to an end. This had repercussions at the United Nations.

CHOOSING A SECRETARY-GENERAL. The efforts of the United Nations, led by Secretary-General Dag Hammarskjöld, to establish order in the Congo were thwarted by commitments that the Communist bloc made to some African leaders. In the chaotic situation the United States strongly supported the approaches of the United Nations. Hammarskjöld gave his life trying to bring peace to the newly established Republic of the Congo; he was killed in an airplane crash on a mission to Africa in 1961. The Soviet Union refused to accept a new Secretary-General, demanding in place of the office a committee of three, one named by the Western nations, one by the Communist nations, and one by the neutral nations. The matter was settled in 1962, when U Thant of Burma was chosen as a Secretary-General acceptable to both the Western and Communist blocs.

FINANCIAL DIFFICULTIES. At the same time that the Soviet Union was making objections to the appointment of a new Secretary-General, it declined to pay its share of the expenses incurred by the United Nations forces maintaining peace in the Congo. Since the United States insisted that no nation in financial arrears should be permitted to vote on matters, the activities of the United Nations almost came to a stop. In 1965 a special committee of the General Assembly started to work on a new plan for the financial support of United Nations activities, which was put into effect in 1966, when it received the support of both the United States and the Soviet Union.

Chapter 16

THE NIXON AND FORD ADMINISTRATIONS—AND PRESIDENT CARTER

Unlike the Kennedy and Johnson administrations, the Nixon administration shied away from a profound commitment to social programs and the civil rights movement. Despite his lack of success in solving domestic problems, particularly that of the economy, Nixon was easily reelected as president, primarily because he had a Democratic opponent who was unable to inspire widespread confidence in his judgment. As for foreign affairs, Nixon achieved notable successes. He brought the Vietnam War to a close and instituted détente[1] with the Soviet Union and the People's Republic of China. But the administration came to a crashing end before its time in the greatest political scandal in the nation's history. Appointed rather than elected vice-president and then elevated to the highest office in the land by the unique resignation of the President, Gerald R. Ford by his manner attempted to wipe out the stain of the Nixon years. He inherited terrible economic problems and severe foreign problems.

In the election of 1976 Jimmy Carter wrested the presidency from Ford, thus signaling the conclusion of the era of Richard M. Nixon in American politics.

NIXON AND THE DOMESTIC SCENE

Nixon turned back the trend of many of the policies on social matters supported by his two immediate predecessors. He vetoed a number of bills related to health and education and impounded funds already appropriated by Congress for economic and social problems of which he himself disapproved. He disappointed those who desired more progress in the enforcement of civil rights legislation, particularly in school desegregation. A

[1]An easing or relaxation of strained relations and political tensions between nations.

253

severe setback in the economy constantly bedeviled the Nixon administration. Soon after Nixon began his second term, his reputation plunged as the Watergate affair unfolded, revealing unprecedented corruption at the highest level of the executive branch.

Election of 1968. On two counts the election of 1968 was significant: it was a natural microcosm of all the political and social turmoil of the decade, stemming primarily from the Vietnam War and the crusade for equality of treatment by blacks and other minority groups; it marked, through Nixon's victory, the start of a distinct era of narrow domestic politics and a turnabout in foreign policy.

DEMOCRATS. In March, 1968, at the close of a television address on the war in Vietnam, President Johnson surprised the nation by saying: "I shall not seek and I will not accept the nomination of my party for another term as your President." Many political commentators felt certain that the decision resulted from his feeling that the voters were dissatisfied with his foreign policies, especially those regarding Vietnam, and with his failure to end racial unrest in the large cities. Before his withdrawal as a candidate for reelection, Johnson had been challenged in the Democratic primaries first by the ultraliberal and vocal anti–Vietnam War Senator Eugene McCarthy of Minnesota and soon thereafter by an increasingly antiwar Senator Robert Kennedy of New York. After Kennedy had won the primary elections in several states, he was assassinated in June, 1968, by an Arab-American who apparently had been infuriated by the senator's strong pro-Israel position. His death opened the way for Vice-President Hubert H. Humphrey, who had entered the presidential race when Johnson withdrew, as a defender of the administration's policies in Vietnam. After a bitter fight between the prowar and antiwar factions at the Democratic national convention in Chicago, the delegates nominated Humphrey for president and Senator Edmund S. Muskie of Maine for vice-president. While the proceedings were taking place, bloody clashes erupted on the streets of Chicago between antiwar and civil rights demonstrators, the vast majority of whom were young people, and the police.

REPUBLICANS. In a well-managed national convention the Republicans quickly nominated Richard M. Nixon for president and Governor Spiro T. Agnew of Maryland for vice-president. Agnew was a border state politician who had publicly assailed militant black activism; his selection thus strengthened the ticket among white southern conservatives.

AMERICAN INDEPENDENTS. Former Democratic governor George C. Wallace of Alabama was nominated for president by the newly organized ultraconservative American Independent Party. Personally selected by Wallace as the vice-presidential nominee of the American Independents was General Curtis E. LeMay, who had recently retired as chief of staff of the air force.

THE CAMPAIGN. The major issues of the campaign were the Vietnam War and urban disquiet. The relatively moderate positions of the two major candidates on these matters were similar. Wallace, however, argued that the only satisfactory solution to the war in Southeast Asia was total American military victory. As for the riots in the cities, he guaranteed that if elected he would end them, with bayonets if necessary. Further, Wallace called for a reversal of the federal government's commitment to desegregation, particularly in the areas of education and housing. Profiting from his experience in the exceedingly close presidential contest of 1960 against John F. Kennedy, Nixon gave skillful direction to the Republican campaign.

NIXON'S VICTORY. In popular votes, Nixon received 31,785,000; Humphrey, 31,275,000; Wallace, 9,906,000. Although the margin of victory in the popular vote between the two major contenders was indeed slim, Nixon received 302 electoral votes to 191 for Humphrey. Wallace carried 45. (When the electoral college balloted, one member who was pledged to Nixon switched to Wallace, finally giving him 46 votes. This action strengthened the demand that the procedure for choosing a president through an electoral college be reconsidered.) Although the Republicans increased their membership in both the Senate and House of Representatives, the Democrats still retained control of both houses.

The Nixon Administration. Nixon was one of the hardest-working of all those who have occupied the White House. He believed deeply in the need for a "strong" president, one who could fathom the desires of the broad base of the American people and bring their will to fruition.

THE PRESIDENT. Nixon was a "loner." Having an inner conviction of the correctness of his own views and wary of the counsel of others, he shut himself off from the wide range of advisers a president usually has, even to the point of avoiding members of the cabinet. Try as he might to appear a "regular guy," his body seemed rigid, his smile forced, and his gestures mechanical.

THE CABINET. Initially Nixon sought for his cabinet individuals of well-established independence of thought and action, a practice he soon discontinued as he attempted to gain a tighter rein on the federal bureaucratic system. The original membership of the cabinet left some diverse constituencies unrepresented; it contained not one black, not one Jew, not one woman. The official family was decidedly conservative. Most of the members were from the business community. William P. Rogers, a New York lawyer and one of the President's closest friends, was named secretary of state. (In 1973 he was succeeded by Henry Kissinger, a former Harvard University professor who was an adviser to the Nixon administration on matters of foreign policy and security.) Republican Representative Melvin P. Laird of Wisconsin was made head of the Defense Department. John N.

Mitchell, a New York lawyer who had been a partner of Nixon's and was a leading bond specialist, became attorney general. Of those serving in the cabinet, he became Nixon's most intimate adviser.

ASSISTANTS TO THE PRESIDENT. As Nixon began his second term, he made numerous changes in the cabinet. In general, the choice of new appointees emphasized the declining power of cabinet officials and the growing influence of the head assistants to the President. White House chief of staff H. R. (Bob) Haldeman was an extraordinarily energetic, "no-nonsense," devoted aide to the President. Domestic adviser John Erlichman was every bit as diligent and as dedicated to Nixon.

Appealing to the "Silent Majority." Nixon sought the base of his support from what he called the "silent majority"—middle-class Americans who had grown weary of "big" government. To those people Nixon represented a rejection of governmental activism, particularly in the areas of civil rights and social welfare.

CIVIL RIGHTS. In his attempt to bring about the entry of the notably conservative Democratic white voters of the Solid South into the Republican party, Nixon embraced what soon came to be called the "southern strategy." This pursuit prompted him to lessen the concern of the executive branch for assiduous implementation of civil rights measures. Further, the Nixon administration recommended to Congress the passage of legislation prohibiting the busing of students solely for the purpose of achieving racial integration in the schools.

THE WELFARE PROGRAM. Nixon recommended drastic changes in the welfare system. In addition to espousing a guaranteed minimum income for every family, he advocated a tightening of the system. For example, every recipient of welfare assistance who was physically able would be required either to accept appropriate employment or to participate in a job-training program. The President's proposals were not approved by Congress.

"LAW AND ORDER." Accommodating himself to the anxiety of the "silent majority" over the often disruptive demonstrations by students against the Vietnam War and the spate of riots in the black sections of a number of cities, plus the rapid increase throughout the nation of violent crimes, Nixon made a strong appeal for the government to focus on "law and order."

SUPREME COURT APPOINTMENTS. Nixon's first nomination to the Supreme Court, that of Warren E. Burger, a conservative judge of the United States Court of Appeals of the District of Columbia, to suceed Earl Warren as chief justice, was soon confirmed by the Senate. The President's next two nominees to the Court, conservative federal judges Clement Haynsworth, Jr., of South Carolina and G. Harrold Carswell of Florida, were bitterly opposed by civil rights groups and organized labor. The Senate refused to confirm Haynsworth, finding that he had heard a case in which he had a conflict of interest, and then rejected Carswell for the same seat on the Court, for having had an undistinguished reputation as a jurist and a record of racist views and action. Thereupon Nixon accused liberal Democratic senators of being biased against the seating of a southerner on the Supreme Court, although those legislators made it known that they would vote for a southern nominee whom they considered qualified. Nixon did succeed in appointing, in addition to Burger, three more conservative members to the Court, one of whom was indeed a southerner. The Court began to lose its liberal stamp. It was turned away from a broad interpretation of the Constitution and a liberal activism that had existed under Warren to a strict interpretation of the Constitution and the exercise of judicial restraint, particularly in the areas of civil rights and law and order.

The Economy. In order to deal with both a spiraling inflation and a deepening recession the Nixon administration imposed a system of wage-and-price controls.

A PROGRAM FOR ECONOMIC RECOVERY. The Nixon administration initially attempted to stem ever-increasing inflation by employing the usual approaches: (1) cutting back on government spending; (2) having the Federal Reserve Banks charge high interest rates to commercial banks, so that the commercial banks in turn would charge high interest rates to the people, and thereby discourage them from borrowing; (3) using influence with businesses to have them curb large increases in prices and with labor unions to have them refrain from demanding large increases in wages. But economic conditions become worse. In addition to inflation, there was recession. The economy was stagnant, with an unemployment rate of almost 6 percent. In August, 1971, Nixon implemented a new economic program with the following provisions: (1) a total restriction for ninety days on increases in wages and prices; (2) a reduction in personal income taxes and a repeal of the excise tax on automobiles, both achieved through congressional legislation, in order to spur the purchase of consumer goods and thus revive the economy; (3) the appointment of a Cost of Living Council to supervise the freeze on wages and prices and to draft proposals for achieving wage and price stability in the future. Labor leaders, led by President George Meany of the AFL-CIO, complained that while wages were frozen, businesses, despite frozen prices, were actually receiving higher profits through the new tax benefits.

PHASE TWO. In October, 1971, just before the ninety-day freeze was to end, Nixon instituted what was soon called Phase Two of the administration's program to halt inflation. This phase included the establishment of a Pay Board, which limited wage increases to 5.5 percent, and the establishment of a Price Commission, which limited price increases to 2.5 percent. Within months labor leaders, particularly Meany once again, complained that although both wages and prices were restricted, business profits were not prohibited from increasing.

Government Reorganization and Reform. The Nixon administration, like many administrations before it, gave some attention to the matter of government reorganization and reform.

RESTRUCTURING THE POSTAL SYSTEM. In 1971 Congress disbanded the cabinet-level Post Office Department, headed by the postmaster general. Established in its place was the United States Postal Service, an independent agency within the executive branch of the government, headed by a postmaster general who was not a member of the cabinet. Rather than relying greatly on financial assistance from the government, as had the Post Office Department, the United States Postal Service was virtually to sustain itself from revenues collected for its services.

THE TWENTY-SIXTH AMENDMENT. During the Vietnam War the minimum age for military service was eighteen. All but a few of the states had long had a minimum age of twenty-one for voting. To consider men old enough to go to war, risking death for their nation, yet too young to vote struck most of the American people as untenable. They decided through their legislators on both the federal and state levels that a change was in order. The Twenty-sixth Amendment to the Constitution, granting the suffrage to citizens who were eighteen years of age or older, was passed by Congress in March, 1971, and ratified three months later. In November, 1971, approximately 11 million Americans between the ages of eighteen and twenty-one were eligible to vote for the first time.

Penetrating Space. The exploration of space was spurred by competition between the United States and the Soviet Union. Each nation sent many spacecraft around the earth, around the sun, to the moon, and to the other planets. Ultimately they engaged in a joint venture in space.

ORBITING THE EARTH. In 1957 the Soviet Union launched the first unmanned spacecraft that escaped the gravity of the earth. In 1958 the United States followed suit. Three years later humans themselves began to travel in space. The first to do so was Soviet cosmonaut Yuri A. Gagarin, who on April 12, 1961, made a single orbit around the earth. The following month American astronaut Alan B. Shepard, Jr., rocketed 115 miles into space. In 1962 John H. Glenn, Jr., became the first American to orbit the earth, doing so three times. In 1965 Virgil I. Grissom and John Watts Young circled the earth three times in a two-man space capsule, which they were able to maneuver from one type of orbit to another. By 1970 the two nations had sent approximately 25,000 unmanned satellites into orbit, of which almost 500 are still circling the earth.

LANDING ON THE MOON. The American program to land a person on the moon was called Project Apollo. In January, 1967, a fire aboard the *Apollo I* spacecraft on its launching pad at Cape Kennedy, Florida, took the lives of Grissom, Edward H. White, and Roger Chaffee. There was intense national grief, and a long delay in plans for the lunar project. But in December,

1968, the *Apollo VIII* carried three valiant men—Frank Borman, James A. Lovell, Jr., and William Anders—on a fantastic journey. During 147 hours their spacecraft traveled the approximately 240,000 miles from the earth to the moon, orbited the moon ten times, and returned to the earth, dropping into the Pacific Ocean.

On July 20, 1969, the ultimate goal of Project Apollo was achieved. Watched on television by hundreds of millions of people all over the earth, astronaut Neil A. Armstrong stepped onto the moon. "That's one small step for [a] man, one giant leap for mankind," he said. Even if the people of the United States and the rest of the earth could not understand all the technical aspects of the moon landing, they did realize that humankind had been given the vision of a larger universe. Soon one of Armstrong's flight companions, Edwin E. ("Buzz") Aldrin, Jr., joined him, while the other, Michael Collins, continued to orbit the moon in their spacecraft. The astronauts brought back from the moon's surface data of immense scientific value. Between July, 1969, and December, 1972, there were five more landings on the moon. The last flight in Project Apollo was made by Eugene Cernan, Harrison Schmitt, and Ron Evans. Cernan and Schmitt roamed over miles of the lunar surface in a specially constructed jeeplike vehicle.

INTERNATIONAL COOPERATION. In July, 1975, American astronauts Thomas P. Stafford, Donald K. Slayton, and Vance D. Brand in their Apollo spaceship and Soviet cosmonauts Aleksei A. Leonov and Valery N. Kubasov in their Soyuz spaceship united their crafts; then two of the Americans entered the Soyuz spaceship and met face to face with the Soviets. This international meeting in space was the dramatic result of the agreement by the American President and the Soviet Communist party general secretary to have their nations cooperate in the exploration of space.

REACHING MARS. In October, 1975, two Soviet robot crafts *Venera 9* and *10* made landings on Venus, which thus became the second body in space to be "visited" by humans, and relayed photographs back to earth before being quickly ruined by Venus's considerable heat and atmospheric pressure. On July 20, 1976, seven years to the day after a person first walked on the moon, the American robot craft *Viking 1* landed on Mars. This was the culmination of an eleven-month voyage to a planet approximately 230 million miles away from the earth. *Viking 1* and the identical *Viking 2*, which landed six weeks later, transmitted photographs of a reddish rock-strewn plain. The two robot crafts were equipped to conduct a number of scientific experiments. They measured such meteorological conditions as atmospheric pressure, temperature, and wind velocity. But making for the greatest interest was that *Viking 1* and 2 scooped up Martian soil and poured it into their miniature biological laboratories to analyze it for evidence of life on another body in the universe. Scientists refrained from concluding whether the experiments indicated that life did or did not exist on Mars; the crafts detected no organisms, yet gathered evidence that chemical processes related to life on earth occur also on Mars. Since Mars has intrigued people for so long both as an object of scientific investigation and as a focus of science fiction (besides being the planet in the solar system where life has been believed most likely to exist), the landing of the two crafts on Mars was considered to be particularly significant in the exploration of space.

Election of 1972. Through a combination of bold moves in foreign policy and what was for him a fortunate choice of the Democratic presidential and vice-presidential candidates and conduct of the Democratic campaign, Nixon won a second term by an overwhelming majority of the popular vote.

DEMOCRATS. The contest in the Democratic primaries aroused much interest among the American people. Senator George McGovern of South Dakota, promising major reforms both in his party and in the nation, won surprising victories in the primaries over other leading contenders—Senator Hubert H. Humphrey of Minnesota, Senator Edmund S. Muskie of Maine, Senator Henry M. Jackson of Washington, and Governor George C. Wallace of Alabama. (Wallace was paralyzed from the waist down after being shot at a primary campaign rally and withdrew from the competition.) McGovern's supporters, among them many students and blacks and other minority groups, worked so effectively that they secured a majority of the delegates to the Democratic national convention and nominated the ticket of McGovern for president and Senator Thomas Eagleton of Missouri for vice-president. Soon after the convention adjourned, party leaders were stunned by the news that Eagleton had been hospitalized for mental depression three times during the 1960s. Reluctantly, McGovern decided to ask Eagleton to resign and seek another running mate. The Democratic National Committee chose R. Sargent Shriver, Jr., former head of the Peace Corps.

REPUBLICANS. Early in 1972 minor challenges within the Republican party to the renomination of President Nixon and Vice-President Agnew were easily turned aside. The delegates to the national convention chose the same ticket that they had four years earlier.

THE CAMPAIGN. McGovern's campaign quickly lost the enthusiasm and momentum that had marked his efforts to win the Democratic nomination. In trying to gain the support of veteran party leaders, most of whom had opposed his nomination, McGovern forfeited some of his influence with the young reformers who had hoped that he would rebuild the Democratic party along ultraliberal lines. In his handling of such issues as unemployment, tax reform, amnesty for draft-evaders in the Vietnam War, abortion, drug abuse, and crime, he gave many voters the impression of either wild radicalism or indecisiveness. Citing the heavy pressure of his presidential duties, Nixon spent little time campaigning. He tried to blunt the charges of the Democrats that his administration showed favoritism to special interests, had brought on inflation, was responsible for the high rate of unemployment, and was involved in a break-in of the Democratic National Headquarters in the Watergate complex. In turn he argued that McGovern, if elected, would embark on unsound economic programs, so cut defense spending that the United States would be reduced to a second-rate power, and end the war in Vietnam so precipitately that American prisoners would be left in North Vietnam and the government of South Vietnam would collapse. For many voters the war issue seemed to be resolved when the governments in Hanoi, Saigon, and Washington announced simultaneously in October, 1972, that they were ready to sign a cease-fire agreement as a prelude to a permanent peace settlement.

NIXON'S LANDSLIDE VICTORY. Nixon received 47,169,000 popular votes to McGovern's 29,170,000. He lost only one state, Massachusetts, and the electoral District of Columbia. Nixon's 60.8 percent of the total vote narrowly missed equaling Lyndon B. Johnson's 61.2 percent of eight years earlier. In the electoral college Nixon had 520 votes and McGovern 17. But far from losing all its strength on the federal level, the Democratic party gained two more seats in the Senate and although relinquishing thirteen seats in the House of Representatives, it still retained a fifty-one vote majority in that body. To many Americans a distressing feature of the election was that only a little over half (55.4 percent) of the eligible voters bothered to cast ballots, a testimony, according to political analysts, to the disenchantment of the electorate with the candidates of both major parties.

A Controversial Vice-President. Spiro T. Agnew was probably the most controversial figure ever to have occupied the second-highest office in the nation.

CONDUCT. The Vice-President attracted attention as a defender of the conservative cause. While Nixon assumed the role of the sedate leader of the nation, it appears that he gave Agnew the part of political counterattacker. Agnew played the part with stinging phraseology. He charged opponents of the Vietnam War with disloyalty, declaring that protests against the conflict were "encouraged by an effete corps of impudent snobs who characterize themselves as intellectuals." He found fault with intellectuals for being skeptical about the traditional values of American society, calling them "nattering nabobs of negativism." He accused the major television networks of distorting the news, characterizing their commentators as a "tiny and closed fraternity of privileged men" who purveyed the ultraliberal biases of the urban Northeast. Although some right-wing members of the Republican party were pleased with Agnew's vituperation, many of the moderates seriously questioned whether their party would be helped by it.

RESIGNATION. Agnew's vice-presidency came to a sudden end after an investigation by the Justice Department produced evidence that as Baltimore county executive and as governor of Maryland he had accepted kickbacks from engineering and other firms doing business with the state. It was further alleged that his receiving of the bribes continued even while he served as vice-president. In October, 1973, he resigned from the government, pleading "no contest" to the charge that he had evaded federal income tax when he was active in Maryland politics. He was sentenced to a three-year probation and fined $10,000. The light sentence was defended on the ground of national interest. Nixon thereupon appointed Gerald R. Ford, minority leader of the House of Representatives, to be vice-president, according to the procedure set forth in the recently ratified Twenty-fifth Amendment.

The Watergate Scandal. The greatest political scandal in the nation's history was the Watergate affair. It destroyed the Nixon administration.

THE BREAK-IN. In June, 1972, five men were arrested inside Democratic National Headquarters in the Watergate, a complex of offices, hotels, and apartments in Washington, D. C. The five, and two others who were later apprehended for participating in the planning of the break-in, were in the employ of the Committee for the Re-election of the President (CRP), an organization that had been set up under the indirect control of Nixon's leading White House advisers. In January, 1973, the seven men were found guilty of conspiracy, burglary, and electronic eavesdropping. Two months later James McCord, one of the convicted burglars, wrote a letter to federal judge John J. Sirica, who had sat during the trial, charging that there had been a cover-up of the burglary by persons at the highest levels of the executive branch. President Nixon declared—and in the months ahead continued to do so—that he had possessed no prior knowledge of the break-in or of attempts to cover up the relationship between the men apprehended in the Watergate and CRP.

THE SENATE SELECT COMMITTEE HEARINGS. During the summer of 1973 the Senate Select Committee on Presidential Campaign Activities, under the chairmanship of Democratic Senator Sam J. Ervin, Jr., of North Carolina, in the course of its investigation of corrupt campaign practices, conducted televised hearings on the Watergate affair. Among the most important witnesses who appeared before the committee were White House chief of staff H. R. Haldeman, White House domestic adviser John Erlichman, special counsel to the President John Dean III, and former attorney general John N. Mitchell. Dean testified that Mitchell, with the awareness of Haldeman and Erlichman, had consented to the burglary, and that Nixon had approved the cover-up. Haldeman, Erlichman, and Mitchell testified that the President had no foreknowledge of the break-in or of the attempts to cover it up. During the course of his testimony the former attorney general described the campaign practices used under the auspices of CRP as "White House horrors." In addition to burglarizing and wiretapping offices of the Democratic party, these "dirty tricks" on Democratic candidates included such tactics as harassing speakers and issuing fraudulent letters and leaflets.

THE DISMISSAL OF THE WATERGATE SPECIAL PROSECUTOR. In May, 1973, Attorney General Elliot Richardson appointed Harvard University Law School professor Archibald Cox as special prosecutor to investigate the Watergate affair and allied acts of political corruption. Cox found much evidence of campaign espionage by CRP, of the use of illegal wiretapping by the Nixon administration, and of large contributions by corporations to the Republican party for efforts expended in their behalf. Meanwhile, during the course of the Senate Select Committee hearings it was disclosed that beginning in 1971 President Nixon's conversations in the White House had been tape-recorded. Cox made vigorous efforts to obtain the tapes of conversations regarding the Watergate affair from Nixon, who in October, 1973, refused to comply, and ordered him dismissed. Attorney General Richardson and the next highest Justice Department official resigned in protest. The dismissal and the resignations, all announced by the White House on the same evening, were collectively dubbed the "Saturday Night Massacre." Nixon's firing of Cox produced outrage across the nation and led the House of Representatives to empower its Judiciary Committee to begin the consideration of impeachment.

THE PRESIDENTIAL TAPES. Reacting to widespread anger and resentment, Nixon appointed Leon Jaworski, a well-respected Texas lawyer, as a new special prosecutor and made available to Judge Sirica tapes that had been sought by Cox. (Two of the nine subpoenaed tapes were claimed not to have existed, and one had an eighteen-minute gap.) Under continuing pressure from the public, in April, 1974, Nixon submitted to the House Judiciary Committee edited typewritten transcripts of his taped conversations on the Watergate affair. Two months later the Supreme Court ordered the President to deliver to Jaworski other, previously subpoenaed, tapes on the cover-up in particular. Nixon's turning over the tapes did not stem the loss of confidence in him. In the summer of 1974 most Americans, according to the polls, were convinced that he had been involved at least in the cover-up of Watergate. There were demands for the President's resignation. But he announced time and again that he was determined to finish his term of office.

THE HOUSE JUDICIARY COMMITTEE HEARINGS. After completing its investigation, the House Judiciary Committee, headed by Democrat Peter W. Rodino, Jr., of New Jersey, in July, 1974 (in televised proceedings), adopted by bipartisan votes three articles of impeachment against President Nixon. The first article, passed by a 27 to 11 vote, charged him with engaging in a "course of conduct" designed to obstruct justice in the Watergate case; the second, passed 28 to 10, charged him with abuse of power; the third, passed 21 to 17, charged him with unconstitutionally defying the subpoenas of the House Judiciary Committee. The next step would have been for the House of Representatives as a whole to consider accepting or rejecting the impeachment articles adopted by its Judiciary Committee and, if it approved the charges, to recommend to the Senate that the President be brought to trial. If found guilty by a two-thirds vote of the Senate, which sits as a court in cases of impeachment, he would have been removed from office.

NIXON'S RESIGNATION. On August 5, 1974, Nixon admitted that he had been aware from the beginning of the attempts to cover up the Watergate break-in and that he had endeavored to prevent the Federal Bureau of Investigation from conducting an inquiry into the burglary. Recommendation by the House that Nixon be tried and his conviction by the Senate were now certainties. On August 9 he resigned. In the history of the nation he was the first President to do so. Vice-President Ford assumed the presidency. Ford soon issued a pardon to Nixon for any crime that he might have committed while occupying the presidential office. In January, 1975, Nixon's leading associates, Haldeman, Erlichman, and Mitchell, were convicted for their participation in the Watergate affair. They thus joined the fourteen former aides to Nixon or employees of the Committee for the Reelection of the President who had already been found guilty of or had pleaded guilty to charges in the Watergate break-in and its cover-up. More serious even than the violent agitation that occurred within the federal government and the near-paralysis of the Nixon administration as it approached its end was the fact that the Watergate scandal caused among the American people a significant loss of confidence in government and a marked lack of respect for public officials.

FORD AND A POST-WATERGATE NATION

Gerald R. Ford viewed himself initially as an accidental and an interim president—and acted almost apologetic about performing his duties. But he soon gained confidence. The major domestic issue faced by the Ford administration was that of the economy, which was wracked by both the worst inflation in peacetime and the worst recession with its accompanying unemployment since the Great Depression of the 1930s. In his vigorous criticism of the number and expense of the various social welfare programs and of the power of the regulatory agencies, the unabashedly conservative President conveyed the image of one who wanted desperately to turn the nation away from "big" government to an embracing of the previous laissez-faire system. As the election of 1976 approached, and Ford decided to seek the presidency in his own right, he appeared to be more concerned about a threat to his nomination from the right wing of the Republican party than to accommodating himself to the economic and social needs of the American people.

The Ford Administration. Ford stripped the presidency of much of its excessive outward display. Eager for an exchange of ideas with both supporters and critics, he made himself available to people of substance in and out of government.

THE PRESIDENT. Ford possessed a friendly manner and kind disposition. He was not an innovator. But his candor, diligence, and modesty earned him a measure of respect from his associates. No dazzler, he was—in a word—uncomplicated.

THE CABINET. The new President immediately dispensed with his predecessor's exceedingly tight control of the executive branch in favor of the more usual approach of diffused authority, with members of the cabinet being free to act fully in those areas of concern for which they were responsible. Within six months after assuming office, Ford had largely reorganized the cabinet by changing four of its eleven members. The official family was given a diversity it had recently lacked, with the appointment of the following: Edward H. Levi, a Jew and a Democrat who was president of the University of Chicago, as attorney general; John T. Dunlop, a Harvard University economics professor who had links with organized labor, as secretary of labor; Carla A. Hills, a woman who led the civil division of the Justice Department, as secretary of housing and urban development; and William T. Coleman, a black lawyer who had served as counsel to or member of several federal government commissions, as secretary of transportation.

LEADING A POST-WATERGATE NATION. As the first Chief Executive after the Watergate scandal, Ford cleansed the air of schemery. He sought the advice of people of divergent views from many sectors of society; he established frequent consultation with members of Congress; he instituted press conferences on a regular basis—all practices that had been allowed to lapse by his predecessor. He quickly put an end to the pervading nationwide bitterness and to the governmental impotence that characterized the last stages of the Nixon administration. He took the people into his confidence. He faltered once in this regard—and badly—when he unexpectedly and precipitately granted Nixon a full pardon without obtaining either an admission of guilt or a revelation of all the facts of the former President's actions in the Watergate affair.

Domestic Issues. Undoubtedly the most serious domestic concern during the Ford administration was the economy. The President had to contend also with such deep-felt matters as the energy crisis, consumerism, and the environmentalist crusade.

THE ECONOMY. The nation was suffering from both inflation and

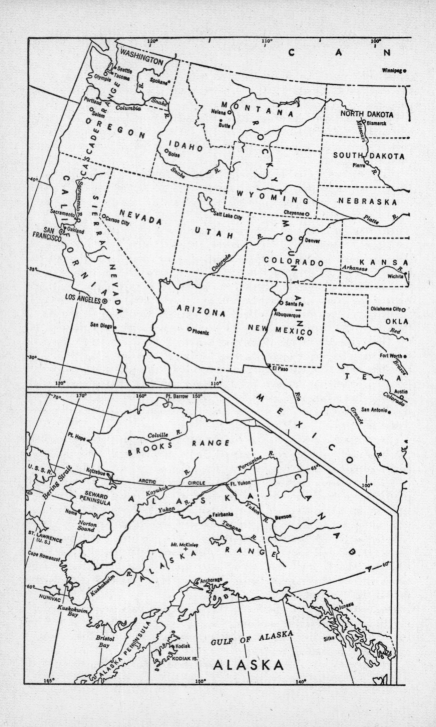

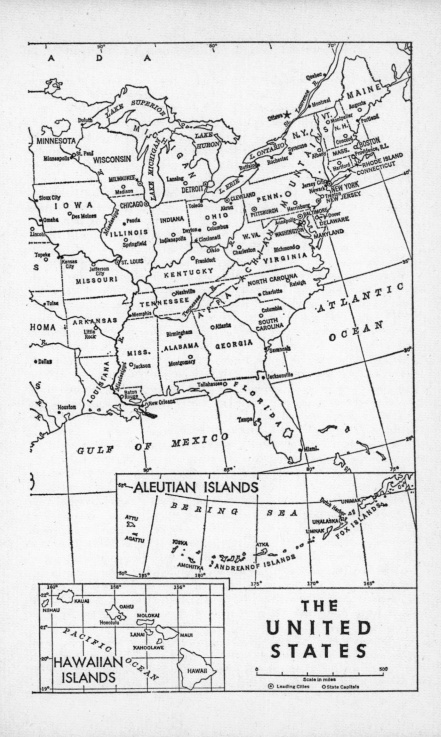

THE
UNITED
STATES

recession at the same time. The Ford administration seemed unsure as to whether the scourge of inflation or of recession needed to be cured first. The President decided it was the former. In order to combat inflation Ford, soon after taking office, advocated such measures as a sharp reduction in government spending, an increase in taxes, and the levying of higher duties on imported petroleum. But at the same time that he assaulted as inflationary a plan of government spending to create employment for needy Americans, he approved programs that either directly or indirectly raised prices. For example, his energy conservation plan was based on the imposition of higher costs for petroleum products, and the government-authorized sale of huge amounts of wheat to the Soviet Union removed much of the crop from domestic consumption and thus increased the cost for the remaining portion. Inflation remained high; at the beginning of 1975 the rate was 9 percent. The devastating effect on people's income of having to pay so much more for the necessities of life produced the worst economic slump since the Great Depression of the 1930s. As for the effects of the recession, the unemployment rate was more than 8 percent throughout 1975, thus making it the most serious recession in three decades. Some government assistance was given to people hit hardest by the recession in the form of tax reductions for those in the lowest income brackets and extensions of the unemployment insurance periods. Ford was soon compelled to do an about-face. He concluded that the recession was just as terrible an affliction to the nation as was inflation. Thus early in 1975 he recommended an antirecession program that included both a tax cut amounting to $16 billion for people with an annual income of less than $40,000 and a plan for public-service employment. But both inflation and recession continued unabated. At the end of 1976 the inflation rate was still 9 percent and the unemployment rate due to the recession was still more than 8 percent.

THE ENERGY CRISIS. Troubled by the skyrocketing cost of gasoline and fuel oil as a result of the price levels established by the Organization of Petroleum Exporting Countries (OPEC), most of whose members were Arab nations, the American people wanted strong action from their government. President Ford proposed raising the price of domestic oil and natural gas to help alleviate the energy crisis. His purpose was twofold: first, to reduce the consumption of those two high-demand, dwindling commodities and, second, to stimulate a search for additional sources by the American oil and natural gas firms. Opposed to the President's plan, yet unable to arrive at an agreement among themselves, the Democratic leaders in Congress, which their party controlled, failed to come forth with a perfected counterproposal.

CONSUMER COMPLAINTS. Ford was severely criticized by consumer groups for his, in their view, lack of sympathy for their cause. According to consumerists, the President was hostile to the establishment of a federal consumer-protection agency and lax in overseeing the enforcement of already existing consumer-oriented laws.

THE ENVIRONMENTALIST CAUSE. The environmentalists found even greater fault with Ford than did the consumerists. Environmentalist groups pointed out that the President had assumed an antienvironmental posture on the use of land for industrial purposes and on the production of nuclear energy, and had backed down on such specific issues as water pollution and automobile emissions standards.

FOREIGN AFFAIRS

The major concern of President Nixon in foreign affairs was the Vietnam War. After implementing a phased removal of American military forces from South Vietnam, he negotiated a cease-fire agreement with the government of North Vietnam. As for other aspects of foreign policy, the Nixon administration engaged in détente with the two leading Communist nations, the Soviet Union and the People's Republic of China, and mediated, after a brief Arab-Israeli war, the creation of United Nations–sponsored buffer zones in the region. President Ford continued the same basic foreign policy as his predecessor, including the pursuit of détente with the Soviet Union and Communist China and the use of United States mediation to help bring permanent peace to the Middle East. Possessing little experience in international affairs, Ford permitted Secretary of State Henry Kissinger to take the lead in this aspect of his administration.

The End of the Vietnam War. The announced policy of the Nixon administration regarding the Vietnam War was, in the parlance of the President and his associates, to "wind down" the American involvement. The war was brought to a halt and a formal cease-fire agreement was signed, but fighting soon erupted again, leading to the collapse of South Vietnam.

VIETNAMIZATION POLICY. In 1969 President Nixon named Henry Cabot Lodge, Jr., who had served as ambassador both to the United Nations and to South Vietnam, to head the American delegation to the peace talks in Paris, replacing veteran diplomat W. Averell Harriman, who had spoken for the Johnson administration. In 1970 foreign-service official David K. Bruce was appointed to succeed Lodge.

While the peace negotiations dragged on, the first American troops were deliberately withdrawn from South Vietnam. The thrust soon thereafter by American forces into Communist sanctuaries in neighboring Cambodia, ordered by Nixon in May, 1970, aroused widespread opposition in the United States. By this time millions of Americans, including hundreds of thousands of students, had participated in many rallies against the continuation of the war. Some radical protesters publicly burned draft cards and raided draft board offices, where they destroyed conscription records.

Throughout the nation there were demonstrations, many of them taking place on college and university campuses, against the government's military policy. In one demonstration in May, 1970, at Kent State University in Ohio students were fired upon by members of the Ohio National Guard and four were killed.

Carefully supervising a program of Vietnamization (training the forces of South Vietnam to assume full responsibility for military actions), the Nixon administration steadily withdrew American troops, until there were fewer than 25,000 in South Vietnam by the beginning of 1973.

CEASE-FIRE AGREEMENT. Although the peace talks in Paris were stalemated, the public discussions had been supplemented by private meetings, often held secretly, between Henry Kissinger, then presidential adviser for foreign policy and security, and Le Duc Tho, chief representative in Paris of North Vietnam. In October, 1972, a cease-fire agreement drafted by these two negotiators seemed to have been accepted by all sides. President Nixon, however, insisted that the terms of the settlement be clarified, and no truce was immediately reached.

In December, 1972, heavy American bombing of the North Vietnamese capital of Hanoi and its harbor at Haiphong was resumed and the government of North Vietnam finally agreed to continue negotiations. In January, 1973, a cease-fire in all Vietnam went into effect. The document that was signed on January 27 provided that (1) all Americans involved in military combat would be withdrawn from Vietnam in sixty days; (2) the United States would remove or deactivate mines it had laid off the coast of Vietnam; (3) American prisoners of war held by North Vietnam would be turned over to American authorities within sixty days; (4) the United States and North Vietnam would respect the right of the people of South Vietnam to self-determination; (5) the administration of South Vietnamese President Nguyen Van Thieu would continue pending an election to be supervised by a council including representatives of the South Vietnamese government, the Viet Cong, and neutralists; (6) all aspects of the agreement would be supervised by an international commission with a 1,160-man force, consisting of troops from Canada, Poland, and Indonesia.

THE COLLAPSE OF SOUTH VIETNAM. Many issues were settled by the cease-fire accord, but tensions between North Vietnam and South Vietnam continued unabated and sporadic fighting between South Vietnamese government troops and the Communist guerrillas within South Vietnam soon began once more. By the beginning of 1974 the fighting was constant and widespread. But it all ended suddenly. In March, 1975, a partial retreat of South Vietnamese troops ordered by President Thieu turned into a rout. Then, on April 30, North Vietnamese troops and Communist guerrillas pushed into and took over the South Vietnamese capital of Saigon. The government of South Vietnam, under Thieu's successor of but a few days, promptly surrendered. Without delay Saigon was renamed Ho Chi Minh City in honor of the dead leader of North Vietnam. Thus more than a century of Western domination, first by the French and then by the Americans, was over.

AMERICAN WAR COSTS. In the Vietnam War approximately 57,000 American men died and about 154,000 were wounded in combat. As for financial expenditures, the United States spent approximately $141 billion.

Détente with the Communist Nations. President Nixon chose the election year of 1972 to begin a policy of détente with the Communist nations.

THE SOVIET UNION. Although hostilities continued in Vietnam, with North Vietnam being supplied with Soviet arms while its ports were being mined and its military areas were again being bombed by the Americans, Nixon was welcomed in Moscow in May, 1972. After discussions between the American President and the Soviet Communist party general secretary, Leonid I. Brezhnev, the two nations agreed to lower trade barriers, to cooperate on health and environmental projects, and to collaborate in space exploration. More significant was the signing of two treaties providing for the limitation of nuclear arsenals. The two accords were the result of the Strategic Arms Limitation Talks, popularly called SALT, which consisted of scores of meetings held at various locations between representatives of the United States and the Soviet Union (beginning in 1970 in Helsinki, Finland) regarding the limitation by the two nations of their nuclear missile systems. The first treaty put on each of the signatories a limit of two sites for their antiballistic missile (popularly called ABM) defense systems. The second stabilized for five years the current level of each nation's offensive nuclear missile systems, both land-launched and submarine-launched. Finally, in Moscow Nixon and Brezhnev pledged themselves to work for an era of peaceful coexistence that might eventually lead to total disarmament.

CHINA. In February, 1972, a few months before his trip to Moscow, Nixon went to Peking to confer with Chairman of the Chinese Communist party Mao Tse-tung and Premier Chou En-lai. After a week of private talks the representatives of the two nations agreed to work to "normalize" relations. This was the first bit of contact between the two countries since a quarter-century earlier, when the Communist Chinese had proclaimed the establishment of the People's Republic of China. (In 1971, several months before the meetings, the People's Republic of China had been admitted to the United Nations and Nationalist China on Taiwan had been expelled.) Sino-American trade and cultural and scientific exchanges were planned. In Peking Nixon and Chou agreed that their two nations would continue in contact in order to arrange further joint efforts.

OTHER NATIONS. The new approach of the Nixon administration toward the Soviet Union and China gave greater significance to the efforts of other nations to decrease tensions between the Communist and the non-Communist worlds. In late 1971 negotiations were begun between North Korea and South Korea to ease the strain between them. A commercial treaty between West Germany and the Soviet Union was concluded in mid-1972. Soon after, restrictions that had been enforced by East Germany on communication between it and the American-, British-, and French-controlled West Berlin, which lay in its midst, were modified.

FORD AND A CONTINUANCE OF DÉTENTE. Despite some opposition from the conservative wing of his party, Ford carried on the policy started by Nixon of détente with the Soviet Union and Communist China. Ford, however, was criticized for perhaps yielding too much, for not fully realizing that détente required some give and some take from each side. Within the framework of détente, Ford pursued vigorously the continuation of the Strategic Arms Limitation Talks with the Soviet Union.

The Middle East. The long-standing tension between Israel and the Arab nations continued threatening to erupt into a war in which the United States could become a participant.

THE "YOM KIPPUR WAR." In October, 1973, Egypt and Syria, with aid from Jordan, conducted a sudden attack on Israel, which was caught by surprise since its people were at the time observing Yom Kippur (the Jewish high holy Day of Atonement). Egyptian forces crossed the Suez Canal to the east bank, into the Israeli-occupied Sinai peninsula, but by the time the fighting ceased two weeks later, Israeli troops had stopped the Egyptian advance and crossed the Suez Canal to the west bank, in addition to repulsing the Syrian forces on the Golan Heights between Israel and Syria.

MEDIATION BY KISSINGER. Under the auspices of the United Nations, in December, 1973, at Geneva, Switzerland, representatives of Israel, Egypt, Syria, Jordan, the United States, and the Soviet Union began discussions on a permanent peace settlement for the region. The following month, with Secretary of State Henry Kissinger serving skillfully as mediator, Israel and Egypt agreed to disengage their troops and to permit the creation of a United Nations–sponsored buffer zone in the Sinai, with Egyptian forces on the east bank of the Suez Canal and Israeli forces deeper into the Sinai. In May, 1974, again through the mediation efforts of Kissinger, Israel and Syria decided on a disengagement of troops and the establishment on the Golan Heights of a buffer zone under the sponsorship of the United Nations.

FORD AND THE ARAB-ISRAELI CONFLICT. Moderating the pro-Israeli position he had held as a representative, Ford maintained that he would be "even-handed" toward Israel and the Arab nations in order to support Kissinger's efforts to achieve a permanent peace in the Middle East. In September, 1975, Israel and Egypt signed an accord by which Israel made a further withdrawal from occupied territory in the Sinai in return for some political concessions by Egypt. The United States agreed to send 200 civilian technicians to a buffer zone between Israel and Egypt where they would operate early warning systems designed to detect any movement in the area by armed forces. The pact was a notable achievement for the Ford administration, which had expended tremendous energy toward its realization. In January, 1976, in the United Nations Security Council the United States vetoed a resolution affirming the right of the Palestinians to "establish an independent state in Palestine" and calling for a complete Israeli withdrawal from all Arab territories occupied as a result of the 1967 Middle East war. The United States argued that if the resolution had passed it would have created unbalanced conditions for negotiating a permanent peace between Israel and the Arab nations. In the spring of 1976 the American and Israeli governments found themselves in conflict. The United States wanted additional diplomatic movement in the Middle East and Israel hoped to defer it. The American position was based on its belief that continued diplomatic activity would be security against renewed fighting in the region.

The United Nations. Within three decades of its founding in 1945 as a deliberative association of 51 members, most of which were Western democratic nations, the United Nations became by 1977 an often unwieldy association of 147 members, almost two-thirds of which were Third World nations (the less developed countries of Asia, Africa, and Latin America). In the mid-1970s the United States was being continually outvoted in the United Nations General Assembly, the body of the world organization composed of all member nations, each of which has one vote. The votes of the less developed countries acting in solidarity could carry any proposition, including the highly-charged resolution of November, 1975, condemning Zionism as a form of racism, which was opposed by the American delegate. Time and again the Western democracies, particularly the United States, were subjected to public invective by Third World delegates, who in private maintained that this should in no way adversely affect the continuation of long-standing economic assistance to their regions from the Western governments. Coming to the defense of the United Nations, Secretary-General Kurt Waldheim cautioned against "disproportionate and excessive disillusionment" with the world organization, declaring that the "new generation of global problems" was "too large and complex to be dealt with by any one nation or group of nations alone."

CARTER AND A NEW DIRECTION

The election of Democrat Jimmy Carter to the presidency marked the beginning of a new era in American politics. The hold of Richard M. Nixon on the nation was now completely severed; although Gerald R. Ford's character and style were far different from Nixon's, he had retained many of his immediate predecessor's staff members and had continued practically all of his policies. If the executive and legislative branches of the federal government, both now controlled by the same party for the first time in eight years, worked together effectively, a period of significant economic and social progress could result. Carter appeared to Americans as a person imbued with a conviction that the strength of the nation stemmed from its commitment to achieving justice for all and to improving the quality of life.

Election of 1976. The Republican candidate came nearer to being rejected by his party for the nomination than any incumbent president since Chester A. Arthur in 1884. After gaining it, he rallied his forces to such a degree that he slashed his opponent's staggering lead in the polls to close to the vanishing point. Finally, he became the first occupant of the White House to lose an election since Herbert Hoover in 1932. The Democratic candidate rose from relative obscurity as a single-term governor to become the first president from the Deep South since Zachary Taylor in 1848.

DEMOCRATS. Fifteen men ran in the Democratic primaries. In a methodically planned and relentlessly pursued effort, former governor of Georgia Jimmy Carter won victory after victory in the primaries over such more prominent contenders as Senator Henry M. Jackson of Washington, Senator Birch Bayh of Indiana, Representative Morris K. Udall of Arizona, and Governor George C. Wallace of Alabama. By the time the Democratic national convention began its proceedings, Carter was virtually assured of becoming his party's standard-bearer. As expected, he was nominated for president on the first ballot. A prolonged search by Carter for a running mate ended in his tapping the ultraliberal Senator Walter F. ("Fritz") Mondale of Minnesota, a move that helped to reconcile liberals within the Democratic party who considered Carter to be somewhat conservative. The delegates to the convention readily named the senator for second place on the ticket.

REPUBLICANS. For months before the Republican national convention met, President Ford had to cope with an intense challenge for the presidential nomination from former governor of California Ronald Reagan, an exceedingly captivating personality who represented the right wing of the party. Before the opening of the convention, Reagan in a bold gamble declared that if nominated he wanted as his running mate Senator Richard Schweiker of Pennsylvania, a person regarded as the most liberal Republican in the upper house. Reagan's move so distressed his conservative supporters that he was immediately compelled to concentrate on retaining what delegate support he already held rather than on increasing it. In a factious convention the delegates chose Ford over Reagan by a strikingly close vote, thus defeating the strongest challenge to an incumbent president within his own party in close to a century. Upon Ford's request, the delegates named conservative Senator Robert J. Dole of Kansas as a candidate for vice-president, which appeased the right wing of the party.

THE CAMPAIGN. There were pronounced differences on a host of issues between the conservatively inclined Ford and the liberally inclined Carter. However, with the Watergate scandal unforgotten, both men tended to avoid dealing with the issues and instead strove to concentrate on portraying themselves as men deserving of trust. Ford declared that his candidacy represented continued quiet at home and peace abroad, and continued reduction of the federal government's involvement in the affairs of local communities. As the campaign drew to a close, Ford's pledge to reduce taxes the following year if elected became the main feature of his stump speeches. The Republican leaders succeeded to a large degree in gradually making Carter himself the overriding issue in the contest. In sharp attacks they characterized the Democratic candidate as irresponsibly advocating massive social programs that would necessitate vast increases in federal government spending and thus be an intolerable burden upon middle-income taxpayers. Further, they described Carter as one who would seriously weaken the nation's security by making considerable cuts in the defense budget. But most of all, they depicted him as a dangerously unknown quantity who was inconsistent on the issues. Carter tried to make Ford's presidential record the focus of the campaign. The Democrat criticized his opponent's handling of an economy marked by high inflation and a high unemployment rate, and his permitting the secretary of state to take the lead in the conduct of foreign affairs rather than assuming it himself. Carter promised the American people full employment, national health care, welfare reform, tax reform, aid to the cities, a new energy policy, government reorganization and reform, and more "openness" in government. During the campaign Ford and Carter engaged in three televised debates, the first such activity between presidential candidates since the 1960 Kennedy-Nixon race and the first to involve an incumbent president. Similar in format to the debates of sixteen years earlier, they drew an estimated 90 million viewers. Political commentators generally agreed that the first debate was won by Ford, the second by Carter, and the third was a draw. Dole and Mondale also participated in a televised debate (it was, at moments, an acrimonious encounter), the first ever between vice-presidential candidates. According to the polls taken at the outset of the campaign, Carter would achieve a landslide victory. But his lead soon began to narrow. Among other things, granting to *Playboy* magazine an interview in which he used earthy language regarding sex and a dull performance in the first debate harmed his candidacy. During the last week and a half of the campaign it seemed as if Ford had gained enough strength to achieve an upset victory. But his cause lost more than a week of precious momentum when he made a clumsy mistake in asserting that Eastern

Europe, particularly Poland, was not under Soviet domination, then had to expend much time and energy retracting the remark in order to soothe the feelings of outraged Americans of Eastern European background who had been appalled by the statement. On the day before the election, the polls indicated that Carter's previous overwhelming lead had dwindled to practically nothing. The contest had become a toss-up.

CARTER'S VICTORY. In popular votes, Carter received 40,180,000 to Ford's 38,435,000. In the electoral college Carter carried 297 votes against Ford's 241, making it the closest electoral vote contest in sixty years. The support to the candidates broke along sectional lines. Carter captured all of the former Confederate states except Virginia; all of the border states except Oklahoma; and most of the large industrial states of the northeast, including New York, Pennsylvania, and Massachusetts. Ford swept most of the Midwest and the entire Far West. Carter achieved his victory by holding together the elements of the Democratic coalition of the New Deal period—organized labor, blacks and other minority groups, Roman Catholics, and the Solid South. The Democratic party continued to enjoy its large majorities in Congress. In the Senate the membership consisted of 62 Democrats and 38 Republicans, exactly what it had been before the election. In the House of Representatives the Democrats controlled 293 seats and the Republicans 142, an addition of three seats to the already substantial margin held by the former. The index of voter participation sustained the downward trend of the few preceding presidential elections; of those eligible to vote, only 53.3 percent did so.

The Carter Administration. Carter continued with even greater resolve than that of Ford the effort begun by the latter to eliminate the "imperial" presidency that had reached its peak during the Nixon tenure. The first indication of this endeavor was the tone of Carter's inauguration, which was informal and modest. Also, Carter was determined to conduct an administration that was "open" and to prevent himself from being made inaccessible to the American people by a highly organized White House staff.

THE PRESIDENT. The constant toothy smile and the soft drawl of his native South belied the toughness and stubbornness of Jimmy Carter (his legal name was James Earl Carter, Jr., but he had discontinued its use long ago). He was diligently methodical in all he undertook. He found deep satisfaction in familiarizing himself with all facets of a governmental issue. Carter did not receive a mandate from every section of the nation; he firmly believed, however, that presidents, through their administrative competence, political skill, and moral persuasion, could become strong leaders of their fellow citizens, thus in effect forging their own mandates.

THE CABINET. Carter wished to give to cabinet members both an important role in policymaking and direct access to the President rather than their having to operate through a power-wielding White House chief of staff, conditions that had not existed during the Nixon administration. In searching for a person to fill each cabinet post Carter considered at least one Washington insider, one outsider, one woman, and one black in order to give to the cabinet as a whole a representative "mix." However, his final choices followed, in general, traditional lines. Named secretary of state was Cyrus R. Vance, a New York lawyer who had been deputy secretary of defense in the Johnson administration. W. Michael Blumenthal, chairman of the Bendix Corporation, a firm producing, among other things, automobile parts, became secretary of the treasury. Harold Brown, a Jew who had been President Johnson's air force secretary and was president of the California Institute of Technology, was made secretary of defense. With the naming of Juanita M. Kreps, an economist and administrative vice-president of Duke University, as secretary of commerce and Patricia Roberts Harris, a black Washington lawyer and former ambassador to Luxembourg, as secretary of housing and urban development, the Carter cabinet became the first one in the nation's history to have more than one woman. Carter's most controversial nomination was that of former federal judge Griffin B. Bell, a close friend and political confidant from Georgia, to be attorney general. The choice of Bell to head the Justice Department was opposed by a number of civil rights organizations, which maintained that Bell, as an aide to a former governor of Georgia and then as a federal judge, had established a record of less than a full commitment to civil rights.

PRESIDENTS AND
SECRETARIES
OF STATE

1.	GEORGE WASHINGTON	1789–1797	Thomas Jefferson	1789
			Edmund Randolph	1794
			Timothy Pickering	1795
2.	JOHN ADAMS	1797–1801	Timothy Pickering	
			John Marshall	1800
3.	THOMAS JEFFERSON	1801–1809	James Madison	1801
4.	JAMES MADISON	1809–1817	Robert Smith	1809
			James Monroe	1811
5.	JAMES MONROE	1817–1825	John Q. Adams	1817
6.	JOHN QUINCY ADAMS	1825–1829	Henry Clay	1825
7.	ANDREW JACKSON	1829–1837	Martin Van Buren	1829
			Edward Livingston	1831
			Louis McLane	1833
			John Forsyth	1834
8.	MARTIN VAN BUREN	1837–1841	John Forsyth	
9.	WILLIAM HENRY HARRISON	1841	Daniel Webster	1841
10.	JOHN TYLER	1841–1845	Daniel Webster	
			Hugh S. Legaré	1843
			Abel P. Upshur	1843
			John C. Calhoun	1844
11.	JAMES KNOX POLK	1845–1849	James Buchanan	1845
12.	ZACHARY TAYLOR	1849–1850	John M. Clayton	1849
13.	MILLARD FILLMORE	1850–1853	Daniel Webster	1850
			Edward Everett	1852
14.	FRANKLIN PIERCE	1853–1857	William L. Marcy	1853
15.	JAMES BUCHANAN	1857–1861	Lewis Cass	1857
			Jeremiah S. Black	1860
16.	ABRAHAM LINCOLN	1861–1865	William H. Seward	1861
17.	ANDREW JOHNSON	1865–1869	William H. Seward	
18.	ULYSSES S. GRANT	1869–1877	Elihu B. Washburne	1869
			Hamilton Fish	1869

19. RUTHERFORD B. HAYES	1877–1881	William M. Evarts	1877
20. JAMES A. GARFIELD	1881	James G. Blaine	1881
21. CHESTER A. ARTHUR	1881–1885	James G. Blaine	
		F. T. Frelinghuysen	1881
22. GROVER CLEVELAND	1885–1889	Thomas F. Bayard	1885
23. BENJAMIN HARRISON	1889–1893	James G. Blaine	1889
		John W. Foster	1892
24. GROVER CLEVELAND	1893–1897	Walter Q. Gresham	1893
		Richard Olney	1895
25. WILLIAM MCKINLEY	1897–1901	John Sherman	1897
		William R. Day	1898
		John Hay	1898
26. THEODORE ROOSEVELT	1901–1909	John Hay	
		Elihu Root	1905
		Robert Bacon	1909
27. WILLIAM H. TAFT	1909–1913	Philander C. Knox	1909
28. WOODROW WILSON	1913–1921	William J. Bryan	1913
		Robert Lansing	1915
		Bainbridge Colby	1920
29. WARREN G. HARDING	1921–1923	Charles E. Hughes	1921
30. CALVIN COOLIDGE	1923–1929	Charles E. Hughes	
		Frank B. Kellogg	1925
31. HERBERT C. HOOVER	1929–1933	Henry L. Stimson	1929
32. FRANKLIN D. ROOSEVELT	1933–1945	Cordell Hull	1933
		Edward R. Stettinius	1945
33. HARRY S. TRUMAN	1945–1953	Edward R. Stettinius	
		James F. Byrnes	1945
		George C. Marshall	1947
		Dean Acheson	1949
34. DWIGHT D. EISENHOWER	1953–1961	John Foster Dulles	1953
		Christian Herter	1959
35. JOHN F. KENNEDY	1961–1963	Dean Rusk	1961
36. LYNDON B. JOHNSON	1963–1969	Dean Rusk	
37. RICHARD M. NIXON	1969–1974	William P. Rogers	1969
		Henry Kissinger	1973
38. GERALD R. FORD	1974–1977	Henry Kissinger	
39. JIMMY CARTER	1977–1981	Cyrus R. Vance	1977
		Edmund Muskie	1980
40. RONALD REAGAN	1981 –	Alexander Haig	1981
		George Schultz	1982

SUGGESTED BOOKS
FOR FURTHER READING

CHAPTER 1: THE RECONSTRUCTION PERIOD

General Works:
Bowers, Claude G. *The Tragic Era* (1929)
Dunning, William A. *Reconstruction, Political and Economic* (1907)
Franklin, John Hope. *Reconstruction: After the Civil War* (1961)
Patrick, Rembert W. *The Reconstruction of the Nation* (1967)
Stampp, Kenneth M. *The Era of Reconstruction* (1965)

Special Studies:
Beale, Howard K. *The Critical Year: A Study of Andrew Johnson and Reconstruction* (1930)
Benedict, Michael Les. *The Impeachment and Trial of Andrew Johnson* (1973)
Bentley, George R. *A History of the Freedmen's Bureau* (1955)
Coulter, E. Merton. *The South During Reconstruction* (1947)
Cruden, Robert. *The Negro in Reconstruction* (1969)
DuBois, W. E. Burghardt. *Black Reconstruction* (1935)
Kutler, Stanley A. *Judicial Power and Reconstruction Politics* (1968)
McKitrick, Eric L. *Andrew Johnson and Reconstruction* (1960)
Trelease, Allen W. *White Terror: The Ku Klux Klan Conspiracy and Southern Reconstruction* (1971)

CHAPTER 2: FROM GRANT TO CLEVELAND: DOMESTIC AFFAIRS

General Works:
Josephson, Matthew. *The Politicos, 1865–1896* (1938)

Morgan, H. Wayne. *From Hayes to McKinley: National Party Politics, 1877–1896* (1969)

White, Leonard D. *The Republican Era, 1869–1901* (1958)

Special Studies:

Hesseltine, William B. *Ulysses S. Grant* (1935)

Hoogenboom, Ari. *Outlawing the Spoils: A History of the Civil Service Reform Movement, 1865–1883* (1961)

Mandelbaum, Seymour. *Boss Tweed's New York* (1965)

Marcus, Robert D. *Grand Old Party: Political Structure in the Gilded Age, 1880–1896* (1971)

Merrill, Horace. *Bourbon Leader: Grover Cleveland and the Democratic Party* (1957)

Nevins, Allan. *Grover Cleveland* (1932)

———. *Hamilton Fish: The Inner History of the Grant Administration* (2 vols., 1936)

Sproat, John G. *"The Best Men": Liberal Reformers in the Gilded Age* (1968)

Woodward, C. Vann. *Reunion and Reaction* (1951)

CHAPTER 3: SETTLEMENT OF THE WEST

General Works:

Billington, Ray Allen. *Westward Expansionism* (1967)

Webb, Walter P. *The Great Plains* (1931)

Special Studies:

Atherton, Lewis. *The Cattle Kings* (1951)

Brown, Dee. *Bury My Heart at Wounded Knee* (1971)

Durham, Philip, and Jones, Everett L. *The Negro Cowboys* (1965)

Dykstra, Robert R. *The Cattle Towns* (1968)

Fite, Gilbert C. *The Farmer's Frontier* (1966)

Hagan, William T. *American Indians* (1961)

Paul, Rodman W. *Mining Frontiers of the Far West, 1848–1880* (1963)

Roe, Frank G. *The Indian and the Horse* (1955)

Shannon, Fred A. *The Farmer's Last Frontier* (1945)

Young, Otis E., Jr. *Western Mining* (1970)

CHAPTER 4: THE RISE OF BIG BUSINESS

General Works:

Cochran, Thomas C., and Miller, William. *The Age of Enterprise* (1942)

Garraty, John A. *The New Commonwealth, 1877–1890* (1968)

Hacker, Louis M. *The Triumph of American Capitalism* (1940)
Kirkland, Edward C. *Industry Comes of Age: Business, Labor, and Public Policy, 1860–1897* (1961)
Tarbell, Ida M. *The Nationalizing of Business, 1878–1898* (1936)

Special Studies:
Benson, Lee. *Merchants, Farmers, and Railroads* (1955)
Cochran, Thomas C. *Railroad Leaders* (1953)
Fine, Sidney. *Laissez Faire and the General Welfare State: A Study of Conflict in American Thought, 1865–1901* (1956)
Fogel, Robert W. *Railroads and American Economic Growth* (1964)
Griswold, Wesley S. *A Work of Giants: Building the First Transcontinental Railroad* (1962)
Hacker, Louis, M. *The World of Andrew Carnegie, 1865–1901* (1968)
Josephson, Matthew. *The Robber Barons* (1934)
Kolko, Gabriel. *Railroads and Regulation, 1877–1916* (1965)
McKelvey, Blake. *The Urbanization of America* (1962)
Nevins, Allan. *Study in Power: John D. Rockefeller* (2 vols., 1953)
Schlesinger, Arthur M., Sr. *The Rise of the City, 1878–1898* (1933)
Taussig, Frank W. *The Tariff History of the United States* (1931)
Temin, Peter. *Iron and Steel in Nineteenth-Century America* (1964)

CHAPTER 5: THE STATUS OF INDUSTRIAL WORKERS

General Works:
Rayback, Joseph G. *A History of American Labor* (1959)
Taft, Philip. *Organized Labor in America* (1964)
Ware, Norman J. *The Labor Movement in the United States, 1860–1895* (1929)

Special Studies:
Bruce, Robert B. *1877: Year of Violence* (1959)
Dick, William M. *Labor and Socialism in America: The Gompers Era* (1972)
Dubofsky, Melvyn. *We Shall Be All: A History of the Industrial Workers of the World* (1969)
Ginger, Ray. *The Bending Cross: A Biography of Eugene Victor Debs* (1949)
Grob, Gerald N. *Workers and Utopia: A Study of Ideological Conflict in the American Labor Movement, 1865–1900* (1961)
Hill, Herbert. *The Racial Practices of Organized Labor* (1965)
Lindsey, Almont. *The Pullman Strike* (1942)
Rosenblum, Gerald. *Immigrant Workers: The Impact on American Labor Radicalism* (1973)
Taft, Philip. *The A. F. of L. in the Time of Gompers* (1957)

CHAPTER 6: THE REVOLT OF THE WEST

General Works:
Buck, Solon J. *The Agrarian Crusade* (1920)
Destler, Chester M. *American Radicalism, 1865–1901* (1946)
Durden, Robert F. *The Climax of Populism* (1966)
Hicks, John D. *The Populist Revolt* (1931)
Pollock, Norman. *The Populist Response to Industrial America* (1962)

Special Studies:
Coletta, Paolo E. *William Jennings Bryan: Political Evangelist, 1860–1908* (1964)
Fels, Rendigs. *American Business Cycles, 1865–1897* (1959)
Glad, Paul W. *The Trumpet Soundeth: William Jennings Bryan and His Democracy, 1896–1912* (1960)
Hoffmann, Charles. *The Depression of the Nineties* (1970)
Hollingsworth, J. Rogers. *The Whirligig of Politics: The Democracy of Cleveland and Bryan* (1963)
Jones, Stanley L. *The Presidential Election of 1896* (1964)
Knoles, George H. *The Presidential Campaign and Election of 1892* (1942)
Merrill, Horace S. *Bourbon Democracy of the Middle West, 1865–1896* (1953)
Nugent, Walter T. K. *Money and American Society, 1865–1880* (1967)
Unger, Irwin. *The Greenback Era* (1964)
Woodward, C. Vann. *Tom Watson, Agrarian Rebel* (1938)

CHAPTER 7: THE UNITED STATES AS A WORLD POWER

General Works:
Battistini, Lawrence H. *The Rise of American Influence in Asia and the Pacific* (1960)
Healy, David F. *U.S. Expansionism: The Imperialist Urge in the 1890's* (1970)
LaFeber, Walter. *The New Empire* (1963)
May, Ernest R. *Imperial Democracy: The Emergence of America as a Great Power* (1961)
Weinberg, Albert K. *Manifest Destiny* (1935)

Special Studies:
Beisner, Robert L. *Twelve Against Empire: The Anti-Imperialists, 1898–1900* (1968)

Campbell, Charles S., Jr. *Special Business Interests and the Open Door Policy* (1951)

Challener, Richard D. *Admirals, Generals, and American Foreign Policy, 1898–1914* (1973)

Dennett, Tyler. *John Hay* (1933)

Freidel, Frank. *The Splendid Little War* (1958)

Healy, David F. *The United States in Cuba, 1898–1902* (1963)

Millis, Walter. *The Martial Spirit* (1931)

Morgan, H. Wayne. *America's Road to Empire: The War With Spain and Overseas Expansion* (1965)

Perkins, Dexter. *The Monroe Doctrine, 1867–1907* (1937)

Pletcher, David M. *The Awkward Years: American Foreign Relations Under Garfield and Arthur* (1961)

Pratt, Julius W. *The Expansionists of 1898* (1936)

CHAPTER 8: THE ERA OF THEODORE ROOSEVELT

General Works:

Beale, Howard K. *Theodore Roosevelt and the Rise of America to World Power* (1956)

Croly, Herbert. *The Promise of American Life* (1909)

Faulkner, Harold U. *The Quest for Social Justice, 1898–1914* (1931)

Mowry, George E. *The Era of Theodore Roosevelt, 1900–1912* (1958)

Special Studies:

Anderson, Donald F. *William Howard Taft: A Conservative's Conception of the Presidency* (1973)

Baker, Richard C. *The Tariff Under Roosevelt and Taft* (1941)

Blum, John M. *The Republican Roosevelt* (1954)

Bowers, Claude G. *Beveridge and the Progressive Era* (1932)

Miner, Dwight C. *The Fight for the Panama Route* (1940)

Mowry, George E. *Theodore Roosevelt and the Progressive Movement* (1946)

Munro, Dana G. *Intervention and Dollar Diplomacy in the Caribbean, 1900–1921* (1964)

Nerr, Charles. *An Uncertain Friendship: Theodore Roosevelt and Japan, 1906–1909* (1967)

Penick, James. *Progressive Politics and Conservation: The Ballinger-Pinchot Affair* (1968)

Pringle, Henry F. *The Life and Times of William Howard Taft* (2 vols., 1939)

———. *Theodore Roosevelt* (1931)

CHAPTER 9: WILSONIAN LIBERALISM

General Works:
Link, Arthur S. *Woodrow Wilson and the Progressive Era, 1910–1917* (1954)
May, Henry F. *The End of American Innocence: A Study of the First Years of Our Own Time, 1912–1917* (1959)

Special Studies:
Blaisdell, Thomas C., Jr. *The Federal Trade Commission* (1932)
Blum, John M. *Joe Tumulty and the Wilson Era* (1951)
———. *Woodrow Wilson and the Politics of Morality* (1964)
Grieb, Kenneth J. *The United States and Huerta* (1969)
Kelsey, Carl. *The American Intervention in Haiti and the Dominican Republic* (1922)
Laughlin, J. Lawrence. *The Federal Reserve Act* (1933)
Link, Arthur S. *Wilson* (4 vols., 1947–1964)
Quirk, Robert E. *An Affair of Honor: Woodrow Wilson and the Occupation of Veracruz* (1962)

CHAPTER 10: WORLD WAR I

General Works:
May, Ernest R. *The World War and American Isolation, 1914–1917* (1959)
Millis, Walter. *Road to War: America, 1914–1917* (1935)
Paxson, Frederic L. *American Democracy and the World War* (3 vols., 1936–1948)
Tansill, Charles C. *America Goes to War* (1938)

Special Studies:
Bailey, Thomas A. *Woodrow Wilson and the Great Betrayal* (1945)
———. *Woodrow Wilson and the Lost Peace* (1944)
Churchill, Allen. *Over Here* (1968)
Coffman, Edward M. *The War to End All Wars: The American Military Experience in World War I* (1968)
Gelfand, Lawrence E. *The Inquiry: American Preparations for Peace, 1917–1919* (1963)
Peterson, Horace C., and Fite, Gilbert C. *Opponents of War, 1917–1918* (1957)
Rudin, Harry R. *Armistice, 1918* (1944)

Seymour, Charles. *American Diplomacy During the World War* (1934)
Stallings, Lawrence. *The Doughboys* (1963)
Stone, Ralph. *The Irreconcilables: The Fight Against the League of Nations* (1970)

CHAPTER 11: THE 1920s: PEACETIME PURSUITS

General Works:
Allen, Frederick Lewis. *Only Yesterday* (1931)
Faulkner, Harold U. *From Versailles to the New Deal* (1950)
Hicks, John D. *The Republican Ascendancy, 1921–1933* (1960)
Leuchtenburg, William E. *The Perils of Prosperity, 1914–1932* (1958)
Nevins, Allan. *The United States in a Chaotic World, 1919–1933* (1950)
Slosson, Preston, W. *The Great Crusade and After, 1914–1928* (1930)

Special Studies:
Bagby, Wesley M. *The Road to Normalcy: The Presidential Campaign and Election of 1920* (1962)
Barrett, Marvin. *The Jazz Age* (1959)
Bernstein, Irving. *The Lean Years: A History of the American Worker, 1920–1933* (1960)
Burner, David. *The Politics of Provincialism: The Democratic Party in Transition, 1918–1932* (1968)
Ellis, L. Ethan. *Republican Foreign Policy, 1921–1933* (1968)
Ferrell, Robert H. *American Diplomacy in the Great Depression: Hoover-Stimson Foreign Policy, 1929–1933* (1957)
Furniss, Norman. *The Fundamentalist Controversy, 1918–1931* (1954)
Galbraith, John Kenneth. *The Great Crash, 1929* (1955)
Josephson, Matthew, and Josephson, Hannah. *Al Smith* (1969)
Mecklin, John M. *The Ku Klux Klan* (1924)
Moore, Edmund A. *A Catholic Runs for President: The Campaign of 1928* (1956)
Murray, Robert K. *The Harding Era: Warren G. Harding and His Administration* (1969)
———. *Red Scare* (1950)
Russell, Francis. *The Shadow of Blooming Grove: Warren G. Harding in His Time* (1968)
Sann, Paul. *The Lawless Decade* (1957)
Schriftgiesser, Karl. *This Was Normalcy, An Account of Party Politics During Twelve Republican Years: 1920–1932* (1940)

Sinclair, Andrew. *Era of Excess: A Social History of the Prohibition Movement* (1962)

Soule, George. *Prosperity Decade* (1947)

White, William Allen. *A Puritan in Babylon: The Story of Calvin Coolidge* (1930)

CHAPTER 12: THE NEW DEAL

General Works:

Brogan, Denis W. *The Era of Franklin D. Roosevelt* (1950)

Leuchtenburg, William E. *Franklin D. Roosevelt and the New Deal, 1932–1940* (1963)

Rauch, Basil. *The History of the New Deal, 1933–1938* (1944)

Schlesinger, Arthur M., Jr. *The Age of Roosevelt* (3 vols. to date, 1957–   )

Wecter, Dixon. *The Age of the Great Depression, 1929–1941* (1948)

Special Studies:

Baker, Leonard. *Back to Back: The Duel Between FDR and the Supreme Court* (1967)

Bennett, David H. *Demagogues in the Depression: American Radicals and the Union Party, 1932–1936* (1969)

Burns, James MacGregor. *Roosevelt: The Lion and the Fox* (1956)

Cronon, Edmund D. *Labor and the New Deal* (1963)

Ekirch, Arthur A., Jr. *Ideologies and Utopias: The Impact of the New Deal on American Thought* (1969)

Freidel, Frank. *Franklin D. Roosevelt* (3 vols. to date, 1952–   )

Graham, Otis L. *An Encore for Reform: The Old Progressives and the New Deal* (1967)

Gunther, John. *Roosevelt in Retrospect* (1950)

McCraw, Thomas K. *TVA and the Power Fight, 1933–1939* (1971)

McKinley, Charles, and Frase, Robert W. *Launching Social Security* (1970)

Patterson, James T. *Congressional Conservatism and the New Deal* (1967)

Pell, Roy V., and Donnelly, Thomas C. *The 1932 Campaign* (1935)

Perkins, Frances. *The Roosevelt I Knew* (1946)

Roosevelt, Eleanor. *This I Remember* (1949)

Roosevelt, Elliot, and Brough, James. *An Untold Story: The Roosevelts of Hyde Park* (1973)

Sherwood, Robert E. *Roosevelt and Hopkins* (1948)

Terkel, Studs. *Hard Times: An Oral History of the Great Depression* (1970)

Wood, Bryce. *The Making of the Good Neighbor Policy* (1961)

CHAPTER 13: WORLD WAR II

General Works:

Buchanan, A. Russell. *The United States and World War II* (2 vols., 1964)
Davis, Kenneth S. *Experience of War: The United States in World War II* (1965)
Fuller, John F. C. *The Second World War, 1939–1945* (1948)
Pratt, Fletcher. *War for the World* (1950)
Snyder, Louis L. *The War: A Concise History, 1939–1945* (1960)

Special Studies:

Ambrose, Stephen E. *The Supreme Commander: The War Years of General Dwight D. Eisenhower* (1970)
Beard, Charles A. *President Roosevelt and the Coming of the War, 1941* (1948)
Borg, Dorothy. *The United States and the Far Eastern Crisis of 1933–1938* (1964)
Eisenhower, Dwight D. *Crusade in Europe* (1948)
Feis, Herbert. *Churchill, Roosevelt, Stalin* (1957)
————. *The Decision to Drop the Bomb* (1966)
Jonas, Manfred. *Isolationism in America, 1935–1941* (1966)
Kimball, Warren F. *The Most Unsordid Act: Lend Lease, 1939–1941* (1969)
Langer, Walter L., and Gleason, Sarell E. *The Challenge to Isolation, 1937–1940* (1952)
Lingeman, Richard R. *Don't You Know There's a War On? The American Home Front, 1941–1945* (1970)
Morison, Samuel Eliot. *The Two-Ocean War* (1963)
Nevins, Allan. *The New Deal and World Affairs* (1950)
Rauch, Basil. *Roosevelt: From Munich to Pearl Harbor* (1950)
Smith, Gaddis. *American Diplomacy During the Second World War, 1941–1945* (1965)
Tansill, Charles C. *Back Door to War* (1952)
Walton, Francis. *Miracle of World War II: How American Industry Made Victory Possible* (1956)
Wohlstetter, Roberta. *Pearl Harbor, Warning and Decision* (1962)

CHAPTER 14: THE QUEST FOR STABILITY AT HOME AND PEACE ABROAD

General Works:

Agar, Herbert. *The Price of Power: America Since 1945* (1957)
Baker, Donald G., and Sheldon, Charles H. *Postwar America: The Search for Identity* (1969)
Goldman, Eric F. *The Crucial Decade—and After: America, 1945–1960* (1961)

Special Studies:

Acheson, Dean. *Present at the Creation: My Years in the State Department* (1969)

Adams, Sherman. *First-hand Report* (1961)

Cox, Archibald. *The Warren Court: Constitutional Decision as an Instrument of Reform* (1968)

Eisenhower, Dwight D. *The White House Years* (2 vols., 1963–1965)

Hartmann, Susan M. *Truman and the 80th Congress* (1971)

Konvitz, Milton R. *Expanding Liberties: Freedom's Gains in Postwar America* (1966)

LaFeber, Walter. *America, Russia, and the Cold War, 1945–1966* (1967)

Lee, R. Alton. *Truman and Taft-Hartley* (1967)

McCoy, Donald R., and Ruetter, Richard T. *Quest and Response: Minority Rights and the Truman Administration* (1973)

Nixon, Richard M. *Six Crises* (1962)

Osgood, Robert E. *NATO: The Entangling Alliance* (1962)

Patterson, James T. *Mr. Republican: A Biography of Robert A. Taft* (1972)

Price, Harry B. *The Marshall Plan and Its Meaning* (1955)

Ress, David. *Korea: The Limited War* (1964)

Ross, Irwin. *The Loneliest Campaign: The Truman Victory of 1948* (1968)

Rovere, Richard. *Senator Joe McCarthy* (1959)

Spanier, John W. *The Truman-MacArthur Controversy and the Korean War* (1959)

Theoharis, Athan G. *The Yalta Myths: An Issue in U.S. Politics, 1945–1955* (1970)

Truman, Harry S. *Memoirs* (2 vols., 1955–1956)

Tsou, Tang. *America's Failure in China, 1941–1950* (1963)

Wilcox, Francis O., and Haviland, H. Field, Jr. *The United States and the United Nations* (1961)

CHAPTER 15: THE NEW FRONTIER AND THE GREAT SOCIETY

General Works:

Burner, David; Marcus, Robert D.; and West, Thomas R. *A Giant's Strength: America in the 1960's* (1971)

O'Neill, William L. *Coming Apart: An Informal History of America in the 1960's* (1971)

Special Studies:

Allison, Graham T. *Essence of Decision: Explaining the Cuban Missile Crisis* (1971)

Draper, Theodore. *The Rediscovery of Black Nationalism* (1970)

FitzGerald, Frances. *Fire in the Lake: The Vietnamese and the Americans in Vietnam* (1972)

Geyelin, Philip. *Lyndon B. Johnson and the World* (1966)

Goldman, Eric F. *The Tragedy of Lyndon Johnson* (1968)

Halberstam, David. *The Best and the Brightest* (1972)

Heath, Jim F. *John F. Kennedy and the Business Community* (1969)

Hilsman, Roger. *To Move a Nation: The Politics of Foreign Policy in the Administration of John F. Kennedy* (1967)

Johnson, Haynes. *The Bay of Pigs* (1964)

Johnson, Lady Bird. *A White House Diary* (1970)

Johnson, Lyndon Baines. *The Vantage Point: Perspectives of the Presidency, 1963–1969* (1971)

Kearns, Doris. *Lyndon Johnson and the American Dream* (1976)

Lewis, David L. *King* (1970)

Manchester, William. *The Death of a President* (1967)

Muse, Benjamin. *The American Negro Revolution* (1969)

O'Donnell, Kenneth P., and Powers, David F. *Johnny, We Hardly Knew Ye: Memoirs of John Fitzgerald Kennedy* (1972)

Schlesinger, Arthur M., Jr. *A Thousand Days: John F. Kennedy in the White House* (1965)

Sidey, Hugh. *A Very Personal Presidency: Lyndon Johnson in the White House* (1968)

Silberman, Charles E. *Crisis in Black and White* (1964)

Sorenson, Theodore C. *Kennedy* (1965)

White, Theodore H. *The Making of the President, 1960* (1961)

――――. *The Making of the President, 1964* (1965)

Wicker, Tom. *JFK and LBJ: The Influence of Personality Upon Politics* (1968)

Wright, Nathan, Jr. *Black Power and Urban Unrest* (1967)

CHAPTER 16: THE NIXON AND FORD ADMINISTRATIONS— AND PRESIDENT CARTER

General Works:

Editors of *The National Observer. The Seventies* (1970)

Freedman, Leonard, ed. *Issues of the Seventies* (1970)

Special Studies:

Bernstein, Carl, and Woodward, Bob. *All the President's Men* (1974)

Carter, Jimmy. *Why Not the Best?* (1975)

Jones, Alan M., Jr., ed. *U.S. Foreign Policy in a Changing World: The Nixon Administration, 1969–1973* (1973)

Kalb, Marvin, and Kalb, Bernard. *Kissinger* (1974)

Kucharsky, David. *The Man from Plains* (1976)

Lukas, J. Anthony. *Nightmare: The Underside of the Nixon Years* (1976)

McCarthy, Mary. *The Mask of State: Watergate Portraits* (1974)

Mankiewicz, Frank. *Perfectly Clear: Nixon from Whittier to Watergate* (1973)

————. *U.S. v. Richard Nixon, The Final Crisis* (1975)

Mazlish, Bruce. *In Search of Nixon: A Psychohistorical Inquiry* (1972)

Mollenhoff, Clark R. *Game Plan for Disaster* (1976)

Osgood, Robert E., and others. *Retreat From Empire?: The First Nixon Administration* (1973)

Panetta, Leon E., and Gall, Peter. *Bring Us Together: The Nixon Team and the Civil Rights Retreat* (1971)

Porter, Gareth. *A Peace Denied: The United States, Vietnam, and the Paris Agreement* (1976)

Rather, Dan, and Gates, Gary. *The Palace Guard* (1974)

Reeves, Richard. *A Ford, Not a Lincoln* (1975)

Safire, William. *Before the Fall* (1975)

Schrag, Peter. *Test of Loyalty: Daniel Ellsberg and the Rituals of Secret Government* (1974)

terHorst, J. F. *Gerald Ford and the Future of the Presidency* (1974)

White, Theodore H. *Breach of Faith* (1975)

————. *The Making of the President, 1968* (1969)

————. *The Making of the President, 1972* (1973)

Wills, Garry. *Nixon Agonistes* (1971)

Index

"ABC Powers" mediation, 120
Abzug, Bella, 247
Acheson, Dean, 208, 218
Adams, Charles Francis, 16, 88
Adams, Sherman, 216–217
Adamson Act, 118
Administrative Reorganization Act, 175–176
Advisory Commission on Civil Disorders, 245
AFL-CIO, 172. *See also* American Federation of Labor (AFL); Congress of Industrial Organizations (CIO)
Agnew, Spiro T., 254, 260, 261–262
Agricultural Adjustment Act (1933), 165, 174, 176; (1938), 174, 177
Agricultural Adjustment Administration (AAA), 165
Agricultural Marketing Act, 148
Agriculture, 25–26, 37–39, 65, 118, 147–148, 153, 165, 173–174, 190–191. *See also* Farmers' discontent
Agriculture, Department of, 25–26
Aguinaldo, Emilio, 91–92
Alabama, 167, 237
Alabama, University of, 237
Alabama claims, 76–77
Alaska, 75, 105, 221
Albania, 225
Aldrich, Nelson W., 104
Aldrich Bill, 26
Aldrin, Edwin E., Jr., 259
Aleutian Islands, 198
Alien Registration Act. *See* Smith Act
Algeciras Conference, 111
Algeria, 196

Alliance for Progress, 248
Allied Reparations Commission, 155
Alsace-Lorraine, 133, 134
Altgeld, John P., 62
Amalgamated Association of Iron, Steel, and Tin Workers, 61
Amalgamated Clothing Workers of America, 172
Amendments, constitutional: First, 132; Thirteenth, 3; Fourteenth, 5, 7, 9, 10, 220; Fifteenth, 8–9, 243; Sixteenth, 106, 116; Seventeenth, 96; Eighteenth, 143, 150, 151, 161; Nineteenth, 97; Twentieth, 170; Twenty-first, 151; Twenty-second, 209; Twenty-third, 240 n; Twenty-fourth, 242; Twenty-fifth, 242, 262; Twenty-sixth, 258
America First Committee, 184
American Defense Society, 125
American Expeditionary Force (AEF), 128
American Farm Bureau Federation, 147
American Federation of Labor (AFL), 59–60, 84, 142, 146, 172, 173
American Independent party, 254
American League to Limit Armaments, 126
American Medical Association, 235
American Neutrality League, 126
American Railway Union, 62
American Rights Committee, 125
American Sugar Refining Company, 28
American Tobacco Company, 101
American Union against Militarism, 126
Ames, Oakes, 15

Anders, William, 258–259
Anthony, Susan B., 43, 97
Anticommunism, 146, 151–152, 210, 213–215, 217–218
Anti-Imperialist League, 88
Anti-Saloon League, 150
Antitrust legislation, 47, 100–101, 117–118
ANZUS Pact, 230
Appalachian Regional Development Act, 241
Arab-Israeli conflict, 231, 250, 272–273
Argentina, 78, 120
Arizona, 96, 97, 127–128, 240
Armstrong, Neil A., 259
Army Appropriation Act, 126
Arrears of Pension Act, 25
Arthur, Chester A., 19, 20, 21, 23
Atchison, Topeka, and Santa Fe Railroad, 50
Atlantic Charter, 186–187
Atlantic Coast Line Railroad, 48
Atomic bomb, 169, 200, 205, 214
Attlee, Clement R., 205
Australia, 197, 198, 200, 230
Austria, 137, 182, 197, 203
Austria-Hungary, 123, 133, 136, 137
Axis satellite nations, 203

Ballinger, Richard A., 105
Baltimore and Ohio Railroad, 48, 61, 145
Bank for International Settlements, 155
Bankhead-Jones Farm Tenant Act, 174
Banking, 116–117, 166–167
Banking Act, 167
Baraka, Imamu Amiri, 244
Barkley, Alben W., 210, 215
Barnett, Ross, 237
Barton, Clara, 43
Baruch, Bernard M., 130
Bataan peninsula, 198
Bay of Pigs, 248–249
Bayard, Thomas F., 24
Bayh, Birch, 274
Beef trust, 45
Belgium, 109, 133, 156, 194, 223, 224
Belknap, William W., 17
Bell, Alexander Graham, 41–42
Bell, Griffin B., 277
Bellamy, Edward, 46
Bering Sea controversy, 77
Berle, Adolph A., Jr., 163

Berlin airlift, 223–224
Berlin Wall, 249
Bernstorff, Johann von, 125
Bessemer, Henry, 41
"Big Four," 134
"Big stick diplomacy," 107
"Billion Dollar Congress," 29
Bimetallism, 68–69, 70–71, 73
Birmingham, Alabama, 238
Bismarck Islands, 197
Black Codes, 4
"Black Friday," 15
Black Muslims, 244
Black Panther Party for Self-Defense, 244
"Black Power," 244
Black Revolution, 232, 236–238, 242–245
"Black Thursday," 154
Blacks, 57, 146, 212–213, 219–221, 254, 256; and gains during 1960s, 236–238, 242–245; during Reconstruction period, 2, 4–5, 7–9, 10–12, 14. *See also* Civil rights; Desegregation
Blaine, James G., 19, 20, 23–24, 27, 29, 77, 78–79
Blair, Francis P., Jr., 14
Bland-Allison Act, 68
Bliss, Tasker H., 134
Blount, James H., 81
Blumenthal, W. Michael, 277
Bolivia, 78
Bonds, war. *See* War bonds
"Bonus Army," 160–161
Borah, William, 136
Borman, Frank, 258–259
Boston police strike, 152
"Bourbons," 10, 12
Bourgeois, Leon, 135
Boutwell, George S., 15
Boxer Rebellion, 82
Boyd, Alan S., 242
Boys of '76, 9
"Brain Trust," 163
Brand, Vance D., 259
Brazil, 120
Brezhnev, Leonid I., 259, 271
Briand, Aristide, 156
Bricker, John, 193
Bristow, Benjamin H., 17
British Columbia, 76
British Guiana, 77, 186
Brown, B. Gratz, 16

Brown, Harold, 277
Brown v. *Board of Education of Topeka*,
    219–220, 221
Bruce, Blanche K., 8
Bruce, David K., 269
Bryan, Charles W., 141
Bryan, William Jennings, 70—71, 73,
    88—89, 100, 103-104, 114, 115, 125,
    152-153
Bryan-Chamorro Treaty, 122
Budget and Accounting Act, 144
Buenos Aires, Declaration of, 179–180
Buffalo, 32, 33
Bulganin, Nikolai A., 225
Bulgaria, 203, 225
Bulge, Battle of the, 197
"Bull Moose" party. *See* Progressive
    party of 1912
Burchard, Samuel D., 24
Bureau of the Budget, 144
Bureau of Corporations, 101
Bureau of Indian Affairs, 33, 245–246
Bureau of Refugees, Freedmen, and
    Abandoned Lands. *See* Freedmen's
    Bureau
Burger, Warren E., 256
Burke Act, 34, 245
Burleson, Albert S., 116
Burlingame Treaty, 23
Burma, 197, 200
Burma Road, 200
Business: effects of Depression of 1929
    on, 160; and New Deal, 164-165. *See
    also* Industry; Railroads
Butler, Benjamin F., 15, 19
Byrd, Harry F., 193
Byrnes, James F., 208

Cairo Conference, 204
California, 23, 35, 71, 97, 110, 246
Calles, Plutarco, 157–158
Cambodia, 251–252, 269
Canada, 76, 77, 150, 184-185, 224, 270
Cannon, Joseph G., 105
"Cannonism," 105–106
Caribbean, 88, 120, 122
Carlisle, John G., 30
Carmichael, Stokely, 244
Carnegie, Andrew, 45
Carnegie Steel Company, 61
Caroline Islands, 198
"Carpetbaggers," 8
Carranza, Venustiano, 120

Carswell, G. Harrold, 256–257
Carter, Jimmy, 253, 273–274, 276–277;
    election to presidency, 274–276
Casablanca Conference, 203
Castro, Fidel, 248, 249
Catt, Carrie Chapman, 97
Cecil, Robert, 135
Central Intelligence Agency (CIA), 208,
    248–249
Central Pacific Railroad, 23, 48, 50
Cernan, Eugene, 259
Cervera, Pascual, 86, 87
Chaffee, Roger, 258
Chambers, Whittaker, 213–214
Chamoun, Camille, 231
Chandler, Zachariah, 19
Chase, Salmon P., 7
Chateau-Thierry, Battle of, 129
Chavez, Cesar, 246
Chennault, Claire, 200
Chesapeake and Ohio Railroad, 146
Chiang Kai-shek, 204, 228–229
Chicago, 42
Chicago, Burlington, and Quincy Rail-
    road, 100
Chicago, Milwaukee, St. Paul, and Pa-
    cific Railroad, 50
Chicanos, 246
Child labor, 58, 118, 164, 173
Chile, 78, 79, 120
China, 23, 51, 80, 82, 109, 110, 111,
    112, 136, 156, 157, 227–229, 230, 250,
    251, 253, 271, 272; in World War II,
    187–188, 191, 198, 200; during post–
    World War II period, 203, 204, 205,
    206
Chinese, 23, 50, 63
Chinese Exclusion Act, 23
Chisholm, Shirley, 247
Chou En-lai, 229, 271
Churchill, Winston, 186–187, 203, 204–
    205, 222
Cigarmakers' Union, 59
Cities, growth of, 42–43
City manager plan, 97
Civil Aeronautics Board (CAB), 175
Civil rights, 4–5, 10, 212–213, 219–221,
    236, 237, 242, 256. *See also* Black
    Revolution; Desegregation
Civil Rights Act (1866), 4-5; (1875), 10;
    (1957), 220–221; (1960), 221; (1964),
    242
Civil Rights Commission, 221

Civil service reform, 16, 21–22, 24, 28, 99, 103
Civil Works Administration (CWA), 164, 171
Civilian Conservation Corps (CCC), 164
Clarendon, George, 76
Clark, Champ, 113–114
Clark, J. Reuben, 158
Clark, Mark, 196
Clark Memorandum, 158
Clay, Lucius, 201
Clayton Antitrust Act, 118
Clayton-Bulwer Treaty, 107
Cleaver, Eldridge, 244
Clemenceau, Georges, 133, 134
Cleveland, Grover, 24, 26–27, 29; and domestic issues, 24–25, 26, 30, 31, 62, 69, 70, 149; elections to presidency, 23–24, 29–30; and foreign affairs, 77–78, 81, 84
Cleveland, Ohio, 95
Coal strike: of 1902, 99–100; of 1946, 209
Cody, William F. ("Buffalo Bill"), 33
Coinage Act, 68
Cold War, 222–231, 232, 248–252
Coleman, William T., 265
Colfax, Schuyler, 14, 15
Collier, John, 245
Collins, Michael, 259
Colombia, 78, 107–108
Colorado, 35, 68, 70, 97
Commerce, Department of, 106–107
Commission on Organization of the Executive Branch of Government. *See* Hoover Commission
Commission plan, 97
Committee on Civil Rights, 212
Committee to Defend America by Aiding the Allies, 184
Committee for Industrial Organization (CIO). *See* Congress of Industrial Organizations
Committee on Public Information (World War I), 131
Committee for the Re-election of the President (CRP), 262–263, 264
Common Market, 236
Communism, 146–147, 151–152, 210, 213–215, 222–230, 248–252. *See also* Anticommunism; Soviet Union
Communist party, 147, 210
Community Credit Corporation, 174

Compromise of 1877, 17–18
Comstock lode, 35
Congo, 252
Congress, 7, 29, 70, 89, 96, 105–106, 114, 135–137, 170, 262–264
Congress of Industrial Organizations (CIO), 172, 173
Congress of Racial Equality (CORE), 236–237, 244
Conkling, Roscoe, 15, 18, 19, 20, 21, 47
"Conquered Provinces" theory, 2
Conscription. *See* Selective service
Conservation, 99, 102–103, 105
Constitutional amendments. *See* Amendments, constitutional
Consumerism, 268–269
Cooke, Jay, 43–44, 45, 50
Coolidge, Calvin, 139, 141, 142, 152; and domestic issues, 144, 147–148; election to second presidential term, 141–142; and foreign affairs, 154, 156, 158
Cooper, Peter, 67
Cooperative Marketing Act, 147
Cooperatives, 58–59, 66
Corporations, 42
Coral Sea, Battle of the, 198
Corregidor, 198
Cost of Living Council, 256
Coughlin, Charles E., 175
Council of National Defense (World War I), 126, 130
Council of Ten, 133–134
"Court Packing" Plan, 176–177
Cowboys, life of, 36
Cox, Archibald, 263
Cox, Jacob D., 14–15
Cox, James M., 139
Coxey, Jacob S., 31
Crédit Mobilier, 15
Creel, George, 131
"Crime of '73," 68
Crop-lien system, 11, 65
Cuba, 83–85, 86–87, 88, 93, 109, 179, 248–250
Cuban missile crisis, 249–250
Cullom, Shelby M., 54
Cullom Committee, 54–55
Currency, 116–117. *See also* Money
Curtis, Charles, 143, 161
Curtis, George William, 21
Custer, George A., 33

Czechoslovakia, 182, 225

Daniels, Josephus, 116
Darrow, Clarence, 152–153
Daugherty, Harry M., 140–141, 142
Davis, Cushman K., 87
Davis, David, 18
Davis, Henry G., 100
Davis, Henry W., 3
Davis, John W., 141–142
Dawes, Charles G., 141–142, 144, 155, 160
Dawes Act, 34, 245
Dawes Plan, 155
Day, William R., 87
Dayton, Ohio, 97
Dean, John, III, 262
Debs, Eugene V., 62, 98
Defense, Department of, 208
De Gaulle, Charles, 224–225, 226
Delaware, 46, 162
De Lôme, Enrique Dupuy, 84–85
Democratic party, 10, 15, 22, 68, 92, 94, 211–212. *See also* Solid South; Election; Elections, congressional
Denby, Edwin, 140, 142
Denmark, 124, 186, 194
Dennis, Eugene, 214
Dependent Pension Act, 29
Dependent Pension Bill, 25
Depression of 1929, 160–161
Desegregation, 212, 219–220, 236, 237. *See also* Black Revolution; Civil rights
Desert Land Act, 37–38
Destroyer-base agreement, 186
Detroit, 245
Dewey, George, 86
Dewey, Thomas E., 185, 193, 211
Diaz, Porfirio, 119
Diem, Ngo Dinh, 251
Dillon, C. Douglas, 234, 240
Dingley Tariff, 104
Direct government, 95, 96
Direct primary, 96
Disarmament, 133, 135, 156, 157, 250, 271
District of Columbia, 240, 261
Dixiecrats, 211
Doheny, Edward L., 140
Dole, Robert J., 275
"Dollar Diplomacy," 112
Dominican Republic, 109, 120, 122, 179

Donnelly, Ignatius, 69
Doolittle, James, 198
Douglas, William O., 210
Draft. *See* Selective service
Drago, Luis M., 109
Drago Doctrine, 109
Drew, Daniel, 48, 52
Dubinsky, David, 172
Dulles, John Foster, 202, 216, 225–226, 230
Dumbarton Oaks Conference, 205
Dunlop, John T., 265

Eagleton, Thomas, 260
East Germany. *See* Germany
Economic Opportunity Act, 241
Eden, Anthony, 204, 225
Edison, Thomas A., 41
Education, federal aid to, 213, 219, 235, 241
Egan, Patrick, 79
Egypt, 230–231, 250, 272–273
Eight-hour workday, 58, 60, 63, 70, 103, 118
Eisenhower, Dwight D., 194, 196–197, 207, 210, 216–217, 224, 228, 232; and domestic issues, 207, 217, 219, 221–222; elections to presidency, 215–216, 218–219; and foreign affairs, 207, 225–226, 230–231
Eisenhower Doctrine, 231
El Caney, Battle of, 87
Election: of 1868, 14; of 1872, 15–16; of 1876, 17–18; of 1880, 19–20; of 1884, 23–24; of 1888, 26–27; of 1892, 29–30; of 1896, 70–73; of 1900, 88–89; of 1904, 100–101; of 1908, 103–104; of 1912, 113–115; of 1916, 126–127; of 1920, 138–139; of 1924, 141–142; of 1928, 142–143; of 1932, 161–162; of 1936, 170–171; of 1940, 185–186; of 1944, 192–193; of 1948, 210–212; of 1952, 215–216; of 1956, 218–219; of 1960, 233; of 1964, 240; of 1968, 254–255; of 1972, 260–261; of 1976, 274–276
Elections, congressional: of 1866, 5; of 1934, 170
Electoral Commission of 1877, 17–18
Electoral Count Act, 25
Elementary and Secondary Education Act, 241

Elijah Muhammad, 244
Elkins Act, 101
Emergency Banking Act, 166
Emergency Fleet Corporation (World War I), 131
Emergency Quota Act, 149
Emergency Relief Appropriation Act, 171–172, 173
Energy crisis, 268
Enforcement Acts. *See* "Force Acts"
England. *See* Great Britain
English, William A., 19
Environmentalism, 269
Equal Employment Opportunity Commission, 242
"Equal Rights" Amendment, proposed, 247
Erdman Act, 63
Erie Railroad, 48, 52, 146
Erlichman, John, 256, 262, 264
Ervin, Sam J., Jr., 262
Esch-Cummins Act, 145
Espionage Act, 131–132
Estonia, 194
Ethiopia, 182
Evarts, William M., 18
European Economic Community. *See* Common Market
European Recovery Program. *See* Marshall Plan
Evans, Ron, 259
Expansionism. *See* Imperialism
Expedition Act, 101

Fair Deal, 207, 212–213
Fair Labor Standards Act, 173, 177
Fairbanks, Charles W., 100, 126
Fall, Albert B., 140
Far East, 82, 110, 111, 112, 187, 204, 205. *See also* China; Japan
Farm Credit Act, 165
Farm Credit Administration (FCA), 165
Farm Security Administration (FSA), 174
Farmer, James, 236, 244
Farmers' discontent, 46, 64–73, 147
Farmers' National Council, 147
Farmers' frontier, 37–39
Faubus, Orval, 221
Faure, Edgar, 225
Federal Art Project, 171
Federal Bureau of Investigation, 264

Federal Deposit Insurance Corporation (FDIC), 166, 167
Federal Emergency Relief Act, 164
Federal Emergency Relief Administration (FERA), 164
Federal Farm Board, 148
Federal Farm Loan Act, 118
Federal Home Loan Bank Act, 160
Federal Housing Administration (FHA), 166
Federal Power Commission, 146
Federal Republic of Germany. *See* Germany
Federal Reserve Act, 117
Federal Reserve Board, 117, 166, 167
Federal Reserve System, 117, 166, 167
Federal Theater Project, 171
Federal Trade Commission, 117–118
Federal Writers Project, 171
Federation of Organized Trades and Labor Unions of America and Canada, 59
Fenian Brotherhood, 76
Field, Cyrus W., 41
Field, James G., 29, 70
Finance, government, 26, 67, 68–69, 131, 144, 166–167, 177–178, 192, 235–236, 257, 265, 268. *See also* Banking; Tariff
Finland, 156, 182, 194, 203
First World War. *See* World War I
Fish, Hamilton, 14, 74, 76
Fish, Hamilton, Jr., 184
Fisk, James, 15, 48, 52
Florida, 9, 18, 143
Foch, Ferdinand, 130
Folger, Charles J., 20
Food Administration: (World War I), 131; (World War II), 190–191
Food and Agriculture Organization (FAO), 206
Food, Drug, and Cosmetic Act, 175
Foraker Act, 89–91
Forbes, Charles R., 140, 141
"Force Acts," 9, 19
Ford, Gerald R., 253, 262, 265, 274–276; and domestic issues, 265, 268–269; and foreign affairs, 269, 272–273
Fordney-McCumber Tariff, 148
Foreign Debt Commission, 155
Formosa. *See* Taiwan
Forrestal, James V., 208

Foster, William, 214
Fourteen Points, 133, 134
France, 87, 109, 111, 112, 251; during
    Cold War, 223, 224, 225, 226, 230–
    231, 250; in World War I, 123, 127,
    129; during post–World War I period,
    133, 134, 135, 156, 157; in World War
    II, 182, 184, 186, 188, 194, 196–197;
    during post–World War II period,
    201, 202, 203, 206
Franco-Prussian War, 43
Frazier-Lemke Farm Bankruptcy Act
    (1934), 165, 176; (1935), 165
Free French, 196–197
Freedmen, 4, 8
Freedmen's Bureau, 4
Freedom Riders, 236–237
Frelinghuysen, Frederick T., 20, 79
Friedan, Betty, 247, 248
Frontier, closing of, 38–39
Frye, William P., 87
Fuchs, Klaus, 214
Fuel Administration (World War I), 131
Fundamentalists, 152–153

Gagarin, Yuri A., 258
Gage, Lyman J., 73
Galveston, Texas, 97
Garfield, James A., 19–20, 21
Garfield, James R., 102
Garner, John N., 161, 170
Gary, Elbert H., 45
General Amnesty Act, 9
General Disarmament Conference, 157
General Motors Corporation, 172, 209
Geneva Naval Conference, 156
"Gentlemen's Agreement," 110
George, Henry, 43, 46
Georgia, 8–9, 16, 167
German Democratic Republic. *See*
    Germany
Germans, 38
Germany, 80, 82, 88, 108–109, 111, 112,
    179, 249, 272; in World War I, 123,
    124–125, 127–128, 129–130; during
    post–World War I period, 133, 134–
    135, 136, 137, 155–156, 179; in World
    War II, 181, 182, 183, 184, 186, 187,
    188, 189, 193–194, 196–197; during
    post–World War II period, 201–202,
    203, 204–205
Ghettos, 244–245

Gilbert Islands, 198
"Gilded Age," 43
Glass-Steagall Banking Act, 166
Glavis, Louis R., 105
Glenn, John H., Jr., 258
Goering, Hermann, 201
Goethals, George W., 108
Gold, 15, 40, 55, 68, 69, 70, 71, 77
Goldwater, Barry, 240
Gompers, Samuel, 59, 60
Good Neighbor Policy, 159, 179
Goodyear, Charles, 41
Gorgas, William C., 108
Gould, Jay, 15, 48, 50, 52
Grady, Henry, 12
Grain Futures Trading Act, 147
"Grandfather clause," 11
Grange, 53, 66
Granger cases, 54, 66
Granger laws, 53, 66
Grangers, 66
Grant, Ulysses S., 8, 9, 13–17, 21
Gray, George, 87
Great Britain, 76–78, 80–82, 108–109,
    111, 112, 119; during Cold War, 223,
    224, 225, 226, 230–231, 250; in World
    War I, 123, 124–125, 127, 129; during
    post–World War I period, 133, 134,
    135, 136, 156, 157; in World War II,
    182, 184, 185, 186, 191, 194, 196, 197,
    200; during post–World War II pe-
    riod, 201, 202, 203–205, 206
Great Depression. *See* Depression of
    1929
Great Northern Railroad, 50, 51, 100
Great Society, 232, 239–248
Greece, 222, 223, 224
Greeley, Horace, 16
Green, William, 172
Greenback party, 54, 67
Greenbackers, 66–67
Greenback-Labor party, 54, 67
Greenbacks, 14, 67
Greenland, 186, 187
Gresham, Walter Q., 30
Grissom, Virgil I., 258
Guadalcanal, 198
Guam, 88, 189, 198
Guantánamo Bay, 93
Guatemala, 78
Guffey-Snyder Bituminous Coal Stabi-
    lization Act, 176

Guiteau, Charles J., 20

Hague Conference: of 1899, 111; of
    1907, 109, 111–112
Hague Court, 111
Haiti, 109, 122, 179
Haldeman, H. R., 256, 262, 264
Half-Breeds, 18–19
Halsey, William F., 198
Hammarskjöld, Dag, 252
Hammer v. Dagenhart, 118
Hancock, Winfield S., 19–20
Hanna, Mark, 71, 73, 100
Harding, Warren G., 137, 139–140, 141;
    and domestic issues, 140–141, 142,
    144; election to presidency, 138–139;
    and foreign affairs, 154, 156
Harkness, Stephen V., 45
Harmon, Judson, 113
Harriman, Edward H., 48, 51
Harriman, W. Averell, 215, 269
Harris, Patricia Roberts, 277
Harrison, Benjamin, 27, 28, 29–30, 47,
    81
Harrison, Francis B., 92
Harte, Bret, 35
Hartley, Fred A., Jr., 210
Hatch Act, 176
Haugen, Gilbert N., 147
Havana, Act of, 180
Hawaii, 75, 79, 81–82, 221–222
Hawes-Cutting Act, 92
Hay, John, 73, 82, 99
Hay-Bunau-Varilla Treaty, 108, 179
Hay-Herrán Treaty, 107
Hay-Pauncefote Treaty, 107, 119
Hayes, Rutherford B., 9–10, 17–19, 21,
    23, 61, 68
Haymarket incident, 61
Haynsworth, Clement, Jr., 256
Haywood, William D., 60
Health care, federal aid to, 213, 235, 241
Health, Education, and Welfare, De-
    partment of, 217
Hearst, William Randolph, 84–85, 100
Hendricks, Thomas H., 17, 23, 25
Hepburn Act, 101, 106
Hess, Rudolf, 201
Hill, James J., 45, 50, 51
Hills, Carla A., 265
Hillman, Sidney, 172
Hirohito, 200

Hiroshima, 200
Hiss, Alger, 213–214
Hitchcock, Gilbert M., 136
Hitler, Adolf, 182, 197
Hoar, Ebenezer R., 15
Hoar, George F., 19, 88
Hobart, Garret A., 71
Hobby, Oveta Culp, 217
Ho Chi Minh, 251, 271
Holden v. Hardy, 63
Holding companies, 46
Holliday, Cyrus K., 50
Home Owners Loan Corporation
    (HOLC), 166
Homestead Act, 37–38
Homestead strike, 61
Hong Kong, 189
Hoover, Herbert C., 92, 131, 140, 143–
    144, 161–162, 208, 217; and domestic
    issues, 144, 148, 151, 159–160, 161,
    167, 169; election to presidency, 142–
    143; and foreign affairs, 92, 154, 155–
    156, 157–158
Hoover Commission: First, 208, Sec-
    ond, 217
Hoover Moratorium, 155–156
Hopkins, Harry L., 164, 171
Hours of Service Act, 63
House, Edward M., 116, 127, 134
Housing Act (1949), 212; (1961), 234
Housing, federal aid to, 166, 212, 234
Housing and Urban Development, De-
    partment of, 241
Howard, Charles, 172
Huerta, Victoriano, 119–120
Hughes, Charles Evans, 95, 126–127,
    135, 139–140, 155, 177
Hull, Cordell, 163, 169, 179, 188, 204,
    205
Humphrey, George M., 216
Humphrey, Hubert H., 240, 254–255,
    260
"Hundred Days," 162
Hungary, 137, 182, 203, 225–226
Huntington, Collis P., 50
Hussein, 231

Iceland, 186, 187
Ickes, Harold L., 163, 165, 171
Idaho, 35, 70, 97
Illinois, 42, 53, 54, 66
Illinois Central Railroad, 48, 51

Immigrants, 23, 38, 41, 42, 50, 51, 57, 110, 149, 215
Immigration, 23, 70, 110, 149–150, 214–215
Impeachment: of Andrew Johnson, 7; proceedings against Richard M. Nixon, 263–264
Imperialism, 74–75, 79–82, 88–89, 91–93, 113. *See also* Spanish-American War
Income tax, 31, 59, 69, 70, 106, 116, 131, 144, 192. *See also* Amendments, constitutional: Sixteenth
India, 197
Indians, 32–34, 245–246
Indochina, 188, 251
Indonesia, 270
Industrial Workers of the World (IWW), 60, 146
Industry, 11, 130, 164–165, 190; devices of, 40, 44–46; effects of, 42–44; government regulation of, 46–47, 99, 100–101, 115, 117–118; nature of, 40–42
Inflation: late nineteenth-century proposals for, 44, 66–69, 70–71; during 1970s, 257, 265, 268
Initiative, 70, 96, 98, 114
Innis, Roy, 244
Insular cases, 89
Integration. *See* Desegregation
Intermediate Credit Act, 147
Internal security, 213–215. *See also* McCarthyism
Internal Security Act, 214
Internal Waterways Commission, 102
International Bureau of American Republics. *See* Pan-American Union
International Conference of American States, 79
International Court of Justice, 155
International Ladies' Garment Workers Union, 172
International Labor Organization (ILO), 206
International Typographical Union, 172
Interstate Commerce Act, 55, 101, 178
Interstate Commerce Commission, 55, 71, 99, 101, 145, 237
International Peace Conference. *See* Hague Conference
Inventions, 41–42

Iowa, 38, 53, 66, 71
Ireland, 76, 124, 137
Irish, 50
"Irreconcilables," 136–137
Isolationism, 74, 138, 154, 183–184
Israel, 231, 250, 272–273
Italy, 82, 108–109, 133, 134, 135, 156, 157, 179, 203; in World War II, 181, 182, 183, 188, 189, 194, 196
Iwo Jima, 200

Jackson, Helen Hunt, 34
Jackson, Henry M., 260, 274
Jackson, Robert H., 201
James, Thomas L., 21
Japan, 51, 82, 88, 109–111, 128, 133, 134, 135, 136, 156, 157; in World War II, 179, 181, 187–189, 197–198, 200, 251; during post–World War II period, 202–203, 204, 205
Japanese, 110
Jaworski, Leon, 263
Jenckes, Thomas A., 21
Jews, 42, 153
Job Corps, 241
Johnson, Andrew, 1, 3, 4, 5, 7
Johnson, Hiram, 95, 115, 136, 182
Johnson, Hugh, 164
Johnson, Lyndon B., 232, 233, 238–240, 254; and domestic issues, 232, 240–243, 245; election to second presidential term, 240; and foreign affairs, 232, 248, 251–252
Johnson, Reverdy, 76
Johnson, Tom L., 95
Johnson Act, 182
Johnson Reconstruction Plan, 3, 4
Johnson-Clarendon Convention, 76
Joint Committee on Reconstruction, 4, 5
Jones, LeRoi. *See* Imamu Amiri Baraka
Jones, Samuel M., 95
Jones Act (1916), 92; (1917), 91
Jordan, 231, 250, 272

Kadar, Janos, 226
Kansas, 36–37, 38, 70, 97, 220
Keating-Owen Act, 118
Kefauver, Estes, 215, 218
Kelley, Oliver H., 66
Kellogg, Frank B., 156, 158
Kellogg-Briand Pact, 156
Kelly, William, 41

Kennedy, John F., 232, 234; and domestic issues, 234–236, 237, 238; election to presidency, 233; and foreign affairs, 232, 248–250, 251
Kennedy, Robert F., 234, 239–240, 254
Kent State University, 270
Kentucky, 16, 71, 167
Kern, John W., 103
Kerner, Otto, 245
Kerr, Robert S., 215
Key, David, 18
Khrushchev, Nikita S., 225, 226, 249–250
King, William L. Mackenzie, 184
King, Martin Luther, Jr., 220, 236, 237, 238, 244
Kissinger, Henry, 255, 270, 272
Knights of Labor, 58–59, 61
Knights of the White Camelia, 9
Knox, Frank, 170
Knox, Philander C., 100, 104, 112
Korea, 110, 204, 272. *See also* Korean War
Korean War, 207, 226–228
Kreps, Juanita M., 277
Ku Klux Klan: during Reconstruction period, 9; during 1920s, 141, 153
Kubasov, Valery N., 259
Kurusu, Saburu, 188

Labor, 32, 41, 56, 63, 64, 70, 118, 146–147, 191, 209–210; aims and tactics of, 57; conflict with management, 60–63, 99–100, 172–173, 209; during New Deal period, 172–173
Labor unions, 57–60, 118, 146–147, 172
Labor, Department of, 106–107
Labor-Management Relations Act. *See* Taft-Hartley Act
Labor Reform party, 54
La Follette, Robert M., 95, 104, 106, 114–115, 136, 142
La Follette Seamen's Act, 118
Laird, Melvin P., 255
Lamar, L. Q. C., 24
Landis, Kenesaw M., 102
Landon, Alfred M., 170–171
Lansing, Robert, 125, 134
Laos, 251–252
Latin America, 78–79, 150, 157–158, 169, 178–180, 230, 235, 248–249. *See also* Good Neighbor Policy; Monroe Doctrine; Roosevelt Corollary

Latvia, 194
League of Nations, 132, 135–137, 138, 139, 141, 143, 154–155, 157
Lease, Mary Ellen, 69
Lebanon, 231
Lee, Robert E., 1
LeMay, Curtis, 254
Lend-Lease Act, 186
Leonov, Aleksei A., 259
Levi, Edward H., 265
Lewis, John L., 172, 209
Liberal Republican party, 15–16
Liberty Loan drives (World War I), 131
Liliuokalani, 81
Lima, Declaration of, 180
Lincoln, Abraham, 1–3
Lincoln, Robert T., 20
Lindbergh, Charles A., 184
Literacy Test Act, 149
Lithuania, 194
Little Rock, Arkansas, 221
Lloyd, Henry D., 46
Lloyd George, David, 133, 134
Lodge, Henry Cabot, 84, 125, 135–136
Lodge, Henry Cabot, Jr., 233, 269
Lodge Reservations, 135–136
Logan, John A., 19, 23
London, Declaration of, 124, 125
London Naval Conference, 157
Long, Huey P., 175
"Long drive," 36
"Long haul–short haul evil," 53, 55
Los Angeles, 96, 245
Louisiana, 9, 18, 220
Lovell, James A., Jr., 258–259
Lowden, Frank O., 139
Lusitania, 125
Luxembourg, 194
Lytton, Earl of, 157
Lytton Report, 157

McAdoo, William G., 116, 131, 139, 141
MacArthur, Douglas, 197–198, 200, 202, 227–228
McAuliffe, Anthony, 197
McCarran, Pat, 214
McCarran Act, 214
McCarran-Walter Act, 214–215
McCarthy, Eugene, 254
McCarthy, Joseph R., 217–218
McCarthyism, 217–218
McCord, James, 262

McCormick Harvester Company, 61
McCrary Bill, 54
McGovern, George, 260–261
McKinley, William, 27–28, 73, 82, 92, 98; and domestic issues, 73; elections to presidency, 70–73, 89; and Spanish-American War, 85, 87–88
McKinley Tariff, 27–28, 30, 31, 81
Macmillan, Harold, 226
McNamara, Robert S., 234
McNary, Charles L., 147, 185
McNary-Haugen Bill, 147–148
McNutt, Paul V., 191
Madero, Francisco I., 119–120
Mahan, Alfred Thayer, 80
Maine, 85
Malay Peninsula, 189, 197
Malcolm X, 244
Manchuria, 157, 227
Manila, Battle of, 86
Mann-Elkins Act, 106
Manufacturing, 40–42. *See also* Industry
Mao Tse-tung, 228–229, 271
March on Washington, 238
Mariana Islands, 198
Marne, Second Battle of the, 129
Marshall, George C., 208, 218, 222–223, 229
Marshall, Thomas R., 114, 126
Marshall Islands, 198
Marshall Plan, 223
Marx, Karl, 98
Maryland, 16, 262
Massachusetts, 53, 77, 261, 276
Matsu Islands, 230
Maximilian, 75
Meany, George, 257
Meat Inspection Act, 103
Medicare, 235, 241
Mellon, Andrew W., 140, 144
Meredith, James, 237
Mesabi range, 40–41
Meuse-Argonne offensive, 129–130
Mexican-Americans, 246
Mexico, 75, 78, 119–120, 127–128, 150, 157–158, 179
Middle East, 230–231, 250, 272–273
Midway, Battle of, 198
Midway Islands, 75
Miller, David Hunter, 135
Miller, Thomas W., 140, 141

Miller, William, 240
Mills Bill, 26
Minimum Wage Act (1949), 212; (1955), 217; (1961), 234
Mining, 34–36, 40
Minneapolis, 42
Minnesota, 38, 42, 53, 66, 71
Mississippi, 8–9, 167
Mississippi, University of, 237
Missouri, 16, 36–37
Missouri, 200
Mitchell, Alexander, 50
Mitchell, John, 99
Mitchell, John N., 255–256, 262–263, 264
Moley, Raymond, 163
Molotov, Vyacheslav M., 204
Mondale, Walter F., 274, 275
Money, 66–69, 70–71, 73
"Money trust," 117
Monopoly, 45–47
Monroe Doctrine, 75, 77–78, 108–109, 136, 158
Montana, 35, 105
Montgomery, Bernard, 196
Montgomery, Alabama, 220
Moore, John Bassett, 155
Morgenthau, Henry, Jr., 163
Morocco, 111, 194, 196, 203
Morgan, John P., 45
Morrill Act, 38
Morrow, Dwight W., 158
Morse, Wayne, 216, 217
Morton, Levi P., 26
Moscow Conference, 204
Moscow Declaration, 204
Muckrakers, 95
"Mugwumps," 24
Muller v. *Oregon*, 63
"Mulligan Letters," 24
Munich Conference, 182
Municipal reform, 96–97
Munn v. *Illinois*, 54
Muñoz Marín, Luis, 91
Muscle Shoals, 167
Muskie, Edmund, 254, 260
Mussolini, Benito, 182, 196
Myers v. *United States*, 7

Nagasaki, 200
Nagy, Imre, 225–226
Napoleon III, 75

Nasser, Gamal Abdel, 230
Nast, Thomas, 15
National Association for the Advancement of Colored People (NAACP), 236, 243, 244
National Civil Service Reform League, 21
National Commission on Law Observance and Enforcement. *See* Wickersham Commission
National Conservation Commission, 102–103
National Cordage Company, 30
National Defense Act, 126
National Defense Education Act, 219
National Greenback party. *See* Greenback party
National Housing Act, 166
National Industrial Recovery Act (NIRA), 164–165, 173, 176
National Labor Reform party, 58, 67
National Labor Relations Act, 173, 177, 210
National Labor Relations Board (NLRB), 173
National Labor Union, 58
National Organization for Women (NOW), 247, 248
National Origins Plan, 149–150
National Recovery Administration (NRA), 164, 173, 176
National Security League, 125
National Union for Social Justice, 175
National Urban League, 243, 244
National War Labor Board (World War II), 191
National Women's Political Caucus, 247
National Youth Administration (NYA), 171–172
"Naval holiday," 156, 157
Nebraska, 38
Negroes. *See* Blacks
Nelson, Donald, 190
Netherlands, 124, 156, 184, 194, 223, 224
Netherlands East Indies, 197
Neutrality: in World War I, 123–126; in World War II, 182–185
Neutrality Act (1935), 183; (1936), 183; (1937), 183, 188; (1939), 183
Nevada, 35, 68, 70
New Deal: evaluation of, 177–178; First,

162–167, 169; philosophy of, 163; Second, 169–176; and Supreme Court, 176–177
New Freedom, 113–118
New Frontier, 232, 233–239
New Guinea, 197
New Hampshire, 53
New Jersey, 46
New Mexico, 127–128
New Nationalism, 115
New Panama Canal Company, 107
"New South," 12
New York, 20, 24, 27, 42, 53, 276
New York Central Railroad, 48, 145
New York City, 15, 17, 161, 247
New York, New Haven, and Hartford Railroad, 48
New Zealand, 230
Newark, 245
Newfoundland, 77, 186
Newfoundland fisheries dispute, 77
Newlands Act, 102
Newton, Huey, 244
Nicaragua, 107, 109, 122, 179
Nimitz, Chester W., 198
Nixon, Richard M., 215, 218, 233, 255–256, 259; and domestic issues, 253, 256–258, 261, 262; elections to presidency, 253, 254-255,260—261; and foreign affairs, 253, 269–270, 271; and Watergate scandal, 253, 262, 263, 264
Noble Order of the Knights of Labor. *See* Knights of Labor
Nomura, Kichisaburo, 188
"Normalcy," 138–144
Norris, Frank, 95
Norris, George W., 105, 167
North Africa, 196–197
North Atlantic Treaty, 224
North Atlantic Treaty Organization (NATO), 224–225
North Carolina, 143, 167
North Dakota, 38, 70, 71
Northern Pacific Railroad, 44, 50, 100
Northern Securities case, 100
Northwestern Alliance, 69
Norway, 194, 224
Nuclear test ban treaty, 250
Nuremburg trials, 201
Nye, Gerald P., 182, 184
Nye Committee, 182

Obregón, Álvaro, 157–158
Office of Defense Transportation (World War II), 191–192
Office of Economic Opportunity, 241
Office of Price Administration (OPA), 191
Ohio, 27, 42
"Ohio Idea," 14
Oil trust, 45
Okinawa, 200
Oklahoma, 142, 276
Old Age Revolving Pension plan, 175
Olmsted, Frederick Law, 43
Olney, Richard, 30, 62, 77–78
"Open-door" policy, 82, 111, 112, 156, 157, 187–188
Oregon, 18, 70, 71, 97, 126
Organic Act, 92
Organization of Petroleum Exporting Countries (OPEC), 268
Orlando, Vittorio, 134
Oswald, Lee Harvey, 239
Outer Mongolia, 204

Pacific, 75, 79–82, 88, 111, 156, 197–198, 200
Pago Pago, 80–81
Pakistan, 230
Palmer, A. Mitchell, 139, 151–152
Panama, 107–108, 179
Panama Canal, 107–108, 119, 120, 122
Panama Canal Tolls Act, 119
Panama, Declaration of, 180
Pan-American Conference: of 1923, 158; of 1928, 158
Pan-American Union, 79
Panay, 187
Panic: of 1873, 43–44, 83; of 1893, 30–31; of 1907, 116–117. *See also* Depression of 1929
Paraguay, 78
Paris, Treaty of, 87–88
Parker, Alton B., 100
Parks, Rosa, 220
Patrons of Husbandry. *See* Grange
Payne Bill, 104
Payne-Aldrich Tariff, 104–105, 115, 148
Peace Corps, 235
Pearl Harbor, 222; Japanese attack on, 188–189
Peik v. *Chicago and Northwestern Railroad*, 54

Pendleton, George H., 21
Pendleton Act, 21–22
Pennsylvania, 27, 41, 42, 162, 276
Pennsylvania Railroad, 48, 145
Pension controversy, 25
People's Party of the U.S.A., 69–70, 71. *See also* Populists
People's Republic of China. *See* China
Perkins, Frances, 163
Permanent Court of Arbitration. *See* Hague Court
Permanent Court of International Justice. *See* World Court
Permanent Joint Board on Defense, 184–185
Perry, Matthew C., 110
Pershing, John J., 120, 128
Peru, 78
Pescadores Islands, 230
Philippine Commission: first, 92; second, 92
Philippines, 86, 87–88, 89, 91–93, 110, 189, 197–198, 200, 203
Physical Valuation Act, 106
Pikes Peak, 35
Pinchot, Gifford, 102–103, 105
Pinkerton detectives, 61, 70
Plantation system, 1, 11
Platt, Orville H., 93
Platt Amendment, 93, 179
Plessy v. *Ferguson*, 220
Plumb, Glenn E., 145
Plumb plan, 145
Point Four Program, 229–230
Poland, 133, 182, 183, 204, 225, 270, 276
Poll tax, 11, 242
Pollock v. *Farmers' Loan and Trust Co.*, 31
Pools, 45, 52–53, 55
Populists, 29, 30, 69–70, 71
"Pork-barrel" appropriations, 20–21, 26
Portugal, 156
Post Office Department, 258
Postal Savings Bank Act, 106
Postal Savings Bank System, 106
Potsdam Conference, 200, 205
Powderly, Terence V., 59
Power, electric and water, 146, 167, 169
Powers, Francis Gary, 226
Presidential Succession Act (1886), 25; (1947), 208–209

Primary elections. *See* Direct primary
Progressive movement, 94–98, 113
Progressive party: of 1912, 113, 114–115; of 1924, 142; of 1948, 211–212
Progressive Republican League, 114
Prohibition, 150–151
Prohibition party, 54, 150
Project Apollo, 258–259
Public Works Administration (PWA), 165
Puerto Ricans, 246–247
Puerto Rico, 87, 88, 89, 91, 246
Pujo, Arsène, 116–117
Pujo Committee, 116–117
Pulitzer, Joseph, 43, 84
Pullman, George, 48
Pullman strike, 61–62
Pure Food and Drug Act, 103, 175

Quemoy Islands, 230
Quezon, Manuel, 92
Quota Act, 149, 214

Radical Republicans, 3–4, 5, 7, 8, 9, 14, 16
Railroads, 32, 41, 59, 69, 98, 118, 131, 145, 191–192; abuses of, 40, 51–53; government aid to, 48, 50; government control of, 40, 53–55, 66, 101, 102, 106; systems, 47–48, 50–51, 145–146
Railroad Administration (World War I), 131
Railroad Brotherhoods, 145
Railroad Labor Board, 145
Railroad Managers' Association, 62
Railroad strikes of 1877, 61
Randolph, A. Philip, 238
Reagan, Ronald, 274
Reagan Bill, 54
Rebates, 53, 55
Recall, 96, 98, 114
Reconstruction, 1–12, 13; and blacks, 2, 4–5, 7–9, 10–12, 14; effects of, 10–12; and South, 1–3, 4, 5, 7–12
Reconstruction Acts, 5, 7–8, 19
Reconstruction Finance Corporation (RFC), 160
"Red Scare," 151–152
Reed, Thomas B., 27, 28–29
Reed rules, 28–29
Referendum, 70, 96, 98, 114

Reid, Whitelaw, 29, 87
Relief and Construction Act, 160
Reorganization Plan. *See* "Court Packing" Plan
Republican party, 3–4, 5, 7, 8, 9, 14, 16, 18–19, 22, 24, 68, 94, 114–115. *See also* Election; Elections, congressional
Resettlement Administration (RA), 173–174
Resumption Act, 67
Reuben James, 187
Reuther, Walter, 238
Revels, Hiram R., 8
Revenue Act of 1935, 177
Rhee, Syngman, 227
Rhineland, 182, 196
Ribbentrop, Joachim von, 201
Richardson, Elliot, 263
Richardson, William A., 17
Rickenbacker, Edward V. ("Eddie"), 129
Ridgway, Matthew, 228
Robinson, Joseph T., 143, 177
Rockefeller, John D., 45
Rodino, Peter W., Jr., 263
Rogers, William P., 255
Roosevelt, Franklin D., 139, 162–163, 203, 204–205, 207, 209; and domestic issues, 159, 163–170, 171–178; elections to presidency, 161–162, 170–171, 185–186, 192–193; and foreign affairs, 93, 159, 178–180; and World War II, 183–184, 186–189, 203–205
Roosevelt, Theodore, 84, 86, 87, 89, 94, 95, 114–115, 125, 126; and domestic issues, 98–103; election to second presidential term, 100; and foreign affairs, 94, 107–112
Roosevelt Corollary, 109, 158. *See also* Monroe Doctrine
Root, Elihu, 73, 99, 135, 154–155
Root-Takahira Agreement, 111
Rosenberg, Julius and Ethel, 214
Rough Riders, 87
Roxas, Manuel, 93
Ruby, Jack, 239
Ruhr Valley, 196
"Rum, Romanism, and Rebellion," 24
Rumania, 133, 203, 225
Rusk, Dean, 234
Russell, Richard B., 215

Russia, 82, 109–110, 111, 123, 133. *See also* Soviet Union
Russo-Japanese War, 109–110, 204

Sacco-Vanzetti case, 152
St. Mihiel salient, Battle of the, 129
"Salary grab," 16–17
Salisbury, Robert, 77–78
Samoa, 79, 80–81
Sampson, William T., 86
San Francisco Conference, 205
San Juan Hill, Battle of, 87
San Mateo v. *The Southern Pacific Railroad*, 47
Sanborn, John D., 17
Santiago, campaign against, 86–87
"Saturday Night Massacre," 263
"Scalawags," 8
Scandinavians, 38
Schecter v. *United States*, 176
Schley, Winfield S., 86
Schmitt, Harrison, 259
Schurz, Carl, 16, 18, 21, 88
Schweiker, Richard, 274
Scopes, John T., 152
Scopes trial, 152–153
Seale, Bobby, 244
Second World War. *See* World War II
Securities Exchange Act, 166
Securities and Exchange Commission (SEC), 166
Sedition Act, 131–132
Segregation. *See* Desegregation
Selective service: in World War I, 128; in World War II, 184, 189
Selective Service Act (World War I), 128
Selective Training and Service Act (World War II), 184, 189
Selma, Alabama, 242–243
Senate: and League of Nations, 135–137; popular election of, 70, 96, 114. *See also* Amendments, constitutional: Seventeenth
Sewall, Arthur, 70
Seward, William H., 74, 75
Seymour, Horatio, 14
Shafter, William R., 86–87
Shantung peninsula, 136
Sharecropping system, 11, 65
Share-Our-Wealth movement, 175

Shepard, Alan B., Jr., 258
Sherman, James S., 103, 114
Sherman, John, 18, 47, 73
Sherman Antitrust Act, 47, 62, 63, 100–101, 117, 178
Sherman Silver Purchase Act, 68–69
Shipping Act, 126
Shipping Board (World War I), 126, 131
Shriver, R. Sargent, Jr., 235, 241, 260
Siam. *See* Thailand
"Sick Chicken Case." *See Schechter* v. *United States*
"Silent majority," 256
Silver, 35, 40, 68–69, 70, 71
Silver movement, 68–69
Simmons, William Joseph, 153
Simpson, Jerry, 69
Sims, William S., 129
Sinclair, Harry F., 140
Sinclair, Upton, 95, 103
Singapore, 189, 197
Sioux, 33
Sirica, John J., 262, 263
Sit-down strike, 172
Sit-ins, 236
"Six-Day War," 250
Slayton, Donald K., 259
Smith, Alfred E., 141, 143, 161
Smith Act, 214
Smith-Connally Anti-Strike Act, 191
Smith-Lever Act, 118
Smoot-Hawley Tariff, 148, 169
Smuts, Jan Christiaan, 135
Snyder, John W., 208
Social Democratic party, 98
Social Security, 174–175, 241
Social Security Act, 175, 177
Social Security Amendments (1950), 212; (1954), 217; (1956), 219; (1958), 219; (1961), 234
Socialism, 98
Socialist Labor party, 98
Socialist Party of America, 62, 98, 142
Solid South, 10, 89, 126, 139, 142, 143, 219, 256, 276
Soil Conservation and Domestic Allotment Act, 174
Solomon Islands, 197, 198
South, during Reconstruction period, 1–3, 4, 5, 7–12. *See also* Solid South
South Carolina, 9, 18

South Dakota, 35, 38, 96, 126
Southeast Asia Treaty Organization (SEATO), 230
Southern Alliance, 69
Southern Christian Leadership Conference (SCLC), 236, 243–244
Southern Pacific Railroad, 50, 95
"Southern strategy," 256
Soviet Union, 258, 259, 271, 272; and Cold War, 222–227, 230–231, 232, 249–250, 252, 253; in World War II, 186, 191, 193–194, 196, 200; during post–World War II period, 201, 202, 203–205, 206, 207. *See also* Russia
Space program, 258–260
Spain, 83–85, 86–88
Spanish-American War, 83–88, 103
Sparkman, John J., 215
Square Deal, 98–103
Stafford, Thomas P., 259
Stalin, Joseph, 200, 204, 205
Stalwarts, 18–19
Standard Oil Company, 45
Standard Oil Company of Indiana, 102
Standard Oil Company of New Jersey, 101
Standard Oil Trust, 45
Stanford, Leland, 50
Stanton, Edwin M., 7
Stanton, Elizabeth Cady, 97
Stassen, Harold E., 211
States' Rights Democratic party. *See* Dixiecrats
Steel trust, 45
Steffens, Lincoln, 95
Steinem, Gloria, 247
Stephens, Uriah S., 58
Stettinius, Edward R., Jr., 205
Stevens, John L., 81
Stevens, Thaddeus, 2, 3, 4
Stevenson, Adlai E. (1835–1914), 29, 88
Stevenson, Adlai E. (1900–1965), 215–216, 218–219
Stimson, Henry L., 104, 125, 157, 158
Stimson Doctrine, 157
Stock-market crash, 138, 154
"Stock-watering," 52
Stone, Harlan F., 177
Strasser, Adolph, 59
Strategic Arms Limitation Talks (SALT), 271, 272

Strikes, 61–62, 99–100, 118, 172–173, 209
Student Non-Violent Coordinating Committee (SNCC), 236, 244
Submarine warfare: in World War I, 124–125, 127–128, 129; in World War II, 187, 192
Suez Canal crisis, 230–231
Sugar trust, 45
Summit conference: of 1955, 225; of 1960, 226
Sumner, Charles, 3
Sumner, William Graham, 43, 88
Supreme Court, 2, 7, 18, 31, 54, 55, 62, 63, 70, 89, 132, 172, 209, 256–257, 263; antitrust rulings of, 47, 100, 101; civil rights rulings of, 10, 219–220, 221; and New Deal, 164–165, 174, 176–177; rulings on railroad legislation by, 54, 66, 102
Sussex, 125
Sweden, 124
Sylvis, William H., 58
Syria, 250, 272

Taft, Robert A., 184, 185, 193, 210, 211, 215
Taft, William H., 92, 94, 104, 114–115, 135; and domestic issues, 94, 104–107, 149; election to presidency, 103–104; and foreign affairs, 112
Taft-Hartley Act, 209–210
Taft-Katsura Memorandum, 110
Taiwan, 229, 230, 271
Tammany Hall, 15, 143
Tarbell, Ida M., 95
Tariff, 22, 26, 27, 28, 30, 40, 45, 65, 70, 71, 115, 116, 269; Act of 1883, 22; Dingley, 104; Fordney-McCumber, 148; McKinley, 27–28, 30; Payne-Aldrich, 104–105; Smoot-Hawley, 148; Underwood, 116; Wilson-Gorman, 31, 70. *See also* Trade Agreements Act
Tariff Commission, 148
Taylor, Glen, 211
Teapot Dome scandal, 140
Technical Assistance Program. *See* Point Four Program
Teheran Conference, 204
Telegraph, 41, 59, 69, 98
Telephone, 41–42, 69, 98

Teller, Henry M., 71, 85
Teller Amendment, 85
Ten Percent Plan, 2
Tennessee, 5, 16, 139, 143, 167
Tennessee Valley Authority (TVA), 167–
  169
Tenure of Office Act, 7, 24–25
Texas, 8–9, 16, 36, 127–128, 143, 238
Texas v. *White*, 2
Thailand, 230
Thant, U, 252
Thieu, Nguyen Van, 270
Third World, 273
Tho, Le Duc, 270
Thomas, Norman, 98
Thurman, Allan G., 26
Thurmond, J. Strom, 211
Tilden, Samuel J., 17–18
Tillman, Benjamin R., 69
Timber Culture Act, 37
Tito, Josip, 225
Tojo, Hideki, 188, 202
Toledo, Ohio, 95
Townsend, Francis E., 175
Trade Agreements Act, 169
Trade Expansion Act, 236
Transportation, 36, 40, 41; in World
  War I, 131; in World War II, 191–192.
  See also Railroads
Transportation, Department of, 241–242
Truman, Harry S., 91, 193, 207–208,
  215; and domestic issues, 207, 208–
  210, 212–215, 219; election to second
  presidential term, 210–212; and
  foreign affairs, 200, 205, 207, 222–
  224, 227–228, 229–230
Truman Doctrine, 222
Trumbull, Lyman, 16
Trusts, 44–47, 100–101, 115, 117–118.
  See also Antitrust legislation
Tugwell, Rexford, 163
Turkey, 133, 222, 223, 224
Turner, Frederick Jackson, 39
Tutuila, 80–81
Twain, Mark, 35, 43
Tweed, William M., 14, 15
Tweed Ring, 14, 15, 17
Tydings-McDuffie Act, 92

U-2 plane incident, 226
Udall, Morris K., 274
Ukraine, 204

Underwood, Oscar W., 113
Underwood Tariff, 116, 148
Unemployment, 31, 44, 160–161, 164,
  171–172, 268
Unemployment Relief Act. *See* Civilian
  Conservation Corps (CCC)
Union of Soviet Socialist Republics
  (USSR). *See* Soviet Union
Union Pacific Railroad, 15, 48, 50
Union party of 1864, 3
Unions. *See* Labor unions
United Mine Workers, 99, 172, 209
United Nations, 155, 203, 205–206, 207,
  227, 231, 252, 273
United Nations Educational, Scientific,
  and   Cultural   Organization
  (UNESCO), 206
United States v. *Butler*, 176
United States v. *E. C. Knight Company*,
  47
United States Postal Service, 258
United States Steel Corporation, 172,
  209, 235
Utah, 97, 115

Van Sweringen railroad system, 146
Vance, Cyrus R., 277
Vandenberg, Arthur, 184
Vanderbilt, Cornelius, 45, 48
Venezuela, 77–78, 108–109
Vermont, 115, 171
Versailles, Treaty of, 132, 134–137, 139
Veterans Bureau, 140
Victory Loan drive (World War I), 131
Viet Cong, 251–252, 270
Viet Minh, 251
Vietnam War, 232, 250–252, 253, 254,
  256, 261, 269–271
Villa, Francisco ("Pancho"), 120
Villard, Henry, 50
Vinson, Fred M., 208
Virgin Islands, 122
Virginia, 8–9, 143, 167, 276
Virginius, 83
Volstead Act, 150–151
Voting Rights Act, 243

Wabash rate case, 54
Wabash, St. Louis, and Pacific Railway

Company v. *Illinois. See* Wabash rate case
WACs (Women's Army Corps), 189
Wade, Benjamin, 2, 3
Wade-Davis Bill, 3
Wagner, Robert F., 173
Wagner-Connery Act. *See* National Labor Relations Act
Wainwright, Jonathan, 198
Waldheim, Kurt, 273
Wallace, George C., 237, 254–255, 260, 274
Wallace, Henry A., 174, 185, 193, 211–212
Walsh, Thomas J., 140
Walter, Francis E., 214
War bonds (World War I), 131; (World War II), 192
War crimes trials, 201, 202
War debts and reparations (World War I), 155–156
War Industries Board (World War I), 130
War Labor Board (World War I), 130–131
War Labor Disputes Act. *See* Smith-Connally Anti-Strike Act
War Manpower Commission (World War II), 191
War of the Pacific, 78
War Production Board (World War II), 190
War Shipping Board (World War II), 192
Warner, Charles Dudley, 43
Warren, Earl, 211, 220, 239
Warren Commission, 239
Warsaw Pact, 224, 225
Washington, 76, 97
Washington Conference, 156
Washington, Treaty of, 76–77
Water Power Act, 146
Watergate scandal, 261, 262–264, 275
Watson, Thomas E., 69, 71
WAVEs (Women Appointed for Voluntary Emergency Service), 189
Weaver, James B., 29, 69, 70
Weaver, Robert C., 241
Welch, Joseph B., 218
Welfare programs, 4, 97-98, 164, 241, 256

West, 51, 79–80; and agriculture, 37–38; and cattle raising, 36–37; and Indians, 32–34; and mining, 34–36; political revolt of, 64, 65–73. *See also* Farmers' discontent
West Germany. *See* Germany
West Virginia, 46, 71
Western Federation of Miners, 60
Westinghouse, George, 48
Weyler, Valeriano, 83–84
Wheeler, Burton K., 142, 184
Wheeler, William A., 17
Wheeler-Howard Act, 245
Whiskey Ring, 17
White, Edward H., 258
White, Henry, 134
White, William Allen, 184
Whitney, Eli, 41
Whitney, William C., 24
Wickersham, George W., 151
Wilhelm II, 133
Willkie, Wendell L., 185, 193
Wilkins, Roy, 236, 238, 243
Wilson, Charles E., 216
Wilson, Henry, 16
Wilson, Woodrow, 94, 95, 113, 115–116; and domestic issues, 113, 116–118, 149; elections to presidency, 113–115, 126–127; and foreign affairs, 113, 119–122; and League of Nations, 135–137; and World War I, 123–126, 127–128; and World War I peace conference, 132–134
Wilson Bill, 31
Wilson-Gorman Tariff, 31, 70, 83
Windom Report, 54
Wisconsin, 38, 53, 54, 66, 96, 142
Wisconsin Idea, 95
Woman suffrage, 97
Woman's Christian Temperance Union, 150
Women's Liberation, 247–248
Women's Peace Party, 126
Womensurge, 248
Wood, Leonard, 93, 125, 139
Wood, Robert E., 184
Works Progress Administration (WPA), 171
Works Projects Administration (WPA), 171
World Court, 135, 154–155
World Health Organization (WHO), 206

World War I: home front during, 130–132; peace settlement after, 132–137; United States armed forces in, 128–130; United States entry into, 127–128; United States neutrality before entering, 123–127
World War II: aggressions leading to, 181–182, 187–189; conferences of, 203–205; dealing with defeated nations of, 201–203; fighting in Europe during, 193–194; fighting in Pacific during, 197–198, 200; home front during, 190–193; national awakening toward, 182–187; United States armed forces in, 189–190; United States entry into, 189

Wright, Fielding L., 211
Wyoming, 35, 36, 97, 105

Yalta Conference, 204–205
"Yellow-dog" contract, 56
"Yellow press," 84
"Yom Kippur War," 272
Young, A. Whitney, 243
Young, John Watts, 258
Young, Owen D., 155
Young Plan, 155
Yugoslavia, 225

Zimmermann, Arthur, 127
Zimmermann Note, 127–128